SAMPSON TECHNICAL INSTITUTE

NORTH CAROLINA
STATE BOARD OF EDUCATION
DEPT. OF COMMUNITY COLLEGES
LIBRARIES

P9-EIE-435

WE WERE THERE
The Story of Working Women in America

HD
6095
W47
1977

Barbara Mayer Wertheimer

WE
WERE THERE
The Story of
Working Women
in America

With the research assistance of
Ida Goshkin *and* Ellen Wertheimer

PANTHEON BOOKS
New York

Copyright © 1977 by Barbara Mayer Wertheimer

All rights reserved under International and Pan-American Copyright Conventions. Published in the United States by Pantheon Books, a division of Random House, Inc., New York, and simultaneously in Canada by Random House of Canada Limited, Toronto.

Library of Congress Cataloging in Publication Data

Wertheimer, Barbara Mayer
  We Were There.

  Bibliography: pp. 399–417
  Includes index.
    1. Women—Employment—United States—History.
  2. Women in trade-unions—United States—History.
  I. Title.
  HD6095.W47   1976   331.4'0973   76-9597
  ISBN 0-394-49590-X
  ISBN 0-394-73257-X pbk.

Designed by Irva Mandelbaum

Manufactured in the United States of America

Since this copyright page cannot accommodate all acknowledgments, they are to be found on the following two pages.

First Edition

Grateful acknowledgment is made to the following for permission to reprint previously published material:

Amalgamated Clothing Workers of America, "Anthem," from *Amalgamated Songbook,* 1968, p. 6.

American Folklore Society: "Pity Me, My Darling," from "Some Types of American Folk Song," by John A. Lomax. Reprinted from the *Journal of American Folklore,* vol. 28, 1915.

American Society for Ethnohistory and Judith K. Brown: Excerpt from "Economic Organization and Position of Women Among the Iroquois," by Judith K. Brown. Reprinted from *Ethnohistory,* vol. 17, nos. 3–4 (summer–fall 1970), p. 164. Copyright © 1971 by The American Society of Ethnohistory.

Arno Press, Inc.: Table from *Women in Industry,* by Edith Abbott, and excerpts from *Autobiography of Mother Jones,* by Mary Field Parton.

Harcourt Brace Jovanovich, Inc.: "Mill Doors" and lines from "Working Girls," reprinted from *Chicago Poems,* by Carl Sandburg. Copyright 1916 by Holt, Rinehart & Winston, Inc. Copyright 1944 by Carl Sandburg.

ILGWU Education Dept.: "The Uprising of the 20,000," from *Everybody Sings,* May 1942, p. 21.

Industrial Workers of the World: "The Rebel Girl," from *Songs of the Workers,* by Joe Hill, 1973, p. 39.

John A. Lomax: 2 verses of "The Pecos Queen," from *Cowboy Songs and Other Frontier Ballads,* edited by John A. Lomax, pp. 369–70. Copyright 1916 by The Macmillan Company.

McGraw-Hill Book Company: Table entitled "Major Occupations in Which Women Were Found, 1850." Reprinted from *Manpower in Economic Growth,* by Stanley Lebergott, p. 520. Copyright © 1964 by McGraw-Hill Book Company.

Montana Magazine; Table entitled "Employment of Women in the West over 21 Years of Age." Reprinted from vol. 24, no. 3 (July 1974), p. 5.

Princeton University Press: "Huswifery," by Edward Taylor. Reprinted from *The Poetical Works of Edward Taylor,* edited by Thomas H. Johnson (Princeton Paperback, 1966). Copyright Rockland, 1939; Princeton University Press, 1943.

Roosevelt University Press: "Bread and Roses," by James Oppenheim, and "The Death of Mother Jones," from *Songs of Work and Freedom*, edited by Edith Fowkes and Joe Glazer, 1960.

The University of Illinois Press: "Let the Girls Sit Down," from *American Labor Songs of the Nineteenth Century*, edited by Philip Foner, pp. 126–7. Copyright © 1975 by Board of Trustees, University of Illinois.

The University of Pennsylvania Press: "We Made Good Wobs Out There," by Vera Moller. Reprinted from *American Folksongs of Protest*, edited by John Greenway, p. 183. Copyright 1953 by the University of Pennsylvania.

The Viking Press, Inc.: "Go Down, Death," from *God's Trombones*, by James Weldon Johnson. Copyright 1927 by The Viking Press, Inc., renewed 1955 by Grace Nail Johnson.

Fannie Harrigan
May 10, 1926—December 16, 1975
Organization Vice-President, New York Metro Postal Union
Member, first graduating class, Trade Union Women's Studies
Friend

PREFACE

I had been mulling over the idea for *We Were There* for some time, but it crystallized on a trip to Michigan in 1973. I was speaking at a conference of trade union women about women in American labor history. During the question period that followed, a short, earnest young woman, who was the first to wave her hand in the air, asked, "Where can we get more information about women in the labor movement? I have never read anything about the women you've told us about today."

I gave the group the titles of several books, each of which had one or more excellent chapters about the efforts of women during the nineteenth and early twentieth centuries to organize labor unions. After listing book number three I stopped, and found myself saying to the young woman, "There is no one book that really talks just about working women in this country. I guess the thing to do is to write one. I'll try."

Her request was based on the fact that the story of working women has rarely been included in history books. In thinking back to our own schooldays, how many of us can recall American history classes where any significant amount of time was devoted to the role of workers, men *or* women, in the building of this country? Perhaps we remember the drawing in our textbook of a mob pulling down the statue of George III near the start of the American Revolution; did we learn that the Daughters of Liberty helped out there? We know that a ragged band of soldiers, mostly farmers, survived the winter (1777–1778) at Valley Forge, but not that women were there as cooks, laundresses, secretaries, and scavengers of food from the surrounding countryside. We read that workers built the railroads across America, but not that slave women as well as men made up many of these work crews. Pioneers crossed the prairies and high Rockies to settle the West, but it was most often their wives who kept the journals that made possible much of our knowledge of those times.

The names of individual working men tend to be recorded on the pages of history only if they fit the Horatio Alger mold: "Poor boy works hard, makes good." Andrew Jackson, Abraham Lincoln, Andrew Carnegie, Herbert Lehman are a few that come to mind. If this is true of working men, it is even more so of working women. While every schoolchild knows about Betsy Ross and how Dolly Madison hung up her laundry in the White House during her husband's administration, where are the accounts of the working women who helped build this country? They fought in every war, nursed the wounded and sick, and answered their country's call for additional workers. They were spies and couriers and "engineers" on the Underground Railroad. They worked fourteen or more hours a day in the mills for a pittance, and braved the wrath of society when, unfeminine though they might be called, they turned out on strike against wage cuts and the speedup of their machines. They have been beaten, jailed, and killed in the cause of the labor movement.

Nor is their story told in *labor* history texts, which give scant mention to women workers and little or no space to the individual women leaders who emerged from their ranks. By and large, these texts discuss women as early millworkers, describe a few major strikes such as that of the 20,000 New York shirtwaist workers in 1909, give a passing nod to the Women's Trade Union League of America, and that is about all.

If it was difficult for the working man to get ahead in this new land of America, to hold a job in the face of periodic recessions, or to organize a labor union against the opposition of both the company and the courts, how much more difficult it was for the working woman! After a fourteen-hour workday she returned to the full responsibilities of her home: bread to bake, water to heat and laundry to wash, clothes to make or mend, supper to cook. Moreover, in society a woman was less than a full citizen: if she was married, the law restricted her right to hold property, to open her own business, to divorce her husband and gain custody of her children. She did not even have control over her own earnings. She could not participate in federal elections until 1920.

As a worker, a woman found that most labor unions would not admit her to membership. Working men did not want women in their craft or on the job: women often undercut wages by working for half the pay of men, and employers frequently tried to use them to break strikes. Equal pay, when first proposed by unions in the middle of the last century, was designed to make it so expensive for an employer to hire women workers that he would revert to hiring only men. Woman's place was at home, and workers only reflected society's precepts when they expressed this view.

Yet women have always been part of America's work force, black, white, or Native American, slave or free. Women leaders have emerged throughout our history, from mills and factories, stores, and offices; they have helped to build the American labor movement. And the working women I have met across the country seek to learn more about this past. We cannot know how far we have come until we know from where we came. To tell this story, however, it was necessary to be somewhat arbitrary in defining just who was a "working woman." Who should be omitted in a book that was to be, not a history of *all* American women, but the story of *working* women and their contribution to America?

Because their stories have been told elsewhere, I have in the main omitted women who worked in the arts and the professions and those who achieved in the fields of social work, suffrage, and reform, although both nurses and teachers are touched on briefly. I have focused on the wage-earning women of America, though I have included as well the women who, for two hundred years before the factory system, worked as economic partners in the settling and developing of this country; the slave women who worked, but not for wages; and the pioneer women, some of whom worked for wages, but most of whom performed a role similar to that of the colonial women two centuries earlier. I am deeply aware that I have only begun to cover these three hundred years of the story of working women. In one small volume, one is forced into count-less sins of omission. Painful decisions have been made about what to include and what, regretfully, to leave out. When possible I have tried to fill some of the gaps with suggestions for additional reading, which will be found in the Annotated Bibliography at the end of the book.

In writing this book I have tried to let the facts speak for themselves and have kept myself out of the story. Nevertheless, the more I researched and the further along I got in the story of America's working women, the more magnificent and courageous and fascinating I found them. I marvel at what they endured and accomplished against such odds.

In the three years it has taken to research and write *We Were There*, I have accumulated many gray hairs and an overwhelming sense of grati-tude to family and friends who have helped and encouraged me through-out. Now that the final chapter of the book has been written, I can undertake the pleasant task of saying thank you to these very special people for their constant support and concrete assistance.

Some of those who have helped me I have never met. Fred W. Thomp-son, author, long-time member of the Industrial Workers of the World and its archivist, is one of these, and to him I am most grateful. I was led to him through another "Wobbly," Tor Cedarval, whom I also thank for his help. Friends across the country—and strangers—have sent me clip-pings, articles, and sometimes manuscripts which I have acknowledged wherever these are used. Pauline Newman, now in her eighties and still active as education director of the New York Health Center of the Inter-national Ladies' Garment Workers' Union, is another whose assistance has been invaluable. I treasure—and shall always remember—our conver-sations about her past, when she took me back to the sweatshop days before the "Uprising of the 20,000" in 1909 and talked about her friends

Rose Schneiderman, Leonora O'Reilly, Mary Anderson, and many others. I am deeply grateful for the pictures from her own collection that she has lent me for this book.

Leon Stein, editor of *Justice*, has been generous with photographs from the files of the International Ladies' Garment Workers' Union, and copied two prints that hang on the wall of his office for use here. Burt Beck, Public Relations Director of the Amalgamated Clothing and Textile Workers Union, has been similarly helpful with photos from the union's files. Anni Hornbostel, Joyce L. Kornbluh, William Scanlon, Anne Rivera, Connie Kopelov, and David and Ellen Wertheimer have helped me with photo research. Philoine Fried generously contributed pictures of her mother, Bessie Hillman, and of her long-time friend Dorothy Bellanca. Other photo sources have been credited elsewhere; to each my deepest thanks.

It is not possible to name all those who have encouraged me along the way, but they know who they are. I shall always be in their debt. I am particularly grateful for the understanding of my editor at Pantheon, Susan Gyarmati. A more supportive, patient human being would be hard to find. Jeanne Morton, copy editor, is another who has been more than kind.

I could not have completed this book without the assistance of Ida Goshkin, librarian and consultant to Trade Union Women's Studies, the program that I direct, who searched out many of the books and materials we have used. Neither her enthusiasm for this project nor her kindness to me have ever waned. Those libraries we have found particularly helpful include: those of the Amalgamated Clothing Workers of America, where librarian Catherine Williams has our deep thanks, and of the International Ladies' Garment Workers' Union, and Dr. Lazar Teper, the union's research director; the Research Library of the New York Public Library; the library of the *New York Times*, where Paul Greenfeeder and Gray Pert were most helpful; the Arthur and Elizabeth Schlesinger Library on the History of Women in America, at Radcliffe College; the Schomburg Center for Research in Black Culture; the Tamiment Library at New York University; the United States Department of Labor Women's Bureau Resource Library in Washington, D.C.; the Yale University Library; and the Library and Women's Resource Center of the National Young Women's Christian Association, where Mrs. Elizabeth Norris, librarian, has our thanks.

A research grant from the New York State School of Industrial and Labor Relations enabled me to have an assistant for a short time, and a mini-sabbatical from the school gave me two quiet months away from the pressure of my job during the summer of 1975 to concentrate all my energies on writing. This would not have been possible, however, without the help of Anne H. Nelson, my associate at Trade Union Women's Studies, Judith Berk, Ida Goshkin, Marta Hernandez, Saundra Kelley, and Dana Schechter, who closed the gap so that the program could continue to go forward while I retreated to write. I owe each of them so much. I also want to thank Sherron Johnson for her typing help early in the project, and the newcomer to our staff, Beverly Collins, for all she has done.

Susan Berresford of the Ford Foundation, which has supported Trade Union Women's Studies from its inception, has been among those whose encouragement has meant a great deal to me, as has that of Lois Gray, Associate Dean, New York State School of Industrial and Labor Relations, Cornell. N.Y.S.S.I.L.R. Dean Robert McKersie has been constantly supportive, and I am grateful for his interest.

Professor Maurice Neufeld of the New York State School of Industrial and Labor Relations, dean of labor historians, read the manuscript, and to his critical and always helpful comments and suggestions I owe more than I can express. In spite of a heavy teaching schedule, he gave me the gift of his time, experience, and judgment, as did my long-time friend Joyce Lewis Kornbluh of the Institute of Labor and Industrial Relations, University of Michigan. A fine researcher and writer, she made numerous helpful suggestions.

My daughter Ellen and my son David Max Wertheimer contributed more to this book than they can ever surmise and have left their imprint on it in many ways. During the two summers of working with Ellen I have found her qualities as a researcher and editor invaluable. I counted heavily on David's editing suggestions, which he gave me generously and with never-failing grace, and on the photographs he took of old pictures for reproduction in the book. The enthusiasm of these two young people for the project was always heartwarming. Nor do I underestimate the strength I drew from their sense of humor.

I value especially the comments and suggestions of my husband, Val, based on his perspective as vice-president of a leading labor union. They were always helpful, as were his patience and his understanding kindness during these months and years.

Even with all this assistance, given so freely and with such love, I know there are errors that remain. For these I alone am responsible, and my failing should in no way reflect upon those who so generously gave their help.

B.M.W.

New York, October 1976

CONTENTS

PART 5 Emergence of the Trade Union Woman: *1900–1914*

ILLUSTRATIONS

Part 1

TWO CENTURIES INTO THE NEW WORLD

Iroquois women at work in a sugar camp. English, Dutch, and French settlers of the seventeenth century learned the art of maple sugaring from Indian women such as these.

Prologue

THE
FIRST AMERICAN WOMEN

O our Mother the Earth, O our Father the Sky,
Your children are we, and with tired backs
We bring you the gifts you love.
Then weave for us a garment of brightness;
May the warp be the white light of morning,
May the weft be the red light of evening,
May the fringes be the falling rain,
May the border be the standing rainbow.
Thus weave for us a garment of brightness,
That we may walk fittingly where birds sing,
That we may walk fittingly where grass is green,
O our Mother the Earth, O our Father the Sky.
     —"Song of the Sky Loom" (Tewa)

She walked softly and straight in her deerskin moccasins, returning to the village after a day of planting corn. Her young child slept in his cradleboard on her back, having spent most of the day hanging on a nearby tree limb while she worked. A member of one of hundreds of Native American tribes scattered across the length and breadth of the continent, she lived much as her ancestors had lived for more than 20,000 years.

Indian tribal life, though it varied widely, always harmonized with nature. The Indian philosophy was to till the land they needed, to fish and hunt to supply their basic wants; they believed that the land was only entrusted to their care during their time on this earth. They knew how much they depended on the lakes and streams and forests, and were careful not to take too much and to waste nothing, lest in anger the Great Spirit punish them for their greed. There was plenty of land. When crop yields told them the land needed a rest, they cleared new fields and moved on.

The first working women in America were Indian women, resourceful in utilizing every aspect of their environment to sustain life. They gathered wild plants for food, herbs for medicines and dyes, clay from the river bed for pottery, bark and reeds for weaving cloth, clam shells for jewelry and wampum. While men hunted and fished, fought wars, built canoes and longboats, wigwams and hogans, and made weapons for

3

the hunt, women tilled the soil and sowed the seed, cultivated and harvested, wove baskets and blankets, tanned animal hides and made clothing, cured meats and dried vegetables, cared for the children, and maintained the home, which they sometimes also built. Indian women were the first people we know who cultivated corn or made maple sugar. They grew cotton, pumpkins, beans, squash, melons, and tobacco.

Not long after his arrival in Jamestown in 1607, Captain John Smith noted how hard the Indian women worked. They always seemed busy, while Indian men had time for talking, games, and tribal governance.[1] Agriculture, so important to the tribes, was usually the responsibility of the women and under their supervision. Thus they could—and did—play a key role in tribal decision-making and barter. Among the Shawnee of the Middle West, women could be chiefs and exerted a peaceful influence, helping the tribe avoid unnecessary bloodshed. A woman in the front lines of an Indian war party served to remind the enemy to spare the helpless. Women's councils among the Cherokee of the Southeast had considerable power, and on occasion overruled a chief if they felt he was angering the Great Spirit. New village chiefs were nominated by the women of the tribe.[2]

Among tribes such as the Nez Percé of the Far West, men and women had equal rights in cases of divorce, which assumed equal division of property. Clans such as the Seri of Lower California were matrilineal; executive power was held by the brothers of the principal woman, and elderwomen controlled clan property.[3] Iroquois women of the Northeast controlled and guarded the public treasury and other tribal property, and could be medicine women, sachems, or chieftainesses. Judith K. Brown describes the important role of Iroquois women:

> Iroquois agricultural activities, which yielded bountiful harvests, were highly organized under elected female leadership. . . . Iroquois women maintained the right to distribute and to dispense all food, even that procured by the men. This was especially significant as stored food constituted one of the major forms of wealth for the tribe. Through their control of the economic organization of the tribe, Iroquois matrons were able to make available or to withhold food for meetings of the Council and for war parties, for the observance of religious festivals and for the daily meals of the household. These economic realities were institutionalized in the matrons' power to nominate Council Elders and to influence Council decisions. They had a voice in the conduct of war and the establishment of treaties.[4]

Despite their central position in the economy, however, Indian women did not have the status of men, nor were they considered men's equals. Highest glory lay in the hunt and in war, and here men could achieve fame in activities not open to women. One of the few tribes in which women did exert unusual influence was the Zuni, a wholly agricultural people. Zuni men worked the fields, whereas the women were considered the proprietors of the land itself. There was little hunting or warfare. Reversing another traditional pattern, husbands came to live with their wives' families.[5]

Indian women assumed almost total responsibility for child care, and their infants were with them constantly. Children played together until they were seven or eight years old, but at that age role differentiation began and boys began to play with each other in imitation of the hunt, sometimes going out with the men, while girls stayed with their mothers to learn the skills they would need as women.

When they reached their teens, boys and girls were ready for initiation into the adult life of the village, which often involved solemn rituals or tests of bravery. Boys who could not pass these tests found themselves assigned, together with the old men, to farm under the direction of the women.

Although few names of individual Indian women have come down to us, their help was critical for the survival of the early European settlers and explorers. They shared their knowledge of agriculture and the gathering and preparation of herbal medicines, teaching the settlers from English towns and cities how to farm the rocky New England soil, what to plant, how to soften deerskin for clothing, how to backpack babies, how to make utensils from gourds and shells, and, indeed, the lore of survival in the wilderness.

1

WORKING WOMEN IN SEVENTEENTH- AND EIGHTEENTH- CENTURY AMERICA

Give ear unto a Maid, that lately was betray'd
And sent into Virginny, O:
In brief I shall declare, what I have suffer'd there,
When that I was weary, weary, weary, weary, O.

That first I came to this Land of Fame,
Which is called Virginny, O,
The Axe and the Hoe have wrought my overthrow,
When that I was weary, weary, weary, weary, O.

Five years served I, under Master Guy,
In the land of Virginny, O,
Which made me for to know sorrow, grief and woe,
When that I was weary, weary, weary, weary, O.
  —"The Trapan's Maiden," early American ballad

Who were America's first immigrant women? Why were they willing to face the unknown hardships of a long sea voyage and life in the colonies? What were they escaping and what did they find?

The first white woman to venture to the New World to live was a Spaniard. Francisca Hinestrosa joined her soldier husband to journey with Hernando de Soto to Florida, only to die in a Chickasaw Indian raid in 1541. Other women from Spain and Portugal arrived in 1550 and 1565 as members of colonizing expeditions that founded the first permanent settlement on what is now the United States mainland: St. Augustine, in 1565. In 1598, far to the west, Juan de Oñate brought four hundred soldiers, almost a third of whom took their families along, out of Mexico to New Mexico, later moving on to what is now Arizona, Colorado, and the eastern part of Texas.[1]

There were seventeen women among the English settlers in the ill-fated colony of Roanoke, Virginia. They vanished when that colony mysteriously disappeared between 1587 and 1591.

More is known about the women who arrived in Jamestown, Virginia, the first permanent English colony, soon after it was settled in 1607. English women came to Massachusetts and Dutch women to New Amsterdam not many years afterward. Black women, too, were part of this early story, from the time the first were brought to Jamestown from Africa in 1619.

Almost all the women who came were working women, and they expected a life of hard toil. Most of them were young; very few were rich. Many came to these shores with their husbands to seek religious freedom; some who were heads of households saw the chance for a new life through farming land that they received on the same basis as men.

Three elements combined to give the earliest women settlers power and responsibility such as they had never known in seventeenth-century England or on the European continent. First, they were in short supply and high demand. Single women were rare, and widows remarried quickly. Second, their role as home managers earned them a new respect. Third, there was an acute shortage of labor, and women performed many kinds of work outside the home from which they were later barred when this shortage ceased. The home was the factory of the day, where women produced almost all that the family needed and consumed: through their own productive and managerial skills the women determined how well their families would live. If they could supply all family needs and then some, they could sell or barter the extra for additional comforts.

Thus, women found a new freedom in the colonies. They could marry whom they pleased, in sharp contrast to the European system of arranged marriages. When they owned land, it often entitled them to vote. Although legally their status was limited, in the new and fluid society many of the laws restricting their lives could not be enforced. However, the strictures surrounding indentured servant women and black slave women in early America created a sharply different experience for them from that of free white women.

The Early Arrivals

One year after Jamestown was settled in 1607, the first English women arrived. Anne Forrest, wife of Thomas Forrest, and her maid, thirteen-year-old Anne Buras, sailed up the James River aboard a supply ship that dropped anchor off the swampy island on which the town stood. We can imagine the two Annes leaning on the deck rail as they watched the town approach. What desperate thoughts they must have had as the stockade of rough wood came into view, each log sharpened to a point at the top, enclosing less than an acre of land on which stood a sad array of cabins built of green lumber and chinked with clay.

To relieve the hard life and chronic complaints of the bachelors of Jamestown, as well as to assure the permanence of the settlement, the Virginia Company soon began to recruit women for the colony. In August 1609, twenty women and children arrived, followed by approximately one hundred more women later that year.[2] Meanwhile young Anne Buras, the maid, had married John Layden, a laborer, in the first colonial wedding. Whether they and their infant daughter Virginia lived through the "starveing tyme" that came the following year, we do not know. Famine, fire, drought, Indian attacks, and sickness reduced the colony from five hundred to scarcely sixty.[3] The survivors packed their belongings, boarded the ship anchored in the James River, and headed for England. However, on the way they met supply ships carrying food and equipment for Jamestown, turned back, and saved the settlement from abandonment.

Anxious to rebuild its struggling colony, the Virginia Company continued to send boatloads of young, single (and, we may imagine, spirited) women to Jamestown as wives for the men. At first these women were allotted their shares of land, but this lowered the number, or perhaps the rapidity, of marriages by making the women independent landowners, and the policy was soon changed. As the women were rowed ashore from each new ship that arrived, the eligible men would line up to greet them, undoubtedly decked out in whatever was left of their finest attire. The price for each woman was 120 pounds of leaf tobacco, worth about $80, which paid her passage over.[4] We are told that the women were not forced to marry against their will, but received housing and food in exchange for laundering and similar services until they decided which man to accept. Most did marry, of course, assuring sons and daughters for the New World.

About the same time that the first Jamestown settlers were struggling for survival, Henry Hudson sailed into what is now New York harbor and claimed the territory for the Dutch. In 1624 the first thirty Dutch families arrived to settle the area where Albany now stands, and a year later the New Amsterdam settlement was founded when the Dutch settlers bought the island of Manhattan for a few bags of trinkets in the famous exchange with the Indians. Here, as in other colonies, the first homes were merely square pits in the ground lined with bark and wood.

The small but bustling fur-trading center on the lower tip of Manhattan Island was cosmopolitan from the start: by 1644 eighteen different languages were spoken there.[5] Women in the settlement took charge of all farming operations, except for the heavy plowing, and became well known for the produce they raised and sold. Since the colony relied primarily on exporting furs traded from the Indians, the men were often away from home, leaving their wives to run the farms and the many small businesses. When the Dutch opened a hospital in New Amsterdam in 1658, a matron was placed in charge, and early in the life of the colony the Dutch licensed midwives and provided houses for them.

In spite of its lively fur trade, the colony grew slowly, for the Dutch West India Company restricted industry. By the time the English took New Amsterdam in 1664, renaming it New York, it had just 7,000 inhabitants.[6]

In 1620 another band of settlers, heading from England for the northern part of the Virginia colony, were blown off course, and the 102 Pilgrims aboard the *Mayflower* made their way into Plymouth harbor. On a chill, damp December day they rowed ashore to face their first New England winter. Their first homes were merely hastily constructed sod huts, sometimes caves, "half a pit and half a tent of earth supported by branches . . . nasty, dirty, dank and cold."[7] Before the winter was over, half the group had died. Scurvy, pneumonia, starvation, and exposure to cold claimed as many as two or three a day, sometimes leaving as few as six or seven adults strong and well enough to care for all the rest.[8] Only four of the eighteen *Mayflower* women lived through that terrible winter, but when spring finally came to New England all eleven of the girls and twenty of the twenty-six boys had survived. At the high price of their own lives the mothers saw to it that the children got the food they needed.

That first spring the remaining Pilgrims plowed the fields and planted, with considerable help from the Indians, who gave them seed and showed them how to cultivate native corn, pumpkins, and beans. The Pilgrim men and women were experienced workers and farmers; within several years they had replaced their primitive huts with thatch-roofed log cabins, including central fireplaces and sometimes hearths and wooden floors. They reassigned land according to the number of people in each household, and Governor William Bradford reported that "the women went willingly [to work] into the fields."[9]

The Pilgrims, however, remained poor. Aften ten years Plymouth numbered only three hundred people; by 1640 they still had only one plow among them.[10] A more affluent group of forty Puritans arrived from England and settled Salem, Massachusetts, in 1628, followed the next year by four hundred others. Seventeen ships carrying 1,000 settlers arrived in 1630 to establish the Boston colony and several neighboring towns. In addition to supplies, the Puritans brought with them a rigid religion, including the tradition of saints and strangers. Only the "saints," or Puritan men, could take part in governing the colonies, and each year it became harder for outsiders—the "strangers"—to join that inner group.

One of the biggest problems the seaboard colonies faced was an acute shortage of labor. Stories of the hardships of colonial life filtered back to England, and it was not always easy to attract skilled workers to the New World. It was largely to meet this growing need that the system of indentured servitude was set up, whereby impoverished single men and women contracted to sell a number of years of their service in the colonies in exchange for payment of their ocean fare to the ship's captain. Sometimes they signed a written contract while still in England, for service of from two to seven years; more often, they took their chances on being "sold" into service when they arrived. Most of these men and women were escaping unemployment and imprisonment, and England was delighted to empty her jails. There are many tales of men, women, and children lured onto ships through false promises or kidnapped off the streets and carried to the colonies to be sold as servants with little hope of ever returning home. The indenture system brought one-half to two-thirds of all immigrants who came to the New World up to the time of the American Revolution.[11]

Immigration from Northern European countries gradually increased later in the seventeenth century. "Redemptioners" came in family groups, paying a part of their passage and planning to work off the rest in the New World. To complete these payments, some sold the services of their children, apprenticing them to a trade. Once they were in the colonies, there was little difference in the treatment accorded the indentured servants from England and the redemptioners from the Continent and Ireland.[12]

Nor did the sea voyage differ for the two groups: it was seven to twelve weeks of horror. Men and women were crowded into holds without ventilation, light, decent food, or sanitary facilities. As many as half the passengers died on the way, especially the children—and whole shiploads of children were sent over, beginning in 1618 with the first two hundred youngsters gathered off the London streets.[13] Why so many died on the way over is vividly described by one redemptioner recruited from the German Palatinate:

> During the voyage there is on board these ships terrible misery, stench, fumes, horror, vomiting, many kinds of seasickness, fever, dysentery, headache, heat, constipation, boils, scurvy, cancer, mouth rot, and the like, all of which comes from old and sharply-salted food and meat, also from the very bad and foul water, so that many die miserable. . . . Add to this want of provisions, hunger, thirst, frost, heat, dampness, anxiety, want, afflictions, and lamentations, together with other trouble, as, e.g., the lice abound so frightfully, especially on sick people, that they can be scraped off the body. The misery reaches a climax when a gale rages for two or three nights so that everyone believes that the ship will go to the bottom with all human beings on board. In such a visitation the people cry and pray most piteously.[14]

Working Women in the Colonies

As new towns and villages mushroomed along the Atlantic seaboard, colonial life took on a more predictable though a no less rugged pattern. A woman's work began at sunup and continued by firelight as long as she could hold her eyes open. For two centuries, almost everything that her family used or ate was produced at home under her direction. She spun and dyed the yarn that she wove into cloth and cut and hand-stitched into garments. She grew much of the food her family ate, and preserved enough to last the winter months. She made butter, cheese, bread, candles, and soap, and knitted her family's stockings. It was her responsibility to gather and dry wild herbs used in food preservation and as medicines; she also served as doctor, nurse, and midwife within her own family and in the community.

Her day began as she coaxed the coals to a flame to cook the first of the three meals she prepared for her large family. Bending over the open fire, summer and winter, she hoisted the heavy cast-iron Dutch oven or water kettle into place on the swinging iron fireplace crane. If she had a well in her own yard she was among the fortunate: many women fetched water from a town well some distance from their cottage.

She had other skills that would prove essential to the victory of the colonies in the Revolutionary War, for the colonial woman was a skilled worker. The small businesses that supplied the growing needs of the rapidly increasing population were usually conducted by husbands and sons within their houses or on their property. For additional labor they depended on their wives and daughters. Thus women learned to shoe horses, cut and trim tin plates, sew uppers onto leather soles, tend the store and keep the books, or operate a saw or gristmill. They could also handle a musket when need be, and often did.[15]

Women married early, produced numerous children, and often died while still quite young. Husbands sought to remarry as quickly as possible, and the new family unit included children by previous marriages in addition to the offspring that quickly arrived. The average colonial family numbered about nine people, some of whom might be maiden aunts, grandparents, indentured servants, and apprentices.

While most women worked full-time in their homes, some earned or supplemented their livelihood through paid employment. One of their earliest occupations was innkeeping. Travel between coastal towns created the need for overnight lodging. Inns and taverns, though sometimes run by husband-wife teams, were often run by women alone. Records from 1643 in Massachusetts indicate that one Goody Armitage was licensed to "keepe the ordinary but not to draw wine."[16]

In seventeenth- and eighteenth-century homes, three generations usually lived under one roof and everyone worked, from maiden relatives to grandparents. Baking, cooking, spinning, and butter churning were women's work, in addition to child rearing, while the grandfather helped where he could and undoubtedly kept an eye on the children.

The first printing press in the colonies, which began operation in 1638, was owned by a woman, Mrs. Jose Glover, in Cambridge, Massachusetts.[17] Women also ran sawmills and gristmills, caned chairs and built furniture, operated slaughterhouses, printed cotton and other cloth, made lace, and owned and ran dry-goods and clothing stores. They worked in tobacco shops, drug shops (where they sold concoctions they made themselves), and general stores that sold everything from pins to meat scales. Women ground eyeglasses, made netting and rope, cut and stitched leather goods, made cards for wool carding, and even were house painters. Often they were the town undertakers, a job rarely held by women today. Records indicate that women worked in paper mills at the equivalent of 75 cents a week plus board[18] and that women barbers served both male and female customers. Still another paid occupation women performed was remaking worn clothing and reknitting the heels and toes in stockings.

In spite of this impressive list, the work women did in their own homes far exceeded in economic importance the other jobs they held. They did not learn their craft and artisan skills from being apprenticed to the trade, as did colonial boys, but from helping husbands, fathers, or brothers on a day-to-day basis in home-centered workshops run mainly by the men. When girls were apprenticed, it was to learn spinning, weaving, and domestic skills.

Textiles from England were expensive and shipments irregular. The young colonies were always short of cloth, and almost every woman spent as much time as she could in weaving homespun. As early as 1640 in New England the production of cloth was encouraged by court order, and women ran spinning schools to train young girls and boys. By 1656 several New England colonies regularly assigned quotas for the production of yarn and cloth to families according to their size.[19] A Salem, Massachusetts court order called on all towns to ensure that "woemen, boyes and girls . . . spin according to their skill and ability."[20]

Cloth production was time-consuming. A woman using every minute of her spare time would need as much as an entire year to card, spin, weave, cut, sew, and fit a suit of homespun for her husband. The religious poem "Huswifery," by Edward Taylor, a seventeenth-century Connecticut minister and poet, reflects how much a part of everyday life these home-centered tasks were.

> Make me, O Lord, thy Spinning Wheele compleat;
> Thy Holy Worde my Distaff make for mee.
> Make mine Affections thy Swift Flyers neate,
> And make my Soule thy holy Spoole to bee.
> My Conversation make to be thy Reele,
> And reele the yarn thereon spun of thy Wheele.

The job of the teacher of early "dame schools" in the mid-seventeenth century involved more than hearing the lessons of neighborhood children. This one supervised a young girl apprentice learning to spin, and kept busy with household chores such as plucking a goose, carefully saving the down feathers for a quilt.

20004297

Make me thy Loome then, knit therein this Twine:
And make thy Holy Spirit, Lord, winde quills:
Then weave the Web thyself. The yarn is fine.
Thine Ordinances make my Fulling Mills.
Then dye the same in Heavenly Colours choice,
All Pinkt with Varnish't Flowers of Paradise.

Then cloath therewith mine Understanding, Will,
Affections, Judgment, Conscience, Memory;
My words and Actions, that their shine may fill
My wayes with glory and thee glorify.
Then mine apparrell shall display before yee
That I am cloathed in Holy robes for glory.[21]

Those women who chose, or were forced, to farm for a living had perhaps an even harder life. Judith Giton in South Carolina is not atypical:

With her husband she grubbed the land, felled trees, and operated a whipsaw. For six months together, she declared in a letter to her brother, she went without bread while working the ground like a slave, and for a period of three or four years she did not always have food when she wanted it.[22]

The women who owned no land and had no family to depend on and no way of opening a small business had the hardest time of all. Throughout the colonies, spinsters usually went to live with whatever relatives would house and feed them. They worked hard in that household for their keep and had no privacy, no voice in making family decisions, and of course, no income.

Although colonial women who were nurses rarely worked at it full-time, those who were midwives often did. Obituaries and tombstones of prominent colonial midwives indicate that theirs was a prestigious occupation. A good midwife would deliver as many as three or four thousand babies during her career. She also played an important role in paternity suits, since she was considered to have had access to the new mother at a vulnerable point in her life, and her word on what she heard at such moments was accepted as evidence in court to identify the real father. Midwifery was protected as a female occupation throughout the seventeenth century. In fact, until the American Revolution most doctors were women. However, the case of Katherine Hebden, a well-known Maryland doctor, indicates the problems these women sometimes had. When it came to suing for nonpayment of fees, her husband, Thomas, had to take the case to court and demand the payment due *him* for medical services rendered by *his wife*.

Along with home businesses that continued to thrive in the eighteenth century, small industries now employed women and children, especially the poor, in work outside the home that was an extension of their traditional tasks. Boston opened spinning schools in 1750 "where the poor may be taught gratis," and a year later a "Society for Encouraging Industry and Employing the Poor" was started with two purposes: promoting the manufacture of woolen and other kinds of cloth, and employing "our women and children who are now in a great measure idle."[23]

Local governments welcomed any merchant contractor who provided work for women and children. A "manufacturing house" in Boston in 1769 employed women at four hundred spinning wheels, and in 1770, with the encouragement of the legislature, Boston's William Molineux hired girls as young as eight for manufacturing wearing apparel. Plans of this sort were applauded, and one of Molineux's contemporaries commented: "The female children of this town . . . are not only useful to the community but the poorer sort are able in some measure to assist their parents in getting a livelihood."[24] New York's Governor Moore reported in 1767: "Every home swarms with children who are set to spin and card." By the time of the Revolution, the United Company of Philadelphia for Promoting Manufacture employed four hundred women at producing cotton thread for the colonies. Not all of these new "factories" paid their workers. Some employers who hired orphans or the unemployed poor viewed this as a "service to the community" to put idle hands to work, and paid no wages.[25]

For women with the necessary skills, domestic service could be a respected and comparatively well paid occupation. The skilled domestic spent a good part of her time in spinning, weaving, baking, and sewing. It is likely that this profession did not lose status entirely until the shortage of women available for this work ended after the Revolutionary War. Spinning and baking were gradually removed from the home to the factory, leaving only the unskilled housework for women domestics.

As early as 1734, maidservants began organizing among themselves to improve their working conditions. John Peter Zenger's New-York Weekly Journal of January 28 of that year carried this notice:

> Here are many women in this Town that these hard Times intend to go to Service, but as it is proper the World should know our Terms, we think it reasonable we should not be beat by our Mistrisses Husband[s], they being too strong, and perhaps may do tender women Mischief. If any Ladies want Servants, and will engage for their Husbands, they shall be soon supplied.[26]

Widows in the New York colony also organized to protest their status. This advertisement from a New York paper makes clear the injustices they sought to remedy:

> We, widows of this city, have had a meeting as our case is something deplorable, we beg you will give it place in your Weekly Journal, that

we may be relieved, it is as follows. We are housekeepers, pay out taxes, carry on trade and most of us are she merchants, and as we in some measure contribute to the support of the government, we ought to be entitled to some of the sweets of it.[27]

Barter remained important until the end of the eighteenth century, and women often traded goods they produced for services or other items they might need. For example:

> Agreed with Mrs. Susannah Shepard, of Wrentham, to make her a chaise for £ 55, she finding the harness, the wheels, leather for top and lining, remainder to be had in goods, at wholesale case price, of her manufacture.
>
> (signed) Stephen Olney.[28]

Women continued to do a brisk business in custom work, spinning and dyeing thread, weaving cloth, and knitting stockings. Those unskilled in any of these arts took in laundry to support themselves or their families when necessary; with soap made of lye and ashes, this was harsh work. Just as in the seventeenth century, many occupations were open to women, as this list from the Southern colonies indicates (although the fact that the women holding these jobs are known by name also suggests that the number who held each kind of job may have been small).

> Rebecca Weyman, upholsterer
> Ann Fowler, upholsterer, also sold paper hangings
> Mary Stevenson, glazier and painter
> Jane Inch, silversmith
> Mary Willet, pewterer
> Anna Maria Hoyland, braziery and tinwork
>   (as her mother before her)
> Maria Warwell, mender
> Cassandra Ducker, owner and runner of a fulling mill
> Mary Wilson, shoemaker
> Elizabeth Russell, shipwright
> Catherine Park, tanyard owner and manager
> Mary Robinson, tanner and leather dresser
> Jane Massey, gunsmith
> Jane Burgess, blacksmith
> Mary Butler, blockmaker, pumpmaker
> Elizabeth Butler, barber
> Margaret Oliver and her mother, butchers
> Elizabeth Kelly, sold and repaired whips
> Martha Clifford, ran a livery stable.[29]

A growing number of women found work in the new boot and shoe industry. This industry was largely itinerant in the seventeenth century, when cobblers traveled from house to house cutting and stitching shoes for the inhabitants. With the growth of towns and cities, shoemakers opened their own shops and met the increased demand for shoes by taking in apprentices to help them. By 1750 a division of labor had occurred, and the job of making uppers was separated from that of making soles. Working in their homes, women began to play an important role in the industry, since they could stitch, trim, and decorate the uppers, particularly on women's shoes.

Some colonial women were printers. In fact, of the 78 colonial newspapers in the eighteenth century, 16 were edited by women.[30] Anne Green, who took over the *Maryland Gazette* when her husband died, may have been the first to advance the case for equal pay for equal work. A mother of six (eight other children had died), she was forty-five when widowed and knew that she would have to maintain all the newspaper's readers and advertisers plus the printing contracts from the state assembly if the paper and her family were to survive. Therefore, the same edition that carried the news of her husband's death carried this announcement:

> I presume to address You for your Countenance to Myself and numerous Family, left, without your Favour, almost destitute of Support, by the Decease of my Husband, who, long abed, I have the Satisfaction to say, faithfully served You in the business of Provincial Printer; and, I flatter myself, that, with your kind Indulgence and Encouragement, MYSELF and SON, will be enabled to continue it on the same Footing. On this Expectation, I shall venture to supply my late Husband's Customers with News-Papers, on the same Terms he did, until I receive Orders to the Contrary, and shall be ready to publish from Time to Time, the Advertisements that shall be sent to the Printing-Office.[31]

She continued to receive the government's printing work at the same rate of pay that her husband had received.

Ann Smith Franklin, the wife of James, Benjamin Franklin's brother, assumed the task of compiling, editing, and printing the *Rhode Island Almanack* when her husband died, and continued it for twenty-three years. Both her daughters and a son worked in the shop with her. She was also the first woman employee of the colonial postal system, becoming postmistress of Boston in 1753.

Mary Katherine Goddard was even better known as a printer and engraver, having learned these skills from her printer-mother, who also taught her to write and edit newspaper copy. At the age of thirty-three, Katherine took over publication of the *Pennsylvania Chronicle* for her brother, William, who had moved to Baltimore to start another paper. As he became increasingly involved with activities related to the Revolution, William turned this second paper over to Katherine, and in 1773 she became editor "on a temporary basis," a position she held for the next ten years.

Even through the difficult years of the Revolution, the paper never failed to come out, and its circulation grew. It has been rated "second to no newspaper of its time in its interest to colonists."[32] In 1777, in recognition of the high quality of her work, Katherine received the order to print copies of the Declaration of Independence for distribution to the thirteen colonies. One of these copies, signed by John Hancock and Charles Thomson, is permanently exhibited in the Library of Congress.

When William Goddard returned after the Revolution, he and his sister found themselves in an important court battle on a freedom-of-the-press issue, finally winning the right to print any opinion in the paper that they wished. In 1784, William bought Katherine's share of the paper from her, and soon afterward she lost the job she had held for fourteen years as postmistress of Baltimore. Feeling keenly that she had a right to her job, she decided to fight to retain it. Her record of loyal service as a postal worker was outstanding; on several occasions she had even subsidized post riders out of her own pocket. She documented this record and sent it with a letter to President George Washington. Undoubtedly, she also had something to do with the petition signed by more than two hundred townspeople of Baltimore requesting her reinstatement. However, neither her letter nor the petition succeeded. Now in her fifties, she opened a dry-goods and stationery store to earn her living, and later also sold books. She died in 1816 at the age of seventy eight, a lonely old woman who had combined unusual mental and intellectual skills with business acumen to serve Baltimore and the new United States "in a way and to a degree that no woman of her period served any other American community."[33]

Sarah Potter Hillhouse of Georgia and Ann Donovan Timothy of South Carolina were two others who edited and published papers during this period, as did Anna Zenger, whose life as a printer's wife took an unexpectedly exciting turn in 1735. Her husband, John Peter Zenger, edited and published the *New-York Weekly Journal*. By supporting the Popular Party in editorials carried in his paper, he contributed to its victory, and for the first time working men took a majority of seats in the Common Council. Immediately, New York's Governor Cosby condemned the paper and jailed Zenger on charges of "seditious libel." During the nine anxious months of his pretrial imprisonment, Anna Zenger continued to edit and publish the paper, at considerable political risk. The happy ending to this important episode in the history of freedom of the press was due in large measure to an eighty-eight-year-old man, distinguished trial lawyer Andrew Hamilton, who saw that freedom was on trial along with Zenger and defended him without any legal fee. Zenger's victory ensured the principle that criticism of the government is not a libelous act if the criticism is true.[34] After her husband's death in 1746, Anna Zenger continued to publish the *Journal* and operate the printing shop.

While some colonial women held a variety of jobs outside the home, by far the majority lived on small farms with a daily round of chores and work similar to those described in a young farm woman's diary of 1775:

> Fix'd gown for Prude, — Mend Mother's Riding-hood, Spun short thread, — Fix'd two gowns for Welsh's girls, — Carded tow, — Spun linen, — Worked on Cheese-basket, — Hatchel'd flax with Hannah, we did 51 lbs. apiece, — Pleated and ironed, — Read a sermon of Dodridge's, — Spooled a piece, — Milked the Cows, — Spun linen, did 50 knots, — Made a Broom of Guinea wheat straw, — Spun thread to whiten, — Set a Red dye, — Had two Scholars from Mrs. Taylor's, — I carded two pounds of whole wool and felt, — Spun harness twine, — Scoured the pewter, — Ague in my face, — Ellen was spark'd last night, — spun thread to whiten, — Went to Mr. Otis's and made them a swinging visit, — Israel said I might ride his jade, — Prude stayed at home and learned Eve's Dream by heart.[35]

We have very little knowledge about the individual colonial women who pioneered on the frontiers as settlers began to move inland, but a few names have come down to us. Abigail Levy Franks, one of the earliest Jewish pioneers, settled in Pennsylvania, and Catherine Montour, who married a Seneca chief, distinguished herself as a negotiator, helping to keep harmony between Indians and the Pennsylvania colonists.

Among the most famous of these frontier women was Mary Musgrove, the bilingual daughter of a Creek Indian woman and an English father, who grew up with a knowledge and understanding of the Indians of Georgia and Florida. James Oglethorpe, founder and governor of the colony of Georgia, hired her as his interpreter and adviser on Indian affairs in 1730. Highly respected and prosperous, she owned a great deal of land and supervised many Indian traders, which helped her to render invaluable service to the colony when it was threatened with attack by the Spanish. The colony might not have survived without the food she procured for the colonists and the Indians she recruited and paid from her own income to fight with them against the Spanish. As the situation with the Spanish became increasingly tense, Governor Oglethorpe sent her to the Florida border to open a trading post that was actually a cover for spying on the Spanish and rallying the Indians and her traders to support Oglethorpe and the colonies against Spain.

Women as Indentured Servants

Indentured servant women found life in the New World dismal. Completely subject to the will of their masters or mistresses, they could neither leave nor marry until their time of service was up, and were severely punished if they tried to do so. Whippings were common, and brandings were inflicted for a second offense. Their terms were extended as punishment if they did marry, or if they failed to show up for work for any reason, or if they bore an illegitimate child, even though this was often the master's own. Indentured servant women received public whippings if they could not prove to the court's satisfaction that those they accused of fathering their children were indeed the fathers. Therefore they often resorted to child murder, even though the law required execution for this crime unless it could be proved that the child had been born dead.[36]

No wonder that a servant woman in Virginia in 1623 wrote: "I thought no head had been able to hold so much water as hath and doth daily flow from mine eyes."[37] And the song of the indentured servant that opens this chapter continues:

> A thousand woes beside, that I do here abide,
> In the land of Virginny, O;
> In misery I spend my time that hath no end,
> When that I am weary, weary, weary, weary, O.[38]

Although it was difficult and costly to prove a court case, indentured servants did have the right, denied Southern slaves, to go to court to protest their treatment. For example, a master accused of beating his maid and then hitting her over the head with a stool for reading a book one Sunday lost her altogether when the court awarded her her freedom.

Following her term of indenture a servant was entitled to "freedom dues," which could be as little as a dress or two, but might include a spinning wheel or loom, some livestock, or even a small piece of land. Most indentured women married as soon as they were freed—they were in great demand—although some continued in their role as houseworkers. Others, however, drifted off and, along with formerly indentured men, came to constitute the bulk of the colonial poor. Some former criminals caused considerable trouble, as did some of the prostitutes shipped over from Newgate prison in London. Gradually the colonies refused to accept any more convicts as indentured servants.

Women's Status, Women's Place

Although colonists everywhere faced similar problems in settling the New World, the colonies developed quite differently. Jamestown never became very large, while the thriving Puritan settlements in Massachusetts numbered 15,000 inhabitants by 1643. This colony's rigid religious dogma viewed women and sexuality as potential dangers to men and dictated that women show complete obedience to their husbands. Idleness was a

sin, and the colony tolerated no free riders. Law and edicts required that
everyone work, and anyone who failed to do so could be whipped or
fined. Town tax laws reinforced the principle that everyone should work.
"Court orders, laws, and public subscriptions were resorted to in order that
poor women might be saved from the sin of idleness and taught to be
self-supporting." One Margarett Page, jailed as a "lazy, idle, loytering
person," was promptly put to work and several families paid to keep her
busy. About the same time Mary Boutwell of Essex was charged with
"exorbitancy not working but liveing idly."[39]

While some women taught dame schools as early as 1635, usually in
their own homes, most Puritan schools were geared to the religious instruction of boys. Girls could use the schools, which began to appear after
1647, only when they were not in use by the boys, for the Puritans felt
that too much book-learning was physically and spiritually harmful for
women and weakened their ability to perform their other duties.

The Puritan attitude toward women is shown in the treatment of Anne
Hutchinson, the first woman we know of in the colonies to organize
others around the belief that women as well as men should be allowed
to think and speak freely for themselves and to play a role in the church.
She had journeyed with her husband and fourteen children to the Massachusetts Bay Colony in 1634, seeking the freedom to practice the religion
she believed God had revealed to her. Once in the colony, her skills as
doctor and midwife were soon in great demand. As she ministered to
women in childbirth she talked of her religion of love. For those women
who could not attend the Sunday church services, she formed a women's
club that held Monday meetings in her home, where she summarized the
preceding day's sermon. Inevitably some of her own ideas crept into these
sessions, which became so popular that she was soon conducting a second
one each week. She fought for the right of women to speak at religious
meetings, and persuaded her own minister, the Reverend John Cotton,
to allow women to take part in church singing.

As she developed a following, the ministers of the colony and Governor
Winthrop came to fear her, and with good reason. Her followers were so
numerous and politically motivated that in 1636 they succeeded in preventing Governor Winthrop's re-election, an act he did not forgive. After
his return to the governorship the following year, he saw to it that Anne
Hutchinson was brought to trial for heretical teachings—a trial where he
served as both prosecutor and judge. Her fate in the colony from that
point on was never much in doubt. Tried not once but twice, the second
time when she was pregnant with her sixteenth child and ill, deserted
by the one minister who had been a loyal friend, with her supporters
frightened into silence, she was forced to accept excommunication

and banishment. When she demanded to know why she was banished, Governor Winthrop silenced her, answering, "Say no more, the court knows wherefore and is satisfied."

Somewhat more relaxed attitudes toward women prevailed in the Middle Atlantic colonies, where educational opportunities were open to both girls and boys in New Amsterdam (at least until the advent of English rule in 1664), and where Quakers and Moravians in Pennsylvania educated both sexes equally and often employed women teachers. However, it was not the children of the workers who received the benefit of this education, by and large, and half the population could neither read nor write. While Virginia opened its first free school in 1642, with neighborhood white children welcomed, there were few public schools even as late as 1700. At the turn of the century only about one in four women in the Southern colonies could read or write.[40]

Women, then, held a unique position in the early colonies, with numerous opportunities to work, and substantial respect and power in their role as supervisors of all home production. But legally their rights were limited. They could hold property only until they married, and after they were widowed. As married women they were legally entitled only to a home, food, support, and protection from violence. They could neither sign contracts nor bring suit. While they had the right to assist their husbands in business, anything they earned or owned belonged to their spouses; technically, this included even the clothes they wore. They could, however, inherit property.

Two colonies provided a somewhat different environment for women from the start: Rhode Island and Pennsylvania. The former was settled by men and women fleeing the tight controls and the rigid religious dogma of the Puritans; the latter, by English Quakers escaping persecution at home. Both these colonies, too, enjoyed unusually peaceful relations with the Indians, paying them for all land on which the colonists settled. Another small community, Gravesend, established on Long Island in 1643, practiced religious freedom and isolated itself from colonial rigidities. Deborah Moody, its founder, had left Massachusetts with a group of settlers who differed strongly from the Puritans and sought to worship in their own way.

Perhaps the first woman to demand a seat in colonial government, an area where no plans had been made to include women, was Margaret Brent. An adventurous woman, she had come to Maryland with her sister Mary and nine colonists in 1638, the earliest record we have of women themselves leading a group of settlers. Each of the Brent sisters settled a large plantation and sent back to England for more workers.

As a farmer, Margaret Brent gained a notable reputation for experimental work in seed production. A persuasive and dynamic speaker, she regularly served as an attorney, and on one occasion her ability forestalled a threatened mutiny of soldiers over nonpayment for their services. She was credited with saving the colony of Maryland from ruin.

In 1647, Governor Leonard Calvert named her his executor, and as such she was entitled to succeed him in the "attorneyship of Baltimore." This would have allowed her a vote in the House of Burgesses, where she felt, in addition, that she was entitled to a vote in her own right as a property owner. She pleaded her case for these votes, but lost. As a result, she protested every action of that session of the Assembly.

The rights of women decreased the lower their economic and social status in the community, though even indentured servant women could plead their cases in court and testify against their masters. Slave women, however, had no rights whatsoever in the South, and few elsewhere. Southern codes locked them and their children into lifelong slavery. Legally they could never marry or inherit property, nor could they sign contracts or learn certain kinds of skilled work. They could not, on their own, leave their owners or plantations, and were returned and severely punished if they did so. Laws forbade slave meetings, and only a few informal plantation schools taught a mere handful of slaves how to read and write. Later, even these schools and any teaching of literacy to slaves were outlawed, although at great personal risk slaves who could read still taught others, as did some whites, particularly women and children.

Slave women in New England, New Amsterdam, and Pennsylvania were sometimes more fortunate. In many cases they received less harsh treatment than in the South, and a number were able to buy their freedom. Twenty-four slave women reportedly held jobs in a Rhode Island creamery, and other slave as well as free black women worked as cooks, maids, and laundresses, while some became skilled spinners, weavers, and knitters. There was no law against northern blacks attending school, although there were few schools for Negroes and only rarely could they attend schools with white children.

By the end of the seventeenth century the colonies had attained an air of permanence. Brick or clapboard homes replaced the early log huts in the towns and cities that now dotted the coast. While the frontier had pushed inland, most settlements still stood within fifty miles of the coast. The population, largely English, also included Dutch, Germans, French Huguenots, Swedish, and Scotch-Irish, as well as black Africans, though the slave population was still small. All of English America contained less than half a million settlers.[41] Industry, firmly home-centered, was conducted mainly by women, while most men farmed. The northern small-farm economy never encouraged slavery, but by the end of the seventeenth century a booming slave trade involved increasing numbers of Puritans and Dutch, and later the English in New York, as owners and captains of slave ships.

As the colonies moved inevitably toward the struggle for independence from England, there was a sense of increasing restiveness. Even with the depression in 1765 and agitation for boycotts and trade embargoes, the colonies were growing rapidly. Already one-seventh of the world's iron was produced in America, as well as over one-half of the manufactured goods the colonists consumed, for which they had formerly depended on England.

The "putting out" system, precursor of the factories of the early nineteenth century, developed to meet the increasing demand for goods. Merchants would contract for work to be done, supplying the raw materials which men and women made into the finished articles in their homes, to be collected at specified times. Cities like Lynn, Massachusetts, became known for shoes; women sewed uppers and men the heavy soles in a system of production that often involved most of the family. Germantown, Pennsylvania, was famous for high-quality knitted products. The iron industry and salt works, still in their infancy, also seemed ready for the major boost they would get from the Revolutionary War.

Yet the family as an economic unit, depending on each of its members and quite self-contained, was the inner strength and secret weapon of the colonies. This would pull the young country through the war. Together with aid from overseas allies like France, it would make possible the birth of the new United States.

2

BLACK WOMEN
IN COLONIAL AMERICA

And God said: Go down, Death, go down,
Go down to Savannah, Georgia,
Down in Yamacraw,
And find Sister Caroline.
She's borne the burden and heat of the day,
She's labored long in my vineyard,
And she's tired—
She's weary—
Go down, Death, and bring her to me.
—James Weldon Johnson,
　"Go Down, Death (A Funeral Sermon)"

What distinguished colonial society from that of Europe or England was its upward mobility. Origins counted for little. If a worker could save money and buy land or open a shop, he could move into the middle class or even higher. Affluence, not birth, was what counted. Only the growing numbers of slaves from Africa and their children had no chance to move up.

Colonial Slavery

In 1619, a Dutch frigate dropped anchor in Jamestown harbor with twenty blacks aboard, at least three of whom were women. Because they had been baptized during the voyage from Africa, English law held that they could not be sold into slavery, so the colonial government bought their contracts as indentured servants.

Desperate for laborers, Jamestown settlers gladly purchased these contracts. One of the black women, Isabella, married one of the black men, Antony, and in 1624 their son, William Tucker, was the first black child born in the English colony.[1] At first black bondsmen worked the prescribed number of years and earned their freedom. They became farmers and artisans, accumulated land, voted, and themselves held servants and sometimes slaves.

But this pattern did not last. Within twenty years after Antony, Isabella, and their shipmates arrived in Jamestown, black indentured servants worked longer terms of service than white and might even have these terms extended for life as punishment for running away. By 1640, Virginia had established slavery as legal, and by 1662 the word "slave" was freely used in Virginia statutes, acknowledging in law what had been a growing practice in the colony: that black people and their children could be held in lifelong bondage.[2]

In rapid succession, many of the early colonies along the Atlantic coast passed similar laws recognizing slavery:

1640	Virginia
1641	Massachusetts
1664	Maryland, New York
1673	The Carolinas
1682	Pennsylvania, Delaware
1708	Rhode Island[3]

In 1667, Virginia law declared that "conferring of baptisme doth not alter the condition of the person as to his bondage or freedome," and so conversion to Christianity was no longer a bar to enslavement.[4]

In New York, too, blacks were early arrivals. Eleven male slaves were among the first group of Dutch settlers founding New Amsterdam, and black women were brought over a few years later. Records indicate that these blacks had some of the rights of indentured servants. For example, in 1661, when a slave couple presented Peter Stuyvesant with a petition for their son's freedom, it was granted. Nor was the bondage of black servants declared "perpetual" until the English took over New Amsterdam in 1664[5] and slave codes restricted the right of black bondsmen to marry in church, own land, or have legal protection of their women against rape.

Slaves came from every part of the vast continent of Africa, bringing with them a multitude of languages, skills, crafts, and cultural heritages. Some came to slavery through capture in native wars, where the victors sold them to black slave merchants. Others were kidnapped or tricked into slavery. Still others were sold by chiefs as punishment for breaking tribal rules.

The journey to America for the newly enslaved Africans involved three stages. The first, the long forced march to the coastal city for debarking, meant pushing night and day over mountains, rivers, and plains. Arriving at the warehouse, or barracoon, slaves were held until enough were collected to fill the ship. Buyers examined them for physical prowess and health, made their purchases, then branded them with a hot iron. Smaller irons were used on the women, who were branded under the breast in order not to diminish their beauty and jeopardize future salability.

As each ship's captain reached his quota of slaves, he would chain them together and row them out for loading. Once on board, he packed them "like books on shelves into holds which in some instances were no higher than 18 inches."[6] One such captain is quoted as saying, "They had not so much room as a man in his coffin, either in length or breadth. It was impossible for them to turn or shift with any degree of ease." For the six, eight, or more weeks of this dread "middle passage," they existed—and many died—like animals. Women seem to have had a higher survival rate than the men, perhaps because they were sometimes brought on deck during the day for the pleasure of the sailors and to launder and cook.

Reverend R. Walsh wrote the following account in the early nineteenth century of conditions that had been typical of slave ships for two hundred years:

> She had taken in, on the coast of Africa, 336 males and 226 females, making in all 562. . . . The slaves were all enclosed under grated hatchways, between decks. The space was so low, that they sat between each other's legs, and stowed so close together that there was no possibility of their lying down, or at all changing their position, by night or day. As they belonged to, and were shipped on account of different individuals, they were all branded like sheep . . ."burnt with the red-hot iron" (one mate told me). Over the hatchway stood a ferocious-looking fellow with a scourge of twisted thongs in his hand, who was the slave driver of the ship, and whenever he heard the slightest noise below, he shook it over them and seemed eager to exercise it. . . .
>   . . . The space between decks was divided into two compartments three feet three inches high; the size of one was sixteen feet by eighteen and of the other forty by twenty one; into the first were crammed the women and girls, into the second the men and boys; 226 fellow-creatures were thus thrust into one space 288 feet square and 336 into another space 800 feet square, giving to the whole an average of 23 inches and to each of the women not more than thirteen inches, though many of them were pregnant. . . . The heat of these horrid places was so great, and the odor so offensive, that it was quite impossible to enter them, even had there been room. . . .
>   . . . On looking into the places where they had been crammed, there were found some children next to the sides of the ship, in the place most remote from light and air; they were lying nearly in a torpid state after the rest had turned out. The little creatures seemed indifferent as to life or death, and when they were carried on deck many of them could not stand. . . .
>   . . . It was not surprising that they should have endured much sickness and loss of life, in their short passage. . . . They . . . had been out but seventeen days, and they had thrown overboard no less than fifty-five, who had died of dysentery and other complaints, in that space of time, though they had left the coast in good health. Indeed, many of the survivors were seen lying about the decks in the last stage of emaciation, and in a state of filth and misery not to be looked at. . . .[7]

Schools of sharks followed slave ships across the Atlantic, feeding on corpses thrown overboard along with those who were too sick to survive, and on those who tried to escape by jumping over the side, preferring suicide to slavery. In spite of severe discipline on board ship, slaves often revolted, although they knew they had no chance of success. John Atkins, ship's surgeon, reports what happened to one woman who took part in such a revolt: "The Woman he [the ship's captain] hoisted up by the Thumbs, whipped, and slashed her with Knives, before the other slaves till she died."[8]

The second stage, or middle passage, usually ended in the West Indies. There the slaves were unloaded, cleaned up, and farmed out to plantations for hardening to field labor. This process, if they survived it, enhanced their value in future sales to colonial plantation owners. But as many as one-third of the slaves, weakened by the long and difficult voyage to the Indies, died during this rigorous introduction to work under the hot sun. Those who lived made the third and final stage of their trip to America within a matter of months, being shipped to the colonies for sale to individual owners, who more and more often were Southern planters.

Even with the increasing traffic in slaves, indentured servants outnumbered them as the chief source of colonial labor through the seventeenth century. In 1648 Virginia had just 300 blacks in a total population of 15,000, and by 1671 this had increased only to 2,000 out of 40,000 inhabitants. By the 1700s, the numbers of indentured servants willing to sign up for grueling Southern work decreased, and slavery grew rapidly. While not all blacks were slaves, by far the largest number were. Between 1680 and 1786, some 2,130,000 slaves made the trip from Africa to the West Indies and America.[9] Most of these ended up in the South, since the small farms and fishing communities of the Northern colonies did not require slave labor.

By the close of the seventeenth century all of New England had a total of no more than 4,500 slaves, while in Maryland and Virginia alone there were some 10,000.[10] The importation of slaves had increased to such an extent that in 1698 South Carolina required planters to purchase or hire one white servant for every six blacks. By the time of the American Revolution, slaves made up two-thirds of South Carolina's population and half of Virginia's.

Colonial codes and laws completely regulated the lives of slaves, differing in harshness according to the percentage of blacks in the population. For example, in New England, where the slave population remained small, slaves could testify under oath against whites and had the right to jury trials. However, South Carolina, with its predominantly black population, patterned its rigid slave codes on the West Indian model and lived in constant fear of slave uprisings.

It is important to recall the nature of these Southern codes: slaves could not legally marry or inherit property, nor sign contracts or leave their owners or plantations. White Southerners were obliged to help in the return of fugitive slaves, and patrolled both urban and rural black dwelling areas, especially at night. The only responsibilities that owners had were to feed, house, and oversee the slaves who belonged to them.

Black Women in the Southern Colonies

One group of women, from the start of their life in America, worked outside their homes on a full-time basis: slave women. About one-third of all slaves were women, most of them sold upon arrival, often without regard for the breaking up of families or even for the separation of young children from their mothers. Most slaves went to work on plantations and farms in the Southern colonies, where they soon came to be preferred to indentured servants. They were cheaper, did not have to be replaced, and received no "freedom dues" since they never became free. Because of their color they were easily identified if they tried to run away. Slave women had the added advantage of producing a continuous labor supply for the growing plantation economy, since slave children under colonial law took the condition of their mothers.

Black women worked in the fields alongside the men, planting and harvesting tobacco, rice, indigo, and, to a limited extent, cotton. (Cotton production, with which the South is always identified, did not become its staple crop until late in the eighteenth century.) Groups of slave women also worked at spinning, weaving, sewing, and knitting. Some slave women were houseworkers: maids, cooks, laundresses, and nurse-maids.

Life in the slave quarters centered around the women. Since slaves could not legally marry and could be sold at the whim of the master, close family relationships among slaves could be broken up at any time, with men sold to new owners more often than women. Thus the responsibility not only for raising the children but for any continuity in family life often fell upon the women. The pattern of the extended family was vital, since mothers worked all day, and their young children were left to the care of grandmothers or old or disabled slaves, except on larger plantations where informal slave nurseries were run by older slave women called "aunties."

Forced to neglect their own children and care for those of their masters, black women often expressed their yearning and resentment in song.

Many a white child was rocked to sleep with some version of this lullaby of sorrow and concern for the black child back in the slave quarters that the nursemaid or "mammy" never had far from her thoughts.

> Hush-a-bye, don't you cry
> Go to sleepy little baby,
> When you awake, you will have cake,   •
> And all the pretty little horses.
> Black and bay, dapple and gray
> Coach and six-a-little horses.
>
> Way down yonder
> Down in the meadow
> There's a poor little lambie,
> The bees and the butterflies
> Pecking out its eyes,
> The poor little thing cried Mammy.
>
> Hush-a-bye, Hush-a-bye
> Go to sleepy little baby.
> When you awake, you will have cake,
> And all the pretty little horses.

When a slave mother was sold, relatives took on the extra responsibility of caring for the children from whom she was often separated. Nor did slave women have any recourse from the sexual abuse they suffered at the hands of white owners and overseers. This was both common and accepted among the white community and imposed a constant burden of exploitation upon black women. It is little wonder that black women as well as men participated in slave revolts, in spite of the almost certain failure of these attempts and the severity of the punishment—usually death by hanging or burning.

Southern slave women worked on plantations with hundreds of slaves, on farms with as few as two or three, and in city households. Plantation slave women went to the fields early each morning, leaving their children behind. These children, often dressed in rough burlap sacks with holes cut for the arms and head, rarely were issued shoes until they were old enough to begin work in the fields—usually at about the age of six or seven. By the time they were twelve, they had regular field assignments.

Plantation slave cabins usually had one room, or sometimes two rooms where two families lived and shared one fireplace. There the women cooked breakfast and dinner, while lunch was sent to workers in the fields.

> The food . . . was issued once a week. . . . Each adult was given a peck of corn and three or four pounds of bacon or salt pork. Fractional amounts, usually one half, were allotted to each child in the family.[11]

Twice a year slaves received their clothes ration. Women were given cloth to make up into dresses and aprons, while men's shirts and pants were sewn in two standard sizes in the plantation sewing room. A typical woman's ration included

> in the fall 6 yards of woolen cloth, 6 yards of cotton drilling and a needle, skein of thread and a half dozen buttons. In the spring 6 yards of cotton shirting and 6 yards of cotton cloth similar to that for men's pants, needle, thread and buttons. Each worker gets a stout pair of shoes every fall, and a heavy blanket every third year.[12]

Men and women could expect to be issued the same kinds of shoes, which almost never fit.

Punishment usually took the form of whippings, which slaves received frequently and for the most minor offenses. The fear of oversleeping particularly haunted field slaves. Awakened from a sleep of exhaustion by a cowhorn at daybreak, slaves had scarcely half an hour to feed the family and get themselves to the lineup for their field assignment. If instead they fell back asleep, they could expect the lash. Often slave women could be seen racing to the lineup carrying aprons and shoes they had not had time to put on in their cabins.

The weariness of the field laborer is captured in this sad, beautiful, and poignant slave song:

> I know moon-rise, I know star-rise;
>   Lay dis body down.
> I walk in de moonlight, I walk in de starlight,
>   To lay dis body down.
> I'll walk in de graveyard, I'll walk through de graveyard
>   To lay dis body down.
> I'll lie in de grave and stretch out my arms;
>   Lay dis body down.
> I go to de judgment in de evenin' of de day,
>   When I lay dis body down;
> And my soul and your soul will meet in de day
>   When I lay dis body down.[13]

Pregnancy usually made no difference in work assignments. Many slave women worked in the fields until close to the time they delivered, sometimes giving birth right in the grass nearby. An exception might be made for a slave woman who was the mistress of the plantation owner, which she often was forced to be, and if it was his child she was carrying. She might then have a lighter work assignment, perhaps as a house slave, preceding and following the birth, for a total of perhaps four weeks in all, together with extra rations. All her children were, of course, slaves, regardless of the father.

Black women in the South served another function, that of wet nurse to the master's children. When one of their own slaves was not available to serve in that capacity, a family would advertise for a slave woman of another owner, or sometimes for a white woman, to be hired by the month or the year as needed.

WANTED

A NURSE with a good Breast of Milk, of a healthy Constitution, and good Character, that is willing to go into a Gentleman's Family. Such a one may hear a very good Encouragement, by enquiring of the Printer hereof.

Two healthy likely wet nurses with their first children to be hired out by the month. Inquire at the Printers.

Wanted by the Month

A HEALTHY CAREFUL NEGROE WENCH for a WET NURSE. One without a child will be most agreeable, or with a child not above six months old.[14]

Slave families most dreaded the slave auction, where they might be separated and sold to new owners with new and unpredictable overseers and new sets of rules to learn at the expense of many a beating. Frances Ellen Watkins Harper (1825–1911), a black abolitionist, poet and lecturer, described the agony of slave sales in this poem titled simply "The Slave Auction":

> The sale began—young girls were there,
>   Defenceless in their wretchedness,
> Whose stifled sobs of deep despair
>   Revealed their anguish and distress.
>
> And mothers stood with streaming eyes,
>   And saw their dearest children sold;
> Unheeded rose their bitter cries,
>   While tyrants bartered them for gold.
>
> And woman, with her love and truth—
>   For these in sable forms may dwell—
> Gaz'd on the husband of her youth,
>   With anguish none may paint or tell.
>
> And men, whose sole crime was their hue,
>   The impress of their Maker's hand,
> And frail and shrinking children, too,
>   Were gathered in that mournful band.
>
> Ye who have laid your love to rest,
>   And wept above their lifeless clay,
> Know not the anguish of that breast,
>   Whose loves are rudely torn away.

> Ye may not know how desolate
> Are bosoms rudely forced to part,
> And how a dull and heavy weight
> Will press the life-drops from the heart.[15]

Because of their ties to their children, slave women did not run away as often as the men, but some did and took an active part in revolts that took place from New York to New Orleans. While we do not know the names of most of the slave martyrs, we do know that in many of the uprisings women fought alongside the men, sometimes with guns and knives, sometimes committing suicide rather than face capture and execution.[16] Men were hanged when caught, but women usually were burned at the stake. This hideous form of torture was probably an attempt to discourage women, who held so influential a position in the slave community, from participating in revolts. Nonetheless, women took part in the planning as well as the actual uprisings, committing arson and sabotage, attempting on occasion to poison owners, and joining in the armed resistance.

The Northern Black Experience

The experience of black women in the Northern colonies differed radically from that of Southern black women. Blacks never exceeded 3 percent of the population in all New England, except for Rhode Island, where they may have been as many as 10 percent. Many were not slaves at all, but free citizens who farmed or worked in the same kinds of jobs as white citizens. Although the largest number of black women working outside the home held service jobs in housekeeping or as laundresses or cooks, many were also spinners, weavers, dressmakers, milliners, hairdressers, or printers, or were involved in other trades open to women at the time.

As early as the mid-seventeenth century, protests against slavery began to gather momentum in the North. In 1652 the Quakers publicly protested the institution of slavery, and in 1688, they issued this statement:

> There is a saying, that we should do to all men like as we will be done ourselves. . . . Here [in America] is liberty of conscience, which is right and reasonable; here ought to be likewise liberty of the body. . . . But to bring men hither, or to rob and sell them against their will, we stand against. . . . Pray, what thing in the world can be done worse towards us, that if men should rob or steal us a way, and sell us for slaves to strange countries, separating husbands from their wives and children. . . . have these poor Negroes not as much right to fight for their freedom, as you have to keep them slaves?[17]

The farther north black people lived, the better their chances of being educated, and the fewer the laws against their schooling. However, towns often passed restrictions against the Indians (evening curfews, for example), and these usually included blacks also. It is not surprising that on occasion Northern slaves and Indians allied themselves against the whites.

Northern sentiment against trafficking in slaves mounted during the second half of the eighteenth century. In part, the colonists feared that eventually they might be outnumbered by blacks unless the trade were halted. Political considerations also had a lot to do with the growth of anti-slave-trade sentiment: through banishing the slave traffic so profitable to England, colonists could lash out at the Parliament which had levied numerous taxes, quartered troops at colonial expense, forbidden all trade except with Britain, and prohibited settlement west of the Appalachian Mountains. Twice Massachusetts tried (1771, 1774) to bar slave trading, only to have the governor of the colony intervene. In 1773 Pennsylvania virtually ended slave importations by imposing a heavy tax on each incoming slave. Rhode Island and Connecticut prohibited this trade in 1774, and Virginia, North Carolina, and Georgia (concerned about the high percentage of blacks in their population) restricted slave trading in 1774 and 1775.

Another strong concern—this on the part of white workers—was the increasing use of black labor at lower wages, and the fear of being replaced by slave labor should the slave trade continue unchecked. By the time of the American Revolution, the colonial black population, most of it in the South, was 700,000 out of the total population of 2,500,000, or 28 percent.

On April 6, 1775, the Continental Congress voted that no more slaves should be brought into the colonies. This reflected both the strained relationship with England and a growing sentiment for freedom, particularly in the North. Jenny Slew's freedom suit is one of the better-known examples of this development, possibly because one of those sitting in the courtroom that day in 1766 when she sued her owner for her freedom was John Adams, later to become the second president of the United States. The court granted Jenny Slew her freedom plus "the sum of four pounds lawful money of this Province."[18]

In spite of the fact that Slew and others like her won individual cases, this route to freedom was difficult, slow, and costly, and group suits by black people inevitably failed. However, it was through court action in the famous Quok Walker case that the Massachusetts State Supreme Court, in 1783, declared slavery unconstitutional.

Records survive of two black women who made unusual contributions during this period. Both had been kidnapped in Africa when very young and sold into slavery. Lucy Terry, born in 1730, grew up as a slave in

Deerfield, Massachusetts. There, in 1746, she penned the first known poem by a black woman, a twenty-eight-line ballad describing the Deerfield Indian massacre.

In 1756 she met and married Abijah Prince, a free man who purchased her freedom, and together they worked his Vermont farm. As time went on they bought a great deal of land and became prosperous. When their oldest son was ready for college he applied to Williams, but was refused admission because of his color. Lucy Prince traveled to Williamstown to appeal to the trustees in a compelling three-hour confrontation, but though they were impressed and moved by her eloquence, they were not willing to admit a black man to the campus.

At the age of sixty-seven Lucy Prince addressed the Supreme Court of the United States, probably the first woman to do so. This action climaxed her long and victorious battle for land rights against a Vermont farm neighbor who had tried to incorporate part of the Princes' land into his own. She appealed her case all the way from her small town court in Sunderland to the highest court of the land, where Justice Samuel Chase, commenting on her victory, told her that she "made a better argument than any he had ever heard—from a Vermont lawyer." She continued to live an active life until her death at ninety-one.[19]

The other black woman, Phillis Wheatley, also began her life in the colonies as a slave. Captured in Senegal, West Africa, when only nine years old, she was sold in the Boston slave market in 1759, but luckily was purchased by John Wheatley, an intelligent and kindly merchant. He and his wife, Susannah, recognizing young Phillis's unusual aptitude for learning, educated her in Latin, astronomy, history, and other subjects in addition to reading, writing, and mathematics. Early in her teens she began writing poetry. Her first book of poems, published in England in 1773, became the second book of poetry to be written and published by an American woman. (The first was by Anne Bradstreet, who came to the Massachusetts colony in 1630.)

Phillis Wheatley's poems received much attention, some of it from men such as Voltaire, Benjamin Franklin, and General George Washington, about whom she wrote one of her poems and whom she visited. When her friend and mistress, Susannah Wheatley, died, Phillis married a grocer named John Peters, who seems to have antagonized her friends and isolated her from them. She and her husband drifted from place to place. Two children born to them died. Poverty finally drove her to go to work in a somewhat seedy boardinghouse during the time her husband was serving a term in debtor's prison. In 1784, broken in health and alone in the world, she and her third child died within hours of each other not long after its birth.

A poet who rarely put her personal feelings into her work, Phillis Wheatley did write one poem about her own experience as a slave. It appeared in the slim volume of her poetry published in 1773.

Poem on Her Own Slavery
(To the Right Honourable William, Earl of
Dartmouth, His Majesty's Principal Secretary of State
for North America, and company)

No more *America* in mournful strain
Of wrongs, and grievance unredress'd complain,
No longer shall thou dread the iron chain,
Which wanton *Tyranny* with lawless hand
Has made, and which it meant t'enslave the land.
    Should you, my lord, while you pursue my song,
Wonder from whence my love of *Freedom* sprung,
Whence flew these wishes for the common good,
By feeling hearts alone best understood,
I, young in life, by seeming cruel fate
Was snatch'd from *Afric's* fancy'd happy seat:
What pangs excruciating must molest,
What sorrows labour in my parent's breast?
Steel'd was the soul and by no misery mov'd
That from a father seized his babe belov'd.
Such, such my case, And can I then but pray
Others may never feel tyrannic sway?[20]

The Northern and Southern black experience in the colonies before the Revolutionary War differed more sharply the farther north one traveled, and reflected the percentage of blacks in the total population, the degree to which white workers felt threatened, and the level of anti-British sentiment—which included efforts to affect British commerce in slaves. On the other hand, the South's dependence on slave labor to maintain its profitable plantation economy steadily increased. The growing proportion of blacks in the population began to threaten the equilibrium of society, and following a brief relaxation after the American Revolution, would lead in the nineteenth century to ever more restrictive laws, increased tensions, conflict with the industrialized North and the West, and finally to a civil war.

3

WORKING WOMEN IN
THE AMERICAN REVOLUTION

"What's the use of women being left behind in a war, if they
can't stay home and do the man's work?"
—Mrs. McKlennar refuses to move into the safety of Eldridge Blockhouse
(Walter Edmonds, *Drums Along the Mohawk*)

Working-class men and women in the 1770s agitated for independence
from England. They were not only vigorous and impatient, they were
sometimes unruly. The policies of the British homeland, which led the
colonies inexorably toward the Revolutionary War, affected them deeply
and adversely. The prohibitions against colonial trade with any other
country than England caused widespread unemployment, raised the cost
of goods, and deeply angered traders and merchants.

Even among themselves colonists were not permitted to trade certain
products, such as hats, wool, or iron, nor could they operate "slitting or
rolling mills or forges or furnaces."[1] The hard times caused by these
restrictions on trade and production might have led families to seek a
new life on the frontier, but still another British edict closed all lands
west of the Appalachian Mountains to new settlement. This reduced the
mobility of city workers, poor farmers, and Southern planters who had
looked toward the West.

Two British colonial taxes, levied to pay for the long though victorious
French and Indian War (1754–1763), succeeded in further unifying the
colonies against English rule. The first came through the notorious Stamp
Act of 1765, which placed a tax on every colonial newspaper and legal
document. Although public pressure forced the repeal of this act, the
harm had been done. When England passed the Tea Act of 1774, giving
a monopoly to the (British) East India Company while retaining the tax
on the company's tea, colonial fury was unprecedented. It resulted in the
famous Boston tea-dumping incident, which a woman, Sarah Bradlee
Fulton, reputedly had a hand in planning.* This was only the first of many

* Sarah Bradlee Fulton, known as the "Mother of the Boston Tea Party," was married to
patriot John Fulton and lived in Medford, near Boston. Although the story may be somewhat apocryphal, it is said that at one of her famous codfish chowder suppers, given at

such "tea parties" that took place in port cities along the coast. Retaliation from England was swift: the port of Boston was closed, court trials were transferred to new jurisdictions, the Massachusetts customs house was moved, the colony's civil government was suspended, and the quartering of troops in colonists' homes was ordered.[2] Couriers saddled their horses and rode out to towns and hamlets with the news. Emergency town meetings were called, and resolutions of support for the people of Boston poured in. Neighboring colonies like Connecticut sent cattle, grain, and other supplies as well as money to help Bostonians during the blockade.

Anti-British sentiment spread and workers organized against British repression. While initial leadership for the Sons of Liberty came from merchants and radicals like Samuel Adams, the Sons and its counterpart organization, the Daughters of Liberty, soon were largely made up of the young working class. Few of the leaders of either group were more than forty-five years old; most were still under forty. Youthful visionaries with a bold and resolute program,[3] they understood earlier than most of the colonists that there was no turning back. Thomas Paine,* worker, civil servant, writer, and patriot, spoke for them when he said, "The period of debate is closed. Arms as the last resource decide the contest."[4]

Nor did the Sons and Daughters of Liberty stand on ceremony. They demonstrated and paraded, organized boycotts, signed petitions, and pledged not to drink tea or buy products made in England. They campaigned for colonists to spin and weave homespun cloth to meet family and army needs, to raise more sheep, prepare more wool, and sew more coats, suits, uniforms, and hats. Their popular slogan was "It is better to wear a Homespun coat than to lose our Liberty."[5]

The Daughters swelled the ranks of the street marches and meetings, joining their voices with the men's in song.

---

the Boston home of her brother Nathaniel, the plan for the Boston Tea Party was born. While Fulton herself did not go to the wharf to help throw the crates of tea overboard, she and her sister-in-law disguised the men who went as Indians, and had hot water ready so they could wash off their disguise immediately upon their return. Sarah Fulton was present at the Battle of Bunker Hill a year and a half later, along with her Minuteman husband, and took charge of nursing the wounded on the village green. This began her wartime activities, which included carrying a message for General Washington through enemy lines—a feat that was recognized later when the general paid her a personal visit to convey his thanks. Harry Clinton Green and Mary Wolcott Green, *The Pioneer Mothers of America* (New York: C. P. Putnam's Sons, 1912), vol. 2, pp. 227–35.

* Paine was also aware of the legal and societal restraints placed on women. In 1775 he wrote that they were, "even in countries where they may be esteemed the most happy, constrained in their desires in the disposal of their goods, robbed of freedom and will by the laws, the slaves of opinion, which rules them with absolute sway and construes the slightest appearances into guilt; surrounded on all sides by judges, who are at once tyrants and their seducers . . . who does not feel for the tender sex?" From the *Pennsylvania Magazine*, August 1775, as quoted in Eleanor Flexner, *Century of Struggle* (New York: Atheneum Publishers, 1970), pp. 14, 15.

Come Rally Sons of Liberty,
Come All with hearts United,
Our motto is "We Dare Be Free,"
Not easily affrighted!

Oppression's Band we must subdue,
Now is the Time, or never;
Let each Man prove this motto True
And Slavery from him sever.[6]

When a mass gathering of the Daughters was interrupted by a man who unwisely chose that time to come forward and denounce the Revolution, the Daughters took hold of him, removed his coat and shirt, spread him with molasses, and plastered him with flower petals.

Perhaps the first woman's auxiliary in the new country, the Daughters were welcomed by the Sons of Liberty, who declared: "With the Ladies on our side we can make every Tory tremble."[7] Adopting the Liberty Tree as their symbol, the Sons and Daughters wore it on medallions around their necks. They held educational meetings to read newspapers, articles, and pamphlets out loud, since many of their number could not read, and they held song fests. It must also be reported that they tarred and feathered not a few Tories, invaded British government office buildings, pressured merchants to support the boycott of English goods, and occasionally burned the homes of British officials. Suffice it to say that the Sons and Daughters were always ready to act!

It was the Sons and Daughters of Liberty who provided key activists in mobilizing popular support for independence and the war effort, while workers from the cities and towns made up many of the long-term fighters in the Continental Army during the years of struggle (1775–1783). Nonetheless, when the call went out in 1774 for the Philadelphia Continental Congress to which every colony would send delegates, the largely voteless artisans and workers were scarcely represented; the distinguished colonists who came together were planters, merchants, and lawyers. Nor were women, blacks, or Indians represented. But the importance of workers to the Revolutionary effort was recognized in the site chosen for the meeting: Carpenter's Hall.

News of Bunker Hill and the battles of Concord and Lexington (April 1775) galvanized the Sons of Liberty, who took over stores of powder and arms, customs houses, and public buildings and raided British ships in the harbors. In the South, too, women as well as men were active patriots, though the total support for the Revolution was less in the Southern colonies than elsewhere. However, Southern women were prominent in public demonstrations for the Revolution. Where formerly they would have been reprimanded for being so forward, journalists commended them openly for their energetic loyalty to the patriotic cause.

> Enthusiastic matrons plunged into the conflict and wrote fiery articles for the newspapers inciting their countrywomen to action. One . . . wrote that when she reflected on the American grievances she was ready to start up with sword in hand to fight by the side of her husband. Other correspondents urged their countrywomen not to be "tame spectators" and reminded them that "much, very much depends on the public virtue the ladies will exert at this critical juncture."[8]

Working women of the colonies played a major role in the Revolution, a partnership role that would not be theirs again until the mid-twentieth century. As Mary Beard describes it, "they wrote letters and spoke hot words to spur on the laggards; they edited and published flaming newspapers; they cheered the crowds which tore down royal insignia; and added their swelling passions to the tumult."[9]

But the words of Edmund Burke, orator and Whig member of the British Parliament during the Revolutionary War years, a man who consistently urged England to grant the colonies full status, described the role of American women in even more vivid terms in a plea to his countrymen in 1779:

> If they had not been rebels, I could have been lavish in praising women, who, reduced by the ruin of civil discord to the most horrid situations of distress and poverty, had generosity and public spirit to strip the blankets, in the freezing season, from themselves and their infants, to send to the camp, and preserve that army which had gone out to fight for their liberty. And shall Britons overlook such virtue, and will they persist in oppressing it? Shall we give them no alternative but unconditional submission? A three years' war has not terrified them, distressed as they are, from their great purpose. Let us try the power of lenity over those generous bosoms.[10]

With only a few infant industries producing goods to supply the young country and its army (in Boston and Philadelphia some four hundred women worked in companies making cotton products, and in South Carolina in 1778 Mrs. Ramage, a widow, opened a mule-powered cotton mill[11]), home manufacturers took on increased importance. Now women as skilled workers came into their own. With years of experience in helping their husbands at the family trade as farmers, printers, blacksmiths, shoemakers, and tailors, or working bellows or grinding corn, they turned their talents to the war effort. "Handy Betsy the Blacksmith" gained a reputation for her skill in making cannon during the war, as well as other kinds of guns. Mrs. Proctor of Salem put her tool factory to work for the colonists.[12] During the critical labor shortage of the war years, women

A Thetford, Vermont, frontierswoman, Mrs. Richard Wallace, wife of an American soldier, took her husband's place on the farm to work it singlehanded, as did so many women whose husbands served with regiments during the American Revolution.

took up the trades their husbands left when they joined the army, and production continued.

Colonial women could load and fire muskets, nurse the wounded, make camp, and cook under the most primitive circumstances. Army camp followers—quite different from what the term might imply today—followed their husbands on the long marches and sometimes into battle. They worked on regular army assignments and received half rations for themselves and quarter rations for their children, who often accompanied them. Many were refugees from towns that had been burned out or areas captured by the British; army rations meant the difference between eating—little as the food allotment might be—and starving.

Women cooked for the troops and nursed the wounded and sick. They mended and sewed and laundered. On the marches they carried their share of supplies and ammunition on their backs. All classes of women followed the Continental Army, from Martha Washington and other officers' wives to the wives of the newest green recruits. Women who could write performed clerical and copying tasks. Others carried water to soldiers in battle, passed bullets to the front lines, and loaded and fired cannon themselves when necessary. At night they crept over the battlefield, scavenging the dead bodies, stripping them of their clothes to help keep the ragged Revolutionary soldiers warm. Margaret Corbin ("Captain Molly") fought and was seriously wounded at Fort Washington. Cited by the Continental Congress for her bravery, she received a pension of half pay and a "compleat suit of cloaths" each year for the rest of her life. When she died about 1800, she was buried at West Point.[13] Molly Pitcher, "Mol O' the Pitcher," whose real name was Mary Ludwig Hays, took her husband's place loading cannon when he was hit and is said to have fired the last shot before Fort Clinton fell. Honored by George Washington, she was pensioned by Congress for her bravery.[14]

Some women fought as soldiers, passing as young recruits. The most famous of these was Deborah Sampson. Born in 1760 in Plympton, Massachusetts, she was bound out as a servant in the Thomas household until she was eighteen. With only a little public schooling, she learned reading and writing from the Thomas children, and when her service ended in 1779, she taught school for six months. In 1782 she decided to join the army and walked more than thirty miles to Boston to enlist in the 4th Massachusetts Regiment, using the name Robert Shurtleff. Tall and strong, she easily passed as a man and took part in several battles. It was only when she was wounded and had to be hospitalized that her identity was discovered. She was discharged in the fall of 1783—and excommunicated by her church for passing as a man. An account of her exploits, called *The Female Review*, was published in 1797. Five years later she toured New England telling of her wartime adventures, and was the first American woman to earn money as a lecturer. She received a small pension from the United States government and lived until 1816.[15]

Some women put their pens to work during the war, and two of these women proved especially influential. One was Mercy Otis Warren, known as the penwoman of the Revolution; the other was Abigail Adams. Their letters to each other and the method they devised to share these with groups who gathered in their homes are sometimes credited with sparking the idea for the famous Committees of Correspondence. These committees drew the colonists together, keeping each town in touch through courier-delivered letters and bulletins on the war effort and on actions taken by the Continental Congress. These would be read aloud in town halls and on village greens to the crowds of citizens who gathered to hear them.

Mercy Warren was also a poet and playwright whose works on the Revolution were both popular and vital to colonial morale. Later she campaigned actively for ratification of the Constitution (1787) and wrote a *History of the Revolution*.

Brilliant and insightful, young Abigail Adams played a role for her eminent husband John, who was involved with the Continental Congress in Philadelphia, similar to that Eleanor Roosevelt was to play almost two hundred years later for her husband in the White House. For the ten years during which John and Abigail rarely saw each other, Abigail served as his eyes and ears. Mary Beard describes it:

> Writing to her husband, during his service in the Continental Congress, she covers all the ground pertinent to the revolt, including profiteering, the will to independence, the problems raised by the arms requirements, recruiting, financing, harvesting, and the desire of her sex for consideration in the new government to be formed.[16]

Portions of these famous letters from Abigail to John give a vivid and often witty view of the days preceding the outbreak of the war, and of some of the problems that emerged after it began.

> *May 7, 1775:* The distresses of the inhabitants of Boston are beyond the power of language to describe. . . . They (the British) have taken a list of all those who they suppose were concerned in watching the tea, and every other person whom they call obnoxious, and they and their effects are to suffer destruction. . . .

> *June 15, 1775:* We now expect our seacoast ravaged; perhaps the very next letter I write will inform you that I am driven away from our yet quiet cottage. . . . Courage I know we have in abundance; conduct I hope we shall not want; but powder—where can we get a sufficient supply? . . .

> *March 31, 1776:* . . . I long to hear that you have declared an independency—and, by the way, in the new code of laws, which I suppose it will be necessary for you to make, I desire you would remember the ladies, and be more generous and favorable to them than (were) your ancestors. Do not put such unlimited power into the hands of the husbands. Remember all men would be tyrants if they could. If particular care and attention is not paid to the ladies, we are determined to (instigate) a rebellion, and will not hold ourselves bound by any laws in which we have no voice or representation.

> *April 14, 1776 (John to Abigail):* . . . Your letter was the first intimation that another tribe more numerous and powerful than all the rest (had) grown discontented. . . . Depend upon it, we know better than to repeal our masculine systems. . . .

> *May 7, 1776 (Abigail to John):* I cannot say that I think you are very generous to the ladies. For whilst you are proclaiming peace and good will to men, emancipating all nations, you insist upon retaining an absolute power over wives. But you must remember that arbitrary power is like most other things which are very hard—very liable to be broken. . . .

> *July 31, 1777:* You must know that there is a great scarcity of sugar and coffee. . . . It was rumored that an eminent, wealthy, stingy merchant . . . had a hogshead of coffee in his store, which he refused to

sell to the committee under six shillings per pound. A number of females, some say a hundred, some say more, assembled with a cart and trucks, marched down to the warehouse, and demanded the keys, which he refused to deliver. Upon which one of them seized him by his neck, and tossed him into the cart. Upon his finding no quarter, he delivered the keys, when they tipped up the cart and discharged him; then opened the warehouse, hoisted out the coffee themselves, put it into the trucks, and drove off. . . . A large concourse of men stood amazed, silent spectators of the whole transaction. . . .[17]

Abigail Adams had had little formal schooling and had educated herself primarily through voracious reading and listening to the lively conversation of the visitors to the home of her minister father. She was deeply concerned about the exclusion of women and blacks from the guarantees of the Declaration of Independence and the Constitution. Strongly against slavery, she opposed its continuation in the newly formed country. She was also troubled by the inequality of educational opportunity for girls, and fought for the right of black children to attend Boston schools alongside white youngsters. In a battle that she waged personally, she won for James, a black servant youth, the right to go to the same school her own children did.

During the war years, with John away, she supervised the family businesses—the farms and dairies—and established herself as a respected entrepreneur. She managed to add to the Adams lands, handled problems of tenant farmers and of refugees from Boston, brought up her children virtually alone, and developed into one of the most perceptive and brilliant letter writers this country has produced.[18]

Only a few of the individual women who contributed to the ultimate success of the Revolution are known to us by name. One of these is Phoebe Fraunces, an unsung black heroine of the war who reportedly saved George Washington from an attempt to poison him in June 1776. Young Phoebe, Washington's housekeeper, was in charge of Mortier House, the general's New York headquarters. One Thomas Hickey, a British spy posing as a deserter to the American side, planned to have Phoebe serve General Washington a dish of poisoned peas. But Thomas made the mistake not only of falling in love with Phoebe but of relating the plot to her, and as she served the poisoned peas to Washington she quietly told him of the plan. It is said that the general threw the plate of peas out of the window into the yard, where chickens ate them and died. Hickey was captured, confessed, and was hanged before a crowd of 20,000 New Yorkers.[19]

While some women achieved distinction and performed heroic deeds, the vast majority worked at their daily tasks and tried to survive. We know they raised increasing numbers of sheep for the wool needed to clothe the ragged army. Estimates are that at the start of the war there was scarcely enough wool in the colonies for caps and stockings, and certainly not enough for uniforms, coats, or other clothing. Women cut and sewed thousands of shirts and pants, knitted countless stockings, and set aside every scrap of used linen for bandages.

Still it was not enough. Through the winter of Valley Forge and succeeding winters the dwindling band of Revolutionary soldiers suffered. In 1780 they were reported on half rations most of the time, and after a strenuous battle numbers of them would faint from hunger. General Greene reported in July of 1782 that "for over two months more than a third of his men were practically naked, having nothing but a breech-clout, and that they constantly suffered from a shortage of food."[20]

Knowing this, women went from door to door collecting supplies, money, medicines, food, and pewter to melt for bullets. They accepted any contribution that could be put to use. They brought food and medicine to soldiers in prison, and were often the only source of supplies for the captives. They nursed their neighbors and buried the dead.

By 1780 women had organized a full-scale system of relief work at the front, which included transporting clothing and supplies over dangerous territory to the army. Esther De Berdt Reed and Sarah Franklin Bache founded a women's "association," which spread from Pennsylvania through New Jersey, Maryland, Delaware, Virginia, and South Carolina, its central purpose being to make clothing and deliver it to the army.[21]

Especially at first, the Revolution had only minority support among the colonists, with about one in three actively working for the patriot cause. Some women supported the Tories as strongly as others did the Patriots. Two of the most famous spies of the War, both Indian women, demonstrate this rift. Molly Brant, supporting the British, was instrumental in keeping the Iroquois tribes on the English side. Nancy Ward, a Cherokee, spied for the colonists.

Women spies and couriers seem to have taken their duties as a matter of routine. Grace and Rachel Martin, soldiers' wives, held up a British courier. Young Deborah Champion rode on a special mission for George Washington, concealing her face in her cloak to pass as an old lady through the British lines. Sybil Luddington, like Paul Revere, rode out to warn colonists that the British were coming.

Little is recorded about black women, especially slave women, during the war, but one in every five women in the colonies was black. Undoubtedly they had an unusually difficult time. While black men initially were barred from serving in the Continental Army even though they petitioned—strongly—to be allowed to join, after 1779 Congress reversed its stand and admitted both free blacks and slaves, who were promised their freedom after the war if they fought. All the colonies except Georgia and South Carolina, which forbade Negro enlistment, filled their quotas by enrolling blacks. By the end of the war, Lomax tells us, over 5,000 black men had died in the fighting.[22] Black women on Southern farms and plantations were worked harder than ever to make up for the men who had left.

Black women in the north, most of them free, struggled as did all women to keep their families together and fed in the face of the disruption and inflation accompanying the war. Many worked as house servants or on farms. Others were skilled spinners, weavers, and knitters. If their husbands were in the army their plight was doubly difficult, since money to pay soldiers was almost always in short supply. Unless a woman worked or went with her soldier-husband as a camp follower, she had no source of food rations whatsoever.

Slaves were courted by both sides. The British offered freedom at the war's end to slaves who remained loyal. Some 14,000 sailed off on British ships following the war, heading for the West Indies and England, but not many gained the freedom they were promised.[23]

With few exceptions the names of black women especially active in the Revolution are lost to us. During this period the poet Phillis Wheatley became an international figure (see chapter 2). We know, too, that over 100,000 black men and women won their freedom as a result of the war, not only through serving in the army but because many escaped to Canada or Florida or resettled in the North. Others were freed by owners who saw the irony of a war for liberation for themselves while other men and women remained enslaved. Still others took to the courts to sue for their freedom.[24]

Indenture as a system virtually ended following the Revolution. Bondsmen who had enlisted earned their freedom, and a few indentured servants came over after 1783.

After the war, antislavery sentiment grew, and by 1792, societies against slavery had been organized in every state. From 1780 on, Northern states began to pass legislation to free slaves, usually by a process of gradual emancipation. Virginia and North Carolina followed with laws to encourage the voluntary emancipation of slaves, and many were manumitted. Perhaps the high point of the freedom momentum came with the Northwest Ordinance of 1787, opening lands north of the Ohio River and west of Pennsylvania to settlers, prohibiting slavery in the entire Northwest Territory, and guaranteeing jury trials, freedom of religion, and fair treatment for Indian tribes.*

* Five states emerged from the Northwest Territory: Ohio, Indiana, Illinois, Michigan, Wisconsin, and a part of Minnesota.

However, 1787 also was the year in which the Constitution of the United States was drafted.

> From the point of view of American Negroes, the Constitution, coming at the close of an era of distinct improvement in their status, must be regarded as a retrogressive document. During the debates at the Constitutional Convention, opposition to slavery and the slave trade was voiced, yet because of the strength of the slave states, the framers of the Constitution gave protection of property rights in slaves higher priority than the protection of human rights.[25]

In three ways the Constitution recognized slavery as an institution: it stated that each slave, himself voteless, counted as three-fifths of a person for taxing purposes and for the apportioning of representatives to sit in the House; it declared that the slave trade might continue until 1808; and it mandated states to help return runaway slaves to their owners.[26] Within six years the cotton gin would be invented, making cotton "king," and Congress would pass a fugitive slave law, two events that had drastic consequences for black men and women.

Women, too, suffered a reversal following the Revolution. As Charles Francis Adams, grandson of Abigail and John and the editor and publisher of their letters, wrote in 1876: "The heroism of the females of the American Revolution has gone from memory with the generation that witnessed it, and nothing, absolutely nothing, remains upon the ear of the young of the present day."[27]

Through the Revolutionary period the colonial woman enjoyed considerably more freedom than her European sisters, and her wartime inspirational as well as economic contributions were widely recognized and respected. But the stricter adherence to Blackstone's codification of English common law by the new American states following the war ended that freedom. Together with the omission of any guarantees to women in the Constitution or the Bill of Rights, married women especially lost any identity of their own. They could not own property—legally even their clothes belonged to their husbands—nor could they sign contracts or bring suit. Any wages they earned were their husband's, and they could not claim custody of their children in the event of divorce. Although widows and single women retained some rights under the law and could open and operate businesses and sign legal documents, no woman had any political rights guaranteed to her.[28] As Julia Cherry Spruill comments, "the Revolution had no permanent effect on the status of women." She quotes Thomas Jefferson in his belief that women belonged in the home, that they would be "too wise to wrinkle their foreheads with politics." The rights of man, she notes, were indeed "applied to men only."[29]

Indian women were especially heavy losers following the Revolution.

Many tribes which had supported the British fled to Canada or moved west. Nor did tribes that had aided the patriots receive any thanks for their efforts; the colonists began at once to move westward, encroaching on Indian land as they went. Legislated guarantees of fair treatment for the Indians living in the Northwest Territory existed only on paper. The story of the conquest of Indian tribes as a result of the opening of the West is well known.

For American women on the Eastern seaboard, however, another momentous revolution was on its way, the Industrial Revolution, which would make wage labor widely available to women. This revolution was to take them out of their homes, inaugurating changes that continue to this day.

4

THE
TRANSITION
1783–1815

It is worthy of particular remark that in general
women and children are rendered more useful,
and the latter more easily useful, by manufacturing establishments than they otherwise would
be.
                    —Alexander Hamilton, 1791

With the war now over, Tories and Patriots had to learn to live together
as Americans. "Witty Kate of the Fort" and Eliza Lucas Pinckney, Southern women who had supported the Revolution, were two who turned their
full attention to helping the country bind up its wounds. Speaking and
writing in a campaign for forgiveness, they sought to minimize retribution
against Tories in the war's aftermath.[1] Many Loyalists and their families
sailed back to England, but many remained, including numbers of American wives of British and Hessian soldiers, who were left behind to face a
life of poverty and loneliness when the troops sailed "home."

The Revolution united the thirteen colonies long enough for them to
acknowledge the inadequacies of the Articles of Confederation that had
been formulated to govern the new country, and to draft a simple but
workable Constitution, ratified September 1788, that went into effect on
March 4, 1789. The Bill of Rights, ten amendments to this Constitution,
became part of the document in December 1791. This guaranteed to
Americans—except for women, blacks, and Indians—those freedoms for
which the Revolution had been waged.

Women were not specifically excluded from the right to vote, except
in Georgia, South Carolina, Pennsylvania, and Delaware. They were
just not *included*. The one exception was New Jersey, which enfranchised
"all inhabitants" over twenty-one who had lived in the state for a year
and who owned property worth at least fifty pounds. This partial en-
franchisement (for property restrictions eliminated many workers, most
women, and the poor) lasted until 1807, when some political scandals in-

volved with voting gave the New Jersey legislature the excuse to restrict suffrage to white males.[2]

Women also began to be excluded from two professions to which they had formerly had access: medicine and the law. Professionalization of these jobs systematically eliminated women through the male-only schooling required even for midwifery, which had been a female monopoly since the early seventeenth century. Pioneer women on the Western frontier, however, would continue to depend on female midwives for some time to come.[3]

Now that the doors to trade and travel were opened wide, Americans rushed through. Post roads crisscrossed the East, and a newly integrated postal service kept people in touch with each other. Cross-country couriers were constantly on the move, and the first woman courier was hired in 1794.[4] Canals were built, opening waterways for travel and trade. The first steamboat belched its way up the Hudson River in 1807, a further stimulus to manufacture and trade. Newspapers and journals of every description kept the reading public informed and agitated.

The country had a currency, albeit its banking system was beset by constant failures. Loans and credit became available, providing added impetus for those who wanted to take advantage of the Northwest Ordinance of 1787 to settle the newly gained public lands.[5] Anyone was eligible who could put together the initial investment of a year's subsistence, the down payment on the land, and the necessary courage for the Western migration.

Men and women flocking to the lands beyond the Appalachian Mountains created a new demand for finished products, which heralded the rise of merchant capitalists. These were enterprising men who purchased raw materials and contracted for their conversion into fabric, clothing, and other necessaries. The "manufacturing" was done almost entirely in the home, by women or as a family occupation. The finished product was then collected and sold by the merchant capitalists to the country stores that served the new settlements and that rapidly became an American institution.

At first this method of production was merely an extension of the war work women had been doing under the "putting out" system, spinning yarn and weaving cloth at home. Gradually, however, it began to change. For example, "sixteen young women and as many girls under the direction of a steady matron" worked at the production of sailduck in Boston in 1789. President George Washington visited this factory, an unusual one for its time. He must have been impressed, for he described in his diary "girls spinning with both hands (the flax being fastened to their waists). Children (girls) turn the wheels for them."[6] Edith Abbott describes this

Women carding and spinning, while the man in the family weaves: a
typical home scene during the "putting out" period before the Industrial
Revolution, circa 1790.

factory building as two stories high and 180 feet long, employing by
1792 some 400 people, most of them women. These women had organized
a mutual aid society undoubtedly patterned after those common among
skilled workers in the trades at that time. This provided the women with
a feeling of solidarity; it is reported that they limited membership to
those whom they voted in, and worked to "promote industry and self-
government."[7]

Settlers who staked claims in the Northwest Territory would be away
for a year or more clearing land, planting the first crops, and building
their cabins. Often wives stayed behind to support this effort. One of the
paying jobs open to them was making "cards" used in combing cotton
and wool. Usually done by women and children, this involved inserting
wire teeth, which they first bent, into holes in leather that had been cut
to a proper shape. Abbott reports that whole families often depended for
their livelihood on this work. Boston boasted the largest card-making
establishment, where 1,200 women and children did piecework by the
dozen, bringing the finished cards to the factory, where other women
checked them out and corrected any defects.[8]

In 1789 a manufacturer in Beverly, Massachusetts, opened a cotton factory to employ women and children "many of whom," he said, "will be otherwise useless, if not burdensome to society."⁹ That same year twenty-one-year-old Samuel Slater illegally slipped out of England, disguised as a farm boy, and sailed to America with the plans for the Arkwright cotton-spinning machinery locked in his memory. He set to work immediately building this machinery for the firm of William Almy and Moses Brown in Providence, Rhode Island. Thus ended England's attempt to hold on to its monopoly of the cotton and wool textile industry, which it had managed to do until then by preventing either machinery or plans from being taken out of the country.

One year later Slater's machinery was ready, and the first American cotton-spinning mill opened in Pawtucket with 72 spindles. Nine children under the age of twelve were the first millworkers, and just ten years later 100 were employed, all between the ages of four and ten.¹⁰ Like so many of the factories that were to follow, this first spinning mill took advantage of the rushing New England streams as its source of power. At this stage, however, the mills only spun the thread. Weaving the cloth was still in large measure a home operation, although the flying shuttle, in use since 1788, had greatly speeded the weaving process.*

Perhaps equally critical to the economic growth of the United States at the time was the invention of the cotton gin in 1793. Although this invention is normally credited to Eli Whitney, there is some evidence that it was actually the work of Catherine Littlefield Greene, widow of General Nathaniel Greene, who entrusted its construction to Whitney, who was boarding with her at the time.

> . . . when wooden teeth would not do the combing work it was she who suggested wire. She did not take out the patent in her own name, it was explained, because "to have done so would have exposed her to the ridicule and contumely of her friends and a loss of position in society, which frowned upon any attempt at outside industry for women."¹¹

The impact on women, both black and white, of this one invention would be hard to overestimate.

In the South it ushered in the reign of cotton, which almost overnight became the staple crop, first in Georgia and South Carolina, then in North Carolina, southeastern Virginia, and Tennessee, and later came to dominate the economies of Mississippi and Alabama. Whereas only 1.5 million

---

* See J. Leander Bishop, *A History of American Manufactures, 1608 to 1860* (Philadelphia: Edward Young & Co., 1864), vol. 1, for interesting details of Slater's ventures, including the fact that it was his wife who first suggested the production of sewing thread from cotton. In 1794 Slater began to manufacture cotton thread for the first time, and it became popular almost immediately because of its strength (p. 60).

pounds of cotton were produced in 1790, twenty years later the South turned out 85 million pounds. With the invention of the cotton gin, one worker could remove the seeds from 50 pounds of cotton in a day, where before it had taken the same worker a full day to remove the seeds by hand from just 1 pound.[12] Huge new tracts of land were cleared and planted in cotton, and the demand for slaves to work the fields and pick the cotton seemed insatiable. Indeed, by the middle of the nineteenth century three-quarters of all slaves would be working in the production of cotton. Not long after the invention of the cotton gin, however, Congress banned the further importation of slaves, effective as of January 1, 1808. Although hard to enforce, the ban did cut the flow of slaves from Africa, but not the demand for slave labor. Thus a new kind of slave traffic developed, as planters in states with an oversupply of slaves (Virginia, Maryland, and Kentucky in particular) turned to selling them in the slave auctions of New Orleans, which rapidly became the center of a lucrative interstate slave trade.

Ships carrying blacks made their way down the east coast to this Gulf port. Other slaves were marched in coffles overland to board flatboats that took them downriver to the slave markets. This new market for American-born slaves made the breeding of slaves important and increased the value of slave women according to their proven ability as "breeders." Advertisements similar to this one appeared regularly in auction announcements and New Orleans newspaper notices:

> *Negroes for sale:* A girl about twenty years of age (raised in Virginia) and her two female children, one four and the other two years old—remarkably strong and healthy—Never having a day's sickness with the exception of the small pox, in her life. The children are fine and healthy. She is very prolific in her generating qualities and affords a rare opportunity to any person who wishes to raise a family of strong and healthy servants for their own use.[13]

The slave broker, too, found himself in business, especially in those states with a surplus of slaves. He would hire out by the day, month, or year any number of slaves that might be needed, and estimates are that some 60,000 slaves a year worked under this system.[14]

One of the aspects of the interstate slave trade that had the deepest impact on black women was the frequent separation of slave families.

> Auction records and manifests of slaves sent to New Orleans, however, prove that separation of families was the rule rather than the exception. When families were advertised for sale, they almost always included only the mother and her younger children, and often not even all of them. Youngsters of ten or twelve were generally considered single. Since even smaller children could be marketed more profitably

individually than in family groups, it was not uncommon for four- or five-year olds to be sold that way.[15]

The more dependent the South became on slave labor, the tighter the strictures governing slave life. The successful Haitian revolt by blacks against French rule during the 1790s received wide publicity, and after each slave revolt in the States the fears of the planters grew. They devised new restrictions, and the conditions of slave life grew increasingly harsh, the punishment for infractions of rules more severe, the efforts to keep slaves illiterate more intense.[16]

The move toward public education for the white population grew during this period, and gradually provisions were made for schools. Part of the money netted through the sale of lands in the Northwest Territories was earmarked for a school in each new township. Not every town could afford a teacher, who up until this point was almost always a man. Although the groundswell for a comprehensive public education system would have to await the development of and pressure from an organized labor movement, nonetheless the idea took root during this post-Revolutionary period.

Individual women opened schools that reached out to those who otherwise could not attend. Catherine Ferguson, a former slave who purchased her own freedom, opened "Katy Ferguson's School for the Poor" in New York City in 1793, with 20 white and 28 black children from the poorhouse.[17] Anne Parrish founded a "Charity School for poor girls" in Philadelphia in 1796.[18] Yet as late as 1790, Boston had only seven public schools. Most children still received their education at home from their mothers, though those families who could afford it employed tutors and sent the boys on to the colleges that began to emerge to serve the sons of the well-to-do.

The big news as the century turned was the water-powered Arkwright mills. By 1807 almost seventy were producing cotton and woolen yarn and linen thread. While only 2 percent of American cloth was made in factories and home production remained the rule,[19] the textile industry had been growing rapidly.

1805	4,500	spindles in use		
1807	8,000	"	"	"
1809	31,000	"	"	"
1810	87,000	"	"	"
1815	130,000	"	"	"20

Major spurs to the growth of the infant textile industry were the Embargo and Non-Intervention Acts of 1808, which excluded imports from England. In 1810 Secretary of the Treasury Albert Gallatin surveyed eighty-seven mills and estimated that some 500 men and 3,500 women and children worked in cotton factories. By 1812, Providence, Rhode Island, was ringed with thirty-three mills, all within a thirty-mile radius of the city. Carts were constantly on the go, bringing yarn to women in their homes for weaving, and picking up finished cloth.[21]

In 1812, the United States found itself once more at war with England, and the stage was set for the Industrial Revolution that was to change the lives of working men and women from then on. That year Francis Cabot Lowell designed a factory to bring under one roof all the processes of textile manufacture: carding, spinning, and weaving. In 1814, Deborah Skinner was operating the first power loom, and one year later, Lowell's factory was ready to open in Waltham, Massachusetts.

But who would work in the new factory? The United States, still overwhelmingly agrarian, needed all its farm labor. The aspiring textile industrialists had to prove that workers they employed in the cotton mills would not deplete this supply. Thus, the *Niles Register* repeatedly assured agricultural interests that men were not needed for factory work, that it was "better done by little girls from six to twelve years old." The Friends of Industry took up the cause, arguing that very few of the millworkers had to be "able-bodied men fit for farming." The millowners wanted, they said, to take advantage of "six hundred thousand girls in the country between the ages of ten and sixteen,"[22] most of them, they claimed, not fit for agriculture anyway, since they were either too young or too weak. They could be saved from idleness and vice by being put to work in the factory. It was pointed out, in addition, that farmer husbands could make good use of the wages earned by their wives and daughters. As noted earlier, under the law these belonged, not to the woman who earned them, but to her husband or to the male head of the family.

By 1814, all four ingredients necessary for the success of the factory system in the United States were present: capital and credit to invest in building and developing factories; a supply of low-cost labor—women and children; water power to substitute for hand power; and machinery, specifically, the power loom.

The young textile industry grew. In 1820 just 12,000 millworkers were reported; by 1830 the number had reached 55,000. Two years later the first reliable statistics on the numbers of women in the cotton mills were issued by the Friends of Domestic Industry, and 39,178 women workers were listed for that date. By 1850 close to 100,000 men, women, and children were employed in cotton mills, and the changeover from the home production of cotton textiles to the factory system was complete.[23] The time of the wage-earning woman was at hand.

Part 2

WORKING WOMEN OF THE NINETEENTH CENTURY

Go listen to the slavish bell
That turns an Eden into hell.
　　　　　　　—Andrew McDonald,
　　　　　　　　in *Voice of Industry*, 1845

A young country preacher led the Taunton, Massachusetts, mill women out on strike in 1829. Salome Lincoln, a weaver at fifteen, a preacher at twenty, financed her preaching activities through her job at the Taunton mill. When the millowners announced a wage cut and the women rebelled, Salome Lincoln was their logical choice to lead the protest march through the streets of Taunton down to the village green.

These sixty young New England women must have shocked the strait-laced townsfolk as they paraded in their mill uniforms: long black dresses, red sashes, and green calashes.* They filed into a hall near the green and urged Salome to speak to them. Eyes flashing, voice ringing, she urged them to pledge to stay out until the wage cut was rescinded. Over the next few days, however, one by one, they trickled back to the mill, all except their leader. She had taken her pledge seriously, and, probably a victim of blacklisting, she never returned to Taunton to work.

Salome Lincoln, the first woman strike leader about whom we have any real information, proved unusual for her time in another way. Defying custom, when she married Elder Junia Mowry she did not retire from her ministerial work, but shared Mowry's preaching career. When she died in 1841, her husband had her tombstone inscribed:

> She spent more than five years as a public laborer in various places; mostly in the south-eastern part of Massachusetts.[1]

The movement of traditional women's work out of the home was only one way in which America was changing. Textile mills now dotted the New England countryside, while power-driven machinery industrialized the cities of the East. At the same time, settlers poured into the newly opened lands west of the Appalachian Mountains. Completion of the Erie Canal in 1825 opened one of a number of waterway links. Land sales boomed; so did speculation, contributing to economic instability and the periodic panics and depressions so common throughout the nineteenth century. The invention of the cotton gin locked the South more firmly

---

* A hood extending beyond the face, supported by a metal hoop.

than ever into its system of slavery, creating continuous pressure for new land for cotton plantations, boosting the interstate slave trade, and pushing the Indians always westward.

Rapid growth marked this period; the United States almost doubled its population in twenty years—from 10 million in 1820 to 17 million in 1840. By 1850 one-half of all Americans had moved west of the Appalachians. This heavy westward migration caused an adverse ratio between younger men and women in cities and towns of the East, helping to ensure a low-wage, unmarried female work force for the growing mills. This ratio held true, however, only for women under the age of twenty-six. After that age most women had married, and female deaths through childbirth corrected the population imbalance.

Cities grew in size and number, until by 1840 one in every twelve Americans lived in a city of 8,000 or more in population, compared with only one in twenty just two decades earlier.[2] The Seventh Census, taken in 1850, reported that New York City (then Manhattan) had a population of 515,547; Baltimore, 169,054; Boston, 136,881; and New Orleans, 116,375. Factory production and the introduction of high-pressure engines began to displace skilled workers, and immigrants competed for the unskilled and semiskilled jobs now available. Working men found city life hard, but working women found it even more so. Seamstresses made 25 to 30 cents a day, compared with the $1.25 a day which male laborers could earn. Wage inequities were reflected in an 1833 Philadelphia survey that showed three-quarters of that city's women workers earning less for 78 hours of work a week than journeymen received for one 10-hour day. Lowell mill wages, about the highest that women could command anywhere in the early part of the century and six times what they could earn at teaching, were only 35 to 50 cents a day, although this also included room and board.[3]

Frequent economic recessions and panics made employment uncertain. No recession up to that time, however, approached in seriousness and suffering the depression of 1837, which lasted five years. It left one-third of the working population of New York City unemployed. Bread riots were common, and wages fell. As late as 1845, one-half the city's women workers still earned less than $2.00 weekly, many less than $1.50, without board.[4]

In the early nineteenth century women worked in more than one hundred occupations, and by 1850 this number had doubled.

A total of 181,000 women were employed in manufacturing, although it was mainly those in cotton and wool production who worked entirely outside the home in the burgeoning factories. Out of a free work force of 6,280,000 men and women, some 1,200,000 were found in manu-

MAJOR OCCUPATIONS IN WHICH WOMEN WERE FOUND, 1850[5]

Occupation	Number of Women
domestic service	330,000
clothing	62,000
cotton textiles	59,000
teaching	55,000
shoes	33,000
wool	19,000
hats	8,000

facturing. Of these approximately 78,000, or 7 percent, were women in the mills.[6]

It was there that many early leaders emerged, unusual women, some of whom went on to become journalists, writers, public speakers, abolitionists, political activists, and feminists. Nineteenth-century working women could not afford the Victorian model of femininity prescribed for the middle and upper classes. Instead they defied tradition, campaigned for the 10-hour day, and often shocked their neighbors as they pioneered for the rights of women a full two decades before the convention for women's rights held at Seneca Falls, New York, in 1848.

5

THE FACTORY BELL
1815–1860

Despite of toil we all agree
Or out of the mills, or in,
Dependent on others we ne'er will be
So long as we're able to spin.
—"Song of the Spinners," *The Lowell Offering*, 1842

The Boardinghouses

The Merrimack River races through New Hampshire and Massachusetts and tumbles over six waterfalls on its way to the sea. Each of these falls provided a site for ambitious nineteenth-century industrialists to develop what soon became New England's leading industry: textiles.

Lowell, Massachusetts, was one such site, a sleepy village of 200 farm families in 1820. By 1826, just three years after the first cloth was produced there by the Merrimack Manufacturing Company, it had mushroomed into a bustling town of 2,000. Its six textile mills employed 1,200 persons, 90 percent of them women.[1]

Who were these women and how were they recruited to millwork? Factory owners knew how angry agricultural interests would be if men were drawn away from farming, yet in the immediate vicinity of the mills the female labor supply was most inadequate. The young women they needed as workers would have to be recruited from miles away and housed "respectably" in town if family permission was to be obtained for their coming to work in the mills.

Thus it was that the boardinghouse plan, known later as the Waltham or Lowell system, evolved. Morally acceptable to farmers, since their daughters would be supervised by matrons (often widows with children to bring up), it was socially enticing to young farm women. Relishing the chance to get out on their own, they flocked to the mills in response to company advertisements and recruiters. They met women with similar backgrounds from different New England towns, tasted independence, earned their own money, and enjoyed the excitement of what must have seemed "the big city." For unmarried women forced to live with relatives, millwork opened the door to self-support. Nor has anyone counted the numbers of brothers these mill women put through college, the farm mortgages they helped to pay off, or the sweethearts they supported while they built their new homes in the West.

This is only part of the story, however. Farm families could no longer count on the "putting out" system, the home weaving of yarn supplied by contractors, for extra income. Wives were still needed on the farms to raise the children and cook, but daughters could be spared for the mills, work that young women found vastly preferable to the other option open to most of them: domestic service. In any event, they viewed millwork as merely an interlude before marriage and family responsibilities. The farm was always there to come home to in case of illness, homesickness, job loss, or—as they would learn—blacklisting.

Each boardinghouse became a close-knit community, a sisterhood, for the mill women seldom were alone. They spent thirteen or more hours a day together at work, their evenings together in the boardinghouse sewing, talking, reading, and singing, and their Sundays together at church and walking by the river. This boardinghouse community became a surrogate family. If a woman did not fit into her particular rooming house, she felt the group pressure and moved. This same pressure, plus the ability to return home whenever they wished, gave these spirited young women the freedom to "turn out," or strike, against company wage cuts that threatened their livelihood and company rules that offended their dignity.

As prices skyrocketed during the 1830s, the matrons could no longer maintain the dormitory atmosphere of the boardinghouses. The $1.25 a week they received for board and room, deducted by the company from the pay of each millworker, proved most inadequate. The mill women soon found themselves crowded six and eight to a room, often three to a bed. The quality and quantity of their food declined; after a long day in the mill, bread and gravy might be their only supper. As their anger and militancy grew, the women came to regard the housemothers as spies who reported their activities and church attendance (or nonattendance) to the company, and evicted them, on company orders, when they went on strike. The regulations that surrounded their lives in and out of the mills rankled. These rules, from one of the earliest boardinghouses, that of the Poignaud and Plant mill at Lancaster, seem typical:

> *Rules and Regulations to be attended to and followed by the Young Persons who come to Board in this House:*
> Rule first: Each one to enter the house without unnecessary noise or confusion, and hang up their bonnet, shawl, coat, etc., etc., in the entry.

Rule second: Each one to have their place at the table during meals, the two which have worked the greatest length of time in the Factory to sit on each side of the head of the table, so that all new hands will of course take their seats lower down, according to the length of time they have been here.

Rule third: It is expected that order and good manners will be preserved at table during meals—and at all other times either upstairs or down.

Rule fourth: There is no unnecessary dirt to be brought into the house by the Boarders, such as apple cores or peels, or nut shells, etc.

Rule fifth: Each boarder is to take her turn in making the bed and sweeping the chamber in which she sleeps.

Rule sixth: Those who have worked the longest in the Factory are to sleep in the North Chamber and the new hands will sleep in the South Chamber.

Rule seventh: As a lamp will be lighted every night upstairs and placed in a lanthorn, it is expected that no boarder will take a light into the chambers.

Rule eighth: The doors will be closed at ten o'clock at night, winter and summer, at which time each boarder will be expected to retire to bed.

Rule ninth: Sunday being appointed by our Creator as a Day of Rest and Religious Exercises, it is expected that all boarders will have sufficient discretion as to pay suitable attention to the day, and if they cannot attend to some place of Public Worship they will keep within doors and improve their time in reading, writing, and in other valuable and harmless employment.[2]

Behind the Façade

The New England mills of the 1820s and 1830s usually fronted on a river, tall, imposing buildings five, six, or even seven stories high. They were also low-ceilinged, poorly lit, and badly ventilated. Overseers insisted on closed windows, often nailing them shut to preserve the humidity they thought kept the threads from breaking. Weaving rooms, unbearably hot in summer, were even more unhealthy in winter, the "lighting up" season. Then workers started up their looms before daylight and worked until after dark, their only light from whale-oil "petticoat" lamps that hung on each loom, mingling their smoky fumes with the thick cotton dust in the air.

From Hannah Borden, reported to be the best weaver of her day, comes our first account of millwork, and we begin to sense the role of the factory bell in the lives of the women. Borden had learned handloom weaving at the age of eight and was quick to adapt her skill to the early power looms of Fall River, Massachusetts, when, in 1817, she became one of its first three weavers.

The factory bell woke her at 4:00 in the morning. Taking her breakfast along, she readied her looms by 5:00, when the bell signaled the start of work. At 7:30 it announced the breakfast break, and called workers back afterward. At noon it rang the half-hour lunch period, and at 12:30 summoned them back. It dismissed them at 7:30 each evening, unless they worked overtime. When they got back to their boardinghouses at night, they were often too tired to eat. At 10:00 the bell rang for bed and lights out. Sundays it called them to church.[3]

Early mill songs reflect the workers' resentment of the bells that ruled their lives.

> The factory bell begins to ring
> And we must all obey,
> And to our old employment go
> Or else be turned away.[4]

Later, another millworker would write:

> It was morning, and the factory bell
> Had sent forth its early call,
> And many a weary one was there,
> Within the dull factory wall.

> And amidst the clashing noise and din
> Of the ever beating loom,
> Stood a fair young girl with throbbing brow
> Working her way to the tomb.[5]

Poetry from mill women? Yes, indeed. Not only were the New England women from the farms literate, but many of them could trace their independent spirit directly to parents and grandparents who had fought in the Revolution. They read the protest journals of the day and followed accounts of strikes on the docks and in the cities, and of the political activities of working men's associations in their campaigns for the ten-hour day and for Andrew Jackson's election.

It was the mill women who made Lowell one of the cultural centers of its day. Many of these women, 80 to 85 percent of whom were under thirty, found the energy at the end of a long workday to organize and attend lectures, forums, and language classes, sewing groups, and literary "improvement circles." Out of one of these circles grew the *Lowell Offering*, the first journal ever written by and for mill women. From the start it seems to have been influenced by the considerable though quiet financial support it received from the owners, who saw in it a useful vehicle for counteracting community prejudice against millwork and for recruiting new workers. The women who wrote for the *Offering*, however, found it an outlet for their talents and a vindication of their role as millworkers;

they portrayed themselves in a dignified light, and this gave status to their work.[6]

But mill life was changing. Tourists to Lowell saw only the bright red factories with their white cupolas, wide flowered lawns, and mill windows lit up prettily at night. They did not see the growing impersonality of industrialization. As absentee owners took over the mills, they left overseers in charge who had total power over their workers. Factory rules became increasingly severe. So little time was allowed for meals— one half-hour at noon for dinner—that the women raced from the hot, humid weaving rooms several blocks to their boardinghouses, gulped down their main meal of the day, and ran back to the mill in terror of being fined if they were late. In winter they dared not stop to button their coats and often ate without taking them off. This was pneumonia season; in summer, spoiled food and poor sanitation led to dysentery. Tuberculosis was with them in every season.

To combat the high turnover in the mills, overseers sought to stabilize the work force and limit worker protest. They fired women for the smallest offense, or for none at all, and imposed mill rules requiring two weeks' notice plus one year's employment at the mill to earn an honorable discharge. Workers who left without this discharge were blacklisted in every mill village.

The Cocheco Manufacturing Company of Dover, New Hampshire, scene of a number of early turnouts, posted these rules for the information of the strikebreakers hired to replace mill women during one dispute. Note the "ironclad" rule, an early form of the "yellow-dog contract," which committed workers not to join a union. The penalty for violation was forfeiture of wages owed the person, which could be as much as four weeks' pay.

CONDITIONS ON WHICH THE OPERATIVES
OR "HELP" WERE HIRED BY THE COCHECO
MANUFACTURING COMPANY OF DOVER,
NEW HAMPSHIRE.

(Decade 1830–40)

We, the subscribers, do hereby agree to enter the service of the Cocheco Manufacturing Company, and conform, in all respects, to the Regulations which are now, or may hereafter be adopted, for the good government of the Institution.

We further agree to work for such wages per week, and prices by the job, as the Company may see fit to pay, and be subject to the fines as well as entitled to the premiums paid by the Company.

We further agree to allow two cents each week to be deducted from our wages, for the benefit of the sick fund.

We also agree not to leave the service of the Company, without giving two weeks' notice of our intention, without permission of an agent; and if we do, we agree to forfeit to the use of the Company two weeks' pay.

We also agree not to be engaged in any combination, whereby the work may be impeded; if we do, we agree to forfeit to the use of the Company the amount of wages that may be due to us at the time.

We also agree that in case we are discharged from the service of the Company for any fault, we will not consider ourselves entitled to be settled within less than two weeks from the time of such discharge.

Payments for labor performed are to be made monthly.[7]

As farm women grew more realistic about work in the mills, recruiting workers became more difficult, and agents in black wagons called "slavers" had to travel ever wider territories to sign them up. If a recruit came from a distance of over 100 miles, the agent received a bonus above the standard dollar a head, for distance helped lessen turnover: women could not return home so easily, and homesick or no, they had to stay in the mill.

Mill Women Strike

Inflation! Depression! No matter which, wages lagged behind prices, and factory owners sought to increase stockholder profits by cutting costs—in particular, the monthly paycheck. Throughout the late 1820s and 1830s workers struck in protest. Mill women took part in these "turnouts" from the start.*

The first record we have of women turning out is that of the 202 women who joined the men in walking out of a Pawtucket, Rhode Island, mill in 1824, and held their own meetings. Women struck on their own for the first time, however, not in the New England mills, but in New York City, when the United Tailoresses formed their own union in 1825 and demanded higher wages.

Dover, New Hampshire, can lay claim to the first strike of mill women on their own. In 1828, several hundred young women shocked the community by parading with banners and flags, shooting off gunpowder, and protesting the company's attempt to enforce new factory rules. They objected to the company's locking the yard gate after the bell had rung and then charging a 12½-cent fine to open it for latecomers; forbidding any talking on the job, giving "disgraceful" discharges for undefined "debaucheries"; requiring church attendance; and specifying fourteen

---

* Early "turnouts" were generally spontaneous and short, over in a few days. Later mill strikes, especially where the family system prevailed, were planned ahead and tended to last far longer. Where workers had no option such as returning home to the family farm following an unsuccessful labor dispute or a blacklisting, the strike was an act of desperation, neither taken in haste nor regarded lightly.

days' notice in order to leave the mill "honorably."[8] The fine for lateness and the threat of blacklisting for dishonorable discharge provoked the most bitterness.

Newspapers from Maine to Georgia carried the strike story. A Philadelphia journal reported that the walkout exhibited "the Yankee sex in a new and unexpected light."[9] Dover millowners advertised for several hundred "better behaved women" to replace the strikers, while some papers made sport of the women for objecting to the ban on talking during work. The strike was soon over, with nothing gained, and the women returned to the mill—minus their leaders, who undoubtedly received "disgraceful dismissals" and were blacklisted.

In nearby Exeter, New Hampshire, in 1831, one of the few successful turnouts took place against an overseer notorious for setting clocks back to get extra work from the women at no extra pay. The company promised that in the future the overseers would regulate their watches!

But most strikes were lost, even those where the women organized ahead of time. When a wage cut was announced at the Lowell mills in February 1834, the women met and laid careful plans. To avoid the blacklist, they gave the required two weeks' notice of intent to leave the mill, then trooped down to the Lowell banks en masse to withdraw their savings. The company-owned banks, unprepared for this "run," were embarrassed (as the women hoped they would be) and had to send to Boston for funds to pay the accounts. Meanwhile the company, not unexpectedly, called in the woman they spotted as the leader and fired her. As she left the mill office, she waved her calash in the air, a prearranged signal to the women watching from the windows, and out they poured, eight hundred strong, to march bravely around the town. One of the women "mounted a stump and made a flaming Mary Wollstonecraft* speech on the rights of women and the iniquities of the 'monied aristocracy.'" The strikers vowed they would "have their own way, if they died for it."[10]

On Saturday, the second day of the strike, they issued a proclamation, their words such a touching mixture of ladylike dignity and revolutionary zeal that they are reprinted here in full:

> Issued by the ladies who were lately employed in the factories at Lowell to their associates, they having left their former employment in consequence of the proposed reduction in their wages from 12 to 25 per cent, to take effect on the first of March.
>
> UNION IS POWER.—Our present object is to have union and exertion, and we remain in possession of our own unquestionable rights. We circulate this paper, wishing to obtain the names of all who imbibe the spirit of our patriotic ancestors, who preferred privation to bondage

* Mary Wollstonecraft: English feminist of the late 18th century.

and parted with all that renders life desirable—and even life itself—
to produce independence for their children. The oppressing hand of
avarice would enslave us, and to gain their object they very gravely
tell us of the pressure of the times; this we are already sensible of and
deplore it. If any are in want of assistance, the ladies will be com-
passionate and assist them, but we prefer to have the disposing of our
charities in our own hands, and, as we are free, we would remain in
possession of what kind Providence has bestowed upon us, and remain
daughters of freemen still.

All who patronize this effort we wish to have discontinue their
labor until terms of reconciliation are made.

Resolved, That we will not go back into the mills to work unless
our wages are continued to us as they have been.

Resolved, That none of us will go back unless they receive us all
as one.

Resolved, That if any have not money enough to carry them home
that they shall be supplied.

> Let oppression shrug her shoulders,
>   And a haughty tyrant frown,
> And little upstart Ignorance
>   In mockery look down.
> Yet I value not the feeble threats
>   Of Tories in disguise,
> While the flag of Independence
>   O'er our noble nation flies.[11]

Each woman pledged to forfeit five dollars (close to a month's pay)
if she went back to work before they all went back together. But the
company did not stand idly by. Sunday brought church sermons against
the strike by company-supported ministers, and on Monday, at a meeting
which it seems likely the company arranged, a Methodist preacher ex-
horted the women to return in gratitude that they had jobs at all. Meanwhile the company publicized its attempts to recruit women from nearby
farms to fill the jobs of those who did not return to work. This threat,
combined with criticism from the local press and clergy, brought the
women back at reduced wages. Only strike leaders were refused entrance.

Just a month later, women at the Cocheco Manufacturing Company
in Dover struck. To the company's advertisement for strikebreakers, the
women responded in a press release:

Girls on Hand.—There are now five hundred of us in the town of
Dover, who are now at work for ourselves, but might possibly answer
the wants and wishes of the "Cocheco Manufacturing Company, at
Dover, N.H.," excepting that we will not consent to work at the reduced tariff of wages to take place on the 15th of March instant, or
even one mill less than the wages lately given. We would just say
to our sex in the country that we are not to live here long without
plenty of work.[12]

Supporting the women in their strike, *The Man*, a daily labor paper, added to their plea:

> We beseech the farmers of our country not to permit their daughters to go into the mills at all, in any place under the present regulations, if they value the life and health of their children.[13]

Probably this turnout was led by the same woman who, a month earlier, had sparked the Lowell strike.* It is certainly an early example of rather sophisticated planning. In an effort to win community sympathy the women forswore parading and stayed quietly in their boardinghouses, except for one mass meeting at the courthouse. There they resolved not to return under the wage cut and to raise money to help any woman who wanted to go home. They chose a committee of twelve to travel to Great Falls, Newmarket, and Lowell to publicize the strike and collect funds, and reported on their meeting to the press. Although the strike was lost, most of the women chose to return home rather than re-enter the mill in defeat.

Meanwhile the Lowell women, wiser after the disastrous strike of 1834, organized the Factory Girls' Association. By the time dissatisfaction in the mills erupted again in 1836, it had 2,500 members. This time mill women struck over an increase in their board charges. Although rising prices certainly made the increase from $1.25 a week to $1.50 necessary, and only half the increase would have come from the paychecks of the women, still it amounted to a 12.5 percent pay cut for them.

Close to 1,500 women walked out in protest. Young Harriet Hanson, only eleven at the time, recalled years later her impressions of that strike:

> I worked in a lower room where I had heard the proposed strike fully, if not vehemently, discussed; I had been an ardent listener to what was said against this attempt at "oppression" on the part of the corporation, and naturally I took sides with the strikers. When the day came on which the girls were to turn out, those in the upper rooms started first, and so many of them left that our mill was at once shut down. Then, when the girls in my room stood irresolute, uncertain what to do . . . I, who began to think they would not go out, after all their talk, became impatient, and started on ahead, saying, with childish bravado, "I don't care what you do, *I* am going to turn out, whether anyone else does or not;" and I marched out, and was followed by the others.
>
> As I looked back at the long line that followed me, I was more proud than I have ever been since at any success I may have achieved, and more proud than I shall ever be again until my own beloved State gives to its women citizens the right of suffrage.[14]

---

* No one seems to know who she was. Could it have been Sarah Bagley? See pages 72-78 on the Female Labor Reform Association.

The strikers, twice as strong in number as in the turnout two years earlier, marched through the Lowell streets singing parodies of popular songs of the day. The best known, to the tune of "I Won't Be a Nun," is:

> Oh! Isn't it a pity that such a pretty girl as I
> Should be sent to the factory to pine away and die?
> Oh! I cannot be a slave,
> I will not be a slave,
> For I'm so fond of liberty
> That I cannot be a slave.[15]

Resolving that millowners would have to communicate with them through the officers of the Factory Girls' Association, and that they would accept no discrimination against strike leaders, they stated:

> As our fathers resisted unto blood the lordly avarice of the British ministry, so we, their daughters, never will wear the yoke which has been prepared for us.[16]

By the end of the month their money ran out. Evicted from their boardinghouses and with no funds, many straggled back to their jobs, although the 250 skilled weavers who went home instead caused considerable havoc to mill production for a while afterward. Strike leaders were fired, and revenge was taken even on young Harriet Hanson's mother, a widowed boardinghouse matron. "Mrs. Hanson," a factory agent told her, "you could not prevent the older girls from turning out, but your daughter is a child, and *her* you could control." Mrs. Hanson was removed from her post.[17]

Perhaps with more help the women might have held out. The National Trades' Union Convention* voted moral support, but more clearly revealed its attitude toward working women by passing resolutions that millwork was physically and morally injurious to women and that hiring them caused unnecessary competition for the men. When it proposed protective laws and equal pay for women, it declared that these would successfully restrict women's jobs, since employers would have to pay women equally and would therefore prefer to hire men. For women who remained in the work force, however, the National Trades' Union recommended that unions take them in and set up all-female locals.

Some unionists saw farther into the future. Seth Luther, New England's leading labor organizer, urged unions to admit women. "It is quite certain," he stated, "that unless we have the female sex on our side, we cannot hope to accomplish any object we have in view."[18] Luther discovered and publicized the fact that mill women often were locked in

---

* The National Trades' Union was a loose federation of local craft unions and city trades assemblies which met in 1834 and 1835. By 1837, it seems to have vanished.

during the day, with serious consequences when fires broke out, and that mill windows were nailed shut and ventilation nonexistent.

The 1840s; The Female Labor Reform Association
and the Ten-Hour Day

> But, if I still must wend my way,
> Uncheered by hope's sweet song,
> God grant that, in the mills, a day
> May be but "ten hours" long.[19]

All labor organization came to a standstill with the depression of 1837. The mills, particularly hard hit in the early 1840s, did not begin to recover until after 1843. At the same time the farm was no longer a refuge for the mill women. Mortgages were being foreclosed, and families depended on every penny the women could send home.

Millwork was different now. The premium system of production bonuses to the overseers added new pressures. Heavier, faster, noisier machines were installed and regularly speeded up, while workers were assigned extra looms to tend and piece rates were cut. Take-home pay for mill women remained at the same level as when the mills first opened in 1823, while the amount each worker was required to produce increased all the time. Some skilled workers had already won the ten-hour day, but mill women still worked a seventy-five-hour week. With jobs scarce, overseers easily forced workers into competing with each other for their favor. Women feared staying out even when they were ill because it affected production and angered the bonus-hungry overseer. Independent, spirited mill women lost their jobs for reading publications the overseer thought radical, or for taking part in the ten-hour movement.

When the long recession shattered their unions, workers turned to organizing politically, focusing on the shorter workday. Although voteless, the mill women had as great a stake in the ten-hour day as the men and eagerly took part in the movement.

One of the most remarkable women of her day surfaced during this campaign. Agitator, labor organizer, journalist, public speaker, adult educator, abolitionist, and political activist, Sarah Bagley appeared on the scene about 1836, coming to Lowell from her native New Hampshire to work in the mills. We know little about her except during the period between that date and 1846, when she slips from view. She believed all women workers should belong to labor unions and was the first to pressure a state legislature into holding public hearings on working conditions, as well as the first to initiate a political campaign by women.

During the first four years of the 1840s, Bagley conducted free classes at night for her sister millworkers and was an early contributor to the *Lowell Offering*, until articles of hers pointing out flaws in the Lowell system were rejected for publication. Late in December 1844, she began meeting with eleven fellow workers to plan an organization to work for the ten-hour day. In January 1845, the Female Labor Reform Association was born. The idea caught on. Within six months some 500 women had joined. Bagley was elected president and her friend and close associate, Huldah Stone, secretary.

A fiery, persuasive speaker, Bagley was as skilled and effective in a small committee meeting as she was addressing a crowd of two thousand, without the aid of microphones, at a Fourth of July rally. She also possessed boundless energy, and knew how to organize and what was important to women in the mill. She had watched the mills grow and change, and had seen overseers speed up the machines and post ever harsher rules, including the hated blacklist. She lived in a boarding-house and knew how it had deteriorated. After a full day in the mill, she devoted her evenings to the Female Labor Reform Association and to organizing the Industrial Reform Lyceum to give a platform to liberal lecturers not invited to Lowell's company-dominated forums. Somehow she found time to initiate fairs and socials to keep her organization together and raise money for its campaigns. Contributing regularly to *Voice of Industry*, the labor paper of the New England Workingmen's Association, she served also as one of its three-member publications committee.

Under her leadership, the Lowell Female Labor Reform Association adopted as its slogan "Try Again," and affiliated with the New England Workingmen's Association, where Bagley and her co-workers represented the mill women at numerous conventions. She knew the lonely path she would have to travel as she violated society's sanctions on women's proper place, but as she said in a speech to the first convention of the Workingmen's Association:

> For the last half a century, it has been deemed a violation of woman's sphere to appear before the public as a speaker; but when our rights are trampled upon and we appeal in vain to legislators, what shall we do but appeal to the people?[20]

By 1845, mill women were eager for a new kind of campaign. They had the Female Labor Reform Association, and a newspaper to publicize their views—the association bought *Voice of Industry* and moved it to Lowell. They had a goal: the ten-hour day; and they had allies in the New England Workingmen's Association. The campaign they evolved was political, and began with petitions to the Massachusetts legislature.

Launched in Fall River in 1842, the petition drives to the state legislature rapidly gathered momentum. In 1843, 1,600 signed a ten-hour-day petition in Lowell. In 1844, 1,000 signed another on hours and against wage cuts. They submitted still another with 2,000 names, until finally the legislature was forced to hold public hearings on working conditions in the mills—the first such investigation ever held by an American governmental body. Six mill women and two men were invited to testify before the legislative committee, and unladylike or not, all six women appeared, including Sarah Bagley.

Like experts, they documented their statements. Eliza Hemingway told of the poor ventilation in the room where she worked with 150 others, of the thick smoke that filled the air from 293 small and 61 large oil lamps that burned morning and night during the "lighting season." Judith Payne reported on her own illnesses due to millwork. Other witnesses told of low wages, rushed mealtimes, and long hours. The testimony brought out the fact that newly arrived immigrant workers, illiterate and uninformed, were paid 18 percent less than the New England mill women.[21]

So keen was the pressure on the legislative committee that it decided to visit Lowell to see conditions for itself. But, with ample warning, the company made sure the mills were clean and sparkling when the committee arrived. The committee's report echoed industry's concern about placing Massachusetts at a competitive disadvantage with textile mills elsewhere, and found nothing unhealthy about the long hours the women worked. It spoke of grassy lawns and fine flowers, and found "everything in and about the mills and boardinghouses . . . to have for its end, health and comfort. . . . Your committee returned fully satisfied that the order, decorum, and general appearance of things in and around the mills could not be improved by any suggestion of theirs or by any act of the legislature."[22] It was small comfort that the committee also stated that it would be nice if shorter hours prevailed, ventilation were improved, and mealtimes extended, for it disclaimed any responsibility for legislating to make these improvements possible.

"Shame, shame," cried the Female Labor Reform Association, and passed unanimously a resolution chastising the committee:

> . . . the Female Labor Reform Association deeply deplore the lack of independence, honesty, and humanity in the committee to whom were referred sundry petitions relative to the hours of labor, especially in the chairman of that committee; and as he is merely a corporation machine, or tool, we will use our best endeavors and influence to keep him in the "City of Spindles" where he belongs, and not trouble Boston folks with him.[23]

A political campaign began such as Lowell had never before witnessed, spearheaded by voteless females determined to punish Colonel William Schouler, chairman of the hearings committee and Lowell's representative to the state legislature. After his defeat, the Female Labor Reform Association publicly thanked the voters of Lowell for "consigning William Schouler to the obscurity he so justly deserves."[24]

Schouler, however, retaliated promptly, digging up damaging information, not about Bagley, but about one of the men with whom she had worked during the election campaign, and damning her by association. She and her beloved Female Labor Reform Association suffered, and not long afterward she withdrew from her leadership role. But not before she had helped organize a new petition for the ten-hour day and against the year-employment rule of the mills. This petition, 130 feet long, with 4,500 signatures, was submitted along with the names of 10,000 workers from other parts of the state who signed similar petitions. But the special legislative committee that resulted from this effort reported even less satisfactorily than the first. Nothing was changed, except that after 1846, the Lowell mills extended the dinner hour by fifteen minutes in the summer, while in 1847 the New Hampshire mills did the same.[25]

We see Bagley's spirit best in the constitution she drafted for the Female Labor Reform Association, the model for similar reform associations that she and her core of organizers* helped to establish in Manchester, Nashua, and Dover, New Hampshire, as well as in Waltham and Fall River, Massachusetts. Article 8 states: "Any person signing this constitution shall literally pledge herself to labor actively for reform in the present system of labor." Article 9 continues:

> The members of this association disapprove of all hostile measures, strikes, and turn-outs until all pacific measures prove abortive, and then that it is the imperious duty of everyone to assert and maintain that independence which our brave ancestors bequeathed us and sealed with their blood.[26]

The preamble to the constitution reveals not only the influence of the Associationists and Utopians, reform groups allied with labor organizations at that time, but also the struggle, as leaders of the Female Labor Reform Association saw it, of worker against owner. Their need to maintain their dignity and self-esteem as factory workers is clear.

---

*Huldah Stone, as secretary of the Female Labor Reform Association, kept in touch with the new associations, writing: "We hope to roll on the great tide of reformation until from every fertile vale and towering hill the response shall be echoed and re-echoed: Freedom—Freedom for all! . . . Yours until death in the cause of labor reform" (*Voice of Industry*, Dec. 27, 1845).

Shall we, operatives of America, the land where democracy claims to be the principle by which we live and by which we are governed, see the evil daily increasing which separates more widely and more effectually the favored few and the unfortunate many without one exertion to stay the progress? God forbid! Let the daughters of New England kindle the spark of philanthropy in every heart till its brightness shall fill the whole earth![27]

Sarah Bagley surfaces one more time as the first woman telegraph operator, a job she took late in 1846 when a station opened in Lowell. Her interest in social reform led her at least briefly to Associationism.* After that she disappears.

Mary Emerson replaced Bagley as president of the Lowell Female Labor Reform Association, which changed its name to the Lowell Female Industrial Reform and Mutual Aid Society, its new constitution calling for initiation fees, weekly dues of six cents, and fines for non-attendance at meetings. More practically based, it set up sick funds and benefits and tried to appeal to the self-interest as well as the idealism of the mill women. It also formed a library, held classes, and continued to publish *Voice of Industry* until late in 1847.

At its convention in 1846, probably in recognition of the role of the mill women in the organization, the New England Workingmen's Association changed its name to the New England Labor Reform League. Three of its eight board members were women: Huldah Stone, recording secretary (with a man to assist her), Mary Emerson, and Mrs. C. N. M. Quimby. The Female Labor Reform Association held equal status with other affiliates in the League from the start.

Sadly, this first convention of the New England Labor Reform League in Nashua, New Hampshire, was also its last. It had focused on more realistic goals than any labor convention ever held. At this meeting Mehitable Eastman from Manchester's Female Labor Reform Association came to the fore, reporting that the women in her mill had decided not to meet separately but to join with the men. "We can devise plans

---

* During this period there were three main groups of utopian reformers: the Associationists, the Land Reformers, and the Cooperators. The first two groups sought a return to the preindustrial era as a solution to workers' problems and the increasing power of capitalism. The third believed that cooperative ownership was the road to achieving control over rising industry. Many trade union leaders, frustrated by the inability of unions to achieve gains, turned to one or another of these reform groups for solutions. In turn, the reformers sought labor union support when it served their purpose. The connection between the various reform groups and unions was an in-and-out one, but so was labor union membership itself during the twenty-year period before the Civil War. It is evident, however, that support of reform groups dissipated the strength of unions and diverted their attention from the basic, bread-and-butter needs of their members. For a concise description of these reform movements the reader is referred to Norman Ware, *The Industrial Worker, 1840–1860* (1924; reprint ed., Chicago: Quadrangle Books, 1964), chaps. 11 to 13.

together to better advantage, seeing men can do nothing without us and we cannot do much without them," she said.[28] She spoke of the intimidation by overseers and the discharge of workers for union activity. As she described worsening conditions, it became clear that Manchester workers counted heavily on achieving the ten-hour day, and she asked the *Voice of Industry* to give more space to practical concerns such as this campaign. Her realism and persuasiveness moved the convention to pass strong resolutions condemning the blacklist and the premium system.

This was not the only highlight of the convention. While it was in session a walkout took place in a Nashua mill against "lighting up," that is, against the long hours that made it necessary during fall and winter to work by oil lamps. When the mill women walked out, however, they found themselves locked in the factory yard. The overseers refused to open the gates until quitting time; the women refused to return to the mill. When the convention delegates learned of this, they marched in a body to the mill gates, shouting for the ten-hour day. The town's one constable, sent to disperse the crowd, was drowned out in catcalls. Rousing cheers greeted the women when the gates finally were opened.

Once more the women won nothing. However, the convention marked a new phase in company-worker relations in New England, for now the owners organized. The next time a strike occurred, in Manchester to protest Sunday work, workers could not even find a hall or a church in which to meet. The owner of the lumberyard where they finally gathered evicted them. When they met in the street, the police broke up the crowd, not hesitating to use their clubs.

The New England Labor Reform League turned to other issues than organizing: to slavery, free land, and free trade, and while violence such as that which occurred in Manchester spread throughout the area, the League took no part in it.

In the late 1840s, the exodus of the militant New England farm women from the mills began. Some went home to marry, some to teach in other New England towns or in the West; some sought work as missionaries or in occupations that were opening to women in offices or stores. As they left—and strikes in 1848 and 1853 contributed to the exodus—their places were taken by increasing numbers of immigrants, particularly the Irish fleeing the potato famine in their homeland.

The steady flow of immigrants to America had become a flood. The fifty-year period between 1776 and 1825 had seen the arrival of 1 million immigrants. But in the single decade of 1840–1850, close to 2 million came, and in the ten years between 1850 and 1860, the number rose to over 2.5 million.[29] The Irish who arrived in America during the twenty years preceding the Civil War totaled 1.7 million, equal to almost one-quarter of the population of Ireland at the time the famine began in 1845.[30] They came in family groups, huddled into the poorest slum tenements in town, and accepted less pay than the New England mill women had received. They knew little about unions and did not contribute to organizing efforts at this point. By the 1860s, the permanent mill population of textile towns formerly on the Lowell plan could hardly be distinguished from those which from the start had operated on the family system and employed men, women, and children as workers.

Families with Children Preferred: The Family System in the Mills

Samuel Slater, it will be recalled, had smuggled himself and plans for the first American spinning frame out of England in 1789 and two years later had launched his own factory, employing children between the ages of seven and twelve. He prospered and in the first quarter of the nineteenth century became the leading textile manufacturer in America. As "mule" spinning equipment* was introduced, Slater took on men to operate it (women's long skirts were said to get in the way†), and evolved a system of advertising for whole families to come to work for him. Company ads would read:

> They wish to hire a weaver, capable of taking charge of water-looms. Also a Family, of from five to eight children, capable of working in a Cotton Mill. None need apply, unless well recommended.[31]

However, employers like Slater rarely asked for references. Their interest was in the number of children per family, and they hired accordingly. Not only did they use children and pay them proportionately less, but if a family took even one child out of the mill to attend school, except as agreed upon in advance, the entire family would be discharged.

Immigrant families, most of whom were poor and anxious to find

---

* The "mule," invented in 1779 in England by Samuel Crompton, got its name because it was a cross between two previous machines, the spinning jenny and the water frame, just as a mule is a hybrid animal. As "mules" developed from a hand-driven to a power-driven operation, men were sought to work them, in part because the machinery was heavier and in part because it took more skill; since men stayed on the job longer than women, they were the ones who received training in this skill. Thus in the Lowell mills, with their largely female work force, "throstle" or ring spinning machinery (both faster and simpler to operate) was retained. In Rhode Island, mules were used from the start, and here the family system developed, the work force including almost as many men as women and children.

† But an old Waltham operator remembered a woman and her daughters who had worked on the mules at the Lawrence mill and who came to Waltham when this type of spinning was introduced there during the early 1840s. The mother was forced out of her job, he reports: "The men made unpleasant remarks and it was too hard for her, being the only woman." Edith Abbott, *Women in Industry* (New York: D. Appleton & Co., 1910), p. 92.

work at once, signed contracts binding each member of the family for a year's work. Slater signed the Dudley family on in 1829:

> Agreed with Abel Dudley for himself and family to work one year from the last day of March past at the following rates, viz: self, four shillings threepence (71¢) per day to tend picker, Mary eight shillings per week ($1.33) Caroline four shillings per week (67¢.) Mary and Caroline have the privilege of going to school two months each, one at a time, and Amos [a younger brother] is to work at four shillings per week when they are out.[32]

If the families did not produce what they had agreed to, they faced eviction from their slum tenements, usually owned by the company.

> As you have failed to furnish the help which we expected when we let you the tenement which you now occupy, we feel bound to give you notice that we shall be looking for a family to occupy it who will furnish help when we want it.[33]

Thus read one such eviction notice, sent in 1842 by the Pocasset Company in Fall River, Massachusetts.

The family system paralleled the growth of company towns on the boardinghouse plan and spread throughout Rhode Island, Connecticut, part of Massachusetts, and the middle Atlantic states and into the Upper South and the Middle West. More than half of all millworkers in the textile industry before the Civil War worked under the family system.

Artist Winslow Homer titled this painting "Bell Time." Entire families in the 1860s worked 14-hour days in the giant textile mills that lined the riverfront of Lawrence, Massachusetts.

Under this system living conditions differed sharply from those the Lowell women knew. Nor were wages paid monthly or even in cash, as they were at Lowell, but in scrip redeemable at company stores where the owners forced workers to trade. There they lost anywhere from 25 to 50 percent of their earnings, especially when they were paid in kind, as sometimes happened. As early as Hannah Borden's time at the Fall River mills, workers forced to use the company stores were cheated. Borden, who insisted on seeing her store account when the charges seemed unusually high, found bills for suspenders and rum she had never purchased.

Benjamin Cozzens, who employed close to 1,500 men, women, and children at his Crompton, Rhode Island mill, automatically deducted 10 percent from the wages of single workers who boarded out and thus did not shop for food in his store. He also posted this notice:

> Those employed at these mills and works will take notice that a store is kept for their accommodation, where they can purchase the best goods at fair prices, and it is expected that all will draw their goods from said store. Those who do not are informed that there are plenty of others who would be glad to take their places at less wages.[34]

The mills, hot and noisy at best, were also dangerous for the children of all ages who worked in the midst of rapidly moving machinery that had no safety guards.* Factory rules were harsh. At the Schuylkill mill near Philadelphia, for example, workers lost one-quarter of a day's pay if they were late for work by as little as fifteen minutes. Instances of corporal punishment of women by overseers were not unknown.

It took the combined earnings of a family to provide food for the table, though usually one young girl was left at home to keep house and care for the youngest children. Pregnant women stayed on the job so close to the time they delivered that babies were sometimes born right in the factory, between the looms. It was work or starve. Yet these same workers fought bitterly against wage cuts and the speed-up. Theirs were desperate strikes, lasting longer than those of mill women in towns like Lowell. They knew the cost before they walked out: hunger and privation. Yet each time

---

* Florence Kelley, in an article written for *The Outlook*, entitled "Industrial Democracy: Women in Trade Unions," tells the story of Mrs. Alzina Parsons Stevens, who had worked in a cotton mill as a young girl in Maine. On her thirteenth birthday she caught her right hand in machinery that mangled it. The company's surgeon amputated part of her finger without anesthesia; nor did the mill even notify her family. Forty years later Mrs. Stevens wrote: "If my interest in the cause of organized labor had ever flagged, if I had ever been in danger of growing discouraged, the sight of that poor finger and the memory of the horror of that day would have been spur enough." Her life was one of devotion to the workers' cause: she learned the printer's trade and was one of the first women to be allowed in the Chicago printers' union. Active in the Knights of Labor, she wrote for the *Toledo* (Ohio) *Bee*, and later founded a federal union including women from different industries. In 1893 she became Assistant State Factory Inspector of Illinois and continued to serve women and children in industry (*The Outlook*, Dec. 15, 1906, pp. 930–1).

they struck, they held out as long as they could, sometimes with the help of other unions in nearby cities.

A rebellion of children heralded the first recorded factory strike, in Paterson, New Jersey, in 1828. One hot July day the company arbitrarily changed the dinner hour from 12 noon to 1 P.M. With much "huzzaing," the children marched out, while their parents cheered them on. By the next day carpenters, masons, and machinists of the town had joined them and turned the strike into a fight for the ten-hour day. However, the employers united to teach the children a lesson, spreading the rumor that they had sent to Newark for militia to protect their property. A week later the children returned to the mill, minus their leaders, who were fired. Not long afterwards, however, the company quietly restored the noon dinner hour.

Seven years later, Paterson workers struck again. Twenty mills joined in the fight for the eleven-hour day (thirteen and one half hours was the norm). They also demanded cash wages instead of coupons on the company store, overtime pay, and an end to excessive fines for lateness. Fifteen hundred children joined their parents, some of them staying out as long as six weeks. Although the company recruited strikebreakers and half the workers straggled back earlier, the strike did succeed in achieving a twelve-hour day, with nine hours' work on Saturdays.

Hours were not the only issue in the early 1830s, as trade union membership grew throughout the East, increasing from 26,250 in 1833 to 300,000 by 1837,[35] when, as noted, most unions disintegrated in the terrible panic and depression which began that year. But during 1835–1836, 140 strikes took place, most of them an urgent protest against wage cuts put into effect at the same time that the cost of living rose 68 percent.[36] Workers under the family system were part of this organizing effort.

In 1833, after an announced 20 percent wage cut in the cotton mills of Manayunk, outside of Philadelphia, the Manayunk Working People's Committee issued a moving but fruitless appeal to the public against this cut and the thirteen-hour day. The following spring, however, the employers posted a notice at the Schuylkill mill that the factory, because of financial problems, would close on March 22. The workers could take no more, and prepared for strike action.

But on March 10, employer tactics became clear. Another bulletin was posted; the company would keep the mill open if workers would accept a 25 percent wage cut. When they saw the notice, men, women, and children walked out as one. Five weeks later the company offered to re-open the mill at only a 15 percent reduction, but the workers refused to return, except for one woman and her six children.

On April 14, still on strike, the workers chose two women and three men to prepare a resolution in support of the walkout, holding "beneath contempt" anyone who went back to work at the lowered rate. Unions in Philadelphia and New York raised strike-relief money, for many of the widows and orphans on strike were close to starvation. As the walkout dragged on, workers offered to return to work at the 25 percent wage cut *if* the company gave them a mortgage on its property. The company responded by bringing in both police and strikebreakers, and the strike was lost some two months after it had begun.

In spite of this disaster, women millworkers in Manayunk struck again in 1835 and again the following year. Each strike ended in defeat. Although men struck with the women in the mills, the labor press of the day tended to report these strikes in terms of the women. Undoubtedly, their desperate condition made good copy, but they were also spunky fighters in a period when society frowned on women acting on their own behalf. However, no names of women leaders in these mill strikes have come down to us, in contrast to the many we know about from New England. The women working under the family system were older and burdened with family responsibilities after thirteen hours a day in the mills. They earned less, ate less well, and were worn out from frequent childbearing. In addition, many were illiterate. What is remarkable is that they supported strike after strike so courageously in spite of the overwhelming hardships they knew they would have to endure.

Society was not alone in frowning on women's participation in labor organizations. While unions often claimed to recognize the potential role of women as members, the National Trades Union conventions of the period reveal more accurately the attitude of unions toward women workers. One convention report focused on the extent to which women had moved into the printing, saddling, brushmaking, tailoring, shipbuilding, and textiles industries; 24 of the 58 labor organizations in the National Trades Union claimed to be affected by women workers in their trades.[37]

How men regarded working women depended on the number of women in the craft. Where they made up a substantial proportion of the work force, men encouraged their organizing. Where women had just begun to enter the industry, they faced open male hostility. Journeymen tailors in New York struck as early as 1819 to keep master tailors from hiring women. In 1835, printers in Boston united to drive "the girls from the business of setting types."[38] However, that same year women bookbinders in New York received union support in their struggle to organize.

Although mill women invariably had the support of the labor movement—after all, they had been in the mills from the start—this did not keep the men from regarding the employment of women and children in the mills as "a servitude degrading to the American character,"[39] and emphatically hoping that someday women would be found working only in the home.

The Struggle over "Contracting Out"

Unions, transitory even among the most skilled crafts, had no enduring bargaining relationship with employers and bore little resemblance to labor organizations as we know them today. With the gradual recovery of business in the 1840s, not only New England mill women but workers generally turned to political action and legislation in their search for reform, particularly for shorter hours. By the 1850s, workers did succeed in achieving laws in some states to limit the hours of work for children and guarantee them several months of school a year, although these laws were seldom enforced. When New Hampshire (in 1847), Pennsylvania, Massachusetts, and other states passed ten-hour laws, each legislature included "contracting out" clauses providing that, when necessary, employers could sign contracts with individual employees to work more than the ten hours permitted under the law. Millowners insisted from the start on workers signing these individual contracts as a condition of employment. Workers signed—but not without a fight.

The story in New Hampshire is typical. Just after the state's ten-hour law was passed in 1847, 2,000 mill women demonstrated, pledging not to sign the "contracts" the owners had prepared for each of them to work whatever hours the overseers ordered. The women resolved on their "sacred honor" to work no more than ten hours a day, but three days before the law took effect the company fired all who had not signed the "contracting out" agreements. Although they knew that discharge meant blacklisting, only one-third to one-half the women signed. As a result, a shortage of skilled weavers forced some mills to close. The situation in Pennsylvania after its ten-hour law passed in the spring of 1848 was similar, except that wages as well as hours were reduced by millowners.

The industrial tragedy of the decade took place in Lawrence, Massachusetts, in 1860. On January 10, at 4:45 P.M., the Pemberton Mill collapsed. Nine hundred workers were inside, most of them women. It took only half a minute for the mill to fold in, leaving a cloud of dust and a huge mass of debris.

Townspeople frantically clawed through the rubble to try to save their relatives, friends, and neighbors, working feverishly into the night. At

11 P.M. a massive fire broke out, but rescue work continued. When the final count was in, 88 had died, 116 were severely injured, and 159 more had some injuries.

There were hearings, of course, and an inquest. Evidence showed that the cast-iron pillars used to support the construction had been too weak from the start for the brick walls and heavy machinery. The engineer in charge of construction, Captain Charles Bigelow, had known this. Nonetheless, the jury "found no evidence of criminal intent." The public outcry following the decision demanded some measure of justice—and Captain Bigelow was censured. That ended the inquest. The surviving workers were left to pick up their lives and find other work as best they could.

By 1860, then, skilled workers had achieved the coveted ten-hour day, but longer hours continued in industries where women and unskilled workers predominated. We turn next to women who worked outside the mills, binding shoes, making straw bonnets, sewing umbrellas, and to city dwellers who earned so little that many turned to prostitution to survive.

6

BINDING SHOES
AND OTHER TRADES

Poor lone Hannah
Sitting at the window binding shoes;
  Faded, wrinkled,
Sitting stitching in a mournful muse.
Bright-eyed beauty once was she,
When the bloom was on the tree;
  Spring and winter,
  Night and morning,
Hannah's at the window, binding shoes.

—Lucy Larcom, in *The Lowell Offering*, c. 1843

Binding Shoes

In each industry in which they worked, women shared three problems: low pay, long hours, and changes brought about by industrialization. For the women who traditionally sewed shoe uppers and decorated slippers, industrialization meant moving from their homes to the factory, from part-time hand-stitching to full-time machine work, and to a division of labor that locked them into the least skilled jobs.

In colonial times, traveling cobblers, or cordwainers, went from house to house, making boots and shoes for entire families, from home-tanned leather supplied by their customers. As cities grew, cobblers joined together into shops, selling any extra shoes they made to wholesalers or retailers. Each shoe, sewn by hand, required both skill and strength to produce.

Women entered the trade about 1750, sewing uppers and decorating women's slippers and shoes, jobs that soon became known as "women's work." Wives could work at home—often the back rooms of the shop—and fit the work into the routine of household chores. By 1795, large numbers of women shoebinders had helped to make Lynn, Massachusetts, the major center for ladies' shoes; that year, the town produced 300,000 pairs of women's shoes. Between 1800 and 1810, the population of Lynn increased by 50 percent, as workers were attracted by its job opportunities.[1]

The invention of the wooden shoe peg in 1811 brought two major changes to the industry: a lower-priced shoe and an even greater employment of women and children. Formerly women shoebinders had sewn the uppers together—the vamp and two quarters—while the men shoemakers had done the heavy, more skilled work of sewing bottoms to uppers. The shoe peg meant that uppers and bottoms of lighter-weight shoes could be joined in a simple operation which, because it employed lower-paid, unskilled women and children, resulted in a cheaper shoe. Hand-sewn shoes continued to be produced by skilled shoemakers side by side with these less expensive shoes. But the latter were so popular that orders went to all the neighboring towns, providing winter employment for fishermen, their wives, and widows like Hannah in the poem above, who looked endlessly toward the sea for her lover's return as she also endlessly bound shoes.[2]

By 1837 there were 15,000 women shoebinders in Massachusetts,[3] as many women as worked in the mills, although most of the former were still part-time while the mill women worked a full thirteen-hour day. Lynn shoebinders in their own homes worked under quite different conditions than the tenement shoebinders of the cities. There, under "garret bosses," they labored in one of the earliest sweated industries.

In 1852, the first sewing machine for leather was introduced in Lynn, drastically changing the industry and affecting the life of every woman in it. Production of hand-sewn shoes fell. Women who wanted work had to move into the factory on a full-time basis or purchase machines to use at home, machines both expensive and cumbersome. Increased production through the sewing machine caused a drop in the number of women in the industry, both in the shoe center of Massachusetts and nationally, as can be seen in the following table:[4]

EFFECT OF THE SEWING MACHINE ON EMPLOYMENT IN THE SHOE INDUSTRY

| | U.S. | | | Massachusetts | |
	1850	1860		1850	1860
Men	72,305	94,515	Men	29,252	43,068
Women	32,949	28,515	Women	22,310	19,215
Total	105,254	123,030	Total	51,562	62,283

Interestingly, the United States Census for 1860 also shows that the over-all percentage of women workers in the country fell from 31 percent in 1850 to 23 percent ten years later, officially attributed to the industrial use of the sewing machine. In 1862, when the McKay machine to sew shoe soles was introduced, one worker could turn out in an hour what it had taken eighty hours to do before.[5] The number of women needed in shoebinding fell still further, while the number of men needed in the other parts of the trade rose.

Cordwaining was skilled work, and the men had always taken pride in their craft. Theirs were some of the earliest union efforts to protect the prices paid for their work and maintain the dignity of the trade. The first key court decision against trade unions, which branded them conspiracies, centered on the cordwainers back in 1806. This held for some thirty-seven years, until the 1842 decision (*Commonwealth v. Hunt*) declared unions lawful and not in and of themselves conspiracies. This case too involved cordwainers: the Journeymen Bootmakers Society of Boston. The ruling of Massachusetts Chief Justice Lemuel Shaw stated that workers had the right to engage in joint action to achieve a legal purpose, even if this meant choosing *not* to work for a company that hired non-union workers. Overnight, a strike for the closed shop became legal.[6]

While they cut and sewed shoes, Lynn shoemakers would talk over political and union issues and try to unite to bargain with their employers. A frequent topic for discussion was the custom many wholesalers had of paying in scrip, good on purchases at a particular dry-goods store where workers always found prices higher than anywhere else. This store-order system led in 1844 to the formation of the Journeyman Cordwainers Society and to the publication of one of the famous labor papers of the day, *The Awl.*[7]

However, the women of Lynn, who bound shoes in their own homes, had little chance to keep in touch with each other, nor did their relatively unskilled work give them any special status. But in spite of their isolation, 1,000 women gathered at the Friends' Meeting House early in 1833 to form the Female Society of Lynn and Vicinity for the Protection and Promotion of Female Industry. The issue was low piecework rates. The preamble to their constitution contains one of the earliest references to the fact that many women supported their families and to their equal right, along with the men, to organize for their common welfare:

> Under these circumstances, driven by necessity to seek relief, a large number of females from this and the neighboring towns, many of whom have families as well as themselves dependent upon their industry for support, and impressed with the belief that women as well as men have certain inalienable rights, among which is the right at all times of "peaceably assembling to consult upon the common good," have assembled accordingly. . . .

Their society, surprisingly modern in structure, provided for officers and an executive board of twelve, for quarterly meetings and an annual officer-election meeting, for a charity fund and dues of 12½ cents a quarter, and for a price list that constituted their demands. Every member signed this scale of prices as her pledge not to undercut fellow workers. Those found in violation would be censured, expelled, or both.[8]

The women in nearby Saugus, Massachusetts, who followed the Lynn example and organized in a similar association, quickly won more money for their work. The Lynn women were not so fortunate: they were forced to strike for a number of weeks. The Cordwainers, to which many of their husbands belonged, came to their help with strike funds and pledges not to work for any manufacturer who did not grant the shoebinders' demands. They organized a boycott throughout the Lynn area, asking citizens to stop buying shoes from the struck firms.

For several weeks employers held out, publicizing their fears of out-of-town competition if they had to pay higher rates. On January 8, the women replied:

> We can only say that we regard the welfare of the town as highly as anyone can do; and that we consider it to consist, not in the aggrandizement of a few individuals, but in the general prosperity and welfare of the industrious and laboring classes.[9]

Just how long the strike lasted we do not know, but at its March meeting the organization held a victory celebration and selected two *men* to represent them at the Boston Trades Union. The difficulties of maintaining a union organization with a membership so scattered can be seen in the story of what happened next. The Society could not get its members to stick to the prices they had won. By its June quarterly meeting the officers announced that three-quarters of the members either had taken work for less money or had failed to pay dues to support the organization. In spite of urgent resolutions passed to rebuild the Society, it died.[10]

Early unions, so isolated from each other, had trouble giving each other assistance. One example of early cooperation among shoeworkers did occur in New York in 1835, when the Ladies' Cordwainers' Society agreed to aid the Philadelphia Cordwainers by not admitting "traveling journeymen" unless they were members in good standing in their home community. These women had need of help themselves soon afterwards. For their work on "southern slippers" they earned only 48 cents a day, from which they had to supply their own silk,* thread, and needles. They struck, and were able to win a two-shilling increase.[11]

Just a year later, Philadelphia women shoebinders and corders walked out, getting strong support from the men, who struck at the same time and declared they would fight all attempts of the employers to "crush the

---

* Costing 12½ cents a yard in New York at that time, the silk was used for the rosettes that decorated the slippers.

ladies' Association."[12] Philadelphia was a strong union town—recall the support given the Schuykill millworkers—and strike-relief funds for the women came from many unions. The walkout lasted two or three months. In June 1836 the women printed up their constitution, which we can assume contained the agreed-upon price list, and all shoebinders were invited to join the new organization. However, like the Lynn Society, this organization did not last long. None of the early unions negotiated real contracts with union recognition or grievance procedure, and they had little organization or structure. Like the mill women, the shoebinders mobilized only around particular issues.

Nothing much is heard from the shoebinders during the depression of 1837–1842. But in 1844, Lynn cordwainers urged the women to attend their meeting, and the *Essex County Whig* joyously wrote up the event:

> That is just what is wanted. The presence of women will aid the cause more than anything else. They are interested in this movement and should be represented at the meetings.[13]

Joining the cooperative movements of the period, shoeworkers did establish a short-lived Producers Cooperative in Lynn in 1845. In 1851, a Cooperative Boot and Shoe Store opened on William Street in New York City, another attempt to give workers a greater share of what they produced.

Then in 1860, the Lynn shoebinders again make the pages of labor history. That year, during a strike of shoeworkers, 5,000 men and 1,000 women marched together in the midst of one of the worst blizzards on record in Lynn. Carrying one hundred banners bright with slogans, and twenty-six American flags, the workers paraded through town to the green accompanied by five bands. Later the women met at a rally of their own at Lyceum Hall, a meeting advertised by giant posters on the walls of city buildings. Come, be free and not slaves, come, snow or no snow, they announced.[14] Some 1,800 women waded through the snow to attend. We can imagine what cheers greeted the reading of a poem written especially for the occasion: "The Song of the Shoemakers' Strike."

Soon 20,000 workers throughout New England had joined the walkout. Newspapers referred to it as the "Revolution in the North" and the "Rebellion Among the Workmen of New England."[15] Other papers compared the participation of the shoebinders to that of the women of the French Revolution.

What did they win? Andrews and Bliss say higher wages, though they compromised with the manufacturers. More important, a shoeworkers' union emerged. But Norman Ware reports the strike a total failure: by

Striking women shoebinders of Lynn, Massachusetts, paraded on March 7, 1860, during the worst snowstorm anyone of the day could remember. Their banners declared "American Ladies Will Not Be Slaves." While the whole town turned out, city guards accompanied them with music and muskets. Firemen brought up the rear.

April 1, he states, all workers not replaced by strikebreakers had gone back. Foster Rhea Dulles claims that employers, while refusing union recognition, did make wage concessions.[16] What really came out of this strike was the organizational experience that would be put to use just a few years later when shoebinders founded the Daughters of St. Crispin (1869), the first national union of women workers.

Bonnets of Straw

The straw hat workers—and their children—also moved from home work to the factory. In 1795 young Betsey Metcalf of Dedham, Massachusetts, only twelve years old, had discovered a way to make braid from oat straw, splitting it with her thumbnail and smoothing it with scissors. Women poured in from nearby towns to learn this technique for making bonnets that sold for half the price of imported ones. It became quite the thing for women to do, and by the 1830s thousands of New England women and children worked at this trade.* Gradually, they were forced to move

* As early as 1821, Mrs. Sophia Woodhouse Wells of Wethersfield, Connecticut, developed straw plaiting out of meadow grass, and wove it into imitation leghorn bonnets that won her the praise of London hat dealers, a silver medal, and 20 guineas as a reward—provided that she furnish them grass seed and detailed instructions for drying and plaiting the grass. She and her husband patented her product and began manufacture of the bonnets. (Bishop, *History of American Manufactures*, vol. 2, pp. 270, 271.)

into factories, where they wove the silk for hat linings and the straw itself all under one roof. A few machines did the work that many women had once been needed to do.

By 1846, straw hat workers averaged only 25 cents a day. Children six to twelve years old were employed to make the braid for the hats.[17] As more and more cheap braid was imported from Europe, the industry provided less and less work. Nonetheless, in 1850 workers formed the Straw and Pamilla Workers Association, born out of the desperate need for a wage scale that would support them. Members chose a Miss Stopford as president and a Miss Roberts as secretary, and sent two delegates that year to the Industrial Congress.

Work which had brought the women 75 cents now earned them just 32 cents. Most women could earn only $2 a week, and even the most experienced worker never made more than $4. Gathering their forces, New York hatworkers presented wage demands to the stores, their only weapon the threat to open a cooperative and sell hats directly, thus bypassing the middleman. Most stores met their wage demands—for the moment. But the association probably disbanded after their momentary success, leaving the hatworkers defenseless while machines continued to take over the industry.

Straw hat workers who flocked to the cities seeking work during the depression of 1837 were not alone. Thousands of women came. Gradually the conditions under which they lived and worked began to attract attention. The artificial-flower makers, for example, were home workers who slaved in their tenement rooms eighteen hours a day, making flowers at 6 cents a gross. Every family member was put to work separating petals; children eighteen months old began their work life at this task. The *New York Daily Tribune* publicized these conditions in 1845:

> Here they find the demand for work greatly oversupplied, and competition so keen that they are at the mercy of employers, and are obliged to snatch at the privilege of working on any terms. They find that by working from 15 to 18 hours a day they cannot possibly earn more than from $1 to $3 a week, and this, deducting the time they are out of employment every year, will barely serve to furnish them the scantiest and poorest food, which from its monotony and its unhealthy quality, induces disgust, loathing, and disease. . . . Their frames are bent by incessant and stooping toil, their health destroyed by want of rest and proper exercise, and their minds as effectually stunted, brutalized, and destroyed over their monotonous tasks as if they were doomed to count the bricks in a prison wall—for what is life to them but a fearful and endless imprisonment, with all its horrors and privations?[18]

The Census of Manufactures indicated that, by 1850, 24 percent of the country's manufacturing workers were women, numbering 225,922 as compared with 731,137 men.[19] Among the worst off of all these women were the umbrella workers, who earned so little and lived so close to the edge of starvation that when they turned out in 1836 over a wage cut from 14 cents per umbrella to 10 cents, the newspapers stated: "In this case we decidedly approve the turnout."[20] Conditions did not improve, and in 1863 *Fincher's Trades' Review*, a labor paper, reported: "No class of female operatives, perhaps, have suffered more from the lack of a just compensation for their labor."[21] New York umbrella workers now earned only 6 to 8 cents per umbrella. If they worked steadily from six in the morning until midnight, they could make twelve umbrellas a day—but out of their earnings they had to pay for needles and thread! In desperation they struck for 2 or 3 cents more per umbrella. Although the *Trades' Review* tried to mobilize New Yorkers to boycott stores not granting this increase, the strike failed. Women so poor, so isolated from each other, and with so little organized support could not hold out for very long.

Women were found—in small numbers, to be sure—as carpenters, plasterers, and blacksmiths, and in other skilled trades. These were exceptions. However, they did remain in one of the crafts they had entered in colonial times, though now relegated for the most part to the unskilled, entry-level jobs. That trade was printing.

The Compositors: Women in Printing

Colonial women knew the smell of printer's ink. Many of them not only ran printing shops, they edited perhaps one-fourth of all newspapers of the seventeenth and eighteenth centuries. As the country grew, so did the number of papers, and women printers, working mostly as compositors, increased in number too.

Apprenticeships in printing, however, were closed to women. This restricted them to the composing room, which had the lowest skill and pay levels in the industry. An 1831 survey of the printing trades in Boston indicated 687 men employed there as printers at $1.50 a day; 395 women at 50 cents a day; and 215 boys who received the same pay as the women.[22]

Men in printing successfully organized unions earlier than in most trades, and at first did their best to bar women from the craft. In 1832, the Typographical Society of Philadelphia protested with such vehemence the plan of one printer to hire women compositors that he had to deny publicly his intent to do so. Print-shop owners less subject to pressure, however, hired women as strikebreakers at lower wages. Women who could not get trained for compositing jobs if they tried to enter by the

Bookbinders about 1870 at work in the "extensive and first-class establishment" of Messrs. Case, Lockwood & Brainard, Hartford, Connecticut. Even though machines had been invented for sewing books, women were still employed in many companies to sew them by hand, securing the forms to the cords at the back of the book.

front door often accepted this back-door route. Some received secret instruction, as Chicago women did from one newspaper owner who used them to replace "troublemakers" among his own newspaper printing crews.

In 1854 the National Typographical Union Convention passed resolutions stating emphatically that it did not encourage the employment of women in the trade. Affiliates such as the one in Philadelphia instructed its representatives "to oppose any recognition of the employment of females as compositors."[23] In spite of this, the number of women in printing increased, finally forcing each local typographical union to come to grips with the problem. One by one they came to see that women workers posed more of a threat to wages and standards outside the union than in it.

The Boston Typographical Union yielded to reality in 1856. At one of its meetings some members offered a resolution:

> That this society discountenances any member working in any office that employs female compositors, and that any member found doing so be discharged from the society.

The meeting refused to pass this, recognizing that women probably were in the industry to stay. Instead it voted a resolution stating:

> Whereas, The impression has gone abroad that this union discountenances the employment of female compositors, Resolved, That we

recommend to the females employed in printing offices in this city to
organize in such a manner as shall seem best to themselves, to prevent
the present prices paid to them from being lowered, and that in doing
so they shall receive the cooperation of this union.[24]

In fact, there were few printing offices without some women. Slowly,
the hand of friendship was extended to them. Today the Typographical
Union proudly lays claim to being the first national union to have
changed its constitution to admit women (1869); the first to have elected
a woman—Augusta Lewis—to a national office, that of corresponding secretary (1870); and the first to demand equal pay for men and women
doing equal work (1873).

Hiring Out: Women's Work

Since the early days of indentured servants, "hiring out" has been primarily women's work. In colonial times it was a legitimate apprentice
trade for a girl, enabling her to learn spinning and weaving. Nor was
domestic service frowned upon: many sisters and daughters of prominent
citizens took on this work for brief periods before marriage. It offered an
acceptable way for spinsters to earn a living.

Early census takers included as domestic servants both nurses and
teachers, so that the actual numbers of women in paid household work are
not clear. However, as early as 1826–1829, the Society for the Encouragement of Faithful Domestic Servants in New York reported its applicants
for work:[25]

white males:	1,080
colored males:	661
white females:	7,630
colored females:	916

Over 80 percent of household servants were women, and of these less
than half were American. During the 1820s and 1830s, most came from
Ireland. As the shortage of servants here continued during the early part
of the nineteenth century, immigrant women earned probably twice what
they could have made in Europe at this kind of work. As late as 1845,
they formed the bulk of domestic workers, two-thirds Irish, another sixth
German.

When servants no longer needed spinning and weaving skills, their
status dropped, and it continued to fall as other skills also became outmoded: cowing, baking, soap making, brewing, and canning. On the
other hand, since the mills drew many New England women away from
domestic work, the wages of servants rose from 50 cents a week in 1815
to $1.25 or $1.50 a week by 1849, and in New York, to $10.00 a month
plus room and board.[26]

Household workers then, as now, had little chance to organize to protect themselves from exploitation. On duty twenty-four hours a day, seven days a week, their living conditions often pitiful, they were at the beck and call of the mistress of the house and at the mercy of the master. Societies to encourage domestic servants emerged after 1830, mainly as employment agencies that also gave prizes to workers who stayed with their families the longest. These societies were less concerned with the welfare of the servants than with satisfying employers, as the advice issued to its roster of servants in early 1830 makes clear:

> Never quit a place, on your own accord, except on such account, that in distress, or death, you think you did right.
> Be moderate in your wages; many very good places are lost by asking too much.
> If you can not pray as well as you would, be sure every night and morning to do it as well as you can.
> Rise early, and your services will give more satisfaction.
> Be modest and quiet, and not talkative and presuming.
> Don't spend any part of the Sabbath in idleness, or walking about for pleasure.
> Watch against daintiness.
> Be always employed, for Satan finds some mischief still for idle hands to do.
> Keep your temper and tongue under government; never give your employer a sharp answer, nor be in haste to excuse yourself.
> Leave every place respectfully; it is your duty.[27]

The *Workingman's Advocate* responded: "The society appears to think that there is a certain species of mankind, born for the use of the remainder; and they talk of improving them as they would a breed of horned cattle."

As factory work offered working-class women options, domestic service continued to lose standing. The freedom to come and go, to have even a few hours a day to call one's own, seemed preferable to the virtual slavery of household service. Black women in the North, barred from almost all factory work, turned to domestic service to earn a living, but immigrant women competed with them for these jobs—and often won.

Even laundresses, always on one of the lowest rungs of the job ladder, faced a crisis around mid-century as steam laundries took over to some extent the work of the individual washerwoman. Laundresses' rates fell lower still, while they continued to bear the cost of soap, starch, fuel to heat the water, and buttons they had to replace. Nonetheless, out of this hot, backbreaking industry one group of laundry workers in Troy, New York, built a strong if temporary union. Kate Mullaney, an outstanding labor leader of her time, emerged out of their struggle.

The Stitchers

"Work—work—work!
My labor never flags;
And what are its wages? A bed of straw,
A crust of bread—and rags.
That shatter'd roof,—and this naked floor—
A table—a broken chair—
And a wall so blank, my shadow I thank
For sometimes falling there!"
—Thomas Hood, "The Song of the Shirt"

Too many women hand sewers wanted work. They competed with each other, stitching a pair of pants for 25 cents, navy shirts for 16 cents each. Then, underbid by other women, they would agree to make them at 10 cents, at 8 cents, even 6¼ cents.[28]

Women have always sewed. In 1725, a Northfield, Massachusetts woman made and sold shirts for Indians at eightpence each and men's breeches at a shilling sixpence. This is our first record of "ready-made" transactions. In most colonial families, women wove the cloth and cut and sewed the garments, while men traditionally made the shoes, hats, and leather gloves.

After 1816, Congress placed a heavy duty on imported ready-made clothing. At the same time the demand increased for cheap work clothes for Southern male slaves and for army and navy uniforms. The fabric for these was woven in the new cotton mills, cut at the "dealer's," and then sent out in bundles to be made up into garments in the homes of the hand sewers. This differed from made-to-measure clothing that was sewn in tailoring shops, or measured, cut, and stitched in the customer's home.

As the reader will recall, tailors struck as early as 1819 against women entering this trade. In 1820, the Emigrant's Directory warned incoming tailors that in New York they would find the trade damaged because women and children worked in it for one-half to three-quarters of men's wages.[29] By 1831, Boston had 300 men, 100 children, and 1,300 women working in tailoring jobs.[30] Especially in periods of economic recession, the prices paid the women would be lower—and there were always other women waiting for their jobs if they refused to accept reduced rates.

These low wages caused New York tailoresses to call their first meetings in April 1825 and to walk out in the first strike of women alone in American labor history. Again in February 1831, they organized "for self-protection against the inevitable consequences of reduced and inadequate wages." When Mrs. Lavinia Waight, secretary of the organization, spoke out, listing the wrongs the women endured, the *Boston Transcript* chastized her for "clamorous and unfeminine declarations of personal rights, which it is obvious a wise Providence never destined her to exercise." The editor did admit that the women could raise their wages through united action, but felt their "bitterness" was unbecoming.[31]

*Working Man's Advocate,** a labor-oriented paper, supported the tailoresses, urging them to set up a cooperative to sell their products for less and earn more at the same time. It voiced a concern of the city's sewing women: the part-time worker who, sewing for pin money, underbid the seamstresses. The paper appealed to "those females who work for low wages, merely for amusement, or to obtain articles of luxury . . . but are not dependent on their labor for a living, to dispense with such things for a season for the sake of humanity, or at least suspend your labor until such labors will command an equivalent that will support life."[32]

Talk did no good, however, and in June 1831, 1,600 sewing women, members of the United Tailoresses Society, struck. Somehow they managed to hold out for five or six weeks, perhaps longer, though we do not know what actually happened.

Throughout the 1830s, tailoresses organized in transitory unions in New York, Boston, Philadelphia, and Baltimore. The Baltimore sewing women issued a strike call in 1833, asking tailoresses and seamstresses in all sections of the city to meet, choose delegates for a city-wide convention, and together seek higher rates. Two years later another new organization formed: the United Men and Women's Trading Society, this time joining tailors with seamstresses in seeking better wages.

In Philadelphia, women workers had the benefit of help from labor agitator and philanthropist Matthew Carey,† who fought especially hard for the sewing women. With his aid they met in 1835 and formed the first city-wide association of women workers that crossed all job lines. The Female Improvement Society for the City and County of Philadelphia included "tailoresses, seamstresses, binders, folders, milliners, stock makers, corset makers, mantua makers, etc."[33] Each industry group formed its own committee and set up its scale of price demands. Among the employers approached with these price lists was the United States secretary of war, since the government paid very little for its army clothes, using its orders as a form of work relief for the destitute. The Philadelphia women gained some small wage increases, although their organization disappeared after this victory.

---

* Edited by George Henry Evans, whose primary interests lay with land reform and not with organizing labor unions.

† Matthew Carey, an Irish-born immigrant, made enough money in the publishing business to devote his life to philanthropy. His special concern was the problems of working women.

The story was the same in Pittsburgh: women would put in an entire day making a shirt and receive 12½ cents. Widows in Cincinnati were "destitute and suffering for the common necessaries of life, because they can not obtain work or a fair compensation for their labor." Working as hard as they could, they made nine shirts in a week—at 10 cents a shirt.[34]

Matthew Carey issued a pamphlet in 1831, setting forth the receipts and expenses of an average sewing woman for a year:

Forty-four weeks at $1.25		$55.00
Lodgings, 50¢ per week	$26.00	
Fuel, 25¢ per week, but say only 12½¢	$ 6.50	$32.50
Remains for victuals and clothes		$22.50

This budget estimated the workday at 16 hours, six days a week, since one day would be "lost through sickness, unemployment, or the care of children." However, Carey was politely taken to task by an anonymous committee of thirty women for overestimating the wages the women could earn. As the committee pointed out, earnings rarely went above $1.12½ cents a week and often fell below. So Carey reviewed his calculations and found that sewing women indeed had just 7 cents a day for food, fuel, and clothing throughout the year, if they were single, but that those who had children to care for and who therefore lost some time from their work, had only 4 cents a day to meet those needs.[35]

Investigating how these women were able to survive, Carey discovered that many begged from charitable societies for money to pay their rent. As soon as their children were old enough, they were sent out to find any kind of job. Little girls helped their mothers sew at home all day and into the night for as long as they could keep their eyes open.

Women rarely received the agreed-upon price for their work and were helpless to fight back. Their pay was cut still further if employers found fault with their work. Sometimes they received "credit on the books" instead of cash, but often they could not collect what was due them. Their work was undercounted; they were told to return the next day or week for their money, or to leave a deposit on the fabric—money that often was never returned.[36]

In 1844, tailors and tailoresses gathered in several overflow meetings in Boston, where they pledged to work together toward a better price scale. A description of their meeting in Boston's Faneuil Hall stated: "The galleries . . . thronged from the lowest to the highest seats with a living panorama of the fair sex who, to their praise be it said, obtain their livelihood by honest industry."[37]

This was just one of many protest meetings that took place that summer and fall in a number of cities, meetings crowded with seamstresses eager to combat employers' attempts to cheat them out of their earnings.

In New York City, striking workers burned the *New York Herald* in effigy at a mass rally because it criticized their protest, after which the paper agreed that employers could probably afford to pay more but cautioned the strikers to "behave well." In Lowell, the *Voice of Industry* commented on a strike of seamstresses in Newburgh, New York: "We hope the rebellion will sweep over the whole country. . . . Shame upon man when weak and friendless women are compelled to appear before the public and give tongue to their wrongs."[38]

Whether the rebellion spread as widely as the Lowell women hoped, mass meetings like the one in New York's City Hall did reflect the desperate plight of the seamstresses. At the New York meeting, Elizabeth Gray appears for the first time as their outspoken and articulate young leader, addressing a meeting of seven hundred women determined to win better wages "by appealing to the public at large and showing the amount of their sufferings." She named employers who payed no more than 10 to 18 cents a day, and another who threatened to send his work to Connecticut for sewing if the women did not accept 20 cents a day in wages. Using a strategy familiar even today, she publicly complimented the employer who had settled with the seamstresses after a turnout of only two hours.

"Was the association open to all who were suffering under like privations and injustice?" one woman asked. It was open to all, she was told, for "only by a firm cooperation could they accomplish what they were laboring for."[39] At this meeting, too, we find one of the earliest records of discussion of the oversupply of urban female workers and the need to open new jobs to them in predominantly male occupations such as clerking in dry-goods stores and bookkeeping.

The Female Industry Association that grew out of this meeting elected Elizabeth Gray president and Mary Graham secretary. It included as members a cross section of women workers in New York: book folders, stitchers, straw workers, lace and fringe makers, crimpers, and sewers of all kinds. Their strike received support from concerned citizens such as Signor Palmo, who donated his opera house for a benefit performance to raise relief money for the women. But in spite of the spirited ring to their words, the women found themselves once again powerless to deal with their employers, while their appeals to the public's sense of justice accomplished little. The next year they met again, this time protesting the price of only 4 cents paid for each shirt they made, "while agents of debauchery circulated among them with offers of ease and plenty." "This is what makes us want to see rich men hoeing corn and rich ladies at the washtub," they proclaimed.[40]

Prices paid the seamstresses continued to drop. Each organizing attempt, begun in determination, lasted only a short while and then evaporated. In 1850, Philadelphia sewers cried out:

To the Humane

The winter is upon us and distress and want stare us in the face. By reason of the low prices for which we are obliged to work many of us are found by the midnight lamp and until daybreak at the needle laboring for a pittance. . . .[41]

They longed to open an association (cooperative) shop, but were too poor even to attempt it.

Finally, in 1851, some 6,000 New York stitchers united to form the Shirt Sewers Cooperative Union. Both the work and the profits were to be divided among the women themselves. One floor up, at number 9 Henry Street, their headquarters bustled with activity. To succeed they needed orders for shirts, and for these the budding cooperative turned to the public. Writing letters carried in friendly newspapers, they described their life and begged for help. Pointing to widows and young women who had no other way to support themselves, they asked for contributions to launch their business and for shirt orders to keep it going.

For once the public heard! Money poured in; a central store was rented, a directress was appointed, and orders for shirts were filled. Within two years the Shirt Sewers Cooperative was regarded "among the successful combinative efforts at work in this city."[42] How long this cooperative lasted we do not know. We do know that the tailoresses of Philadelphia in 1850 also organized a cooperative to make and sell clothing and sewing services. "We are industrious and willing to work," they stated, "but paid as we are, we can not get enough to support life." Two sewers, Marion Tainter and Elizabeth Richards, had the courage to sign for the tailoresses.[43] Women like abolitionist Lucretia Mott and men like author George Lippard helped the Philadelphia sewers to organize an industrial union, which for a time did well, sponsoring labor education programs and sending delegates to the National Industrial Congress. For the two years that there are records of its existence, tailoresses received a fairer return for their garments than they ever had before.

However, even these attempts at solving the problem were exceptional. The "sweating system," involving whole families, took firm hold during the 1850s: men, women, and children, working together twelve to sixteen hours a day, would earn a dollar among them. Even then the *New York Tribune* reported, after an investigation, "the worst feature about seamstresses' wages is the all-too-prevalent fashion of those who employ them never giving them their pay."[44] And some young women, in complete desperation, worked for food and lodgings only.

Sewing Machine: Blessing or Curse?

Invented by one man, perfected by another, the sewing machine has had a stormy history. The Frenchman Barthélemy Thimonnier, who patented the first machine to sew cloth, almost lost his life when an angry mob destroyed his machines because they threw hand sewers out of work. For each measure of freedom the sewing machine has brought the home-maker, there has been a corresponding industrial problem. True, it meant lower-priced ready-made merchandise, but employers soon saturated this market and large-scale unemployment resulted. Hand sewers felt it first: thrown out of work, their wages cut,* they faced intense competition for jobs plus the financial burden of purchasing their own machines. For many this meant lifelong enslavement to the moneylender or to an employer who might advance the purchase price of this new invention at exorbitant interest rates.

Elias Howe's sewing machine (1846) and Singer's foot treadle, which improved it (1851), gradually brought hand sewers into the factory. Although for the rest of the century the pattern persisted—garments taken home in bundles, sewed in tenement sweatshops, then returned to the contractors for payment—by 1850, 4,228 garment manufacturing establishments employed 96,600 workers, of which 61,500 were women.[45] Four kinds of needlewomen worked in the sewing trades in the 1850s:

> 1. Journeymen dressmakers, who worked in the factories sixteen hours a day for $1.25 to $2.50 a week.
>
> 2. Dressmakers, who worked in the customers' homes and earned from 62½ cents to $1.00 a day.
>
> 3. Apprentices, who paid their employers to teach them the trade, working a year without pay or board. However, they rarely learned much except straight sewing and ended their year quite unskilled.
>
> 4. Home sewers, those who called for and delivered bundles of work. These were the most numerous (10,000 in New York City alone in 1854), endured the worst working and living conditions, and received the lowest pay.[46]

But capmakers, the lowest paid of all garment sewers, earned as little as 14 cents a day for fifteen to eighteen hours of work. Out of this they rented or bought their machines, as well as thread and needles, and paid for machine repairs. Early sewing machines frequently got out of control and tore into the fabric. Contractors, of course, charged the sewers for each torn garment, and these women lived in constant fear of accidents.

---

* Needlework that paid women 97½ cents in 1844 brought them only 37½ cents in 1845. (Ware, *Industrial Worker*, p. 50). With the invention of the heavy cutting knife, several garments could be cut at one time, and men took over the cutting market. They worked in the shops where the bundles of cut goods were picked up by home workers for stitching.

Yet needlewomen continued to flood the market. An advertisement in a Philadelphia paper shows the lengths to which they went:

> Wanted—by a young girl, a competent dressmaker, the loan of $100.00 for which she will give one year and a half of her time as a dressmaker and seamstress.[47]

The introduction of the sewing machine, with which one woman could do the work of six sewing twenty hours a day each, coincided with massive immigration, especially from Ireland, and with the recession of 1848. While prices again began to rise in the 1850s, the wages of sewing women did not. In fact, employers used the availability of immigrant labor and the intense competition among the women for work as reasons to cut rates still further. Only by increasing the hours per day that they worked could the women keep their low earnings at the same level.

It is small wonder that many turned to prostitution.

The Desperate Women

Where the wages of women reduced them to starvation levels, prostitution sometimes offered the only alternative. In 1858, Dr. William Sanger surveyed 2,000 prostitutes in New York City's jails. (The total number of prostitutes in New York at the time was estimated at 6,000, or 1 for every 64 adult males in the population.)

One-quarter of the women Sanger surveyed were sewers: tailoresses, milliners, seamstresses, vestmakers, dressmakers, hat trimmers, or flower makers. Although almost half of the total, some 933, worked as servants, earning $5 a month or less for being on call twenty-four hours a day, Sanger found no single group as badly off as the sewers. "Working from early dawn until late at night," he wrote, "with trembling fingers, aching head, very often an empty stomach, the poor seamstress ruins her health to obtain a spare and insufficient living."[48] He did not see that she had any way out. Milliners and women working in paper-box factories seemed just as badly off. So did tobacco packers and book folders. Over half of those he interviewed had averaged only $1 a week before turning to prostitution. Another 336 women had earned no more than $2 weekly.

Three out of every four were under twenty-five years of age; almost half were between fifteen and twenty. A high number, 63 percent, were foreign-born, and more than one-quarter were uneducated. Three-fourths were single or widowed. Of the 490 married women in his survey group, 103 reported desertion or refusal of support by husbands, or alcoholic spouses.

Prostitutes also died young. Sanger found that the women, once they entered the trade, lasted an average of four years. Nearly half had had syphilis at one time or another and had given birth to at least one child. More than half of all the children born to them were illegitimate. Infant mortality among them was four times higher than the average for New York City.

The more Sanger learned, the angrier he became. He saw that not enough jobs were open to women at decent levels of pay and that women were barred from numerous occupations they could easily have filled, such as clerking in department stores. Instead, women held the dullest, poorest-paid jobs. Sanger castigated employers for buying labor at the lowest possible price, and consumers for saving pennies at the expense of the workers, whose wages and working conditions they never thought to ask about before they bought.

Far ahead of his time, he advocated medical care for prostitutes with no shame attached to it. He had found that in France remedial and preventive measures had sharply reduced the incidence of venereal disease. Pointing to the experience of countries that had tried to regulate prostitution punitively and failed, he opposed punishment as a preventive and strongly endorsed the licensing of prostitutes.

But Sanger's words fell on deaf ears. Prostitution continued to flourish. By 1870, an estimated 10,000 prostitutes roamed New York's sidewalks; by 1890, the number had increased to 40,000.[49] Their "Hello, dear, won't you come home with me?" shocked visitors to the city. Young immigrant girls just off the boats from Europe joined the American women who streamed to the cities seeking decent work at decent pay. Unsuccessful at finding either, they were recruited or lured, or sometimes virtually kidnapped, into prostitution.

Working Women and the
Seneca Falls Convention, 1848

Early one summer morning in 1848, a young gloveworker from a village in Seneca County helped hitch the farm team to the wagon, climbed aboard, and with a few stops to pick up five or six friends along the route, started toward Seneca Falls, New York. Nineteen-year-old Charlotte Woodward* was one of a number of women who worked at home sewing mittens and gloves from deerskin tanned and cut in shops of towns nearby.

The glove sewers had read a small announcement carried five days earlier by the *Seneca Courier*, inviting the public to a two-day convention to begin July 19. It was billed as a women's rights meeting for the purpose of talking about the social, civil, and religious rights of women. The first

---

* Charlotte Woodward was the only woman who attended the Seneca Falls Convention of 1848 who lived to see women's suffrage ratified and to vote in a national election.

day, the notice read, was for women only. The second was open to the public, and a well-known abolitionist and lecturer, Lucretia Mott, would speak.

Charlotte Woodward, years later, described that day:

> I do clearly remember the wonderful beauty of the early morning when we dropped all our allotted tasks and climbed into the family wagon to drive over the rough roads to Seneca Falls. At first we traveled quite alone under the overhanging tree branches and wild vines, but before we had gone many miles we came on other wagonloads of women, bound in the same direction. As we reached different cross-roads, we saw wagons coming from every part of the county, and long before we reached Seneca Falls we were a procession. . . .[50]

Three hundred attended that meeting, of which forty were men. What made Woodward and her friends leave their farms during the busy haying and harvesting season to travel to Seneca Falls and join the gathering? Young and spirited, they were also angry. Woodward explains her feelings:

> We women work secretly in the seclusion of our bed chambers because all society was built on the theory that men, not women, earned money and that men alone supported the family. . . . But I do not believe that there was any community in which the souls of some women were not beating their wings in rebellion. For my own obscure self I can say that every fibre of my being rebelled, although silently, all the hours that I sat and sewed gloves for a miserable pittance which, as it was earned, could never be mine. I wanted to work, but I wanted to choose my task and I wanted to collect my wages. That was my form of rebellion against the life into which I was born.[51]

Woodward rebelled on two counts. First, married women had few property rights in New York State, and husbands were virtually free to spend their wives' earnings as they saw fit. Second, her own interests and ambitions lay not in glove sewing but in typesetting and printing. However, women were not admitted to apprenticeships in printing, nor were small-town print shops interested in hiring women. Even if there had been a job open for a woman, she probably would not have been free to leave the farm to take a job in town.

Undoubtedly a number of the women at Seneca Falls were working women like Charlotte Woodward. Others were farm women who worked hard in the home and fields and contributed their economic input to the family. They had practical, concrete reasons for their interest in women's rights. Not all of them went so far as to favor suffrage for women, which was the only resolution that did not pass the convention unanimously. But Charlotte Woodward did, and put her name to the Declaration of Principles before the convention ended. Among those principles was one Lucretia Mott had offered: "That the speedy success of our cause depends upon the . . . untiring efforts of both men and women for securing to women an equal participation with men in the various trades, professions and commerce."[52]

Working Women at Mid-Century

Part Two has viewed the role of white working women as the Industrial Revolution changed the face of America. Factories had replaced the home in the production of fabrics, shoes, hats, and clothing, while women followed their work to the mills. In many cases this meant shifting from part-time work at home to full-time labor in the factory, where wages were often so low that children joined their parents to help support the family. In almost all instances the wage system and piece rates replaced the prices workers used to set for the work they performed. Where factories needed large numbers of employees, urban growth followed. Families who lost their farms in the economic recessions that plagued the nineteenth century trooped to the cities. A factory population emerged.

The early New England textile workers in the boardinghouses differed from other working women of the time: they were younger, usually single, better educated, and had the option of returning to the family farm whenever they wished. By the 1850s most had left the mills to marry, to become missionaries or teachers, or to take jobs in white-collar trades. But the women who replaced them and formed a permanent factory population had no such choices. Many were immigrant women, poor and not well educated, who took any job at any wage in order to help support their families in this new and strange land.

Women were used to long hours of work. But in the factories, they came face to face not only with thirteen-hour workdays and low wages but with unhealthy and dangerous working conditions. Machines rarely had safety guards. Fingers, skirts, and long hair caught in them, causing serious injury and sometimes death. With factory work, too, came an increasing distance between the employer and the individual worker. "I regard my work-people just as I regard my machinery," said one factory agent. "When my machines get old and useless, I reject them and get new, and these people are part of my machinery."[53] Hired agents or overseers replaced the individual owner, who was now only one of a number of stockholders in a corporate structure.

Strong trade unions did not develop. The wonder is that the societies and associations that did form around particular crises, only to vanish within a few months or at best within a couple of years, were able to challenge the employers to the extent that they did. While the most famous of these organizations was undoubtedly the Lowell Female Labor

Reform Association, with Sarah Bagley at its head, we have noted some of the others. Those that fought for women like the seamstresses and umbrella workers, women who still worked mostly at home and in isolation from each other, are among the most amazing. So poor that they could hardly keep bread on the table, with no resources to withstand unemployment, somehow they managed to mobilize and strike even when they knew they had almost no chance of success.

Thus far, Part Two has dealt almost entirely with white working women of the Northeastern and Middle Atlantic states, where industry first took hold. During this period the Southern states remained predominantly rural, concentrating on the production of cotton, tobacco, and sugar. Their plantation economy firmly tied to slavery, they depended on exporting their crops and importing many of the manufactured products they needed. Northern industry in turn leaned heavily on Southern orders for shoes and cheap cotton work clothes for male slaves, and for the sale to the South of cotton yard goods that slave women made into clothing. The North depended to a considerable extent on the South's raw cotton for its mills.

It is no surprise that many industrialists joined forces with slaveholders to point out to millworkers how unhealthy the abolitionist cause was for them: that freed blacks would most certainly come North to take their jobs, and that in any event Southern planters would cut off orders to mills where workers gave assistance to fugitive slaves. Owners, too, watched with great interest whenever slaves were brought in as strikebreakers in Southern iron mills and textile plants.

In spite of this pressure, many Northern workers strongly supported the abolitionists and, together with Quakers and the nonslave black population, helped to organize the growing number of stations on the Underground Railroad. From their meager earnings, mill women along with other workers gave generously in support of this cause.

We turn next to the black women of America, slave and nonslave, before the Civil War, virtually all of whom were working women.

7

IN FACTORY AND FIELD:
Black Women and Slavery
in America 1808-1860

When the sun comes back and the first quail calls,
Follow the drinking gourd,
For the old man is waiting for to carry you to freedom
If you follow the drinking gourd.

The river bank will make a very good road,
The dead trees show you the way,
Left foot, peg foot traveling on,
Following the drinking gourd.

The river ends between two hills,
Following the drinking gourd.
There's another river on the other side,
Follow the drinking gourd.

Where the great big river meets the little river,
Follow the drinking gourd.
The old man is a-waiting for to carry you to freedom,
If you follow the drinking gourd.*

—"The Drinking Gourd," slave song

Slavery was big business in the South. While Northern industry was expanding, with workers moving in a steady stream to the cities to take up factory jobs, the South grew increasingly dependent on its slave economy and key agricultural crops, particularly cotton. As a result of the use of slave labor, the South had the lowest wage scales in the country. Moreover, it had so downgraded the idea of manual labor that even mill women brought from Lowell to train and supervise slaves in Southern cotton mills returned North in despair, no longer able to perform their work with pride.

The South stayed agricultural by design. Power was centered in the

* Slave songs invariably had double meanings. John Greenway, in *American Folksongs of Protest* (New York: A. S. Barnes, Perpetua Books, 1960), explains that "The Drinking Gourd" is "an audible map of the local branch line of the Underground Railroad. The 'Drinking Gourd' is, of course, the Big Dipper—north. 'Peg foot' refers to an old white man with a wooden leg who led the Negroes north" (p. 99).

hands of some three thousand leading slaveholders, men who held the largest numbers of slaves and most of the good plantation land. They controlled systematically every Southern institution: churches, schools, newspapers, courts, legislatures, even business and the small farmer. Southern factory owners met with strong planter opposition to any plans to reorganize their plants, hire free labor, and compete in efficiency with Northern industry. For the plantation system depended not only on control of the 4 million slaves throughout the South, but of the 8 million whites as well, the majority of whom were poor farmers and workers. Use of free labor would mean higher wages, strikes, and workers who might also organize politically and present a threat. Planters had a high stake in keeping the South agricultural.

Slavery as a business thrived, while the pressures to produce more and more cotton led to deteriorating conditions under which slaves lived and worked in the antebellum South. At the same time, both the number of slaves and the fears of the whites who ruled over them increased. A look at the distribution regionally and racially of the 32 million people in the United States in 1860 highlights why the South lived in such fear:[1]

UNITED STATES POPULATION IN 1860 BY REGION AND RACE

Region	White	Free (nonslave) black	Slave black
South	7,033,973	258,000	3,838,765
Northeast	10,438,028	155,983	18
North Central	8,899,969	69,291	144,948
West	550,567	4,450	29

Close to one-half of all Southerners were black, enslaved, and voteless. While the largest number of black Americans were Southern slaves, a half-million blacks who were technically "free" lived lives so circumscribed that Benjamin Quarles's term "nonslave" seems more appropriate. They contributed out of all proportion to their numbers to the developing fight for freedom. Nonslave black women, many of whom devoted their lives to the cause of abolition, were also among the first to see the connection between rights for blacks and rights for women.

Slavery: Big Business of the Antibellum South

> When we all meet in heaven
> There is no parting there.
> When we all meet in heaven
> There is parting no more.[2]

A British traveler in the South prior to the Civil War was awed by the thriving Gulf port of Mobile, Alabama, where each day wagons streamed into the city, piled high with cotton to be loaded on board ships bound for the mills of Europe and the North. He wrote:

> People live in cotton houses and ride in cotton carriages. They buy cotton, sell cotton, think cotton, eat cotton, drink cotton, and dream cotton. They marry cotton wives, and unto them are born cotton children. . . .[3]

Although seven out of eight slaves worked in the Deep South, mostly in the cotton fields, tobacco, sugar, rice, hemp, and especially corn were all important crops. The South in 1850 produced some 60 percent of the nation's corn.

At mid-century the price of slaves was still going up, which indicated the extent of Southern dependence on slave labor. A planter who had paid $500 for a slave in 1800 paid $1,500 by 1860. This was true even though the numbers of slaves increased from 700,000 in 1790 and 2,100,000 in 1830 to 4,000,000 in 1860. These slaves were held by fewer than 400,000 owners in a Southern white population of 7 million, and of these, 88 percent held an average of only two slaves each. More than half of all slaves were held by just 12 percent of Southern families.[4]

In 1808, the Constitutional ban on slave importations went into effect. The South, however, never faltered in maintaining slavery as a thriving industry. It achieved this in four ways: slave trading between the states, slave smuggling, slave breeding, and the hiring out of slaves.

The interstate slave trade got help from the courts. Just one year after the ban on importing slaves became effective, a South Carolina court held that "the young of slaves . . . stand on the same footing as other animals."[5] Thus the courts upheld the practice of taking slave children from their mothers for sale to new owners. Moses Grandy, who was born into slavery, told what happened to his mother when she resisted the sale of one of his brothers.

> My mother, frantic with grief, resisted . . . she was beaten and held down: she fainted, and when she came to herself, her boy was gone. She made much outcry, for which the master tied her up to a peach tree in the yard, and flogged her.[6]

Slaves might be sold by one owner directly to another, or by dealers at auction centers like those in New Orleans. Two hundred separate markets there disposed of slaves brought in daily from the Upper South, via the overland route to the Mississippi River and to New Orleans by boat, or on ships sailing from Southern ports on the Atlantic. The threat of sale and separation from their families was a major source of control over slaves.

When the federal ban on importing slaves went into effect in 1808, slave smuggling replaced the open traffic in blacks from Africa, and continued until 1859, when the *Clotilde* sailed into Mobile Bay, Alabama, the last ship to unload its smuggled cargo of slaves in the United States. The import ban left it to each state to determine what to do with smuggled cargoes, and Southern states did little to enforce the law. Fines for violators, if caught, were minimal. Seized cargoes were usually sold, the money going to the state's treasury or, on occasion, to the informer who reported the illegal shipment. For blacks aboard these ships this was a distinction without a difference, since smuggled cargoes reaching port were advertised as soon as they landed, and slave sales, though more guarded than formerly, took place promptly.

However, these incoming cargoes did not meet the ever-increasing need of the Deep South for slave labor to grow cotton. Consequently, some owners set about buying young "stock," much as cattle breeders would do, and compelling these slaves to "mate." A slave woman might bear her first child at the age of thirteen, and by the time she was twenty have had five children. To encourage rapid "breeding," some owners promised freedom to slave mothers when they had borne ten or fifteen children.[7] That the owner often helped this process along is evidenced by census figures of 1860 that show 588,000 slave children with white fathers.

Some owners were reluctant to break up slave families and tried to sell them as a unit. Most were not. However, the fact of sale and separation could not keep blacks from developing close family ties. Advertisements for runaways often stated that the slave in question probably had headed for a spouse or children from whom he or she had been separated. That family ties were strong is also evidenced by the great sacrifices made by slave mothers and the heavy risks they ran to keep their children together. Ex-slave and abolitionist leader Frederick Douglass wrote of his own mother:

> I never saw my mother, to know her as such, more than four or five times in my life; and each of these times was very short in duration, and at night. She was hired by a Mr. Stewart, who lived about twelve miles from my home. She made her journeys to see me in the night, travelling the whole distance on foot, after the performance of her day's work. She was a field hand, and a whipping is the penalty of not being in the field at sunrise. . . . I do not recollect of ever seeing my mother by the light of day. She was with me in the night. She would lie down with me, and get me to sleep, but long before I waked she was gone. . . . She died when I was about seven years old. . . . I was not allowed to be present during her illness, at her death, or burial.[8]

As the purchase price for slaves rose, hiring out slaves became an increasingly good business. Slave rental fees doubled from $100 a year in 1800 to $200 or more by 1860. Skilled workers, always in short supply in the South, went for as much as $600 a year.[9] Renters had no responsibility for slaves in old age or illness, for the slaves were rented only for as long as needed, by the year, month, week, or day. Renters furnished only maintenance and medical care.

Hired slaves worked in the factory as well as the field. Twenty percent of the 160,000 to 200,000 slaves used in industry were "rented,"[10] as were many city slaves. On the plantations, owners sometimes permitted trusted slaves to hire themselves out, but required them to turn over most of their pay to their masters.

Women in the Fields

From ex-slave Lewis Clarke comes this firsthand account of field work:

> The bell rings, at four o'clock in the morning, and they have half an hour to get ready. Men and women start together, and the women must work as steadily as the men, and perform the same tasks as the men. If the plantation is far from the house, the sucking children are taken out and kept in the field all day. If the cabins are near, the women are permitted to go in two or three times a day to their infant children. The mother is driven out when the child is three to four weeks old.[11]

Overseers, supervising plantations for absentee owners, often were the cruelest in the plantation hierarchy. Moses Grandy, when an ex-slave, wrote of their treatment of women slaves:

> On the estate I am speaking of, those women who had sucking children suffered much from their breasts becoming full of milk, the infants being left at home; they therefore could not keep up with the other hands: I have seen the overseer beat them with raw hide, so that the blood and milk flew mingled from their breasts. A woman who gives offence in the field, and is large in the family way, is compelled to lie down over a hole made to receive her corpulency, and is flogged with the whip, or beat with a paddle, which has holes in it; at every stroke comes a blister. One of my sisters was so severely punished in this way, that labor was brought on, and the child was born in the field. This very overseer, Mr. Brooks, killed in this manner a girl named Mary. Her father and mother were in the field at the time.[12]

As the numbers of slaves in the population rose, so did the fear of slave rebellion. The Denmark Vesey revolt of 1822 and that of Nat Turner in 1831 brought in their wake Black Codes that restricted slave life even further. Laws prohibited both manumission (the freeing of slaves by their owners) and the purchase by slaves of their own freedom. Any slave who, in spite of the law, became free after these codes were passed had to leave the state. Slaves had no legal standing and could not sue in court, nor testify against whites, nor own property. No slave could hit a white person, even in self-defense, but the killing of a slave was rarely punished. Rape of a slave woman by a white man caused raised eyebrows only if the owner thought someone else had harmed his property, and it was not unusual for a slaveowner to be waited on by a slave who was his own child.

The codes forbade slaves to leave the plantation without special permission. They were not allowed weapons, nor, in Mississippi, could they beat drums or blow horns, since it might be a signal for revolt.[13] Social contact with nonslave blacks and with whites was discouraged; visiting in the homes of either was not allowed. Nor could slaves hire themselves out without permission, or hold meetings, or gather in groups of any kind. After slave revolts, when fear among whites ran highest, slaves were forbidden even to talk with each other. Regulations required that a white be present at Sunday church meetings of slaves, and after 1830 even these services were discouraged. Instead, owners took their slaves to the white church, there to sit in segregated pews under the master's watchful eye.

Most of all, whites feared educated slaves, and it became a crime to teach a slave to read or write. Many a slave nursemaid, however, learned from her young white charges and then taught small groups of slaves late at night, deep in the woods, at the risk of severe punishment if she were caught. Slave children, routinely assigned as companions and guardians to white children, learned from them and taught their elders. Although some owners did teach their slaves to read, and a few plantation slave schools existed, by and large slaves remained illiterate. In antebellum Georgia, for example, only one in every eighty slaves could read and write.[14]

A system of patrols, on which whites served in rotation, enforced the Black Codes. The patrols operated rather laxly for the most part, but when unrest was in the air, slaves caught out of bounds without permission might be whipped or even killed on the spot. While these punishments deterred some blacks, others rebelled, even when they knew their revolts were doomed to failure. More subtle forms of protest were common, such as feigning illness, deliberately making mistakes or misunderstanding instructions, breaking or losing tools, chopping the cotton plants, or arson, even though severe and arbitrary punishment might, and often did, follow.

And slaves ran away. One of the most daring escapes, that of Ellen and William Craft in January 1849, is reported in a letter from abolitionist and ex-slave William Wells Brown to William Lloyd Garrison, editor of a leading abolitionist paper, *The Liberator*, January 12, 1849:

> One of the most interesting cases of the escape of fugitives from American slavery that have ever come before the American people, has just occurred, under the following circumstances:—William and Ellen Craft, man and wife, lived with different masters in the State of Georgia. Ellen is so near white, that she can pass without suspicion for a white woman. Her husband is much darker. He is a mechanic, and by working nights and Sundays, he laid up money enough to bring himself and his wife out of slavery. Their plan was without precedent; and though novel, was the means of getting them their freedom. Ellen dressed in man's clothing, and passed as the *master*, while her husband passed as the *servant*. In this way they travelled from Georgia to Philadelphia. They are now out of the reach of the blood-hounds of the South. On their journey, they put up at the best hotels where they stopped. Neither of them can read or write. And Ellen, knowing that she would be called upon to write her name at the hotels, &c, tied her right hand up as though it was lame, which proved of some service to her, as she was called upon several times at hotels to "register" her name. In Charleston, S.C., they put up at the hotel which Gov. M'Duffie and John C. Calhoun generally make their home, yet these distinguished advocates of the "peculiar institution" say that the slaves cannot take care of themselves. They arrived in Philadelphia, in four days from the time they started. Their history, especially that of their escape, is replete with interest. They will be at the meeting of the Massachusetts Anti-Slavery Society, in Boston, in the latter part of this month, where I know the history of their escape will be listened to with great interest. They are very intelligent. They are young, Ellen 22, and William 24 years of age. Ellen is truly a heroine.
>
> Yours, truly,
William W. Brown
>
> *P.S.* They are now hid away within 25 miles of Philadelphia, where they will remain until the 6th, when they will leave with me for New England. Will you please say in the *Liberator* that I will lecture, in connexion with them, as follows:—
>
> At Norwich, Conn., Thursday evening, January 18
> At Worcester, Mass., Friday evening, January 19
> At Pawtucket, Mass., Saturday evening, January 20
> At New Bedford, Mass., Sunday afternoon and evening, January 28.[15]

Another famous slave escape occurred on Christmas Eve, 1855. Young Ann Wood—some accounts say she was still in her teens—led a group of boys and girls north out of Virginia. Armed and driving a wagon, the young people were fully prepared to fight for their freedom and die if they had to. Slavecatchers stopped them, but the fugitives pointed their guns and threatened to kill as many of the posse as they could before they themselves died, and they were permitted to pass. Two of their number, on horseback, probably did not make it: shots were fired and they were never seen again. The rest found their way to Philadelphia and freedom.

Though no one knows the number for certain, between 40,000 and 100,000 slaves escaped to the North and Canada* via the Underground Railroad during the years preceding the Civil War. Most of these came from the Upper South. One route went through Ohio and Indiana, one through Maryland, Delaware, and Philadelphia. Along the way, men and women, black and white, risked their lives to assist the "passengers" from one "station" to the next. Fugitives traveled with "conductors"; "station-masters" sent word ahead as to how many adults and children were in each group by indicating the number and size of "parcels" to expect.

Harriet Tubman, Moses of Her People

Harriet Tubman was the Railroad's most famous conductor. Called "Moses" by the slaves, she made nineteen journeys back to the South in the years following her own escape in 1850, to bring over three hundred slaves out of Maryland. Because of the passage of the Fugitive Slave Act in 1850,† almost all of her passengers had to be taken across the border to Canada. Gradually she became a legend, until at last the price on her head in the South reached $40,000 for the person or persons who could capture her, dead or alive.

Born in 1820 on a Maryland plantation in Dorchester County, Harriet Ross began to work at the age of six, when her owner hired her out to a poor family and his wife, a weaver, and shortly after that, to another family as nursemaid. These jobs netted her measles, pneumonia, near-starvation, and a lifelong crisscrossing of scars from beatings about her neck. When she could take it no more, she ran away. For five days she

---

*In Canada they were safe. Canadians, who had never held many slaves, outlawed slavery in 1833. Although the United States requested help from the Canadian government several times after the passage of the Fugitive Slave Act in 1850, the Canadians refused any assistance whatsoever. Not only fugitive slaves turned gratefully to Canada after 1850 but also a number of nonslave men and women, who were afraid they could not prove their freedom and would be in danger of capture and removal to the South if they remained in the States. By 1855, there were 30,000 blacks who had settled in the Lake Ontario area of Canada. Robert S. Starobin, *Blacks in Bondage* (New York: New Viewpoints, 1974), p. 146.

† The Fugitive Slave Law, passed in 1850, was a "Compromise" whereby California was admitted as a free state and the slave trade was abolished in Washington, D.C. The South, in exchange, got support for the return of runaway slaves from any state in the union. All law enforcement agents had to assist in their removal, and a penalty of $1,000 was levied against any United States marshal who did not arrest fugitives if asked for help. No warrant was required for this arrest. The only proof a judge needed was the owner's statement that this was his property. There was no jury trial, nor could the runaway testify on his or her own behalf. Anyone who aided the Underground Railroad, even by as little as giving food to fugitives, could be jailed for five years and fined $5,000. Saunders Redding, *They Came in Chains* (Philadelphia: J. B. Lippincott Co., 1950), pp. 118–19.

hid in a pigpen, fighting the pigs for scraps of food. Half-starved, she was returned—after a severe beating—to her home plantation, and was used for outdoor work from then on.

By the time she was eleven, she could split rails and chop wood like a man. As she worked beside her father, cutting and hewing, he taught her about the forest: how to walk so quietly that not a twig crackled underfoot, which plants made good food and sustained life, and which roots had the power to heal. The North Star became her friend.

A turning point in her life came when she was fifteen. Ordered by an overseer to hold a runaway slave so he could be tied up for a beating, she refused, blocking the doorway to help the fugitive escape. The overseer, aiming a two-pound metal weight at the runaway, missed, hitting Harriet on the head instead. The concussion she received left her semiconscious for months, with a deep gash that finally healed but marked her for life. The accident also left her with unpredictable and inconvenient fainting or sleeping spells.

At twenty-four she married John Tubman, a free black. Just five years later, she faced the prospect of being sold to a Georgia slave trader, and pleaded with her husband to join her in running away. He refused. Sad and disillusioned, she described later how she made her decision:

> I had reasoned this out in my mind; there was one of two things I had a right to, liberty or death; if I could not have one, I would have the other; for no man would take me alive; I should fight for my liberty as long as my strength lasted, and when the time came for me to go, the Lord would let them take me.[16]

She used the code of spirituals and her beautiful singing voice, deep, husky, and rich, to tell her family that she was leaving. She sang:

> When that old chariot comes
> I'm going to leave you,
> I'm bound for the promised land,
> Friends I'm going to leave you.
>
> I'm sorry, friends, to leave you
> Farewell, Oh, farewell!
> But I'll meet you in the morning
> Farewell, Oh, Farewell!
>
> I'll meet you in the morning
> When I reach the promised land;
> On the other side of Jordan,
> For I'm bound for the promised land.

That night she went. The first person to befriend her, a white woman, began her lessons about what the Underground Railroad really was: a series of friendly homes between long night marches and daytime hideouts in the woods; warmth between spells of cold; food between stretches of eating only berries and plants; a fire and dry clothing between the icy rivers waded and rain endured without shelter; money to replace worn-out sandals. In the course of the next ten years she would come to know the route well and use all the forest lore she had learned from her father. The North Star would guide her, as would her own mystical faith in God. But loneliness and uncertainty sometimes almost overwhelmed her. When she reached the North during her own escape she felt, "I was free, but there was no one to welcome me to the land of freedom. I was a stranger in a strange land. . . ."[17]

Each trip North tested her ingenuity; each situation demanded something new. A talented actress and mimic, disguises came to her on the spur of the moment: at one time she was an old woman, bent-over and shaky; at another, a farmer setting out for market with two chickens tied together by the feet. She hid in wagons with false bottoms, where she and her passengers lay covered over with bricks. On one of her last trips, to bring her aged mother and father to freedom, she rode brazenly out in the open, past signs offering handsome rewards for her capture. There were times in the woods when she had to point her gun at fugitives who lost courage and wanted to turn back. She always carried paregoric to quiet the babies so that their cries would not reveal her little band, hiding in the woods by day, to slavecatchers riding by.

She went South twice a year. To finance these trips, she worked as a

Harriet Tubman, greatest "engineer" on the Underground Railroad and Civil War fighter, is shown here as an old woman in Auburn, New York.

cook in a Cape May, New Jersey, hotel during the summer, hoarding her wages and tips. The winters she spent in the town of St. Catherine's in Canada, where she worked and helped the ex-slaves she had brought North to find jobs and adjust to a cold climate and new country.

In 1858 she mounted the lecture platform for the first time and was an instant success. Everywhere she spoke the audiences stood and cheered and wept. Invariably, this simple woman in her plain gray dress moved them. She came to number among her friends all the great leaders of abolition, among them Frederick Douglass, the Grimké sisters, Lucretia Mott, William Lloyd Garrison, and John Brown.

Her work continued throughout the Civil War as scout, spy, and nurse. At the Combahee River she led a band of three hundred black soldiers on a raid to free eight hundred slaves—the only woman in American history ever to have led troops in battle. She nursed ex-slaves and wounded black soldiers in hospitals, using her knowledge of herbs to save many seriously ill with dysentery.

Following the war she returned to the small home she had bought in Auburn, New York. There she raised money for a school for freed slaves, and became interested in women's suffrage. Her home was a haven for the poor and the aged. To help support this work, her friend Sarah Hopkins Bradford wrote two books about her, in 1869 and 1886.

In 1869, Harriet Tubman married again. Her husband, a veteran twenty years her junior, died in 1888, after having been ill and dependent on her during most of their marriage. Because she had not been officially in the government's employ during the war, she was denied a pension for her war work, but she finally received a small monthly sum as the widow of a veteran.

During the last years of her life she was Auburn's beloved celebrity. As she peddled homegrown vegetables from door to door, each family asked her in to tell stories of the Underground Railroad. Her memory never failed her, nor did the rich flow of her words, with their Biblical cadence and allusions. She died in 1913, old, perhaps lonely, but admired by the hundreds who knew her. A year after her death, the entire town closed down for a day devoted to the memory of its most distinguished citizen. The tablet that Auburn citizens placed in front of the town courthouse reads:[18]

IN MEMORY OF HARRIET TUBMAN.
BORN A SLAVE IN MARYLAND ABOUT 1821.
DIED IN AUBURN, N.Y., MARCH 10, 1913.
CALLED THE MOSES OF HER PEOPLE,
DURING THE CIVIL WAR. WITH RARE
COURAGE SHE LED OVER THREE HUNDRED
NEGROES UP FROM SLAVERY TO FREEDOM,
AND RENDERED INVALUABLE SERVICE
AS NURSE AND SPY.
WITH IMPLICIT TRUST IN GOD
SHE BRAVED EVERY DANGER AND
OVERCAME EVERY OBSTACLE. WITHAL
SHE POSSESSED EXTRAORDINARY
FORESIGHT AND JUDGMENT SO THAT
SHE TRUTHFULLY SAID
"ON MY UNDERGROUND RAILROAD
I NEBBER RUN MY TRAIN OFF DE TRACK

AN' I NEBBER LOS' A PASSENGER."
THIS TABLET IS ERECTED
BY THE CITIZENS OF AUBURN.

Slave Women in Industry

The first Southern cotton mill opened in 1789, its work force composed of slaves rented from nearby plantations. By 1860 more than 5,000 slaves, most of them women, worked in cotton and woolen mills under white supervisors, who included the women from Lowell mentioned earlier. Slave women also worked in turpentine camps and sugar refineries, in food and tobacco processing, in rice milling, and in the manufacture of hemp. They worked in foundries and saltworks, pulled trams in the mines, and put ore into crushers and furnaces. They were lumberjacks and ditchdiggers. As early as 1800, slave women made up half the diggers on South Carolina's Santee Canal. They helped build the Louisiana levees and worked on slave crews laying track for the Southern railroads.[19]

Industrial slaves worked a six-day week, twelve to sixteen hours a day. Even seven-day weeks were not uncommon. Food was even more of a problem than it was for agricultural slaves, for although their rations were similar, slaves in industry could not count on table scraps, nor were they likely to have garden plots on which to grow vegetables to supplement their diet. In jobs such as rice milling, workers could expect the broken rice not fit for market, but few jobs provided these extras.

Clothing allotments were poor. So was housing. Workers lived in shanties and cooked over an open pit in the middle of the floor. The smoke rose slowly, eventually drifting out through a hole in the roof, which also let in the rain. Medical care hardly existed. Pneumonia, typhus,

Slave women before the Civil War perform stemming operations in a tobacco factory.

tuberculosis, scarlet fever, diphtheria, dysentery, and other diseases swept through the shanty communities. The occasional clinic, built near the factory, was crowded and dirty. Maternity beds and those for infants and children were placed in the same room with all the other patients, and this resulted in unusually high maternal and infant mortality rates.

Working conditions were harsh and dangerous; supervision was tight and severe. Nonetheless, industrial slaves resisted. There were slowdowns, carelessness, sabotage, stealing, and even refusal to work, though at great risk to personal safety. Factory overseers withheld food and clothing rations to discipline the slaves, and forced them to sing, not only to prevent their talking and plotting, but also to increase production.

There was one advantage for slaves in industrial work. Through a system of "overwork," or overtime, they could earn small amounts of money which were their own. However, this system served also to lock them into their jobs, for all regular work had to be completed before overwork could begin. Nonetheless, a substantial number of industrial slaves broke away to escape to the North. Fugitives, if caught, were subject to severe beatings and painful shackling.

Considering the low cost of renting or owning slaves, it is not hard to see why factory owners at first preferred this system to hiring free labor, white or black. Slaves could not quit, organize, or strike. When necessary, they could be—and were—used as strikebreakers in labor disputes. As word of this practice traveled North, Northern workers recognized the danger to their own jobs in low-cost slave labor, particularly in the event of a strike, and many became strong supporters of the abolitionist cause.

Slave women were considered as valuable in the factory as in the field, for their children at a young age could be put to light factory jobs. Then, too, women and children cost less to feed. Owners estimated their cost at two-thirds that of men. They were more docile and were thought to perform some operations better, for example in tobacco and hemp production, where they made up a high proportion of the work force. Nevertheless, it was generally true that factory production using slave labor turned out to be less efficient in the South than production in the North with free labor.

Slave Women in the Cities

Proportionately more individual Southern city dwellers held slaves than Southern rural whites, although they held a much smaller number per family. In Charleston in 1820, three-quarters of all white families owned slaves, and in Richmond, two-thirds.[20] Between 1820 and 1840, however, the ratio began to change, until by the Civil War city families had a far smaller stake in the continuation of slavery than did plantation families.

With the exception of Richmond, where a number of male slaves worked in heavy industry, a majority of the urban slave population was female. This was due, in part, to the fact that black men had some opportunity to "hire out" as bondsmen and earn the money to buy their freedom—and the law required them to leave the state as soon as they had done so. While slaves in the city had more mobility than those on plantations and could attempt escape more often, slave women, with ties to their children, were less able to take advantage of this mobility.

City slave women worked at a wide variety of jobs, as chambermaids, vendors, nursemaids, hairdressers, seamstresses, laundresses, and servants. While they needed passes wherever they went, frequently they had their own homes (albeit these were shacks), worshipped in their own churches, and mingled more easily with nonslave blacks as well as with other slaves. The possibilities for learning to read and write, as well as the opportunity to acquire training in a trade, improved in the city, for the more skilled a slave, the more she could command for her master in hiring out. Because of their value to their owners, city slaves often seemed to have more security than nonslave blacks, who formed a class of a quarter of a million men and women who walked a perpetual tightrope and were unwelcome wherever they went.

Nonslave Blacks in the South

"They are not slaves indeed," wrote the English actress Fanny Kemble from a Georgia plantation, "but they are pariahs, debarred from every fellowship save with their own despised race, scorned by the lowest ruffian in your kitchen. They are free, certainly, but they are also degraded, the off-scum and the off-scouring of the very dregs of your society."[21]

Nonslave blacks lived cautious lives. White workers viewed them as a threat to their jobs and wages. Labor unions barred them. Slaveholders regarded them with suspicion as a source of help to escaping slaves and as potential leaders of slave revolts. "Free negroism . . . is not a condition . . . which the higher law of nature grants," wrote Van Evrie, referring to free blacks as "social monstrosities."[22] Southern legislatures viewed them as lazy, inclined to loose morals, and likely to become public charges, and passed laws governing every aspect of their lives. While the states hoped in this way to force nonslaves to leave the South forever, ironically these workers provided both skilled and unskilled labor that was much in demand.

The biggest problem of nonslaves was staying free. Often they were enslaved for infractions of the many rules surrounding their lives, or kidnapped and sold. They had to carry passes and identification papers at all times; anyone without these was presumed to be a slave or a runaway. Some Southern states required registration of all free blacks; others mandated white guardians for them. States restricted their in-migration and sometimes they could not even move into another county. They could carry no arms without a license, and by 1835 in most Southern states, they had lost all rights to free assembly. States often prohibited societies of free blacks other than religious and required the presence of a white minister for their church services. Contacts with slaves were restricted or forbidden altogether. They could not buy alcohol. By law, nonslave blacks were compelled to work, and "vagrants" could be imprisoned and then farmed out as laborers to work off their fine.

In spite of these restrictions, a number of nonslave blacks successfully pursued trades and professions, owned homes,* and educated their children—but not in public schools. Their tax money supported schools their children could not attend, and there were few public schools for black children. In some states it was even unlawful to teach nonslaves. Nor could they testify in court cases involving whites, or serve on juries.

These conditions applied, of course, to black men and women alike. Anyone with a dark skin was presumed a slave unless he or she could prove otherwise. The Virginia Supreme Court of Appeals stated:

> In the case of a person visibly appearing to be a negro, the presumption is that he (she) is a slave . . . the plaintiff in a suit for freedom must make out his title against all the world.[23]

As late as 1860 in Lexington, Kentucky, slave dealers tricked two young women out of their freedom papers, and no amount of pleading by a Baptist minister who knew them well could save them from the auction block and sale to a firm of slave traders.

The Black Woman Worker of the North

The importance of the Northern black washerwomen in the pre-Civil War period cannot be overstated. It was she who supported her family when her husband, even though he might be skilled in his trade, could not find work. Barred from unions, male black workers found that whites refused to work with them, while employers, fearing retaliation, would not hire them. An 1847 survey of 4,249 black women workers in Philadelphia found that most were washerwomen and household workers. Eleven percent (486) worked in the needle trades, and 213 others had jobs as hairdressers, milliners, midwives, and nurses.[24]

---

* They were permitted to own property and to make contracts.

As waves of immigrants landed in New York harbor and displaced even the lowest-paid blacks, abolitionist leader Frederick Douglass cried out: "Every hour sees the black man elbowed out of employment by some newly arrived immigrant whose hunger and whose color are thought to give him a better title to a place."[25] This held true for black women as well, and they finally went from door to door offering to work as laundresses, cooks, nursemaids, or domestics at almost any wages the mistress of the house would pay.*

Nor was unemployment the only problem that Northern blacks faced. They had no political power and no police protection. Mobs victimized them, as in Pittsburgh in 1834 and again in 1835 and 1839, when fires were set in black neighborhoods. Race riots occurred in the 1830s and 1840s in Cincinnati, Philadelphia, and New York City. By focusing on one experience, that of white Quaker teacher Prudence Crandall, the depth of this negative feeling can be seen.

In 1833 in Canterbury, Connecticut, thirty-year-old Prudence Crandall decided to open her school for girls to one black woman who sought teacher training. The local outcry was so fierce when she admitted young Sarah Harris that she closed her school, but she promptly reopened it two months later as a boarding school for black girls. The town exploded. When Crandall refused to close the school, the forces of law were mobilized to force her to shut it down. First, she was jailed on charges of vagrancy. Next, a law was passed barring the teaching of out-of-state blacks. When this failed to stop her, the town ruffians had their day. The mob stoned teachers and students and shoveled manure into the school well. Doctors refused to take the young women as patients, shopkeepers would not sell the school food, and students were barred from the local Congregationalist church.

For eighteen months Prudence Crandall and some of the students held on, aided by abolitionists from far and near who sent food, carted water and supplies, and raised money. The end came, however, when one of the townspeople set fire to the school cellar and when, shortly after, a number of them attacked the building with heavy clubs and iron bars, demolishing window sashes and smashing windowpanes. While Crandall was forced to give up the school, she never abandoned the fight for the abolitionist cause.[26]

Northern blacks, however, had a number of important rights denied to

* This was especially aggravated during the early years of the Civil War, when Northern mills closed down for lack of cotton and factory women flooded the cities seeking work— any work—displacing black women by the thousands from their menial jobs, the only jobs they had been able to get.

blacks in the South. They could protest injustice and use the courts. Most important, perhaps, they could form organizations, hold meetings and conventions, publish newspapers, write books, and work for the abolitionist cause.* Some of the most significant contributions to this cause were made by ex-slaves who wrote (or dictated, for some, like Harriet Tubman and Sojourner Truth, could neither read nor write) books and articles that educated the public concerning the evils of slavery. Between 1810 and 1860, over one hundred serious works ranging from fiction to autobiography were written by ex-slaves and nonslave blacks.[27]

A number of black women leaders emerged as teachers and speakers in the abolitionist cause. Frances Maria Stewart was one, the first American woman public lecturer, black or white, who left us the texts of her speeches. Born in Hartford, Connecticut, in 1803, orphaned and bound out to a clergyman's family when only five years old, she worked there until she was fifteen. Although she had little formal schooling, she read every book in this ministerial household that she could get her hands on, which gave her speeches their religious tone. When she had been married only three years, her husband died. Cheated by his lawyers out of the money he left her, she turned to writing and speaking to support herself. She championed the cause of education for free blacks, to enable them to sue for their rights. "Knowledge is power," she reminded her audience. She castigated white Northerners for reducing free blacks to near-slavery by denying them both jobs and schooling.

Embittered by the criticism of black men, who disapproved of her as a woman who spoke in public, she became one of the first to talk of the double-edged sword of prejudice: race and sex. In 1833, faced with this opposition to her public appearances, Maria Stewart put aside her lecturing career and turned to teaching in the public schools of New York City. After the Civil War she worked in a freedman's hospital and later opened a Sunday school for some seventy-five children.

Mary Ann Shadd, teacher, editor, journalist, and lawyer, was born in 1823 in Wilmington, Delaware. Her father's antislavery activities inspired all of his children to dedicate themselves to this cause, including young Mary Ann, who, as a teacher, moved to Canada and championed the cause of blacks living there to escape the Fugitive Slave Act. She was the first black woman in North America to edit a weekly paper, *The Freeman*, of Toronto, Canada. During the Civil War, she traveled thou-

* It is interesting to note that the New York Female Anti-Slavery Society refused to admit black women, who also could form only segregated auxiliaries to this society in Albany, Rochester, Nantucket, and Lexington, Ohio. August Meier and Elliott Rudwick, *From Plantation to Ghetto* (New York: Hill & Wang, 1966), pp. 105–6.

Susie King Taylor, laundress, teacher, Civil War nurse, and author.

sands of miles across the United States recruiting black soldiers for the army. Following the war, as a widow with a young daughter to support, she moved to Washington, D.C., where she taught and later was appointed principal of a grade school. At the age of forty-six, she entered Howard Law School, graduating in 1883 as the only black woman in her class. In spite of criticism for "unladylike" behavior, she never stopped her public-speaking activities nor her support of increased educational opportunities for blacks.[28]

Susie King Taylor, born in the South, served in the first Negro regiment during the Civil War as nurse, teacher, and laundress. In her *Reminiscences of My Life in Camp* she described the lengths to which her family went when she was a child to see that she received an education:

> I was born under the slave law in Georgia, in 1848, and was brought up by my grandmother in Savannah. . . . We were sent to a friend of my grandmother . . . to learn to read and write. She was a free woman and lived . . . about half a mile from my house. We went every day about nine o'clock, with our books wrapped in paper to prevent the police or white persons from seeing them. We went in, one at a time, through the gate into the yard to the kitchen, which was the schoolroom. She had twenty-five or thirty children whom she taught, assisted by her daughter. . . . The neighbors would see us going in some times, but they supposed we were there learning trades, as it was the custom to give children a trade of some kind. After school we left the same way we entered, one by one. . . .[29]

Later a white playmate offered to give Susie King lessons if she promised not to tell anyone. Still later, her grandmother arranged for the landlord's son to continue her education. Her ability to read and write proved immediately useful in the forging of passes for blacks in her home town of Savannah.

Among the many black women teachers of this period, Maria Becraft and Sarah Mapps Douglass were two of the most brilliant. Maria Becraft was only fifteen when she opened the first boarding school for black girls in Washington, D.C., in 1820, fully thirteen years before Prudence Crandall's abortive effort in Canterbury. In this same year Sarah Douglass launched her day school for black children in Philadelphia, and she too was young—just fourteen. Sarah Douglass was later to pioneer in curriculum development, introducing science and physiology into the program in order to open opportunities for her students beyond a traditional home economics and trade education. As head of the primary grades of the Institute for Colored Youth, she trained many of the black women who later became teachers in the Philadelphia school system. A founding member of the Philadelphia Anti-Slavery Society, she combined a lifelong interest in education with work for the abolition movement and, after the war, for freedmen. She never halted her own education, entering medical school in 1855 to ensure that the science courses she introduced into her school were the best her students could obtain anywhere. She died in 1882.[30]

Frances Ellen Watkins Harper, abolitionist, worker on the Underground Railroad, teacher, public lecturer, poet, and author, was born in 1825 of nonslave parents, who died when she was only three. Her Baltimore uncle, a brilliant man who combined a passion for the abolitionist cause with talents as a preacher, linguist, and educator, was the only parent she knew. Frances Watkins showed her own talent early, and by the time she was fifteen had published a book of poetry and prose pieces. In 1853, as a teacher in Ohio, she became active in the Underground Railroad—the same year that her home state passed a law subjecting nonslave blacks coming into Maryland to sale into slavery. Her first antislavery lecture was delivered in New Bedford, Massachusetts, and entitled "Education and the Elevation of the Colored People"; it brought her a contract to lecture throughout the state for the Maine Anti-Slavery Society. Her career as a public lecturer next took her through Pennsylvania, New Jersey, New York, and Ohio. During her talks she often read some of her own poems, which grew in popularity along with her stories and articles. The proceeds from her writing invariably went to help runaway slaves.

She married in 1860 and withdrew from the lecture circuit, but returned to it after her husband's death four years later in order to support herself and her young daughter. She spoke out vehemently against racial violence, especially the lynchings which took place following the war. She also worked to promote Negro suffrage, and after 1875, strongly advocated women's suffrage as well. Later in her life she took up the cause of black young people in the cities, and served as director of the

American Association of Colored Youth. William Still, a noted abolitionist, knew her well and described her as a lecturer who "speaks without
notes, with gestures few and fitting. Her manner is marked by dignity
and composure. She is never assuming, never theatrical."[31] J. W. Logues, a
worker on the Underground Railroad, wrote to William Still from Syracuse, New York, in 1856: "Miss Watkins is doing great good in our part
of the State. We think much of her. She is such a good and glorious
speaker, that we are all charmed with her."[32]

The Crossroads: America in 1861

By 1861, black men and women were employed in over 130 jobs and
trades, although only a small proportion were skilled workers. The outlook
for their children had not improved much in fifty years. If anything,
conditions for slaves had worsened, aggravated by rising political tensions
and white fears of slave rebellion. Restrictions grew more rigid and punishments more severe in order to maintain the slave system intact.

The agitation of the decade preceding the Civil War was also reflected in the black communities of cities throughout the North, as increasing numbers of fugitives from the Upper South stopped off on their
way to Canada, or sometimes stayed on with relatives in spite of the risk
of seizure and return. It was in the midst of this ferment that the women
discussed in this chapter and others rose to prominence, women who supported themselves and their families through teaching, nursing, writing,
cooking, lecturing, and doing other people's laundry, but also devoted
their talents, time, and wages to the cause in which they believed. Many
of these women knew each other, and it is likely that at one time or another all of them were in touch with Frederick Douglass, ex-slave, orator,
newspaper editor,* and leader. Douglass knew, long before others, that
there would be bloodshed and war over slavery.

In 1852 an antislavery journal, the *National Era*, carried a year-long
serial, *Uncle Tom's Cabin*, by abolitionist Harriet Beecher Stowe. It was
then published as a book, with instant success: in its first year it sold
300,000 copies. As a play it ran to packed houses throughout the North,
and was translated into German, French, Italian, Polish, and Chinese.
The story, based on accounts of ex-slaves and the daily excesses of the
Fugitive Slave Act, rang true. Its impact was both immediate and en-

* Douglass was a lifelong friend of the women's rights movement. Editor of the Rochester
(New York) *North Star*, he carried on the masthead of its first issue: "Right is of no sex;
truth is of no color." His paper ran an announcement of the 1848 Seneca Falls Women's
Rights Convention, which many newspapers did not take seriously. He attended this convention and played a key role in support of Elizabeth Cady Stanton's resolution calling for
votes for women.

during. Everyone read it, old and young, year after year. In the South it was both furiously condemned and widely read.

One seemingly small event, an abortive raid on the arsenal at Harpers Ferry, West Virginia, by abolitionist John Brown and a small band of zealots, had repercussions that polarized North and South, drawing Southern leaders together as no preceding event had yet done. Southerners now realized that their system could not survive as long as they were part of the United States and that there would be no safety from slave rebellions except in a confederation of slave states able to eliminate all alien influences. But in the North, John Brown became a martyr and symbol who, on the gallows, did more for the abolitionist cause than he could ever have done had his raid on Harpers Ferry succeeded.

Abraham Lincoln was elected president of the United States in 1860. In December 1860, Southern states began the process of seceding from the Union, the Union that Lincoln had pledged himself to uphold. Although the lines had been drawn, not everyone in the North embraced the cause of union or freedom for slaves, nor did everyone in the South support the Confederacy and its system of slavery.

During the Civil War that followed, the role of women began to change, so significantly, when viewed in retrospect, that this period marked a watershed for them as well as for the country as a whole. During the war, women in the North and the South entered the work force, many for the first time, taking the place of men called to military duty and helping to meet the demands of a wartime economy. Women, many of whom had been widowed, and some in new jobs that did not exist before the war, became a permanent part of the work force and began to organize trade unions more like the ones we know today.

Part 3

WORKING WOMEN IN WAR AND PEACE
1861–1886

In 1861 the nation was divided against itself. Women in the North and the South served as nurses, spies, teachers, and soldiers. While the South was ravaged by the war, the North essentially prospered, and the boom which followed ushered in the Industrial Age. Many of the women who had taken jobs outside the home for the first time during the war stayed on. Their ranks were swollen with widows from the South, who came North to find work.

A migration of another sort, from North to South, took place as women answered the call for teachers to educate the newly emancipated black men, women, and children. For a brief time there was some hope that Reconstruction would work. But with the election of Rutherford B. Hayes in 1877, home rule was restored to the South, and blacks were almost as badly off as they had been under slavery.

The war had opened new occupations for Northern women in office work, government employment, and retail stores, but women also continued in the jobs that were traditionally theirs. Sewing women, still the lowest-paid workers, often could not collect from their employers even the little they were owed. Their situation became desperate, and it was to help women with a problem as basic as collecting their wages that the Working Women's Protective Union was formed to supply free legal assistance.

In 1873 the country entered one of the worst depressions in its history, marked by riots, widespread suffering, and outright starvation. At the same time, America had become a land of corporate giants that employed armed guards and private armies to defeat workers' attempts to organize trade unions. Nonetheless, a secret labor federation, the Noble Order of the Knights of Labor, came out into the open and during the 1880s proceeded to organize hundreds of thousands of workers, for the first time including in the ranks of unionists black workers and women. Some of the women leaders who came forward during this period were fiery Kate Mullaney of the Troy Collar Laundresses; Augusta Lewis, who organized Women's Typographical Union Number 1; and Leonora Barry, organizer and head of the women's department of the Knights of Labor.

8

WOMEN IN THE CIVIL WAR AND RECONSTRUCTION
1861–1877

It shall flash through coming ages!
It shall light the distant years;
And eyes now dim with sorrow
Shall be clearer through their tears.

—Frances Ellen Watkins Harper, "President Lincoln's
Proclamation of Freedom"

On December 20, 1860, South Carolina seceded, the first of the eleven states that formed the new Confederacy of 9 million persons. More than one-third were slaves. Four slave states remained with the Union: Maryland, Delaware, Kentucky, and Missouri. In 1863, West Virginia broke away from Virginia to join them. The nineteen free states, which included 61 percent of the total population of the United States, held overwhelming superiority in industrial production (81 percent of the total for the United States in 1860), in farm production (67 percent), and in railroad trackage (66 percent).[1]

Meanwhile the South attempted to build its own industry, but since it depended on supplies from Europe—eventually cut off in large part by the Union blockade—Southern industry remained embryonic. Its lack of steel and iron-making capacity was the prime reason for the collapse after 1863 of its railroad system, never very adequate at best. Its army shrank (20 percent deserted between 1864 and 1865), and the Confederacy faced runaway inflation and a near-worthless currency. The war brought to the defeated South poverty, destruction, and disorganization. For a time its superior military leadership and the fact that it was fighting a war of "independence" on home territory gave it a tactical advantage, but this did not last.

Women, North and South, worked on the battle front and behind the lines as army nurses, firmly establishing the profession for the first time. At least four hundred women fought as soldiers. Women were also spies and smugglers as well as cooks and laundresses for the troops. Women

132

remained active after the war, traveling South to teach and work with freed slaves. Regrettably, only a few of their stories can be touched on here.

Women of the North in the Civil War

The wartime work of women commenced with the first cannon fired. In April 1861, when Dr. Elizabeth Blackwell and her sister, Dr. Emily Blackwell, called a meeting in New York City to organize the Woman's Central Relief Association, three thousand women became involved in the war effort almost overnight. The Blackwells began to train nurses for service with the army—the first time American women had received formal training for this kind of work.* By mid-1861, this association had helped to initiate the United States Sanitary Commission, which functioned throughout the war to raise money for medical supplies and to recruit nurses for war duty. However, these nurses tackled more than care of the wounded, for the army camps had problems of health and sanitation that were as dangerous to the men as the wounds they received in battle. Bringing order out of filth and chaos was a major job on arrival. Debris, garbage, and litter were everywhere, open trenches substituted for latrines, and dysentery, typhoid, and malaria plagued every camp.

The Sanitary Commission, precursor of the American Red Cross, developed a remarkable network of branches. The Chicago center, for example, coordinated 1,000 aid societies that raised money and organized women to roll bandages, make clothing for the troops, and collect medical supplies and foodstuffs. Cleveland and Cincinnati worked with their own network of 500 branches.[2] But the work of the societies and branches did not stop there. They sent packages to the men at the front and helped their wives back home find jobs. They secured back pay, pensions, and work for discharged soldiers, and looked after those permanently disabled while in the service. Mary A. Livermore and Jane Hoge, social workers moved by the suffering they saw in army hospitals, became the guiding spirits of the Chicago branch. They surprised even themselves when their first Sanitary Fair netted $80,000 instead of the $25,000 they had anticipated.† The movement to raise money through fairs caught on,

* After a long struggle, Elizabeth Blackwell had succeeded in getting admitted to a medical college in the United States and had become the first woman to graduate from an American medical school.

† These two women, coordinating a mammoth fund-raising venture, discovered that they, as women, could not sign a contract for any of the facilities or services they needed to produce the fair. Following the war both women worked on behalf of women's rights, but Mary Livermore in particular believed that suffrage would open the way to political activity through which women could deal with poverty and related problems, such as alcoholism and prostitution. She became a popular lecturer and writer, speaking until she

and before the war was over the Sanitary Commission had raised $50 million.[3]

Nursing as a profession in the United States owes its start to the numbers of mainly middle-class women who became nurses in the Civil War. The training of nurses began in Germany in 1836, but nursing emerged as a true profession when, during the Crimean War (1853–1856), Florence Nightingale brought hygiene into hospital practice and wrote the classic work on nursing that became the bible of Civil War nurses. The first American schools of nursing opened in 1873.

In addition to the nurses trained by the Blackwells, Dorothea Dix recruited and supervised hundreds of women who gave devoted service. Born in 1802, Dorothea Dix grew up in a frontier town in a region that is now Maine. She had achieved a national reputation before the war as a prison reformer and advocate of humane treatment for the insane. Visiting jails across the country, she prepared "memorials" for state legislatures detailing the degrading, squalid conditions under which prisoners lived, the auctioning off of the destitute insane as a source of free labor, and the crowding and cruelty in the treatment of mentally ill and criminals alike.[4] As a result of her lobbying efforts, a number of states enacted laws protecting the insane and establishing hospitals for their treatment rather than their punishment.

When war broke out, Dix volunteered her services to the government and was appointed Superintendent of Army Nurses. She set about recruiting immediately, adopting rigid standards that she felt would protect the morals of her nurses at the front and avoid repercussions back home. At first, only women over age thirty who met her definition of plainness were accepted. Nurses had to be physically strong, were permitted no jewelry or ribbons, and had to agree to wear brown or black only and to stop wearing hoop skirts, which got in the way of their work. No one, however, could have anticipated the length or bloodiness of the Civil War, and at one point any woman willing to undertake the exhausting work of night and day nursing was enlisted, Dix asking only, "Are you ready to work?"

> These women . . . worked as long as they could stand. Then, if they had no homes near enough to go to, they slept for a while in some corner, on the floor, in their bloodstained clothes. Their morning toilet was a dash of cold water on their faces, a little soap, if there was any, on their hands, and they were ready to work again. They washed

---

was seventy-five. One of her lectures was delivered over eight hundred times. She spoke without notes in a deep, resonant voice that earned her the title of "Queen of the Platform." Edward T. James and Janet W. James, eds., *Notable American Women, 1607–1950* (Cambridge, Mass.: Belknap Press, 1971), vol. 2, p. 412.

wounds and fed the helpless, they wrote letters for the men who could not write and listened to the last words of the dying. They made many mistakes, they often got in the way of the surgeons, some were inefficient . . . all lacked experience and training. . . . [But] gradually . . . through their efforts, chaos became order, filth gave place to cleanliness, so that before a week had passed unfit buildings had become workmanlike hospitals.[5]

The nurses Dorothea Dix signed up received $12 a month plus food and travel. Many others received no pay at all.

Clara Barton, herself a fearless and tireless nurse, trained her own teams of nurses for work at the front. Born in 1821, she had once worked as a copyist in the United States Patent Office, and had been discharged along with two other women because the secretary of the interior thought it improper to mix the sexes in a public office.[6] During the war she recruited and collected medical supplies quite independently of the United States Sanitary Commission, and would appear unannounced at the front during battles, ready to work. She once wrote home: "I wrung the blood from the bottom of my clothing before I could step, for the weight about my feet."[7]

As the Sanitary Commission got better organized, Barton's role as a nurse became less important, but she had established such a reputation with wounded soldiers who wrote of her in letters home that, following the war, hundreds of families sought her help in locating their sons and husbands who were missing in action. As a result of the records that she had kept on the wounded and imprisoned, she was able to trace hundreds of missing soldiers, and eventually to mark the graves of some 13,000 who perished in the notorious Andersonville Prison in Georgia. Later, as founder and first president of the American Red Cross (1882), she would incorporate this "missing persons" service as a permanent part of the organization's activities.

The women who came to nurse their own wounded sons or husbands behind the lines often stayed to nurse the thousands of other soldiers who poured into the makeshift hospitals. Mary Ann Bickerdyke, fondly called Mother Bickerdyke by the soldiers, was one of these women. Distributing relief supplies to an army hospital in Cairo, Illinois, in 1861, she was appalled at the primitive conditions under which the wounded were treated. She rolled up her sleeves and stayed, asking no one's permission. Sometimes alone, sometimes with other volunteers whom she recruited, particularly teachers Mary Jane Safford and Eliza Porter, she worked throughout the war, mostly at emergency hospitals on the front lines, but interspersing these activities with speaking engagements to raise money and supplies for the Sanitary Commission.

A frontier woman from Ohio and Illinois, she spoke directly and brusquely with an ungrammatical eloquence to those in charge, and had no patience with army bureaucracy. A surgeon once asked her on what authority she presumed to act in his hospital. She is said to have responded, "On the authority of Lord God Almighty; have you anything that outranks that?" She waged a personal war against corruption and inefficiency, and saw to it that a number of inept medical personnel were fired. Her energy knew no limits. When food supplies at a hospital were inadequate, she scoured the countryside around, collecting food on the hoof, along with fresh eggs and milk.[8]

She rode hospital trains going North, collected supplies, supervised their distribution, moved forward with the advancing army. After the war, she continued to work with veterans, some of whom she helped to resettle on free land in Kansas, where she moved with them and opened a boardinghouse. Her co-worker Mary Safford called her to New York in 1870 to work in the slums there for the Protestant Board of City Missions, but she did not stay long. Her final years were spent in her beloved Kansas, where she died in 1901 at the age of eighty-four.[9]

Among the most famous of the war nurses was Annie Wittenmeyer, who organized hospital diet kitchens for the sick and wounded and who worked after the war to get the Fifty-second Congress to pass a law granting pensions for army nurses, which it finally did. Another, Mary Edwards Walker, was a doctor who served first as a war nurse and then as a spy. She was captured, exchanged as a prisoner of war, and then commissioned as a first lieutenant and assistant surgeon, the highest rank held by a woman during the war. Annie Etheridge, another war nurse, was decorated for her services but discharged in 1878 from her clerkship in the Detroit Treasury Department because she married. Belle Reynolds was inspired by her nursing work to enroll in medical school after the war, and practiced medicine in Illinois and California. Mary Safford also became a doctor following the war, and was the first woman surgeon to perform an ovariotomy.

Quaker women were leading abolitionists and suffragists out of all proportion to their numbers in the American population, and served in key roles during the Civil War. Perhaps because their religion accepted men and women as equals, educated both, and encouraged both to speak out at meetings for worship, Quaker women learned to move with self-assurance. Cornelia Hancock and Laura Haviland were among the many who served with distinction in the war and continued to make unusual contributions in the following period.

Numbers of women went with their husbands to war camps and stayed on with the regiments when they marched to the front. Matrons of the regiment had semiofficial functions as cooks, laundresses, and secretaries, keeping records and writing letters. Other women foraged for food, carried military dispatches, and sometimes took the place of men wounded in battle. Approximately 400 women fought in the war disguised as men. Some were detected only when wounded, some never at all. Georgianne Peterman, age seventeen, served two years as a drummer boy. There is the story of one soldier, wounded and captured by the Confederate army, who was returned to the Union side with a note that read: "As the Confederates do not use women in the war, this woman, wounded in battle, is returned to you."[10]

Some camp followers used their hoop skirts to smuggle liquor to the soldiers, and some contrived tin bustles that held as much as five gallons each trip. Women served as spies and scouts; a number of them, like Elizabeth Van Lew, operated behind Confederate lines. Among her activities, Van Lew helped Union soldiers escape from prison and hid them behind a specially constructed secret panel in her Richmond, Virginia, home. Pauline Cushman, captured by the South and sentenced to die as a spy, was barely freed in time by Union troops. Soldier Sarah Emma Edmonds, alias Franklin Thompson, had had prior experience with disguises when she ran away from marriage at the age of fifteen and supported herself as a Bible salesman. Mary Elizabeth Bowser, a freed slave, hired out as a servant in the household of Confederate President Jefferson Davis and regularly sent messages to the Union side.[11]

Mrs. Dabney (there seems to be no record of her first name) and her husband, a black man serving with the Union army as a cook, proved one of the most remarkable spy teams of the war. Dabney was intrigued with the army telegraph equipment, and begged those operating it to explain to him how it worked. Shortly after they did so, his wife asked to go over to the Confederate line and become a laundress for the wife of a high-ranking Southern general. Soon her husband began relaying the most remarkable information about rebel plans to the officers in his camp. He knew almost to the hour what movements the enemy planned, and even what proposals they had under discussion. How he got this information remained a mystery until the officers could contain their curiosity no longer and asked what his secret was. Taking them up a hill behind the camp, he pointed across the river to Lee's headquarters.

> That clothes-line tells me in half an hour just what goes on at Lee's headquarters. You see my wife over there; she washes for the officers, and cooks, and waits around, and as soon as she hears about any movement or anything going on, she comes down and moves the clothes on that line so I can understand it in a minute. That there gray shirt is Longstreet; and when she takes it off, it means he's gone down

about Richmond. That white shirt means Hill; and when she moves it up to the west end of the line, Hill's corps has moved upstream. That red one is Stonewall. He's down on the right now, and if he moves, she will move that red shirt. . . .[12]

The clothesline telegraph proved one of the most useful in the war.

Anna Ella Carroll, a young and brilliant writer on political issues, was sent by President Lincoln to the Western theater of the war in 1861, ostensibly as a journalist. In reality, her assignment was to survey military installations and collect information for the president about a possible campaign down the Mississippi River. The more she investigated, the less she thought of the plan. Instead, she drew up an alternate plan for a campaign along the Tennessee River to drive a wedge between Confederate forces. While she never received official credit for this plan, which was adopted and followed successfully, it seems probable that she was the first to come up with the design.[13]

Sojourner Truth, Orator for Freedom

One of the outstanding orators in American history, Sojourner Truth stood "six feet tall in all her ebony majesty."[14] She was born Isabella Baumfree, a slave in Ulster County, New York, about 1797. Because her first owner and his family all spoke Dutch, so did Isabella, even before she learned English.

In 1826, one year before she would have been free under New York State law, she ran away and was taken in by a Quaker family whose name, Van Wagener, she adopted. Later she left them to move to New York City to work. It was there that she joined a fanatic religious group, which dissolved not long after she joined it, in the midst of some irregularities with which she reputedly was not involved. When Benjamin Folger, a white man, slandered her concerning her connections with the group, she sued him for damages and won her case. About this time, too, with the help of some Quaker friends, she won legal proceedings for the return of her son, Peter, who had been sold illegally into slavery in the South. Because of these two successful experiences, she had a lifelong faith in the power of the law.

Full of a new mystical belief that never left her, she changed her name to Sojourner Truth, and set out from New York with just 25 cents in her pocket. She walked eastward, preaching as she went, and stopping to work only long enough to earn the money to take her on her way again.

When she learned of the refusal of the World Anti-Slavery Convention meeting in London in 1840 to admit eight women delegates, Sojourner Truth became a staunch supporter of women's rights. Later she voiced her concern for "prison reform, labor reform, and temperance" as well.[15] She became so well known that by 1850 her biography had been written and published by her friend Olive Gilbert,* while two other books in print devoted considerable space to her preaching.

Her earthy humor, sharp tongue, and quick wit never failed her. As a well-known antislavery speaker, she drew her share of hecklers. One, an Ohioan who supported slavery, said to her once, "Old woman, do you think your talk about slavery does any good? Do you suppose that people care what you say? . . . Why, I don't care any more for your talk than I do for the bite of a flea." Sojourner Truth answered him, "Perhaps not, but the good Lord willing, I'll keep you scratching."[16]

Her voice was deep, resonant, and powerful, with a distinct Dutch accent. Even in a day when there were no microphones, there was never a hall too big for Sojourner Truth's voice. One day in Indiana when she was addressing a group that included supporters of slavery, a doctor rose to suggest that she was, in fact, a man in disguise, and demanded that a committee of women take her backstage and verify that she was a woman. The hall dissolved in an uproar, just as the proslavery group had hoped it would. But over the roar of the crowd, Sojourner Truth shouted, "My breasts have suckled many a white babe, even when they should have been suckling my own." Ripping open her dress, she said to the now hushed audience, "I will show my breasts to the entire congregation. It is not my shame but yours that I should do this. Here, then, see for yourselves. Do you wish also to suck?"[17]

There were times when proslavery groups clubbed her, as in Kansas, and stormed the halls where she spoke, as in Missouri, but nothing stopped her. One of her most famous speeches was given at the women's rights convention in Akron, Ohio, in 1851, where she was selling copies of the story of her life by which she supported herself. Nettled by the comments of a minister who had described women as helpless creatures inferior to men, she gave what is perhaps one of the great extemporaneous speeches of all time. It is presented here as it was recorded by Mrs. Frances Gage, who chaired the meeting that day. The majesty, cadence, and thunder of these words have rarely been matched. With each repetition of her phrase "Ain't I a woman?" the audience responded with more shouts of "Yes, yes." When she finished, the women rose and cheered and wept in gratitude and shame—for they had not wanted her to speak, yet she had turned the meeting around for them singlehanded.

> Well, children, where there is so much racket there must be something out of kilter. . . . What's all this here talking about?

* Sojourner Truth could neither read nor write.

SOJOURNER TRUTH.

Sojourner Truth about 1853. This drawing was the frontispiece of her *Narrative*, which she peddled to support herself as she traveled and preached freedom for blacks and rights for women.

That man over there says that women need to be helped into carriages, and lifted over ditches, and to have the best place everywhere. Nobody ever helps me into carriages, or over mud-puddles, or gives me any best place! And ain't I a woman? Look at me! Look at my arm! I have ploughed, and planted, and gathered into barns, and no man could head me! And ain't I a woman? I could work as much and eat as much as a man—when I could get it—and bear the lash as well! And ain't I a woman? I have borne thirteen children, and seen them most all sold off to slavery, and when I cried out with my mother's grief, none but Jesus heard me! And ain't I a woman?

Then they talk about this thing in the head; what's this they call it? That's it, honey (intellect). What's that got to do with women's rights? . . . If my cup won't hold but a pint and yours hold a quart, wouldn't you be mean not to let me have my little half measure full?

Then that little man in black there, he says women can't have as much rights as men, 'cause Christ wasn't a woman! Where did your Christ come from? *Where did your Christ come from?* From God and a woman! Man had nothing to do with Him.

If the first woman God ever made was strong enough to turn the world upside down all alone, these women together (here) ought to be able to turn it back, and get it right side up again! And now they are asking to do it, the men better let 'em.

Obliged to you for hearing on me; and now old Sojourner Truth ain't got nothing more to say.[18]

During the war years Sojourner Truth worked in Union army hospitals and camps for freed slaves, but concentrated a good part of her efforts on the soldiers of the black regiment from Michigan, which was

NARRATIVE

OF

SOJOURNER TRUTH,

A

NORTHERN SLAVE,

EMANCIPATED FROM BODILY SERVITUDE BY THE
STATE OF NEW YORK, IN 1828.

WITH A PORTRAIT.

"Sweet is the virgin honey, though the wild bee store it in a reed;
And bright the jewelled band that circleth an Ethiop's arm;
Pure are the grains of gold in the turbid stream of the Ganges;
And fair the living flowers that spring from the dull cold sod.
Wherefore, thou gentle student, bend thine ear to my speech,
For I also am as thou art; our hearts can commune together:
To meanest matters will I stoop, for mean is the lot of mortal;
I will rise to noblest themes, for the soul hath a heritage of glory."

NEW YORK:

PUBLISHED FOR THE AUTHOR.

1853.

then her home. She traveled up and down the state for them, collecting clothing and food. On the first Thanksgiving after the Emancipation Proclamation, she and her friends baked Thanksgiving dinner for the entire regiment. As she served the soldiers, the voice that had sung so many gospel songs across the country hummed a new song, her own version of the "Battle Hymn of the Republic," and it is likely that before the dinner was over the entire regiment was singing with her:

> We are the hardy soldiers of the First of Michigan,
> We're fighting for the Union and for the rights of man,
> And when the battle rages, you'll find us in the van,
>   As we go marching on.[19]

For a year during the war, she worked as a counselor for the Freedman's Relief Association. Following the war, she continued to fight—and won— her campaign to integrate streetcars in Washington, D.C. She spoke out for women—this time for black women—in New York City in 1867:

> There is a great stir about colored men getting their rights, but not a word about the colored women; and if colored men get their rights, and not colored women theirs, you see the colored men will be masters over the women, and it will be just as bad as it was before. So I am for keeping the thing going while things are stirring. . . .[20]

In old age, instead of retiring to her home in Michigan, she campaigned for land in the West to resettle blacks from the South, now caught in the backlash following Reconstruction. She believed that America owed the Negro people a debt that could never be paid, but free land would at least make amends.[21]

> We (the ex-slaves) have been a source of wealth to this republic. Our labor supplied the country with cotton, until villages and cities dotted the enterprising North for its manufacture, and furnished employment for a multitude, thereby becoming a revenue to the government. Beneath a burning southern sun have we toiled, in canebrake and the rice swamp, urged on by the merciless driver's lash, earning millions of money; and so highly were we valued there that should one poor wretch venture to escape from this hell of slavery, no exertion of man or trained bloodhound was spared to seize and return him to his field of unrequited labor. . . . Our nerves and sinews, our tears and blood, have been sacrificed on the altar of this nation's avarice. Our unpaid labor has been a stepping-stone to its financial success. Some of its dividends must surely be ours.[22]

Her campaign for free land failed, although she is credited with encouraging a number of Southern blacks to migrate to Kansas and Missouri. She returned to Battle Creek in 1875. The year of her death, 1883, she said, "I ain't gonna die, honey, I'se going home, like a shooting star."[23]

Following the Civil War, Abraham Lincoln wrote of the role women played in making the Northern victory possible:

> I have never studied the art of paying compliments to women; but I must say, that if all that has been said by orators and poets since the creation of the world were applied to the women of America, it would not do them justice for their conduct during this war.[24]

Women of the South

The bravery and sacrifice of the women of the South during the war is well known. Most Southern women, wives of tenant farmers, worked the farms while their husbands fought. Some continued to hire out as they had in the past, to sew or do housework on nearby plantations. For the most part, they had vital agricultural and family responsibilities and could not leave to serve as nurses and war workers to the same degree that many women in the North could. It was women in the cities of the South who were more likely to fill these roles.

Belle Boyd became a courier for General Stonewall Jackson and a Confederate spy at the age of eighteen. Beautiful "Wild Rose" O'Neale (Greenow) controlled a five-state network of over 50 spies, 48 of whom were women and young girls, and was in touch with a host of blockade runners as well as important senators and government officials on the Union side. It is said that Union army officers would seek her help in getting promotions! Even in jail she continued to operate her network. She died a dramatic death at sea one stormy night in 1864 when her small boat capsized during an attempt to run the Union blockade.[25]

Loretta Janeta Velazquez disguised herself as a man in order to fight in the Confederate army alongside her husband, but even after he was killed she continued as a soldier. Following the war she wrote about her adventures, including a detailed description of how she disguised herself. Together with a New Orleans tailor, she designed a number of wire net shields to wear next to her skin to give her a man's shape. She wrote:

> If I had undertaken to wear pantaloons without some such contrivance, they would have drawn in at the waist and revealed my true form. . . . So many men have weak and feminine voices that, provided the clothing is properly constructed and put on right, and the disguise in other respects is well arranged, a woman with even a very high-pitched voice need have very little to fear on that score.[26]

Over this netting she wore a tight-fitting shirt and straps across the shoulders and chest. Around her waist she wore a band "with eyelet holes arranged so that the pantaloons would stand out." When her apparatus failed to work properly one day she was discovered, and spent the next ten days in jail.

Women in the South, too, nursed the wounded in hospitals and on the battlefields and tried to raise money for medicines and food. Only the Union blockade prevented the carrying out of a wild scheme designed by Confederate women to raise hard currency for the South through the sale to Europe of their hair, which they pledged to cut in the hope of bringing in as much as $40,000,000.[27]

With the Southern cotton crop reduced by two-thirds in 1862, and by four-fifths by 1864,[28] with the Union blockade preventing supplies from entering the South, women turned again to home production. They rummaged in their attics and brought out spinning wheels and looms that had not been used for a generation, setting to work to make cloth for uniforms as well as for home use. They made tea from herbs, dyes from roots and berries, and coffee from dried, ground potato cubes. As the war dragged on, the South lost all ability to transport food and supplies. Shortages for soldiers often were acute, even though women sacrificed at home to send food to the front. Confederate currency was so unstable that farmers hesitated to sell their produce, while dealers waited for prices to go up before they released supplies. Meanwhile tools used in farm production deteriorated, horses and mules were commandeered for the army, and many slaves who had not run away waited for the Union soldiers to free them, producing as little as they could—their own form of sabotage.

Whenever possible, male and female slaves were put to work in iron furnaces, in cotton and woolen mills, and in small-town factories, where they made friction matches, engine parts, army boots, shoes, hats, and saddles. They worked the mines and processed salt. Black workers sensed their increased power and sometimes refused to work. In 1862, for example, they struck for wages on the Woodland Plantation and won. Increasingly they refused to be whipped, withholding their labor until all threat of the lash was withdrawn.[29]

Women and Reconstruction

The cost in lives during the Civil War was the highest of any war in the history of the United States, 50 percent higher than the figure of 407,000 American deaths in World War II. The North lost 360,000 men, the South 260,000, or one in every four Confederate soldiers. Over 1 million men were killed or wounded, or died of disease contracted in camp.

The South was destitute and bitter. Sherman's March to the Sea had left nothing but scorched earth behind. Coastal cities were in shambles, transportation had collapsed, roads and bridges were destroyed, crops lay in ruins. In some areas the population was close to starvation, especially the ex-slaves, or freedmen. Southern mills had in most cases closed or burned down, throwing thousands of women out of work, women with no other means of support. Alabama alone had 80,000 widows who needed work.[30]

While inflation had been hard on the Northern working class, by and large the North was flushed with victory and prosperity. Business profits from war production were high, railroads and industry booming, cities growing fast. However, the South's problem now confronted the North as well: how to reunite the country, house the homeless, provide jobs, land, and education for the freedmen, and especially how to incorporate them into the fabric of society. Most had never handled money, negotiated for jobs and wages, bought food or clothing, found homes for themselves, or attended school. Few of them understood how laws affected them.

Reconstruction had begun in 1862 with the appointment of acting military governors in states that had been retaken, such as Tennessee. During the war, President Lincoln had set up several departments of Negro affairs to administer programs for freedmen. Josephine Griffin perhaps more than anyone else saw the need for a central bureau to help freedmen start a new life, preferably, she felt, in Northern cities or on Western farms. An ardent antislavery worker and women's rights advocate from Connecticut, she had moved to Washington, D.C., as general agent for the National Freedmen's Relief Association, an organization that provided temporary shelter and supplies for the many blacks coming through Washington immediately following the war. In part through her persuasive efforts and her personal contact with President Lincoln, the Freedmen's Bureau* was launched in March 1865 to supply relief, provide education, and administer abandoned lands in the South. Its great task began, the work which Lerone Bennett, Jr., has called "an Urban League, CIO, WPA, and Rosenwald Foundation all rolled up into an early NAACP."[31]

During its short life (1865–1869), the Bureau provided 1 million freedmen with medical help, founded 46 hospitals in fourteen states in its first two years of work, supplied 21 million persons, many of them destitute whites, with food, and established schools that operated day and night. By 1869, 600,000 blacks of all ages were attending elementary schools, and four major universities—Howard, Hampton Institute, More-

---

* Officially, the Bureau of Refugees, Freedmen and Abandoned Lands of the War Department.

house, and Fisk—had been founded to train black teachers.[32] For freed-men wanted two things: land, and education for themselves and their children.

Charlotte Forten, a black teacher from Philadelphia, was one of seventy teachers who, as early as 1862, went South to the Georgia Sea Islands to teach. Planters there had fled when Union troops occupied the islands, and abolitionists seized the chance to set up what today would be called a "pilot project" for educating the slave population that had been left behind. Forten wrote:

> I never before saw children so eager to learn. . . . The older ones, dur-ing the summer, work in the fields from early morning until eleven or twelve o'clock, and then come to school, after their hard toil in the hot sun, as bright and as anxious to learn as ever. . . .[33]

This proved true throughout the South. One agent of the Freedmen's Bureau wrote from North Carolina in 1866:

> The colored people are far more zealous in the cause of education than the whites. They will starve themselves, and go without clothes, in order to send their children to school.

Another agent reported:

> A child six years old, her mother, grandmother, and great-grandmother, the latter over 75 years of age . . . commenced their alphabet together and each one can read the Bible fluently.[34]

Mothers would bring their children to the schoolroom and tell the teachers that they would do their youngsters' share of work on the farm if their children could only learn to read and write.

Women teachers, black and white, were the backbone of the Freed-men's Bureau. Converging on the South from all directions, they taught under the most difficult circumstances. Elizabeth Bond, in Louisiana, wrote in April 1864:

> I opened school here in a rough log house, thirty feet square and so open that the crevices admitted light sufficient without the aid of windows. The furniture consisted of undressed plank benches without backs, from ten to twelve feet long, and in the center of the room stood an old steamboat stove about four feet long which had been taken out of the river.[35]

Another teacher wrote:

> Did well enough till it rained, since then I have walked three miles a day (to school) ankle deep in thick black mud that pulls off my shoes. Nothing to eat but strong pork and sour bread. . . . The school shed has no floor and the rains sweep clean across it, through

A freedmen's school in Vicksburg, Mississippi, 1866. Mrs. Green teaches an eager assortment of students of all ages to read and write.

the places where the windows should be. I have to huddle the children first in one corner and then in another to keep them from drowning or swamping.[36]

But huddle the children they did, and stay they did, and teach they did during those five years. White opposition to their work mounted, and they were subjected to personal ridicule and disturbances at the schools. They could get no credit at local stores, could not find rooms to rent, and sometimes had to stand up to violence.

Pupils were stoned on their way to and from school. Bricks and missiles were thrown through the windows while schools were in session . . . a schoolhouse was broken open on successive nights for months . . . a white teacher was whipped in public, another was run out of town, and several black families were evicted from their homes because they sent their children to school. Schools were burned, and threats of violence to teachers were common.[37]

But the teachers would not give up. Where there was no schoolhouse, they went from plantation to plantation, from cabin to cabin, holding classes where the students were. Two sisters managed to cover eighteen plantations in this way, taking along with their books all the clothing, slates, and other equipment for their students that their broken-down carriage would hold.

Everything was in short supply, especially teachers. To fill the gap, teachers trained their more advanced students to teach others. W. E. B. Du Bois called the work of the Freedmen's Bureau teachers the Ninth Crusade:

> Behind the mists of ruin and rapine waved the calico dresses of women who dared, and after the hoarse mouthings of the field guns rang the rhythm of the alphabet. Rich and poor they were, serious and curious, bereaved, now of a father, now of a brother, now of more than these, they came seeking a life work in planting New England schoolhouses among the white and black of the South. They did their work well. . . .[38]

Reconstruction, however, failed to give freed men and women the land they needed to be independent of their former owners. The Bureau distributed perhaps a million acres to 30,000 freedmen, but most of this land had to be returned to its former owners after they were pardoned by President Andrew Johnson. "Forty acres and a mule" was a dream that was not to come true. Instead, a system of tenant farming or sharecropping evolved, with many former slaves hiring themselves out, the men for nine to fifteen dollars a month plus food, the women for five to ten dollars a month. Most blacks had little choice but to return to the plantations at terms set by their former owners.[39]

The Bureau also tried to assist freedmen in obtaining fair contracts for hiring out their labor. This proved a frustrating task. There were never enough agents to protect the freedmen from the Black Codes passed by almost every Southern state, codes designed to rehabilitate the plantation economy and maintain control over the newly freed black population. In varying degrees of severity, depending on the proportion of blacks in the state, these codes provided, on the one hand, for the rights of blacks to "make contracts, sue and be sued, own and inherit property, and testify in court." On the other hand, they prohibited blacks from voting, serving on juries, testifying against whites, carrying arms, using certain public buildings, or working in occupations other than agriculture, domestic service, or menial jobs.[40]

States took special advantage of the illiteracy and desperate need for work of most black men and women. Louisiana's Black Codes, for example, prohibited vagrancy and provided that workers should make contracts for hiring out. These contracts had to be read to workers in front of witnesses before signing. In theory this sounded like protection against forced labor; in fact, it was quite the opposite. The contracts were long and committed workers to a year of service to the employer. They included every other condition of work. If employers were convicted of nonpayment, for example, they could be fined double the amount owed the worker. But an illiterate worker with no money could not do much about suing. The worker, on the other hand, could have his or her wages deducted if ill, and double the amount if the illness was "feigned." Rations would be deducted as well. Workers who refused to work for more than three days could be put to forced labor without pay on roads or levees until they agreed to return to the employer. Hours were spelled out: ten a day in summer, nine in winter, with the worker responsible for all care of animals and tools, including payment for repairs. There were fines of 25 cents an hour for all time lost from work; $2 a day for leaving home without permission; and $1 for "disobedience"—defined as swearing, quarreling, or fighting. Any item stolen or damaged had to be paid for at twice the value. No visitors were allowed during work hours. Disagreements were to be settled by the employer, with the right of appeal to the nearest justice of the peace and two others, one chosen by the employer, one by the worker. Dismissal by the employer could be appealed in a like manner.[41]

These contracts were invariably long, confusing, and impossible to remember in detail after a hasty reading. By the end of the year of work contracted for, the freedmen were almost always in debt to the employer (a debt more often than not invented by the employer) and in no position to refuse to sign the agreement for another year. Finally, the employers would suggest that it was simpler if a ten-year contract were signed. The alternative being unemployment and possible imprisonment for debt, the workers could not refuse. With the ten-year agreements came virtual slavery, a system of peonage that allowed no chance to break out and that lasted well into the twentieth century.

The Freedmen's Bureau fought the Black Codes, but the Bureau itself came to an end in 1869 and was not renewed by Congress beyond that date. The Republican-controlled Congress fought the codes as well, but the civil rights legislation that it passed in 1866 over President Johnson's veto was declared unconstitutional in 1875. The Fourteenth and Fifteenth Amendments to the Constitution, which tried to establish personal and voting rights for blacks on a permanent basis, were limited by Supreme Court decisions that interpreted them narrowly. In 1883 the Court declared civil rights legislation passed in 1875 unconstitutional.

The door was open for the Ku Klux Klan, which had held its first convention in 1867, to continue its intimidation and lawlessness and for the states to pass Jim Crow laws that institutionalized segregation for almost one hundred years to come. The Klansmen rode at night, hooded in white with bright red crosses emblazoned on their chests. If terrorizing blacks and sympathetic whites who tried to stand up for the freedmen's rights did not work, threats and violence came next. Homes were burned, blacks whipped, mutilated, raped, and lynched. In the period before 1874, over 5,000 blacks died for their political beliefs, while the Klan ensured that the ballot box was for whites only and the gains of Reconstruction were totally undermined.[42]

9

WOMEN ON THE HOME FRONT AND IN THE INDUSTRIAL ERA *1861-1881*

Welcome, sisters, to our number,
  Welcome to our heart and hand;
At our post we will not slumber
  Strong in Union we shall stand.

No angry passions here should mar
  Our peace, or move our social band,
For friendship is our beacon star,
  Our motto, union, hand in hand.

—"Song of the Sewing Women," 1865

Initially the Civil War brought economic dislocation to the North. As their supply of raw cotton from the South was cut off, mills from New Hampshire to Pennsylvania, employing some 75,000 or more women, closed down,[1] and women flocked to the cities seeking work. Soon, however, New England fields were dotted with sheep that supplied Northern mills with wool, while some cotton came North again as Southern states were retaken. By late 1862, industry was booming with wartime production of clothing, boots, shoes, saddles, munitions, and supplies for the army.

Economic need drove more and more women to the factories, for with husbands and sons in the army, thousands of women had no other means of support. The spiraling cost of living forced others to seek employment. As the war dragged on, they were joined by thousands of widows also looking for work. The effect was to depress wages.

The Stitchers and the Sewers

At the height of the wartime industrial boom, there were working women throughout the cities of the North who lived close to starvation, 30,000 of them in New York City alone. Among the most desperate were the sewing women. As sewing was the only work they knew how to do,

151

they vied with each other for jobs. Laboring 15 hours a day, many could earn only 17 to 24 cents, whether they worked on shirts, underwear, umbrellas, or tassels. From their earnings they had to pay for the thread they used and for any lost or damaged goods. Moreover, they often were unable to collect from their employers even the little that was owed them. Finally, in 1863, the condition of the sewers was so acute that *Fincher's Trades' Review*, the labor paper edited by Jonathan Fincher, a labor leader from the machinists' and blacksmiths' union, began to campaign actively for union support to help the women organize. It was not easy to get. The attitude of one St. Louis journeyman tailor typified that of most men in unionized trades: he urged all unions to resist any entrance of women into trades where they worked alongside men, stating that women workers belonged only in jobs "more congenial to girls."[2]

Luckily a number of New York trade unions felt otherwise and sponsored a mass meeting in November of 1863 to bring working women together to discuss ways to increase their earnings and collect the money that their employers owed them. Union leaders and working women shared the platform and urged organization as the only way to get more for their work. Resolutions were passed pledging funds to help the women unionize.

It is likely that a successful strike of women shirtmakers that month was a direct outgrowth of this meeting. The following spring the sewers organized a "benevolent association," the Working Women's Union, and elected two sewers, Ellen Patterson and M. Trimble, as recording secretary and president, respectively. While its constitution did provide for sick benefits, the real purpose of the small band of 100 founding members was to organize a union of sewing-machine operators in the city. As Ellen Patterson put it:

> We have organized to improve our social condition as far as possible, and in no case to allow employers to reduce our wages, and, lastly, as soon as we have the numbers and the funds, to have an advance of wages and shorter hours.

The group held picnics, fund-raising events, and organizing meetings, and in January 1865 sponsored its first mass rally. Its members regularly attended meetings of the New York Trades' Assembly (similar to today's City Central Labor Council), which promised its support and told the women that their "influence was indispensable" in getting their men friends to join unions.

> If they (your men friends) do not join, then have nothing to do with them, and tell them you do not wish to associate with any gentleman who refuses to aid in a movement calculated to benefit his fellow-men.[3]

The sewing women, ignoring the patronizing tone of this bit of advice, used the occasion of the large gathering to induct eighteen new members into the Working Women's Union. They joined hands in a ring around the new members and sang the song that appears at the beginning of this chapter. Between the singing of the first and the last verse, their president addressed the new members:

> Sisters . . . you will be expected to attend our stated meetings and are bound to observe our laws by the strongest of human ties—your sacred honor . . . be careful to cultivate a forgiving spirit; write the errors of your sisters in sand, but engrave their virtues on the tablets of endur-
> ing memory. . . .
> This chain which you now behold is a bond of that union that should always exist among working women. Remember that union is power; a good many can help one when one can not help the many. Behold, the chain is now broken that you may be added as another link.[4]

Similar Working Women's Associations of sewers organized in Boston and Philadelphia, where they published the *Women's Journal* and collected petitions requesting an increase in wages from government contractors. Although they won 20 percent more on their work, they proclaimed that it was hardly enough to make a difference and continued agitating, petitioning, and organizing. Finally they designated a committee to go to Washington and visit President Lincoln. The president, moved by the information they brought him on their wages and living conditions, directed the quartermaster in charge of government clothing contracts to "manage the supplies of contract work for the Government made up by women so as to give them remunerative wages for their labor."[5]

Word of the visit encouraged the Cincinnati women to send a petition to President Lincoln on their own behalf:

> Cincinnati, O., Feb. 20, 1865.
> To His Excellency, Abraham Lincoln, President of the United States: The undersigned, wives, widows, sisters, and friends of the soldiers in the army of the United States, depending upon our own labor for bread, sympathizing with the Government of the United States, and loyal to it, beg leave to call the attention of the Government, through his Excellency the President, to the following statement of facts:
> 1. We are willing and anxious to do the work required by the Government for clothing and equipping the armies of the United States, at the prices paid by the Government.
> 2. We are unable to sustain life for the price offered by contractors, who fatten on their contracts by grinding immense profits out of the labor of their operatives. As an example, the contractors are paid one dollar and seventy-five cents per dozen for making gray

woolen shirts, and they require us to make them for one dollar per dozen. This is a sample of the justice meted out to us, the willing laborers, without whom the armies could not be promptly clothed and equipped.

We most respectfully request that the Government, through the proper officers of the Quartermaster's Department, issue the work required directly to us, we giving ample security for the prompt and faithful execution of the work and return of the same at the time required, and in good order.

We are in no way actuated by a spirit of faction, but desirous of aiding the best government on earth, and at the same time securing justice to the humble laborer.

The manufacture of pants, blouses, coats, drawers, tents, tarpaulins, etc., exhibits the same irregularity and injustice to the operative. Under the system of direct employment of the operative by the Government, we had no difficulty, and the Government, we think, was served equally well.

We hope that the Government, in whose justice we have all confidence, will at once hear us and heed our humble prayer, and we will ever pray, etc.[6]

Sewing women mobilized everywhere, in Baltimore, Chicago, Boston, Woburn and Worcester, Massachusetts, and Troy, New York. In July of 1864 several of them were fired for union activity in Buffalo. In Detroit they had better luck in setting up a scale of prices to ask for their work. The Sewing Women's Protective Association there was strong enough to open an office and, with the help of the Detroit Trades' Assembly, to buy sewing machines for women to use right in the union hall. Customers brought their work to the sewers directly, and the women avoided the contractor's machines and low price scales. With this option the women were strong enough to negotiate higher prices even for work done through the contractor. Next, Detroit unionists joined in support of working women who had trouble collecting their wages, threatening what amounted to a total boycott by workers from every trade unless employers made amends. One Boston newspaper commented about the needlewomen of Detroit in 1865: "Let such unions be formed among sewing women everywhere. They are sure to succeed if they are in real earnest as spunky women know how to be."[7]

It was no accident that sewing women more than any other women workers tried to organize. They were starving, and their need to find a way to press for higher prices for their work was critical. After domestic workers, sewers were the largest group of women working outside the home. They were victimized by the contract system, where the government paid a price per dozen to a contractor for sewed garments. Whatever the contractor could save over what he paid to have the garments made, he kept. Squeezing the sewing women meant extra money in his pocket.

They also suffered from the introduction of the industrial sewing machine that came into its own during the war. At the beginning of the war, 38,000 sewing machines of the Singer and Wheeler types were in factory use; at the war's end, 63,000. The shirt that took fourteen hours to make by hand now took one hour by machine.[8]

Working Women's Protective Unions

At the same time that labor unions began to show an interest in helping women organize, the *New York Sun* called a meeting for sewing women of the city to inform the public of the starvation level at which so many of these women lived. Prominent citizens attended to hear women testify about conditions that existed right in their midst. No one could have anticipated the outpouring of women. Hundreds came from all over the city. The hall overflowed with "hoop-skirt makers, shirt sewers, vest makers, sewing machine operators, press feeders, silver burnishers, photographers, and umbrella sewers." [9] The information gathered at this meeting led to the appointment of a committee of working women and distinguished citizens to try to develop a way to help the city's women wage earners. This committee held further hearings and took long testimony from women who told of 12-hour days where they paused only for a cup of tea and a piece of bread, and earned 16 64/100 cents for the day's work. One woman who earned 11 cents a day making underwear stated: "If I get to bed about daylight, and sleep two or three hours, I feel satisfied." Another supported a sick husband and four children on earnings of 12½ cents for 10 hours' work, and had to supply her own thread. The plea of many was voiced by one woman who cried out, "Oh, if we could always get paid for our work, we could get along."[10]

Out of the investigation the Working Women's Protective Union emerged, combining a number of functions so successfully that it was still in operation well into the 1890s. It was not a labor union, nor was it directed or staffed by wage-earning women. The prime movers were middle- and upper-class women concerned particularly about the powerlessness of working women, who had neither knowledge of the law nor money to hire lawyers to collect the wages due them.

The Protective Union provided working women with free legal services. Often prominent New York City lawyers represented them in court. In its first fifteen years of work, the Protective Union handled 27,292 grievances, managed to settle 20,000 out of court, and recovered $24,647.49 for the women it represented. It also lobbied for passage of a law providing penalties for employers who did not pay their workers. Armed with this law, the union's threat to prosecute achieved many out-of-court settlements.[11]

Protective Unions in a number of cities served as employment agencies, their "registry systems" always having many more applicants for jobs than they could place. In addition to finding jobs for women (during its first year it placed 3,500), the New York City Protective Union trained women for "seven branches of labor of a mechanical character not generally occupied by them."[12] By 1870 the union was placing women in 75 different kinds of work,* and receiving upwards of 10,000 applications for jobs a year. While it taught hand sewers how to operate sewing machines so they could increase their earnings, and tried to improve women's pay and hours, it never saw its role as one of encouraging women to organize unions, nor did it effect much change in their working conditions.

The "Genteel" Trades

During the Civil War, inflation forced a number of unmarried girls and young women into the job market. They headed first for those trades considered the most proper, including (according to *Harper's Bazaar*) cutting paper collars, making hoop skirts, mounting photographs, making candles, burnishing silver, trimming hats, setting type, fitting shoes, and working in retail stores, offices, telegraph establishments, and for the government. Wherever women were hired in these trades, wages fell.

Retail stores are one example. Women had worked in stores ever since the first "she-merchants" of colonial America. But as stores grew in size, owners hired young men as clerks, on the theory that women customers preferred to be waited on by men. There were exceptions to this rule. As early as 1853, Arnold Constable hired women clerks on a regular basis. He had visited Paris and found women successful at selling, undoubtedly for two reasons: they were young and educated and added "class" to the store, and they worked for less money. Macy's, then on Fourteenth Street in New York City, also used women for selling as well as in cashier and bookkeeping positions.[13]

An additional pressure to use women as store clerks came from industrial leaders and newspapers, who strongly urged it in order to free more young men to settle in the West, thus developing its new market possibilities. Writers referred to youths "frittering away (their) strength and emasculating (their) manhood behind the counters of our retail shops." It was the Civil War that accomplished almost overnight what public

---

* Although this by no means represented all the areas in which women were employed. As early as 1850 the census had shown women in 175 different industries.

pressure had not: the industry lost many of its young men and absorbed numbers of women and girls. Storeowners quickly worked out a method not only for paying women less but also for keeping wages down indefinitely. Philadelphia stores, for example, took on young women for six months' training at no salary, then paid them $2 a week for the next six months. For the second year the clerks received $3 a week, and after that period they could expect to be discharged, making room for a whole new group of trainees at no wages. The most an experienced saleswoman could earn was $5 a week, according to a survey by the *Workingman's Advocate* in 1866.[14]

A workweek of 112 hours was not uncommon for saleswomen. Sundays were a holiday in name only. The store opened for individual customers during the day on Sunday, and Sunday evenings proved the best time for inventory work. As novelist Reginald Kauffman wrote:

> If Katie were late, she was fined ten cents for each offense. She was reprimanded if her portion of the counter was disordered after a mauling by careless customers. She was fined for all mistakes she made in the matter of prices and the additions on her salesbook, and she was fined if, having asked the floorwalker for three or five minutes to leave the floor in order to tidy her hair and hands, in constant need of attention through the rapidity of her work and the handling of her dyed wares, she exceeded her time limit by so much as a few seconds.
>
> There were no seats behind the counters, and Katie, whatever her physical condition, remained on her feet all day long, unless she could arrange for relief by a fellow-worker during that worker's luncheon time. There was no place for rest save a damp, ill-lighted "Recreation Room" in the basement. . . .
>
> "It ain't a cinch, by no means"—thus ran the departing Cora Costigan's advice to her successor—"but it ain't nothing now to what it will be in the holidays. I'd rather be dead than work in the toy-department in December . . . and I'd rather be dead an' damned than work in the accounting department. A girl friend of mine worked there last year . . . an' didn't get through her Christmas Eve work till two on Christmas morning, an' she lived over on Staten Island. She overslept on the 26th, an' they docked her a half-week's pay. . . ."[15]

Following the war, saleswomen began to organize, working with the (men) Clerks' Early Closing Association to try to cut their long hours. While the men won a seven o'clock closing except for Saturdays, when they worked from 8:00 in the morning until 11:00 at night, the women did not.* Hardest of all to bear was the lack of any facilities for sitting

* As late as 1898 one salesclerk reports: "My hours were from five in the morning until ten (at night) and on Saturdays until half past eleven o'clock at night, and then I was expected to post my books on Sunday morning." George G. Kirstein, *Stores and Unions* (New York: Fairchild Publications, 1950), p. 6, quoting the Retail Clerks *Advocate*, March 1898, p. 3.

down. Sitting down, as one employer put it, "would make the trade appear dull."[16] Susan B. Anthony, a supporter of working women and an agitator for their rights, urged in her paper *Revolution* that customers patronize only those stores where employers furnished stools and allowed their workers to sit while selling. Not until 1890, with the formation of the Consumers' League, would an organized attempt be made to use selective buying as a way to force employers to do this.

After 1880, paralleling the growth of the ready-made clothing industry following the war, department stores became big business. The number of saleswomen jumped from 7,462 in 1880 to 142,265 by 1900, an increase of 1,800 percent in twenty years. Seventy-five percent of all women employed in these stores were young, between fourteen and twenty-five years old, their average age twenty-two years.[17] Two major fears of store women were of getting too "old" to be acceptable, and of losing their jobs as soon as they married, even if they continued to need the work.

Salesclerks working behind the counters were the elite among store workers. Young girls, often only twelve or fourteen years old, held jobs as runners, or cash girls, carrying the customers' money to a central cashier on the floor and returning with the change for the salesclerk to present to the customer. These young girls also swept floors and dusted counters. They earned $1.50 a week, and regarded this work and low pay as necessary steppingstones to a stock girls' or clerk's position when they "grew up."

The Woman Office Worker

During the Civil War the government, now a major employer, gave hiring preference to war widows and children of soldiers killed in action. Increasingly, women also held jobs as clerks and copyists who copied speeches and documents for Congressmen. In 1866, Congress set their salaries at $900 a year, while men doing similar work were receiving from $1,200 to $1,800 a year.[18] Four years later Congressional legislation changed that situation when it provided one schedule for clerks, with the same wages for men and women in each category. For the most part, however, men and women usually did not perform the same work, and as late as 1868 no women were employed in the War Department, the Treasury, or the Post Office Department (though women worked in the post offices themselves, as they had since colonial times).

The story of women entering the field of office work is, again, that of employers discovering that women could do the job as well as men and would work for less. Bookkeepers in the 1860s received $500 a year if female, closer to $1,800 a year if male.[19] It was Susan B. Anthony's

Revolution that pointed out case after case of women earning less than half of what men received for the same work.

The first women stenographers transcribed into longhand the notes taken in court by men. The growth of business and industry, however, opened the door for the employment of women in secretarial as well as typing work. With the introduction of the commercial typewriter in 1873 and of the shift-key model in 1878, business schools began to train women as typewriters (as those who operated typing machines were called at first), stenographers, and bookkeepers. So rapidly did opportunities for women open in these jobs that by 1900 one-half of all women in high schools were enrolled in business courses and over half of all business school students were women.

WOMEN IN OFFICE WORK, 1870–1900[20]

Year	Number of women	Percentage of women in trade
1870	9,982	3.3%
1880	28,698	5.7%
1890	168,808	16.9%
1900	238,982	75.7% (of all stenographers and typewriters; 12.9% of clerks and copyists; 28.6% of bookkeepers and accountants)

Two-thirds of all stenographers and typists were between fifteen and twenty-four years of age. Ninety percent were thirty-five years old or less. Eight out of ten were unmarried and lived at home.[21] Employers quickly underscored the sharp distinction between factory work and employment in the "genteel trades" when they refused to hire for office work foreign-born women and even those who had been born here but whose parents were immigrants. Families scrimped and saved, changed their names, and lied about their origins to give their daughters the training that would enable them to enter the new world of office work, even with its low pay and long hours, rather than see them face the drudgery and physical dangers of factory employment.

Women in Teaching and Nursing

Following the Civil War women were in the majority in two professions: teaching and nursing. While public education had been firmly established in the North, many of the men in teaching had served in the army during the war and were lured afterward into industry or business where they could make far more money. This left the profession to women. However, women were not new to teaching. They had been moving gradually into teaching jobs since the 1830s, as new schools opened and the men who would have taught in them decided to head West instead. Between 1830 and 1860, almost a quarter of all native-born American women had done some teaching at one time or another in their lives. The turnover rate was high, for as soon as women married they had to resign. But women teachers were popular with local communities. They were cheap and submissive, and rarely caused trouble. Paid 30 to 50 percent less than men, they showed endless patience with poor living conditions, overcrowded one-room schools, and inadequate teaching equipment.

Most communities in the North had elementary schools by the close of the Civil War, but there were still only 200 high schools in the whole country in 1870, and ten years later just 800.[22] By that year, two-thirds of all elementary school teachers were women, most of them untrained, although a few teacher-training institutions had opened before the war.* As training became available, the profession of teaching gained in status. Fannie Jackson Coppin, a black educator who headed the Female Department of the Philadelphia Institute for Colored Youth, was one of the postwar pioneers in teacher training and in industrial arts. By 1880 there were 81 percent more women teachers than there had been ten years earlier.

The need for black teachers was still acute, particularly in the South where the effects of the war on education had been disastrous. The entire school system had to be rebuilt. In addition, the South had never provided any education for black children, which Reconstruction now mandated. In order to maintain its separation of the races, the South had to support a dual school system, and few black teachers were available.

Nursing as a profession also developed rapidly during the postwar years, in large measure because of the remarkable women who had served as nurses during the war. Traditionally a job performed at home by women, nursing was about to receive recognized training and a new status.† The first woman to receive a degree from the first school of nursing was Linda Richards, who was graduated in 1873 from Dr. Susan Dimock's New England Hospital for Women and Children in Roxbury, Connecticut. Richards had always wanted to be a nurse, and seems to have been in demand even as a teen-ager to nurse her Vermont neighbors whenever they needed help. During the war years she worked in a straw factory,

---

* The first state-supported normal school opened in 1839 in Lexington, Mass.

† The 1870 census reported 1,154 trained nurses, including practical nurses and midwives, who were in the census counts until 1900. Between 1880 and 1890 there was a 187% increase in these figures.

dreaming of a nursing education. In 1870 she scraped the money together to go to Boston City Hospital as an assistant nurse, where she believed she could find the training she sought. However, what she found there were nurses who were unsupervised, untrained, and unkind, and she left after three months. Dr. Dimock's hospital offered the education she needed. After graduating, she taught at nursing schools in New York and Boston, where she learned to deal with the opposition of doctors who objected to any training for nurses. She devoted the rest of her life to teaching nurses in this country and in Japan.[23]

The "Daughters of Toil" and
the National Labor Union

The first congress of the National Labor Union, held in Baltimore, Maryland in August 1866, made history. Not only did it found the first national labor federation, but it also focused some of its attention on working women, passing a resolution in support of the sewing women and "daughters of toil in the land," and asking women's cooperation with the National Labor Union in return. William Sylvis, president of the Molders' International Union and the dynamic young leader of the National Labor Union (he was elected its president in 1868) appealed for the organization of women workers and for equal pay for equal work, even though he knew that only two national unions at that time even permitted women to join.*

Following this appeal, the second annual congress passed a historic resolution directed at women workers, urging them to "learn trades, engage in business, join our labor unions or form protective unions of (your) own, and use every other honorable means to persuade or force employers (to) do justice to women by paying them equal wages for equal work."[24] For the first time delegates representing a cross section of skilled workers endorsed the principle of equal pay for equal work. They urged Congress and state legislatures to enact this principle into law for women in public employment. State labor conventions throughout New England and New York passed resolutions on equal pay for women.

But it was not all altruism. Equal pay for women would make men's jobs more secure; it removed the incentive for hiring women. Workers

---

* It is interesting, however, that of the 65 delegates to the first NLU Convention, only 2 actually represented national unions, though there were eighteen such unions in existence. Some 55 of the delegates were from local unions or city bodies and the remainder from 8-hour leagues. Close to half were from the Baltimore-Washington, D.C., area. At each of the NLU Congresses through 1875, a majority of the delegates were from local rather than national unions. David Montgomery, *Beyond Equality: Labor and the Radical Republicans, 1862–1872* (New York: Alfred A. Knopf, 1967), pp. 176, 182.

believed that employers meant to substitute women for men, and predicted that it would take only a few years to reduce "wages for mechanical labor down to the pittance now received for needle-work." Labor papers carried stories reporting women's wages as perhaps a quarter those of men, while the New York Working Women's Association, which suffragist Susan B. Anthony* had been instrumental in organizing, proclaimed rag-picking the only business in New York City "where women have equal opportunities with men."[25]

At its 1868 Congress the NLU admitted four women delegates, Susan B. Anthony and Mary Kellogg from New York Workingwomen's Protective Unions Number 1 and 2, Mary MacDonald of the Women's Protective Union of Mount Vernon, New York, and Elizabeth Cady Stanton, secretary of the Woman's Suffrage Association. A lengthy fight over whether or not to seat Stanton (who represented an organization that was not really a union) resulted in the delegates voting to seat her but passing a resolution stating that this in no way meant a Congress endorsement of women's suffrage.

Kate Mullaney, head of the Troy Collar Laundresses Union, also attended and received an ovation from the delegates for her work in Troy. She was elected second vice-president of the NLU, and although she was later declared ineligible on a technicality,† this did not diminish the fact that for the first time a national federation of labor delegates had chosen a woman for a top position.

---

* Susan B. Anthony, prime mover behind the Women's Loyal National League during the war and later founder of the National Woman's Suffrage Association, published *Revolution*, a weekly women's rights journal. During the few short years of her connection with it, it supported wholeheartedly the organization of working women, the eight-hour day, and equal pay for equal work. Unhappy about the attitude of unions toward women, she supported any moves that indicated a change on their part. She once wrote: "Every woman should scorn to allow herself to be made a mere tool . . . to undermine just prices of men workers, and to avoid this, 'union' is necessary. Hence I say, girls, stand by each other and by the men who stand by you." (Israel Kugler, "The Women's Rights Movement and the National Labor Union, 1866–1872," unpublished PhD. dissertation, New York University School of Education, 1954, p. 242, quoting the *Revolution*, Feb. 4, 1869). Anthony got into repeated difficulties with trade unions on the suffrage issue. She saw an immediate connection between the political power of the ballot and women improving their conditions of work. The NLU, however, was not ready to endorse suffrage for women, even though William Sylvis saw the value of at least partial suffrage for women so they could vote on "moral issues relating to Sunday labor, granting license to sell rum, the use of tobacco, a reduction of working hours, or any question intimately concerned with the domestic and social happiness of women" (editorial in the Molder's *Journal*, July 1866). For his time, this was a courageous position for a labor leader to take. Anthony also got into difficulty with the National Typographical Union over training women printers outside of union apprenticeships (which were not open to women), thus enabling them to serve as strikebreakers at times, and because she hired them in her own printing shop, which was non-union.

† The first vice-president also came from New York State, and the constitution barred the NLU from having these two offices filled by two members from the same state (Kugler, "The Women's Rights Movement," pp. 430, 431).

At the 1870 NLU Congress in Cincinnati, four women served as delegates, and Mrs. Willard from the Sewing Girls Union of Chicago was elected to the post of second vice-president, to be re-elected the following year.[26] Delegates Mrs. Ermine Lane of Boston, Miss Martha Walbridge and Miss McDermott submitted a resolution, unanimously passed by an overwhelmingly male Congress, to

> demand for our toiling sisters the same rate of wages that we receive for ours.
> We also ask all who are represented in this convention, and also all working-men of our country, to do all in their power to open many of the closed avenues of industry to women, and welcome her entering into just competition with men in the industrial race of life.[27]

In 1869, just as Sylvis was beginning to build the NLU membership, he died. Whether he could have prevented its subsequent decline is doubtful. Its initial successes with eight-hour legislation and repeal of the contract labor act (used to import immigrant workers as cheap labor and as strikebreakers) preceded a sharp division between those delegates concerned with trade union issues and those more interested in politics and forming a labor party. However, it had taken an important first step in recognizing women as a permanent part of the work force. It had focused attention on the issue of equal pay for equal work and had paved the way for the admission of women into two national unions, the Cigar Makers and the National Typographical Union.

Lady Segar Makers

During the war the Lady Segar Makers in Providence, Rhode Island, had organized. At its September 1864 meeting the organization's members voted to boycott a non-union employer and sent a letter to *Fincher's Trades' Review* in Philadelphia in order to publicize the action. The union's secretary wrote:

> We voted almost unanimously that in consideration of the fact that 10 members of our union had gone to work with some 17 or 18 rat girls, to pronounce it a rat shop and to advertise it as such, and we hereby caution all cigar makers, whether male or female, against making any engagements with W. H. Huntoon & Son, as the majority of the girls at work are rat girls, and they are working far below union prices.[28]

Women were not new to cigar making. The first cigar factory in the country opened in Suffield, Connecticut, in 1810 and employed only women. Early colonial farmers had raised tobacco from the seventeenth century, their wives turning the dried leaves into cigars, mostly for home consumption.* Before the Revolution, the bulk of the tobacco crop constituted a prized export to the mother country, where it was manufactured into cigars and snuff by skilled workers. The War of 1812, with its embargo on British goods, gave the cigar industry an additional foothold in America, and by 1832 Massachusetts had ten cigar factories employing 238 women, 48 men, and 9 children. From the start women earned only 35 to 50 percent of men's wages and performed the least skilled work, mostly stripping the leaves, rarely rolling the finished cigar. The men who constituted the skilled cigar makers organized, and as early as 1835 seem to have recognized the danger of striking without the support of the unskilled women in the factories. Philadelphia Journeymen Segar Makers, for example, urged the women to join them in seeking higher wages:

> Resolved, that the present low wages hitherto received by the females engaged in segar making is far below a fair compensation for the labor rendered. Therefore, Resolved, that we recommend them in a body to strike with us and thereby make it a mutual interest with both parties to sustain each other in their rights.[29]

By 1860 most cigars were produced in the North, while the South was the center for growing the tobacco. Slaves planted, harvested and dried the tobacco. Slave women and children worked in the factories stripping and sorting the leaves for rolling into cigars. Before 1861 many cigar makers were self-employed, for a worker needed little capital to get together the tools and the supply of tobacco needed to go into business for himself. However, in 1861 a federal revenue tax gave an advantage to larger businesses, while new machinery turned the rolling of cigars into a less skilled operation, increasing production to such an extent that the self-employed cigar maker could not compete. The machinery also invited the hiring of unskilled women at lower wages. Not only were the women hired for less, but employers saved additional money in the plant: few of the women took advantage of the time-honored industry custom that smokes were on the house!

The National Union of Cigar Makers, aware that the trade was changing, opened its doors to women and black workers in 1867, though it still focused its organizing efforts on skilled craftsmen. Since few women or blacks in the factories held these skilled jobs, few could join the union. However, eight years later the union added a clause to its constitution for-

---

* In 1790, Mrs. George Benjamin Miller, a widow, took over her husband's tobacco business and became famous as a leading manufacturer of fine-cut chewing and smoking tobacco. The enterprise became Mrs. G. B. Miller & Co., and remained so until 1848. Bishop, in A History of American Manufactures (3rd ed., 1868), writes: "Talent and energy . . . enabled her to overcome all opposition, and so popular did her productions in a short time become, that for several years she had the field almost exclusively to herself" (p. 515).

bidding any local union to refuse membership to anyone because of "sex or system of working," meaning factory or home work. The union's *Journal* granted, in an 1878 article, that women as union members were as loyal as any men. They "picketed the factories faithfully, from early morning till late in the evening, in stormy weather, rain and snow, and piercing cold. The *Journal* also publicized the union's policy of equal pay for equal work. Several locals withdrew from the national union over the issue of admitting women, and Baltimore Union No. 1 wrote Adolph Strasser to say: "We have combatted from its incipiency the movement of the introduction of female labor in any capacity whatever. . . ."[30]

An event external to the trade changed the industry more than the union's leaders could have predicted. The Austro-Prussian war of 1867 destroyed the Bohemian tobacco factories, where women held the skilled jobs in the industry. Thousands of these women skilled at cigar making emigrated to America to earn the money to send home for the men and children to follow. They came in groups of five or six, and worked in these groups in their own tenements under a commission system. When their families came from Europe to join them, the women taught the men, who had been field workers back in Bohemia, how to strip tobacco and roll cigars. Children were put to work at the simpler operations and became a new source of cheap labor for the industry, threatening the jobs held by American men. An entire tenement sweatshop system in the cigar-making industry developed.

These new workers were trapped. Totally dependent on the employer who owned the raw material and sold their product, they found that often he also owned the tenement where they lived, charged them high rents, and held over them the power to evict. From an 1885 New York City study of the conditions of working women comes testimony on how these cigar makers lived:

> These people worked till twelve p.m. or one o'clock a.m., then slept by the machine a few hours, and commenced work again. (Women sat) surrounded by filth, with children waddling in it, whose hands, faces, and bodies were covered with sores . . . even on the lips of the workers.[31]

Following the severe depression of 1873–1877, the union conducted a series of strikes in which employers saw the opportunity to use women as strikebreakers in the factories. The Cincinnati union voiced its anger:

> We first used every endeavor to get them in the union, but no one would join; therefore we passed the resolution that if they would not work with us, we would work against them; but I think we have taught them a lesson that will serve them another time.[32]

The most bitter strikes of all took place in New York City, where over half of all cigar workers were female, most of them Bohemian women. In New York, some women had been brought into cigar factories as well as providing the bulk of tenement industry labor in cigar making. The New York strikes focused on trying to end the tenement system in cigar making,* and the *Cigar Maker's Journal* reports that a large number of women took part in these walkouts. When the Bohemian women struck with the factory men, employers promptly hired American men and women to replace them. This time it was women who became embittered when men continued to work. The *Cigar Maker's Journal* wrote: "Mrs. Treish left her husband, a scab; the union was dearer to her than her family. Brave woman!"[33] Adding to their bitterness was the fact that many of them were evicted from their employer-owned tenements and literally thrown onto the streets.

Organizing the tenement shops proved almost impossible. There were so many of them, each involving families who lived in fear of starvation if their income were cut or their rent raised by an angry employer. Nor were the cigar workers in the factories eager to have the tenement workers, most of them women, in the union, primarily because they were seen as a major threat to union pay scales. It is not surprising, therefore, that in his anuual report for 1879, Adolph Strasser, the union president, turned to protective legislation as a way to keep down the number of women in the industry.

> We can not drive the females out of the trade, but we can restrict this daily quota of labor through factory laws. No girl under 18 should be employed more than eight hours per day; all overwork should be prohibited; while married women should be kept out of factories at least six weeks before and six weeks after confinement.[34]

If employers were forced to follow strict rules that applied only to women, they would undoubtedly prefer men, who carried with them no limitations. Nonetheless, the percentage of women in cigar making continued to rise, from 10 percent of all cigar workers in 1870 to 17 percent in 1880 to 28 percent by 1890. By the turn of the century, 37 percent of all cigar workers were women.[35]

Women Workers and the Typographical Union

The second union to admit women was the National Typographical Union, founded in 1852 and the oldest national union still in existence today. Women had been printers since the first colonial printing presses

---

* The problem was complex. In getting rid of the cigar sweatshops the union protected the jobs of its members but left the tenement women without work and starving.

were installed, but it was not until 1853 that they began to be hired into the printing industry in any numbers, and then it was frequently for strikebreaking purposes. New York printers went on strike against *Day Book* that year, and the owner advertised for "girls to learn the compositors' trade." On April 11, he wrote:

> On Saturday we stated that we did not know what we should do, but should trust to our wits to get us out of the tight place the Printers' Union had put us in. We did not trust in vain—they came to our aid, as they always have in an emergency. We advertised for girls to learn to set type, determining to teach them the art rather than submit to the tyranny of any trade union in the universe. There were more than 40 girls applied for situations at our office this morning to learn to set type. We engaged four of them. . . . We see no reason why they will not make good compositors and earn their eight or ten dollars a week, which will be to them good wages.[36]

Just four months later, and unrelated to the strike, the *Tribune* announced that a Mrs. Phoebe Patterson of New York proposed to establish a printing office where the typesetting would be done by women.[37] Women were not strangers to printing. But neither were they members of the union, and invariably they received less pay.

In the early 1860s, the National Typographical Union urged locals to help women organize, but one woman printer, Augusta Lewis, did not need any urging. With the help of Susan B. Anthony and the Working Women's Association of New York City, she called the women compositors together for a meeting on September 28, 1868, at the office of *Revolution*. Women's Typographical Union Number 1 was founded officially on October 12 of that year. Young Augusta Lewis was elected president. The local received its charter from the National Typographical Union, together with offers from New York Typographical Union Number 6, and particularly from one of its young leaders, Alexander Troup, to hire a hall for the women printers to meet in and to furnish funds and equipment to help them get their organization off the ground.

Anthony could not contain her enthusiasm. She wrote:

> Girls, you must take this matter to heart seriously now, for you have established a union, and for the first time in woman's history in the United States, you are placed, and by your own efforts, on a level with men, as far as possible, to obtain wages for your labor. I need not say you have taken a great, a momentous step forward in the path to success. Keep at it now, girls, and you will achieve full and plenteous success.[38]

By January 1869 some 30 women printers had joined, but the local never did succeed in enrolling many more than 40 at its height. Anthony sup-

ported Women's Typographical Union Number 1 not only by printing
its meeting notices and promoting it among women compositors, but also
by writing signed articles in *Revolution* pointing out the improvements
in wages that unionizing would bring. She also urged women not to expect any special treatment on the job if they also wanted equal pay:

> Make up your mind to take the "lean" with the "fat," and be early
> and late at the case precisely as the men are. I do not demand equal
> pay for any women save those who do equal work in value. Scorn to
> be coddled by your employers; make them understand that you are
> in their service as workers, not as women.[39]

Augusta Lewis was the unquestioned leader among the women compositors. She had grown up and gone to school in Brooklyn. During the
depression of 1867, when she was nineteen, she set out to earn her own
living. A good writer, articulate and well educated, she was able to get
a job as reporter for the *New York Sun.* After a typesetting apprenticeship
on the *Era,* she took a compositor's job on the *New York World.* When
the National Typographical Union struck the *World* in 1867, the women,
who were not members of any union, stayed on their jobs. Although they
had been cajoled into doing so by the publisher, they found that after the
strike, when the men returned to work, most of them were fired. Although
Lewis was not discharged, she walked out with her co-workers when they
were dismissed. During her next few jobs with small printing concerns,
she came to see that women needed to organize, and joined with Anthony
and Elizabeth Cady Stanton in 1868 to form the Working Women's Association "to act for its members, in the same manner as the associations
of workingmen now regulated the wages, etc., of those belonging to
them."[40]

When the NTU struck the book and job printing houses in 1869,
Lewis succeeded in persuading a number of women printers not to take
the jobs of the strikers, even though the employers advertised that they
would even pay female compositors the full journeyman's wage if they
would scab.

One of those who continued to give Lewis and Women's Typographical
Union No. 1 the most encouragement was Alexander Troup, now
national secretary-treasurer of the union, whom Lewis married in June
1872. The women's local had difficulties from the start. Non-union firms
would not hire its members, nor pay them equally with the men if they
did give them jobs. Even though equal pay was a NTU principle, union
foremen felt that the men would be better off without women as com-
petitors, and they too tried to avoid hiring them. Nor could women get
apprenticeships, and as a result they could never rise above the compositor's job level to become journeymen printers.

In 1870, twenty-two-year-old Augusta Lewis was elected corresponding secretary of the National Typographical Union, a job that involved organizing, developing contacts with women printers, and analyzing problems in the printing industry. As part of her job she surveyed conditions in the industry and presented her findings in a well-documented report to the next union convention. Looking out from the speaker's platform on the sea of male faces, she tried to explain to the delegates how difficult it was for women printers in the union to find jobs, the problems they faced, and the kind of help that they needed from the men but had not found forthcoming.

> A year ago last January Typographical Union no. 6 passed a resolution admitting union girls (of local 1) in offices under control of No. 6. Since that time we have never obtained a situation that we could not have obtained had we never heard of a union. We refuse to take the men's situations when they are on strike, and when there is no strike if we ask for work in union offices we are told by union foremen "that there are no conveniences for us." We are ostracized in many offices because we are members of the union; and, although the principle is right, disadvantages are so many that we cannot much longer hold together. No progress has been made in the past year. Women receive 40 cents for all kinds of work. A strike among them would prove disastrous. . . . It is the general opinion of female compositors that they are more justly treated by what is termed "rat" foremen, printers and employers than they are by union men. . . .[41]

Never a large or very strong local, Women's Typographical Union Number 1 lasted just nine years. By the time it ceased operation, however, women had been admitted to a number of NTU locals around the country on an equal basis with men.

Lewis's working life did not stop with her marriage. She continued as a journalist, became an ardent suffragist, and maintained her interest in social reform. She and Troup lived in New Haven, where he edited the *New Haven Daily Union*. Writing about her early days in the union, she said in 1911: "Considering the prejudice against women in industrial occupations at that period, I wonder at our temerity and success."[42] As of today, Lewis is still the only woman to have held a national office in the International Typographical Union.

Daughters of St. Crispin

The women of the shoe towns did not compete with the men for jobs. Entire families worked making the shoes, men and women performing different work. Women handled the shoebinding; men cut the leather and did the heavy stitching. When the McKay machine for sewing uppers to shoe soles was introduced in 1862, many of the shoeworkers had left to fight in the Civil War. It was women, therefore, who were recruited to work the new machines, run at first by foot power and undoubtedly heavy to operate.

Not many years after the war the shoebinders drew up a petition to the men in the Knights of St. Crispin (a national union of male shoe-workers) asking their help in forming a union. By July 1869 the women shoeworkers had formed what was the first national union of women workers in the country, the Daughters of St. Crispin.* At the first national meeting of the Daughters in Lynn, Massachusetts, July 28, 1869, some thirty delegates represented eleven lodges, some from cities as far away as San Francisco and Chicago. By December, the Daughters had grown to inclue twenty-four lodges, with applications from fourteen more, three of them in Canada.[43]

At their second convention the following year, the Daughters adopted this resolution:

> *Whereas the common idea among employers has been and still is that woman's labor should receive a less remuneration, even though equally valuable and efficient, than is paid men even on the same qualities of work; and*
>
> *Whereas in every field of human effort the value and power of organization is fully recognized: Therefore be it*
>
> *Resolved by this National Grand Lodge of the Daughters of St. Crispin, That we demand for our labor the same rate of compensation for equal skill displayed, or the same hours of toil, as is paid other laborers in the same branches of business; and we regard a denial of this right by anyone as a usurpation and a fraud.*
>
> *Resolved, That we condemn and promptly veto one sister's making a percentage on another sister's labor.*
>
> *Resolved, That we assure our fellow-citizens that we only desire to so elevate and improve our condition as to better fit us for the discharge of those high social and moral duties which devolve upon every true woman.[44]*

Despite their determination, they still felt they had to soften the resolution with the assurance that equal pay and treatment would make them better able to perform their womanly duties.

The organization soon faced two tests of its ability to survive. In Stoneham, Massachusetts, in 1872, 300 Daughters from three factories struck

---

* Crispin and Crispianian, the patron saints of shoemakers, date back to the eighth century. Two royal Roman brothers, so the story goes, journeyed to the French city of Soissons, converting the populace to Christianity while supporting themselves by shoe-making. Condemned to death by the Roman emperor Maximianus, they escaped for a time, but finally were caught and beheaded. For centuries the guilds of shoemakers played a leading role at the annual festival of Saint Crispin, October 25. (*Encyclopaedia Britannica*, 14th ed., 1929, vol. 6, p. 727.)

for higher rates for their work. They held out for two weeks, calling off the walkout only when it became clear that strikebreakers would be brought in to take their places. Two union leaders were fired and blacklisted throughout the area. In Lynn, home of the shoe industry, a larger strike occurred the same year, beginning in two of the binding shops but spreading to the entire city. In this fight the women showed their organizational skills. They enlisted the support of the Knights of St. Crispin, used mass meetings to unite the women, organized a committee representing every shop, distributed leaflets to women in all the shoe factories of Lynn, and made full use of the press. The strike was won!

It often happened that shoebinders who tried to organize in the Daughters of St. Crispin were fired for union activity. Two walkouts of the Knights of St. Crispin in 1871, in Syracuse and Baltimore, were in sympathy over discharges of women for organizing. However, by 1872 the Daughters as an organization began to decline, and the depression of 1873 brought all its union activity to a halt. One attempt to reorganize was made in 1876 in Lynn, but its days as a national organization of women shoeworkers were over. Still, their union experience would prove valuable when they joined the Knights of Labor in great numbers after it opened its doors to women in 1881. The largest single group of women in the Knights was the shoebinders.

The Collar Laundresses of Troy

Once upon a time, Troy, New York, was the center for the production of detachable collars and cuffs, the shirts that went with them, and the laundries that washed, starched, and boxed them for the stores. The story is told that as early as 1827 the wife of a retired Methodist minister, Mrs. Hannah Lord Montagu, got so tired of washing her husband's shirts each time the collar became soiled that she invented the detachable collar. Out of this idea her husband developed collar and cuff making into a succcessful business.

> These collars were at first all made by his wife and daughters at home, but he soon began to give out work to the women in the neighboring families, who received with each lot of collars a card carefully specifying: "In pay you buy my goods at my prices." The minister-storekeeper was not long the only collar manufacturer in the field, and Troy became the center of a great industry (at first largely a home industry, but by the period under consideration it had been transferred to the factory).[45]

Washing and starching the collars was as important to the industry as making them in the first place,[46] and by 1835 collar laundering began to be one of the leading occupations for the women of Troy.* The work involved standing "over the wash tub and over the ironing table with furnaces on either side, the thermometer averaging 100 degrees, for wages averaging $2.00 and $3.00 a week."† From these wages were deducted fines for any damage or soiling of the collars or cuffs. However, the laundresses did not put up with this for long. Troy was a union town, its workers taking their lead from the Molders and the Sons of Vulcan (boilers and puddlers),‡ the most active unions in the iron mills of the city. The women saw at first hand what labor organization could do for the men in their families, and fiery Kate Mullaney soon had over 400 fellow workers organized into the Troy Collar Laundry Union.§ The union was successful in increasing the earnings of the laundresses from their $2 and $3 level to $8 to $14 a week, although their workday remained anywhere from 12 to 14 hours long. The union demonstrated its strength in April 1866, when it contributed $1,000 to striking molders, a

Here Kate Mullaney and the Troy collar laundresses worked on "an endless, innumerable mass of daily accumulations [which] if whirled abroad upon the air before some tempest . . . would whiten a whole country with a linen snow-storm of tens of thousands of flakes, in cuffs, and wristlets, and collars, and fronts, and habits for ladies and gentlemen . . . at the rate of acres per day."

remarkable sum of money for that period. Their union spirit was not confined to Troy, for that same year they sent $500 to bricklayers on strike in New York City.[47]

Mullaney knew the leading unionists of her day, and was active in the National Labor Union. The reader will recall that she had been elected its second vice-president in 1868, though later removed on a technicality. Some accounts state that she was appointed national organizer of women

* Andrews and Bliss state that the industry also included the manufacture of the shirts and ladies' blouses that carried detachable collars as well as of the collars and cuffs.

† The laundering of collars and cuffs involved eleven processes: washing with soap to remove "the manufacturer's dressing from the goods"; bleaching with "hyperchloride of soda"; adding "dilute of sulphuric acid" to further bleach the collars; another washing in

for the NLU, others that she became assistant secretary. In any event, there is no indication that she was actually assigned to work in either capacity. She knew Susan B. Anthony and supported woman suffrage. She was convinced that the political power of the ballot would mean more respect for the collar union from forces in town like the Troy press, which berated the women's organizing efforts while supporting those of the men.

The union men of Troy regarded the collar laundresses as "the only bona fide female union in the country," and when the women faced a bitter fight with the employers over a demand for a wage increase in May 1869, Troy unions rallied to the women's support. The Molders Union voted $500 a week to help the women hold out during their strike, which involved close to 500 workers. It pledged "to continue the same for weeks to come rather than see such a brave set of wenches crushed under the iron heel of these laundry nabobs."[48]

While employers united to break the strike and destroy the union, the workers of Troy gave it their full support. Seven thousand attended a mass rally, and townspeople and storeowners backed the women. As the strike dragged on with no end in sight, Mullaney and the union organized a cooperative "Union Linen Collar and Cuff. Manufactory" to provide work for members and combat employer attempts to starve them out. The enterprise began production, sending its output to a New York merchant who had agreed to arrange for its sale.[49]

All might have gone well, with the women holding out indefinitely thanks to the support of other Troy unions, except for the untimely death of William Sylvis, which sent the Iron Molders into a tailspin and focused their attention on their own union troubles more than on the Troy Collar Laundresses. At precisely the same time, struck companies advertised that they were putting a new paper collar on the market, and the laundresses saw their jobs coming to an end.[50] Not only did the employers break the strike, but the women voted to dissolve their organization, probably the price exacted for getting back their jobs.*

---

suds; boiling; "rubbing and rinsing"; blueing and "rolling"; a starching with thin starch; a starching with thick starch; drying; and finally, ironing. Horace Greeley and others, *The Great Industries of the United States* (Hartford, Conn.: J. B. Burr & Hyde, 1871), p. 542.

‡ Puddlers convert cast iron into wrought iron.

§ Nancy Ducatte reports that the issue around which the women organized was the introduction of starching machines, scalding hot to handle, which cut prices received for their work almost in half. Nancy Ducatte, "The Shirt and Collar Industry and Kate Mullaney," Troy, N.Y., undated paper, p. 4. Copy available in the library of Trade Union Women's Studies, Cornell University, 7 East 43rd Street, New York, N.Y. I am indebted to Anne Rivera of the Amalgamated Clothing and Textile Workers Union for this material.

* The leading manufacturer of collars, cuffs, and the shirts to which they were attached was George B. Cluett, Brothers and Co., which remains today as Cluett and Peabody,

Within a short time after the union broke up, the cooperative laundry closed. Once again a union of women workers that had started in high hopes and with a good chance of success failed over the long run to survive. Women organizing on their own against employers united to defeat them did not have the financial strength, political force, or staying power to establish a permanent organization. Not long after the strike, Mullaney left the East to join the Sisters of St. Joseph Convent in Carondelet, Missouri, where she died in 1876.

Speedup in the Mills

When the cotton mills were ready to rehire after the initial slump of 1861, most of their former workers had found other jobs. Their places were taken by immigrant men, women, and children, who were assigned additional looms at no rise in piece rate. The women were forced to work faster and faster to keep pace with the machines.[51] Conditions in the mills deteriorated during the Civil War. In 1866, a tragic night fire in a mill near Providence, Rhode Island, that operated twenty-four hours a day caused panic among the mill's 600 workers, many of whom jumped from upper-story windows to escape the flames and were killed. The investigation following the fire revealed doors and windows locked shut. The same year a similar tragedy occurred in a mill in Woonsocket, Rhode Island.

It was far from easy for the immigrant mill women to organize. Most did not speak English, and to reduce the danger of organization, supervisors saw to it that they worked next to someone from a country whose language they did not understand. Working hours remained from sunup to dark six days a week. It took the wages of an entire family to eke out a living.

Nonetheless, millworkers did try to organize, and often their strikes were long and bitter. In 1869, 800 millworkers at the Cocheco Mills in Dover, New Hampshire, walked out over a wage cut. This was the strike

---

makers of the famous Arrow shirts. Now a unionized concern, in 1869 it led the way in holding out to defeat the Collar Laundresses. Greeley and others, *Great Industries of the United States* (p. 544), describe the dispute just two years after it had taken place:

> A few years ago, a so-called "Workingwomen's Union" was set up among the hands, and at once went to work to raise wages. Apparently there was a measure of justification for the step, since the required advance was granted, as was another within a few months. A third, however, met with a prompt refusal; the manufacturers, though not organizing into any formal body, agreed to put a stop to the performances, the Mssrs. Cluett being among the very first in taking this ground. The demand of the "union" was peremptorily refused, work stopped, the ill-advised strikers were let alone until they returned to work at previous rates, and the Union was exterminated, as no member of it would be employed.

that brought Jennie Collins onto the New England labor scene. Left homeless at the age of fourteen, Collins had gone to work in the mills of Lowell in 1842. From there she had tried domestic work in Boston, then turned to earning her living as a seamstress. During the Civil War she found time after work to volunteer at Boston's military hospitals and to organize her fellow workers to do the same.[52] Without much formal education herself, she launched a workers' education program reminiscent of the days of Sarah Bagley, and taught free evening history classes for women workers.

Known as a champion of the cause of working women, Collins was active with the New England Labor Reform League and organized the Working Women's Club of Boston. When the Cocheco women struck, she rallied to their aid, trying to organize a boycott against all products of the Cocheco mill. "We working women will wear fig-leaf dresses before we will patronize the Cocheco Company," she declared.[53]

The strike was lost. However, Jennie Collins continued to speak for suffrage and for protective laws for women, and opened a center in Boston for working women. This was financed by money from employers, who were perhaps eager to get Collins out of circulation as a labor organizer. She took in needy women and provided both recreation and education programs for any who came. In addition, she organized what amounted to an employment office for women seeking work. To supplement the center's income, Collins wrote and lectured widely, continuing her work even when ill with tuberculosis, which finally took her life when she was fifty-nine years old.[54]

At least once during the postwar period mill women won a strike, although it was only a short-lived victory. In January 1875, women weavers in Fall River, Massachusetts, formed their own union, rebelling against a decision of the union of men weavers, who had voted to accept a 10 percent wage cut. The women excluded all men except newspaper reporters from their organizing meeting and voted not to take any reduction in wages. They chose three mills to strike against, while accepting the wage reduction in the other mills "under protest" in order to permit those workers to support the strikers for as long as necessary to win their common fight. When the men in the mill learned of the plan, they voted their support.

This strike was a major undertaking: 3,500 looms and 156,000 spindles were affected, while those millworkers who stayed on the job supported the 3,215 strikers until their victory late in March. However, less than five months later the employers again announced a 10 percent wage cut, and this time almost all the mills struck. By September the children of the strikers were starving. Workers marched silently to the city hall to beg food for their families, only to be met by the police. At the end of

October they were forced to return to work and accept a wage cut greater than the 10 percent employers had originally announced. In addition, they had to sign an "iron-clad oath" not to join any union in the future. Strike leaders were blacklisted throughout the area.[55]

Black Women Workers in the Postwar Era

Most black women worked as cleaning women, cooks, nursemaids, laundresses, building cleaners, and chambermaids, although some were hairdressers, seamstresses, and midwives. A number of black women became teachers and went South during Reconstruction to work with freedmen. In 1864, Rebecca Lee became the first black woman doctor to be graduated from medical school.

A group of black working women is credited with forming the first labor organization in Mississippi, the Washerwomen of Jackson, who established themselves in June of 1866 and sent this resolution to Jackson's mayor:

> That on and after the foregoing date, we join in charging a uniform rate for our labor . . . the statement of said price to be made public by printing the same, and any one, belonging to the class of washerwomen, violating this, shall be liable to a fine regulated by the class.[56]

Those black men and women who could get out from under the tenant-farming and sharecropping system continued to migrate to the cities seeking work and moved westward to Kansas and the coast. White workers looked on these black migrants to the city with suspicion and fear. Employers saw them as a source of strikebreakers. White unions maintained the bars to their membership, and only a few locals such as the Boston carpenters admitted black workers (1866). Even unions like the Cigar Workers, who in 1871 specifically declared that black cigarmakers could join, left it to each local to interpret just who was a "cigarmaker," and in effect, discrimination continued.

While in 1866 the National Labor Union invited black workers to join, there is no record that blacks felt welcome, since few of the union locals forming the NLU admitted them. The National Colored Labor Union, organized in December 1869, admitted women from the start and opened its doors to unskilled workers. Although few women held the kinds of jobs that led to organization or union membership, nonetheless Mrs Mary A. S. Carey was elected a member of the executive committee and several women delegates attended the first convention. The report of its committee on women's labor contained the plea that this federation profit "by the mistakes heretofore made by our white fellow citizens in omitting women . . . that women be cordially included in the invitation to further and organize cooperative societies."[57] The report, which endorsed equal rights for women workers, was adopted unanimously.

At the 1869 NLU congress, a majority of the unions represented agreed to accept blacks, but in separate locals, and the NLU seated nine black delegates. The ensuing decline of the NLU and its disagreement with the National Colored Labor Union over support of the Republican Party (which the NCLU favored) versus the formation of a labor party (NLU-endorsed) left little room for close cooperation between these two labor groups. Not until the organization of the Knights of Labor in 1881 was the door to union organization opened to black workers on an equal basis. When the door opened, black workers did not hesitate to enter.

The Depression of 1873–1877

Except for the Great Depression of 1929, this country has never known a more serious economic catastrophe than the depression of 1873–1877. By the end of the four years, 3 million workers were out of work. One out of every five workers was jobless; two-fifths worked no more than half a year; and only one in five was steadily employed, although not necessarily for full weeks.[58] Those with jobs faced wage cuts, while the jobless went hungry. During the winter of 1873, an article in *Harper's Weekly* reported that 900 died of starvation, while 3,000 deserted their infants, leaving them on doorsteps.[59] Workers were reduced to collecting rags, rummaging through garbage for food scraps, and living in shanties built of boxes and discarded lumber.

Those with shanties to return to at night were more fortunate than the thousands of homeless in cities across the country who slept in doorways and in parks. The unemployed paraded and rioted for bread. In Chicago, 20,000 marched with signs asking for "bread for the needy, clothing for the naked, houses for the homeless."[60] Even under police attack, workers demanding relief in New York, Omaha, and Cincinnati refused to disperse. But no organized relief was forthcoming.

Union membership plummeted from 300,000 in 1873 to perhaps 50,000 by 1878. Workers lived in constant fear of losing their jobs. Employers used lockouts, the iron-clad rule, the blacklist, and strikebreakers to keep unions out.

One cold January day in 1874, workers gathered for a rally in Tompkins Square Park on New York's Lower East Side. It was a peaceful group,

made up mostly of unionists and their families. Unbeknownst to them,
their permit to meet in the park had been withdrawn by nervous city
authorities only hours before. When they arrived at Tompkins Square they
were charged by mounted police, who rode down men, women, and children, using nightsticks in what one worker who observed them called "an
orgy of brutality."[61] Among those who witnessed the tragedy was a young
man named Samuel Gompers who would, in 1886, become the first president of the new American Federation of Labor. His experience in Tompkins Square impressed him deeply and undoubtedly contributed to shap-
ing the structure of the American Federation of Labor and his own
union philosophy. Years later in his autobiography, *Seventy Years of Life
and Labor*, he wrote of that night:

> I was in no way connected with the arrangement of this demonstration.
> . . . As the fundamentals came to me, they became guideposts for my
> understanding of the labor movement for years to come. I saw how
> professions of radicalism and sensationalism concentrated all the
> forces of organized society against a labor movement and nullified in
> advance normal, necessary activity. I saw that leadership in the labor
> movement could be safely entrusted only to those earning their bread
> by daily labor. . . . I saw the danger of entangling alliances with
> intellectuals.[62]

This suspicion of intellectuals determined in part Gompers's attitude, thirty
years later, to the National Women's Trade Union League.

Worker resistance continued throughout the depression years. A series
of strikes climaxed in the nation-wide railroad strike during the summer
of 1877. Of this strike the *Baltimore Sun* reported:

> There is no disguising the fact that the strikers in all their lawful
> acts have the fullest sympathy of the community. . . . The singular
> part of the disturbance is in the very active part taken by the women,
> who are the wives and mothers of the firemen. They look famished
> and wild, and declare for starvation rather than have their people work
> for the reduced wages. Better to starve outright, say they, than to die
> by slow starvation.[63]

The strike spread. Before it was crushed, all major cities were involved,
100,000 workers had walked out, and troops had been ordered to Washington, D.C., in fear that a national insurrection was taking place.
Twenty men, women, and children were killed by the militia in Pittsburgh, twelve in Baltimore, and similar troop attacks against strikers took
place elsewhere.

While the strike was lost, and its leaders blacklisted on every railroad
for years to come, out of the tragedy came new worker solidarity. Unions
that had died during the depression, or had been forced underground,

began to revive. As the country pulled out of the trough and employment gradually rose, an organization that had begun in secret in 1869 now came out in the open. The Noble and Holy Order of the Knights of Labor, the first labor federation in the country actively to seek to organize unskilled workers, women, and blacks, held its 1881 convention in Detroit and announced itself to the workers of America.

10

WOMEN IN THE KNIGHTS OF LABOR *1881–1886*

Toiling millions now are waking—
See them marching on!
All the tyrants now are shaking,
Ere their power's gone.

Storm the fort, ye Knights of Labor,
    Battle for your cause;
Equal rights for every neighbor—
    Down with tyrant laws!

—Song of the Knights of Labor*

By 1880 the United States had become the world's leading industrial nation, a land dominated by trusts and monopolies. It could hardly keep up with the rapid growth in population, the rush to its cities with new inventions like the electric light, the telephone, the transatlantic telegraph, the typewriter. Railroads crisscrossed the country. Steel mills belched smoke day and night. Electricity was applied to industry: transformers, dynamos, motors. An age of specialization began: some stores sold meat, others candy, others baked goods. Canning of meats and vegetables was introduced. So were the department store, standardized packaging of goods, and brand-name advertising.

Rapidly growing cities meant more slums, filled by the numbers of immigrants, almost half a million a year now, who came to America to start a new life and provided a never-ending supply of cheap labor for the giant firms that made a few Americans very rich. This was the day of the "robber barons," the railroad, steel, and mining magnates whose lives contrasted so sharply with those of the average working men and

* The Knights of Labor sang this song at all their meetings. The tune is familiar to today's trade unionists as "Hold the Fort."
    Hold the fort, for we are coming,
      Union men be strong
    Side by side we battle onward,
      Victory will come.
The song was adopted by the Emergency Brigade, headed by Genora Johnson, during the Flint (UAW) campaign to organize automobile workers in the General Motors Company, scene of one of the major sit-down strikes, 1936–1937.

women their empires employed. Railroad tycoon Jay Gould spent $1,000 a week to maintain his yacht; Mrs. William Vanderbilt, a quarter of a million dollars on a single ball. At the same time, workers in 1880 averaged only $300 a year in wages (down from $400 a year in 1870),[1] and worked such long hours that they could hardly take advantage of the 2,500 public libraries which Andrew Carnegie began in 1881 to endow.

The numbers of women and children in the work force increased by 38 percent between 1870 and 1880, and in the next ten years by 51 percent. Outside of domestic work and agriculture (for the country was still primarily rural and would be for some years to come) most working women were clustered in the sewing trades, in teaching, and in cotton and woolen mills. Women also worked as laundresses, as waitresses, and in other service jobs. The numbers in store and office jobs, while increasing, still did not figure prominently.[2]

Women in the cities faced deterioration in their living and working conditions. Their workday was 12, 14, or more hours long, often spent in tenement dwellings under the most insanitary conditions, making clothing, cigars, or flowers or trimming hats. Nor were workers outside the urban centers much better off. Company stores flourished in the mill villages, where workers received payment in scrip and children went to the mills or mines as soon as they were able. In the South, blacks, most of them on farms and plantations, often earned no more than 50 to 75 cents a day. Paid in scrip redeemable only at the planter's commissary, they would find that after harvesting their sharecropped cotton they owed their employer more than he owed them because of the inflated prices he charged.[3]

The risk of industrial accidents increased as faster machinery was introduced without safety guards. No laws made employers responsible for factory injuries. A worker who lost a finger or hand, or worse, bore the cost. The first factory law for machine safeguards, passed in 1877 by Massachusetts, and similar laws passed during the next ten years by fifteen other states, provided limited enforcement and minimal fines. When the federal government established a Bureau of Labor in 1884, for the first time elementary data on hours and working conditions became available and provided ammunition for reform.

The final quarter of the nineteenth century saw heightened employer resistance to union organization. Companies hired private armies of guards and labor spies that reported on meetings and hounded active unionists. Workers were intimidated, fired, and blacklisted for union organizing. Scabs were brought in to break strikes, workers were locked out in labor disputes, and the hated "yellow-dog contracts" were introduced. In the late 1880s, employers also discovered the use of court-ordered injunctions to prevent boycotts and keep union organizers from talking with their workers near the factories,[4] and added these to their antilabor arsenal.

Rise of the Knights of Labor

In view of the hostile climate for organizing in the post–Civil War period, the secrecy that surrounded the birth of the Noble and Holy Order of the Knights of Labor is understandable. By keeping its operations clandestine, the nine Philadelphia garment cutters who formed the order sought to avoid employer retaliation. Assembly Number 1, Knights of Labor, adopted elaborate rituals for inducting new members, to impress upon them the importance of maintaining secrecy. The organization grew slowly, but by 1878 it felt strong enough to hold its first general convention. Founded on the precept of its first president, Uriah S. Stephens, that "the most perfect government is one in which an injury to one is the concern of all,"[5] the constitution adopted at that general assembly called for equal pay for equal work and for no child labor under the age of fourteen. The next year the general assembly of the Knights took up a resolution to admit women to the order, but the convention tabled the resolution.

Not until 1881, the same year that the Knights came out into the open, did it also vote to extend membership to women over the age of sixteen.* Once the doors to membership opened, women joined in great numbers until, by 1886, 192 women's assemblies had been organized.[6] In addition, women joined a number of formerly all-male assemblies. Some 50,000 women were members of the Knights at its 1886 membership peak, approximately 10 percent of all the organization's members. However, this was barely 2 percent of the more than 2.5 million women aged ten years and up listed by the 1880 census as gainfully employed.[7] Of the all-female assemblies, 91 were "mixed" (including workers of different trades). Single-trade women's assemblies included:

19 assemblies of shoeworkers
17 of cotton and woolen mill workers
12 of housekeepers
5 each of sewing women, tailoresses, and laundresses
4 each of knitters, collar and shirt ironers, dress and cloak makers

* All male workers of every race and creed had been welcomed in the Knights from the beginning, except Chinese. The only trades excluded were stockbrokers, lawyers, gamblers, and liquor salesmen. Black workers were found in both segregated and integrated assemblies.

2 each of hatters, shirt operatives, paper box makers, weavers

1 each of "bookbinders, carpet makers, cigar makers, farmers, feather curlers, gold cutters, Government employees, lead pencil workers, rubber makers, leather sewers, potters, and cabinetmakers."[8]

Although few black women worked in the job categories given above, those who did so joined men's assemblies in the Knights of Labor. However, there were several all-female assemblies of laundresses, chambermaids, and housekeepers in five Southern states and the District of Columbia.*

Shoeworkers were the first to organize a women's assembly in the Knights: Garfield Assembly 1684 in Philadelphia. Mary Hanafin, a founding member of Garfield Assembly, made a singular contribution during the few short years in which the Knights were active in focusing the organization's attention on women workers. A saleswoman, probably of ladies' shoes, she first emerges as one of the active members fired from her job for participating in the Knights. Before the women shoeworkers had organized their assembly, the men in the factory, already members of the Knights, had assured them that this activity would not endanger their jobs. When the women leaders were fired, therefore, they were surprised. This surprise turned to distress when the men advised them not to take any action to fight the dismissals. Mary Hanafin decided otherwise, and standing firm against the employer the women won back every leader's job.[9]

Mary Stirling, another shoeworker from Philadelphia, was elected one of eight representatives from her district to the general assembly of 1883. She seems to have been the only woman delegate to attend (another was elected from Rochester, New York, but could not get to the meeting), and was the first woman delegate ever to attend a Knights' convention. She is recorded as having taken an active part in the business of the meeting and in the election of officers, and as having received "three votes for general worthy foreman."[10] The following year two women attended: Mary Hanafin from Philadelphia and Louisa Eaton of Lynn, Massachusetts, presumably also a shoeworker.

Three women delegates attended the 1885 general assembly session,

* These were in Louisiana; Washington, D.C.; Richmond, Norfolk, Danville, and Petersburg, Virginia; Raleigh, North Carolina; Jacksonville and Pensacola, Florida; and Arkansas, where there were three women's assemblies, one of women farmers. In all, 60,000 black workers, most of them men, were members of the Knights in four hundred all-black assemblies. When the number of black workers in integrated locals is added to the 60,000 figure, perhaps 90,000 black workers belonged to the Order, two-thirds of them in Northern states. John Bracey, August Meier, and Elliott Rudwick, *Black Workers and Organized Labor* (Belmont, Calif.: Wadsworth Publishing Co., 1971), pp. 11, 19.

two shoeworkers and Hanafin. At this meeting Hanafin took the floor to move that all three women be appointed a committee on women's work, to conduct a survey and gather statistics about working conditions of women. She also ran for the executive committee of the order, but she received only two votes, probably those of the other two women delegates. However, her motion for a committee on women's work passed, and its three members at once set about conducting the survey and preparing their report for the next year's general assembly. The women had had no experience at this type of work, but wrote to each women's assembly in the Knights, compiling figures that showed that women averaged $5 a week in wages and worked 10 hours a day. Shoeworkers made slightly more money than did women in other industries.

As a result of the interest the committee created, sixteen women were among the 660 delegates attending the 1886 general assembly, the largest number of women ever to attend a single convention during the lifetime of the organization. Of the sixteen, five were shoeworkers, five worked in textile mills, and two were dressmakers.* All sixteen were appointed a committee to hear and make recommendations on the survey of working women conducted during the preceding year. Mary Hanafin, as president of this committee, reported to the convention that the committee had constituted itself "a permanent organization, the object of which will be to investigate the abuses to which our sex is subjected by unscrupulous employers, to agitate the principles which our order teaches of equal pay for equal work, and the abolition of child labor."[11] From among the sixteen the women elected Mary Hanafin president, Mary O'Reilly (mill-worker) vice-president, Nellie Hardison (shoebinder) treasurer, and Leonora Barry (hosiery worker) general investigator. Their recommendations to the convention included setting up a women's department in the Knights, its purpose being to "free from the remorseless grasp of tyranny and greed the 1000's of underpaid women and girls in our large cities, who, suffering the pangs of hunger, cold and privation, oft times yield and fall into the yawning chasm of immorality."[12] The department was to maintain a full-time general investigator on salary, the expense to be covered by the Knights. All the committee's recommendations were accepted by the convention.

Who were these women who initiated the women's department of the Knights of Labor? Those who were shoebinders, active in the Knights since the year women were admitted to the order, had had prior experience in the Daughters of St. Crispin. They knew how to organize and conduct local union business as well as how to operate in a large con-

---

* The other four were a saleswoman, a machine operator, an ironer, and a housewife.

Some of the women delegates to the 1886 convention of the Knights of Labor, including Mrs. George Rodgers, holding her two-week-old daughter, Lizzie, whom she had brought with her on the long, sooty trip from Chicago to Richmond, Virginia.

vention. All of the women who came as delegates were leaders, elected from district assemblies that represented thousands of workers from local assemblies in each area. Then as now, attending a convention was a prize; running for election as a delegate was in itself a political undertaking within the district structure.

Elizabeth (Mrs. George) Rodgers, a delegate from Chicago and a leading woman in the Knights, has the distinction of being its first woman member. Mrs. Rodgers was the mother of twelve children and brought her baby of two weeks with her to the convention. She was a member of the Knights as a housewife,* and was the first woman to be elected a master workman of a district assembly. This job included presiding over 600 Knights, male and female, representing 40,000 members.[13] She had organized a union of working women in the 1870s, years before the Knights admitted women, and served as president of this union for two years. An elected delegate of the order to the Illinois State Trades Assembly, she represented her own Knights assembly at district meetings and served as a judge in the Knights of Labor district court. As an outstanding Chicago unionist, Mrs. Rodgers received the 1886 general assembly nomination to run for the post of general treasurer of the Order, but declined.

When Mrs. Rodgers was interviewed during the convention by temperance leader Frances Willard, also a member of the order, she was asked

---

* Housewives were considered workers eligible for membership in the Knights.

how she felt as the first woman to join the Knights. She replied: "My husband always believed that women should do anything they liked that was good and which they could do well. . . . I said to myself, 'there must be a first one, and so I'll go forward.' "[14]

Another of the women delegates, Mary O'Reilly, a millworker from Providence, Rhode Island, served as secretary in the women's department established by the Knights following the 1886 convention. She left that post only after Pennsylvania passed the country's first factory inspection bill and appointed her to the post of deputy factory inspector. She was one of the first women to serve in such a high government position and certainly the first millworker ever to do so.[15]

It was Leonora Barry, hosiery worker from Amsterdam, New York, who emerged as the foremost delegate at this 1886 convention. Her four-year stint as general investigator for the women's department and the records she left give insights into the lives and work of women during the 1880s that would be lost to us otherwise.[16]

Leonora Barry, General Investigator

Born in Cork, Ireland, in 1849, Leonora Kearney came to America as a child of three. When in her teens she taught school for several years, and in 1871 she married William Barry, also from Ireland. Barry died while their three children were still young, and shortly after his death their youngest child also died. To support her children, Leonora Barry moved to Amsterdam, New York, and went to work in a hosiery mill. She found that after her first full day of work she had earned just 11 cents. Her wages for the first week came to only 65 cents, and with that she had to support a family of three. As soon as she heard about the Knights of Labor, with its platform of equal pay for equal work, and as soon as women were admitted, she joined. With her abilities and her interest, it was not long before she was elected master workman of her assembly of 927 women, a representative to its district assembly, then a delegate to the 1886 general assembly meeting in Richmond, Virginia. There she met with the fifteen other women delegates and worked closely with them on the committee that recommended her appointment as general investigator, commissioned to "go forth and educate her sister working-women and the public generally as to their needs and necessities."[17]

Her job was a new one. It had never before existed on the American labor scene. There were no road maps or guides. Putting one son in boarding school and leaving the other with a relative, she plunged into her new work. Hundreds of letters came from women asking for help in establishing assemblies, and organizations of all kinds asked her to lecture. She herself felt it important to investigate and publicize factory conditions of women workers, but here she ran into a stone wall. Many employers refused her entrance to their plants, and she had no authority to force them to let her in. When she discovered that women who spoke to her about their working conditions during her investigations often were fired for doing so, she became cautious, reluctant to jeopardize women's jobs further. Meanwhile her correspondence both with women's assemblies and individual women workers grew. Her report of October 1888, for an eleven-month period, shows the range of her activities:

> 537 requests for her to help women organize
> 213 appointments filled
> nearly 100 different cities and towns visited
> new assemblies organized
> 100 speaking engagements met
> 789 communications received asking for advice or information;
>   all answered by Barry or her secretary, Mary O'Reilly
> 1,900 leaflets distributed
> 97 telegrams received and answered[18]

Sometimes her work was more like that of a business agent. For example, in Dubuque, Iowa, she helped two unions of overall workers to eliminate the employer practice of charging workers for electricity to run their machines and for the thread, needles, and oil they used. She estimated that this meant at least a 15 percent wage increase for each worker. Although Barry refused to lobby as we know it today (she thought it unladylike) and refused to buttonhole legislators or visit them in their offices, she did help to get a state factory inspection law passed when she testified before the Pennsylvania legislature.

Her work included establishing two cooperative shirt factories, one in Baltimore and the other in New York. Cooperatives were warmly supported by the Knights as an alternative to the wage system. Practical in her approach, Barry also began an insurance department, both to help women in need and to build their loyalty to the order. However, this idea was not widely accepted, Rhode Island being one of the few places where it caught on and the program was managed successfully. She also organized boycotts of products made by non-union labor.

The Knights supported women's suffrage as well as temperance, and Leonora Barry was a popular speaker at suffrage and temperance meetings. Through her public lectures she promoted increased education and industrial training for women (to enable them to find jobs other than in the low-paid unskilled fields), state factory inspection laws, abolition of the tenement system, and laws prohibiting child labor. She warned that mills were moving South and making wide use of child labor at a time when laws in the North were just beginning to limit it.

The educator in her tried to train women in union administration as she organized new assemblies. In 1887 she was made a general officer of the Knights, with an office at the order's headquarters in Philadelphia, and in 1888 her title was changed to "general instructor and director of women's work," with her salary raised from $12 a week to $4 a day, six days a week, plus travel expenses, a handsome amount for that time.[19]

But Barry was frequently discouraged. The problems she encountered in organizing had been faced by union leaders before her, and have been faced by others since her time. Meetings often were poorly attended, while "hundreds of people living within sight of the (meeting) hall either stayed home or fell over each other in their efforts to secure seats at a 10-cent show that was running in the town." She came to believe that women should be urged to "organize as a part of the industrial hive, rather than because they are women." Even when women had the training for jobs where they could earn more money, they would not take them, prevented by apathy and hopelessness. As Barry commented: "Through long years of endurance [they] have acquired, as a sort of second nature, the habit of submission and acceptance without question of any terms offered them, with the pessimistic view of life in which they see no hope."[20]

She saw women who made good wages but who would not extend a helping hand to those less fortunate. She sympathized with the women who resisted organization because of their fear of being fired, but not with those who held back because it was not their idea of a proper role for women. She felt that if women worked, they should be organized. She heard over and over from women the argument that they were only working for a little while, until they married and could leave their jobs forever.

She found, too, that women's assemblies repeatedly wrote to the Knights' headquarters asking to be allowed to elect a man as president, excusing themselves by saying that they lacked the experience, or that a man could do the job better. So many of these requests came in that the order printed permission forms to send out routinely to the women's assemblies. While she blamed tradition and women's education for many of their attitudes, on occasion she spoke out against "the neglect and indifference of their brother toilers" as one reason progress among women was so slow.[21]

In addition, Barry had to contend with criticism leveled against her by her own church. A Roman Catholic, she was deeply hurt when several priests, led by Father Peter McEnroe in Pennsylvania, termed the Knights a "vulgar immoral society" because it hired a woman organizer, and called her a "lady Tramp." Barry answered in an angry letter refuting the "slanderous attack upon my character and motives as a representative of a grand and Noble Order pledged to the service of humanity."[22] She proclaimed her right as "an Irishwoman, a Catholic, and an honest woman" to help her working sisters.

Although her contact with the Knights of Labor ended in 1890 with her marriage to Obadiah Lake,* Leonora Barry remained active in the causes of temperance and suffrage, playing a particularly important role in the successful Colorado campaign for state suffrage in 1893. A well-known and popular lecturer who combined charm and humor with her gifts as a public speaker, she was associated with two lecture bureaus, who booked her widely. Because of her past reputation with the Knights, she was often fondly called Mrs. Barry-Lake. She continued her speaking activities until 1928, when she was forced to withdraw from public life because of mouth cancer. She died two years later at the age of eighty.[23]

Women's Strikes in the Knights of Labor

In spite of the official position of Terence Powderly, who followed Uriah Stephens as Grand Master Workman of the Knights, that the organization should support peaceful resolution of labor disputes rather than strikes, members of the order were often forced to strike. The most frequent causes were wage cuts and discharges. Strikes were often long, bitter, and violent, and only occasionally received support from the national Knights. In August of 1885, New York cloak and shirt makers walked out in what the *New York World* called "not a strike but a revolt for bread and butter." Men and women held separate meetings, but as the *New York Times* reported, "they were united in action," and won wage increases and shorter hours.[24] Women's assemblies of textile workers and hatmakers struck in 1884, with each new strike gaining the reputation for women that led Powderly to call them "the best men in the Order." Women supported their union brothers on the picket line, giving scabs what was known then as the "ditch degree" and "water cure": while some groups of women tossed strikebreakers into ditches, others dumped buckets of water over them.[25]

The Yonkers, New York, strike of carpet weavers, 90 percent of

---

* Leonora Barry, who believed that women should work only when necessary, resigned from her post with the Knights when she married. Two other factors influenced her decision to leave: her husband worked in St. Louis, and she was both discouraged and disillusioned over what was happening to the order at that time. Internal dissension coupled with rapid membership loss did not bode well for its future.

whom were female, began because an employer fired a number of women who had joined the Knights. On a cold February day in 1885, 2,500 women walked out and formed a picket line around the mill. Of these 2,500, only 700 belonged to the Knights, but within a few days all had joined. Police violence backfired into sympathy for the women. During their protest, three women strikers were arrested and charged with walking near the struck plant; Ellen Tracy, Lizzie Wilson, and Mary Carey became a perfect issue around which the Knights rallied citizen strike support.

With public feeling so high, it seemed clear that no jury would convict the young women. To avoid an acquittal, the court tried to rule for a juryless trial. An appeal to a higher court forestalled this, a jury trial was ordered, and the women were acquitted. New York's labor movement united in a big dinner to honor the bravery of these women strikers. Among the 2,000 who attended were delegates from almost every union in the city, who watched the women each receive a medal stating:

IN HONOR
of the
ARREST OF A PICKET
in the
YONKERS STRIKE
May 18, 1885.[26]

The strike, a long one, lasted until the end of August, when workers returned without union recognition. The threatened wage cut, however, was withdrawn and a number of important grievances resolved. The reputation of women as militant members of the Knights of Labor was confirmed.

Significance of the Knights of Labor

In 1886 the Knights of Labor was at its peak, and claimed more than 700,000 members. However, its astounding growth from 50,000 in 1884 to this figure two years later meant that much of its claimed membership was on paper only. The Knights never had much control over or contact with its many new assemblies. For a number of reasons—lost strikes, idealistic investments in cooperatives that failed, battles with the emerging American Federation of Labor, poor leadership, and an increasing emphasis on agrarian workers—the Knights went rapidly downhill and in the 1890s no longer was a force in the labor movement. As an organization it was unable to fight the growing power of giant corporations and monopolies that used ever harsher tactics to defeat unionization.

Nonetheless, the role of the Knights of Labor in labor history during its nine short years of major influence should not be underestimated. For the first time an organization had reached out to almost all workers, skilled and unskilled, welcoming blacks and whites, men and women, and organizing them on a grand scale never before known in this country. It developed a legislative program which it sought to have enacted, and it brought together other concerned groups to promote laws that would settle labor disputes peacefully, end child labor and sweatshops, limit hours of work and night work for women, establish employer responsibility for work-related accidents, and effect mine and factory inspection and safety rules. Several states did adopt statutes in some of these areas. The Knights' strong interest in education led it to sponsor lectures that focused attention on these problems in an effort to arouse a public conscience about working conditions in America.

For women, the Knights was nothing short of revolutionary. Its women's department received the support of the order's national officers, who tried to put it on a permanent footing, encouraged it to report at each general assembly, and made its director a general officer of the organization. This was often in sharp contrast to the attitude of the average Knight, who usually did not cooperate with the women's department very enthusiastically, if at all. The order promoted equal pay for equal work, though with limited success. However, the New Jersey Commissioner of Labor stated in 1886: "Since the girls have joined the Knights of Labor here they make the same wages as men."[27] One of the best women available for the post of general investigator was named to it, and when she left in 1890, the Knights tried to fill the job with another qualified woman. Only the fact that Mrs. Alzina Stevens turned down their offer led the order to abandon the women's program. There is evidence that as long as she held the post, Leonora Barry had the freedom to develop her program and conduct organizing and educational activities as she saw fit. Recalling the handicaps of travel in the 1880s—the long, sooty, uncomfortable train trips, the horse-and-buggy rides in the rain, communication by telegraph and letter rather than by the easy convenience of the long-distance telephone—we can wonder that Barry accomplished all that she did. It would be many years before women again found the same welcome and open door in a labor organization.

Part 4

THE
WAGE-EARNING
WOMAN *1886−1910*

As the United States approached the twentieth century, its cities were crisscrossed with streetcars and elevated trains, Chicago and New York talked with each other over long-distance telephone, and automobiles were coming onto the popular market. Americans smoked three billion cigarettes in 1900, and consumer industries burgeoned. To supply services along with these goods, service industries developed and prospered, opening new jobs for women in stores and offices, laundries, beauty parlors, restaurants, and hotels.

Meatpackers had learned to use every part of the slaughtered animal in what was now one of the country's most dangerous industries, dangerous to the workers employed in it and to the consumers of its products. Commercial bread had become so accepted that housewives found themselves no longer baking—and who had ever thought that bread would come from a factory! The developing rayon industry brought with it a rush to produce ready-made women's wear, similar to the explosion into ready-mades in the men's clothing industry fifty years earlier. And cotton shirtwaists had become "the uniform" for the office girl and department-store clerk.

America was modernizing. Mail service improved. Hospitals were built, requiring more nurses to staff them. Schools were constructed for the children of the immigrants who continued to come to this country at an astounding rate, 12,053,538 between 1890 and 1910.

In 1890 almost 4 million women worked outside the home out of a total work force of 22 million, nearly one in every seven women in the country. Close to 1 million of these women were nonwhite, most of them still working in Southern agriculture, in household work, and in laundries. Only 3 in 100 nonwhite working women earned their livelihood in factories.

By 1900, women held jobs in 295 of the 303 separate occupations listed by the Twelfth Census. The overwhelming majority of these women were single and supported themselves. The married women who worked outside their homes did so out of economic need; as few as 5 percent of them were able to count on their husbands' earnings alone to support the family.

Some women, clustered in certain industries and jobs, sought organization into unions. In 1895 they made up 5 percent of all union members, although two economic recessions (1893–1897 and 1907–1909) plus em-

Women pushcart vendors were common at the turn of the century on
New York's Lower East Side.

ployer anti-union drives would reduce this to barely 3 percent by 1910
(perhaps 64,000 women out of a total of 1.5 million trade unionists). In
the period covered in Part Four, many national and international unions
still refused to accept women as members, and few of these unions
organized in the relatively unskilled occupations where most women
worked. Nonetheless, women did organize when they could, forming 546
local unions in communities throughout America. Most of these were chartered directly by the American Federation of Labor as federal locals, for as
small, independent locals they had a low survival rate. Unions of button
workers and of court reporters, of goldleaf cutters and of suspender workers, of theatrical wardrobe attendants and of domestic workers formed for
a brief period and were gone. However, women also composed more than
half of the union membership in five industries: women's clothing,
gloves, hat and cap making, shirtwaist and laundry, and tobacco.

Even though a number of industries had opened new jobs for women
at the turn of the century, including white-collar and clerical jobs, and
women were coming into the work force in increasing numbers, most still
found themselves at the lowest wage and skill levels. In 1899, men in
manufacturing industries averaged $587 a year, while women could ex-

pect to average $314. Black women earned only about one-half the wages of white women.

Part Four turns, then, to the period between 1886 and 1910, from the birth of the American Federation of Labor to the early years of the twentieth century.

By 1910 new jobs had begun to open for women. Here a group of street-car conductors pose for the camera.

11

WOMEN WORKERS AND THE EARLY AMERICAN FEDERATION OF LABOR *1886–1910*

Shall song and music be forgot
   When workers shall combine?
With love united may they not
   Have power almost divine?
Shall idle drones still live like queens
   On labor not their own?
Shall women starve while thieves and rings
   Reap where they have not sown?

—Sung by Chicago women unionists, Labor Day parade,
   September 1903

Scrubwomen sang proudly as they marched down Chicago's Michigan Avenue in the Labor Day parade of 1903 together with 30,00 other women unionists. Ellen Lindstrom led 8,000 garment workers, Catherine Groggins headed the line of 3,300 teachers, and the candymakers had a float on which they made marshmallows and tossed them to onlookers along the way. The parade included working women in twenty-six different trades, from cracker packers and coremakers to women who made feather dusters and fifty women horseshoe nailers.[1] For Chicago in 1903 had more working women in labor unions than any other city in the country at that time.* How did it happen, and what impact did the new American Federation of Labor have on the organization of women workers who, at the turn of the century, made up one-fifth of the American work force?

Formation of the American Federation of Labor

Samuel Gompers, who with Adolph Strasser formed the Federation of Organized Trades and Labor Unions in 1881, first discussed working women and their need for organization at the federation's second

---

* However, this record membership—31,400—dropped to 10,000 over the next five years. By 1908 unions remained in only 9 of the 25 trades that they had formerly covered. Economic recession, the open-shop movement, unsuccessful strikes, .and the AFL's lack of encouragement toward women's unions took their toll.

convention. He assured women that their organizations would in the future be accepted "on an equal footing with trade organizations of men."[2] This may have been because Mrs. Charlotte Smith, president of the Woman's National Industrial League, began attending the federation conventions in 1882. Little is known about Mrs. Smith or her league except that it supported opening more occupations to women, equal pay for equal work, and a cooperative effort by all labor unions to achieve shorter hours.[3] Though she was not granted a seat at a federation convention until 1884, she was present—possibly the only woman there—and undoubtedly pricked the consciences of the leaders by reminding them that there were 2.5 million working women in America.

It may have been Charlotte Smith's urging that caused the 1883 convention to go on record in favor of unions for women and to invite women to join the federation in supporting equal pay for equal work. They passed a similar resolution in 1885. It should be realized, however, that (as with the printers and cigar makers discussed in Chapter 9) the issue of equal pay was complicated. Unions were not strong enough to enforce such a policy except in the crafts where no women worked anyway. If it had been promoted aggressively in industries where women worked, it would still in most cases not have affected the women, for as yet they rarely held any but the most unskilled jobs. Moreover, if the unions had insisted on equal pay where women and men did perform the same work, employers would have hired men, not women; they had introduced women into these job categories only to save money. Thus while the principle was sound, it cannot be seen without its ramifications; the key result of equal pay, unless it had carried with it equal access to jobs, would have been to throw women out of work.

In 1886 American labor history marked a red-letter year. The Federation of Organized Trades and Labor Unions re-formed into the American Federation of Labor, a loosely knit body of autonomous national and international unions dedicated primarily to organizing and protecting crafts and skilled workers. A new kind of labor organization, it believed in unions achieving immediate objectives themselves rather than counting on the government to pass regulatory legislation which was rarely enforced. It opposed organizing competing unions in the same trade (dual unionism) and supported the closed shop to protect its members from the rising tide of immigrant workers. While its leaders professed a socialist philosophy, the organization's official political stance was to reward labor's friends and punish its enemies, and to avoid forming a separate labor party that would dissipate its strength. (The AFL Executive Board abandoned this policy only twice: in 1924, when it supported Robert LaFollette, Sr., in his bid for the presidency on the Progressive

Party ticket, and again in 1952, when the AFL convention endorsed
Adlai Stevenson and the Democratic ticket.)

The AFL was pragmatic, it held its member unions together, and it
survived. Differing from the Knights of Labor in its view of strikes, it
knew it would have to achieve its ends through using this weapon; that it
would face court injunctions and employer opposition. It was ready to
give its member unions support and to utilize boycotts wherever these
would be effective. Through its emphasis on separate craft unions, it
fostered worker solidarity within each trade, and it believed that going too
far outside the craft or trade would weaken the support that union members were willing to give each other.

Women in the Early AFL

From the start, women seem to have been eligible for membership in
the AFL. The 1888 convention report of AFL President Samuel Gompers
urged all unions to help organize women. Where a craft union did not
cover the job category of women in a particular trade, the AFL was prepared to charter a federal local directly affiliated with the federation itself.
But federal locals rarely had the same bargaining strength alone that they
would have had as part of a national union.

Some national unions did permit women to join, but only if they
organized their own locals. In these instances, women usually sat in on
negotiations but were largely ignored when agreements were reached.
Women complained: "The men think that the girls should not get as
good work as the men and should not make half as much money as a
man."[4]

On the other hand, where women were accepted into local unions
along with the men, they frequently found union dues so high that at
their unskilled level and low pay they could not afford them. Where they
were admitted on a reduced-dues schedule, it meant both reduced benefits and a lesser voice in union affairs.

Conflicts occurred where a national union did not admit women, yet
its jurisdiction covered a craft in which women worked. Such a situation
faced women boot and shoe workers of Pontiac, Illinois. In a letter of
appeal to the AFL national office, the women explained that they wanted
to join the Boot and Shoe Workers union but found the dues too high.
They requested the AFL's help in persuading the union to reduce its
dues. When asked to lower them, the union declined, its secretary-treasurer
stating: "[These women] evidently want to organize on the bargain-
counter plan, and we can well do without such members." Next, the
women appealed to the AFL to charter them directly as a local, but the

Boot and Shoe Workers union protested this so vehemently that the AFL refused.[5] It was not long before the women, discouraged everywhere they turned for help, lost their organization.

This was not the only way that national and international unions kept women out. They restricted apprenticeship programs to men, thereby limiting women to unskilled jobs which often made them ineligible for union membership. One of the protests that President Gompers received about this stated:

> It is an evil combination. Lack of skill keeps many of us from entering the unions of skilled craftsmen, and rigid apprenticeship regulations prevent us from becoming apprentices to the trade and thereby rising to the rank of skilled workers.[6]

Most international unions did not have constitutional clauses excluding women from membership, but they had no way of enforcing their open-door pronouncements on their affiliated local unions, which continued to do just as they pleased. Not only would many of them not admit women, but they also would not accept women's transfer cards from other local unions in the same international. Local unions had autonomy and often shaped their policies to exclude women and black workers.

Gompers also received letters from men protesting policies in effect in some of these local unions. The president of United Mine Workers District 5, Pittsburgh, wrote:

> Several groups of the working women of the Pittsburgh area requested me to give them information on how they could get organized. I contacted the various unions of the trades involved, after which the women themselves approached them. I have learned that these women were told that there was no room for them in the unions they approached. Most of the women are so discouraged that they are ready to abandon the plan to organize, and I wonder if there is not some way that they could be attached to the American Federation of Labor directly.[7]

Nor were women particularly welcome at local union meetings even when they were members. These meetings, long held to be the province of the men, often conveyed the atmosphere of a club rather than of an organization conducting union business. Cigar smoke filled the hall, which was located as often as not above a saloon frequented by the men, and meetings sometimes turned boisterous. Often they lasted until far into the night, which was hard on women who had household chores to perform before going to work the next morning. It cramped the style of men to have women present; nor was women's participation in the conducting of union business appreciated. It took an unusually aggressive woman to get the floor and make herself heard, although her help as recording secretary was usually accepted. Where women had only half the voting rights because they paid lower dues, their participation was invited even less.

From 1890 on, however, women did not stand idly by. That year the AFL convention was attended by its first woman delegate: Mary Burke, charter member and first vice-president of the Retail Clerks International Protective Association.* She introduced a resolution urging the AFL to appoint several women organizers to help unionize women workers, but her motion, duly passed, was not implemented for several years, and then only halfheartedly.

Among the Federal Labor Unions chartered by the AFL directly, the most famous and important was Ladies Federal Labor Union Number 2703, granted its charter in June 1888. Elizabeth Morgan, its secretary and prime mover, was an organizer reminiscent of Sarah Bagley, mill-worker and organizer of the Lowell Female Labor Reform Association. Into Local 2703 Morgan brought women workers from a wide range of occupations: clerks, bookbinders, candymakers, typists, dressmakers, music teachers, gum makers, laundresses, and others. In the next four years, out of this "mixed" local grew twenty-three separate unions of women in individual trades (shirtmakers, shoeworkers, watchmakers, bookbinders), for each group of ten workers from one trade was spun off into a new local to organize women in that occupation.[8]

Elizabeth Morgan, whom some accounts name as Hannah M. Morgan, was born in Birmingham, England, in 1850 and became a millworker like her parents when she was eleven. She married Thomas Morgan in 1868 and they came together to this country a year later. Thomas Morgan found work as a machinist in Chicago and joined the National Union of Machinists and Blacksmiths. During the depression of 1873, while the family suffered through fifteen weeks of his unemployment, the Morgans became avowed socialists. Elizabeth Morgan had joined the Sovereigns of Industry, a transitory cooperative society, and in 1881 became a charter member of the Chicago Knights of Labor.

In 1888, Elizabeth Morgan was elected secretary of Ladies' Federal Labor Union Number 2703, which she had been instrumental in organizing. In a letter to Samuel Gompers, she wrote:

> My education is but poor, but I will do the best I can as I like many other children had to work when but 11 years old. I went to work in a Mill and worked from 10 to 16 hours a day and for that reason I am not very good to write. . . .[9]

* Mary Burke also chaired the opening session of the founding convention of the Retail Clerks in 1888.

With the women of Local 2703 behind her, Morgan used her influence and ability to organize the Illinois Women's Alliance, uniting women's groups interested in suffrage, temperance, health, housing, and child labor reform into a coalition to promote state legislation in these areas. Its success was remarkable. New laws strengthened the Compulsory Education Act of Illinois and appointed truant officers, some of them women. Five women factory inspectors for the state were appointed; new school construction was authorized; and one Women's Alliance member was assigned to the Chicago Board of Education. The alliance worked for laws prohibiting the employment of children under fourteen, and in 1890 the Chicago City Council enacted a bill to this effect. A year later the state passed a similar bill, but a lack of enforcement powers rendered it ineffective.

One night at a union meeting Morgan heard Cloak Makers Union president Abraham Bisno describe the "sweating dens" of Chicago's clothing industry. She promptly organized an investigation of these conditions through the Women's Alliance, and got the Chicago Trades and Labor Assembly to print 10,000 copies of the alliance report. For the first time the public read about wage cuts that meant near-starvation; fourteen- and sixteen-hour working days; crowded, filthy, unhealthy working conditions; and children who worked beside their parents, learning to pick out basting stitches when they were five years old or even less. Popular outcry was loud and vigorous, but Elizabeth Morgan suggested that consumers may have been more worried about the unclean condition of the clothes they purchased than about the conditions of the men, women, and children who made them.

When she learned that Congress planned an investigation into sweatshop conditions, she sent the congressional committee chairman a copy of her report, and so it happened that the committee opened its hearings in the city of Chicago, with Elizabeth Morgan as its first witness.[10] Governor John Altgeld launched a separate state inquiry into Chicago's sweating system, and ultimately the state legislature passed the Factory and Workshop Inspection Act (the Sweatshop Act). Elizabeth Morgan and two active reform leaders, Florence Kelley and Jane Addams, with the support of the trade unions of Illinois, had been victorious. But the battle was not yet over. Employers now formed the Illinois Manufacturers Association specifically to fight the provision of the new Sweatshop Act that limited the working day for women to 8 hours. A test case heard by the Illinois Supreme Court upset the hours limitations law; *William E. Richie* v. *The People* became the first court decision of this kind in the country. However, Governor Altgeld appointed Florence Kelley, former director of the

Consumers' League, to enforce the factory inspection portion of the law, and in 1893 Alzina Parsons Stevens* became her assistant. The dedication of these women was responsible for starting Illinois on the long, slow road toward enforcing those provisions of the new legislation not affected by the court decision.[11]

In 1894, Elizabeth Morgan was the only woman delegate at the AFL convention, representing the now-famous Ladies Federal Union Number 2703. This convention made history in two ways. First, it went on record in support of resolutions Morgan initiated to strengthen state compulsory school-attendance laws, to promote the 8-hour day for women and children, and to abolish the tenement sweatshop system.† Second, Morgan was nominated and ran against P. J. McGuire, first vice-president of the AFL (the man who had led the 8-hour movement in 1886), for his post in the federation. While she received just 226 votes and McGuire won with 1,865, labor journalist Alice Henry put it in perspective when she called it "a vote for those days large enough to reflect credit equally upon the woman for whom it was cast and on the men who cast it."[12]

Chicago women were not the only ones to organize in the early 1890s. Between 1895 and 1905, women are known to have conducted 83 strikes completely on their own, winning 35, partially succeeding in 11 other instances, and failing in 37. Out of a total of 15,726 strikes recorded during that period, women took part in 1,262, for women would often support men on strike even when they themselves were not involved in the dispute.[13]

One of the more celebrated women's strikes was that of the Shirt, Waist and Laundry Workers Union of Troy, New York. Angry over wage cuts that brought their earnings down to 50 cents a day, women workers in the United Shirt and Collar Company walked out in January 1891. Before long, more than 500 women who worked in other shirt and collar plants in Troy joined the strike and turned to the state AFL for help. Soon they had organized a local union directly chartered by the

---

* Alzina Stevens's background is described in the footnote on p. 80 above. As chief factory inspector of Illinois Florence Kelley made good use of Stevens's past experience in organizing, writing about women workers, promoting the union label, and speaking on the problems of women in factory work. Florence Kelley, "Industrial Democracy," *Outlook,* December 15, 1906, pp. 930, 931.

† These were issues, however, that presented reformers with a dilemma. Laws for shorter hours said nothing about maintaining wage levels; pay cuts resulting from shorter hours meant starvation to workers living in sweatshop poverty. Forcing sweatshops to close if they did not improve their working conditions meant loss of jobs for women who had no other way to earn a living. The pathetic wages of children working in the tenements in violation of school-attendance laws often meant the difference between the family's eating or not. The sweatshops were evil; so was starvation. In a time long before unemployment insurance and government provision of welfare and jobs in periods of economic recession, there were few options for unskilled workers, especially women.

AFL and elected Mary Evaline, their twenty-three-year-old leader, president, and Dora Sullivan vice-president. To meet employer intransigence, the state AFL announced a boycott against the United Shirt and Collar Company, and this threat brought victory, at least initially. The company signed an agreement including a new set of wages, and soon the other struck companies capitulated. The AFL, seeing its chance to organize thousands of women workers in the state, put Mary Evaline on its staff as special organizer for collar and cuff workers and added Dora Sullivan shortly afterward in a campaign that organized several locals of shirtworkers in this mid-state garment center. However, within a few years the situation had changed completely. The United Shirt and Collar Company had broken the union during a long and bitter eleven-week strike. Membership in the Troy Shirt, Waist and Laundry Workers Union had dropped drastically. In an effort to rebuild, the union sought help from the central labor body of Troy, but found that the predominantly skilled workers there were uninterested in helping them and even hostile. The union's president, Walter Charriere, complained of this attitude in a letter to Samuel Gompers on February 8, 1904:

> A major handicap to our already exceedingly difficult task of organizing our craft throughout the country arises from the fact that in many localities the Central Labor bodies dominated by unions composed almost exclusively of men refuse to recognize our locals and the women delegates duly elected by them. . . . the female members of our craft . . . with the evidence now apparent that the unions of men in the Central Bodies are hostile to them and unwilling to support them, are even more timid. . . . it is causing many of our members to think of leaving organized labor. Hence our appeal to you that you take this up at your earliest convenience.[14]

In 1891 the only two women delegates to the AFL convention were put on a committee on women's work, one as chairman, one as secretary. Quite possibly, they were the only two people on the committee. Nonetheless, Eva McDonald Valesh, editor of a Minnesota labor paper, and Ida Van Etten, representing the Working Women's Society of New York, recommended that the convention create the post of National Organizer for Women at a salary of $1,200 a year plus expenses; that the AFL appoint a woman to fill it; and that it make her a member of the AFL executive council. In her report to the convention, Van Etten closed with this plea to organize women workers:

> Thus it can readily be seen that women-workers either must become organized and receive not only equal pay for equal work, but also equal opportunities for working, or they will, by degrees, naturally form an inferior class in every trade in which they enter. . . . In this condition they will be a constant menace to wages; they will be used,

in case of strikes and lockouts, to supply the places of union men; and, in short, we shall witness the horrible spectacle of workers whose interests are identical being used against each other for the purpose of lowering the general condition of their class.[15]

The convention referred the resolution favorably to the executive council to act upon.[16] In 1892, bindery worker Mary E. Kenney was appointed the first woman organizer for the AFL, although the council declined to make it a post with executive council status.*

Mary Kenney, born in Hannibal, Missouri, in 1864, was one of the children of Irish working-class immigrants, her father a railroad worker, her mother a cook. After the fourth grade in school, she was apprenticed to a dressmaking establishment, where she worked for two years without receiving any pay. She was fourteen when her father died and she found work in a bindery in order to support her sick mother. There she rapidly learned all the operations in bookbinding that the company would teach to a woman. When she went to Chicago in the 1880s, she had no trouble in finding a bindery job. She promptly joined Ladies Federal Local Union Number 2703, and proceeded to organize women in her industry into Woman's Bookbinding Union Number 1. She moved into Hull House, where she got to know Jane Addams and enlisted her help in organizing work and in setting up a working girls' boarding club. Kenney is described as a beautiful young woman with red-gold hair and deep blue eyes, and as a persuasive and dynamic public speaker.

She must have been persuasive indeed, for the AFL was a struggling young federation with little money and less inclination for organizing women workers, yet it added her to its staff for this purpose. Regrettably, after only six months, it commended her for her work but asked her to leave, pleading tight finances. Kenney had courage as well as persuasiveness. Few women had ever been full-time paid labor organizers before, and undoubtedly she met with resistance to her role as well as to her message—hardly a popular one—as she traveled through upstate New York and then on to Boston in her efforts to organize women workers.

When her job was terminated she returned to Chicago, where she worked briefly with Florence Kelley, newly appointed factory inspector of Illinois, and helped to promote a state woman suffrage bill (which failed to pass).

After her marriage in 1894 to John O'Sullivan, Boston labor editor and organizer, she and her husband lived in Boston's Denison House, a settlement house similar to Hull House, and she continued to work, encouraged by her husband to do so even after they had four children. She

* The executive council traditionally has been composed of elected presidents of selected affiliated national and international unions, not of appointed staff such as organizers.

helped rubber workers and laundry and garment workers in their organizing efforts. In 1902, after the death of her husband in a tragic accident, Mary O'Sullivan had to find work to support her young children and turned to managing real estate. Conducting classes for the tenants and a summer program for young working women were pet projects of hers. In 1903 she was one of the founders of the Women's Trade Union League (see Chapter 15), and in 1912 (see Chapter 19) she defied the AFL at the time of the Lawrence textile strike in order to remain in Lawrence and help the Industrial Workers of the World (IWW). In 1914 she was appointed inspector for the Massachusetts Board of Labor and Industries, a post which she held until she retired in 1934. She died nine years later at the age of seventy-nine.[17]

It was not long after the executive council had asked Mary Kenney to leave that Gompers tried again to place a woman organizer on the AFL staff, hiring Miss E. E. Pitt, a Typographical Union member from Boston and an experienced volunteer organizer. Early in 1894 Gompers requested that the executive council appropriate funds for four more women organizers. Not only was he voted down, but Miss E. E. Pitt was removed from her organizing job. The council gave several reasons for this, reasons that may have a familiar ring even today. First, it claimed that it would not be possible to find qualified women to fill the four jobs. Second, it stated that the money could be spent more effectively by hiring men as organizers. Finally, it pointed to the number of specific requests for organizing help that were coming in from unions composed largely or entirely of men, as compared with the vague suggestion that women organizers might be successful in unionizing more women.[18] The AFL council recognized that even those unions that admitted women often had to schedule lower dues for them and did not find it profitable to increase their numbers of women members to any great extent. Although in 1898 the AFL did hire a woman organizer, Eva McDonald Valesh, she was expected to fill the dual role of union organizer and assistant editor of the *American Federationist*, official publication of the AFL.[19]

Basically, both the executive council and Samuel Gompers himself believed that married women should not be working at all. The *Woman's Home Companion* interviewed Gompers in 1905, asking him whether he felt that wives should contribute to their families' support by working outside the home. Though in later years he would change his mind, he answered the question emphatically in the negative:

> No! . . . In our time, and at least in our country, generally speaking, there is no necessity for the wife contributing to the support of the family by working . . . the wife as a wage-earner is a disadvantage economically considered, and socially is unnecessary.[20]

He spoke for the organized skilled workers of America, it is true, who undoubtedly agreed with him that a woman's place was still at home. However, they were not alone. Society in general frowned on married women working, and husbands felt they had failed if they could not support their wives and families. Most working women looked forward to the moment when they could leave their jobs and devote their full time to homemaking. Nor were women unionists who became leaders the role models that they are today. As will be seen, most of them were forced to choose between marriage and their work in the labor movement, and many remained single throughout their lives, bucking the pressure they must have felt to marry and raise a family. Dedicated to their work, they were nonetheless often lonely, and were in a sense outcasts who found friendship and encouragement with each other while devoting almost all their waking hours to their work.

By 1910, in spite of society's attitude, growing numbers of women worked outside the home and composed 21 percent of the country's total work force. It would not be long before they would be a force in the labor movement.

12

WOMEN'S WAGES, WOMEN'S WORK

You never come back.
I say good-bye when I see you going in the doors,
The hopeless open doors that call and wait
And take you then for—how many cents a day?
How many cents for the sleepy eyes and fingers?

I say good-bye because I know they tap your wrists,
In the dark, in the silence, day by day,
And all the blood of you drop by drop,
And you are old before you are young.
        You never come back.

                    —Carl Sandburg, "Mill Doors"

At the turn of the century, one-half of America lived in cities. Except in the crowded tenement sections of the biggest of these, such as New York and Chicago, women still cultivated vegetable patches, raised rabbits and chickens in their back yards, and canned much of the food their families ate during the winter months. Many supplemented family incomes by taking in boarders. In 1890 the United States Bureau of Labor found that this was true for one in every five working-class families. For some families, it constituted the entire income. In Perry, New York, for example, almost every family took in six or more workers who came from outlying farms to work in the town's woolen mill.[1]

Sewing, another home occupation for women, might involve dressmaking, mending, or making over worn-out, outgrown, or outmoded garments. Especially in the cities, women brought work home from garment factories, or made cigars, artificial flowers, and caps, often in tenement sweatshops. They also took in laundry. While the 1890 census found more than 200,000 laundresses, mostly black women who often worked in their employers' homes, it neglected to count the many women who provided laundry service to boarders on an individual basis.[2]

The same census reported 1.2 million women in domestic service as housekeepers, office cleaning women, maids, cooks, or hotel chambermaids. Most were young and single and worked as live-in help, earning from $2 to $5 for a workweek one-and-a-half times as long as that of a factory

209

worker. Half were foreign-born or had parents who were. One in four was black.[3]

By 1900, one-fifth of America's 25 million women were in the work force.[4] At least half of all workers in textile mills and tobacco factories were women, while in the garment industries they outnumbered the men. Women worked in the shoe industry, in food processing and canning, and in heavy industries such as foundries and tin-plate mills. In every case they held "women's jobs," for the most part unskilled, offering little chance to learn a trade or move up the job or pay ladder. Even where women held jobs requiring considerable skill, such as coremaking in foundries, which took two years to learn, they earned just one-half the wages of non-union men doing the same work and one-third those of union men. Yet nearly one-quarter of Pittsburgh's coremakers were women in 1907, when government inspector Elizabeth Butler studied women workers in that city. She found the men in the industry fearful that

Women and children lug home bundles that will keep them sewing far into the night. By 1890 the tenement sweatshop system was in full force, as this *Harper's Weekly* drawing shows.

women were undercutting their jobs, yet unwilling to admit women into their union and to permit union men to work in the same plants with women. Thus in the core room of the largest foundry in Pittsburgh, all fifty of the workers were women.[5]

Women had entered the burgeoning electrical industry, doing not only routine work such as winding coils but also heavy work such as splitting mica. They shaped bolts and screws, braided and twisted cable in the cablemaking companies (at a starting wage of 50 cents a day), and worked in hinge factories and enameling plants. In tin-plate mills, women and boys performed unskilled work as "openers." They wore gloves with a heavy lead piece in the palm, with which they took hold of a sheet of welded plates, beat it on the ground to separate the parts, and then made an opening. Forcibly tearing the plates apart, they held

In immigrant families crowded into squalid tenements, everyone worked as soon as he or she was able. From an 1883 drawing in *Harper's Weekly*.

part of the sheet down with one knee while they tore the metal with the other.[6]

Factory women, like women in domestic service, tended to be single and young. Three out of four were under twenty-five years of age, and fewer than one in twenty were married (though one in twelve domestic workers were married women). They were almost always white, for few black women—or men—were accepted for factory jobs. Three-fourths were either foreign-born themselves or had foreign-born parents.

This was the era in which reformers, settlement-house workers, and journalists began to expose the inhumanity of tenement sweatshops and factory work, particularly the conditions under which women and children were so often employed. In 1893 Helen Campbell wrote, in *Women Wage-Earners*, of the conditions turned up by the Massachusetts Bureau of Labor. They had found

Women workers, many of them Scandinavian immigrants, shown in the rag-sorting room of a Minnesota paper mill about 1910.

employees packed "like sardines in a box"; thirty-five persons, for example, in a small attic without ventilation of any kind. Some were in . . . basements where dampness was added to cold and bad air. . . . In one case girls were working in "little pens all shelved over. . . . There are no conveniences for women; and men and women use the same closets, wash-basins, and drinking cups, etc." . . . In another a water-closet in the center of the room filled it with a sickening stench. . . .

Matchmakers, from an 1871 drawing in *Harper's Weekly*. As early as 1838, "phossy jaw" was known to be an occupational disease of workers in match factories; it destroyed the lower part of the face. Not until 1912 was federal legislation passed against the use of phosphorus in this industry.

> . . . Feather-sorters, fur-workers, cotton-sorters, all workers on any material that gives off dust, are subject to lung and bronchial troubles. In soap-factories the girls' hands are eaten by the caustic soda, and by the end of the day the fingers are often raw and bleeding. In making buttons, pins, and other manufactures . . . there is always liability of getting the fingers jammed or caught. For the first three times the wounds are dressed without charge. After that the person injured must pay expenses. . . .
>
> In food preparation girls who clean and pack fish get blistered hands and fingers from the saltpetre. . . . Others in "working stalls" stand in cold water all day. . . .
>
> In match-factories . . . necrosis often attacks the worker, and the jaw is eaten away. . . .

Helen Campbell continues:

> The Factory Inspection Law for the State of New York, in detail much the same as that of Massachusetts, is sufficiently full and explicit to secure to all workers better conditions. . . . There is, however, constant violation . . . and this must remain true for all States, until the number of inspectors is made in some degree adequate to the demand. . . .[7]

Massachusetts was not the only state to investigate conditions of women workers. New York, Connecticut, California, and others followed suit. In 1888 the United States Bureau of Labor issued a report on women wage earners in 22 cities and 343 firms. In each city it found wages low. In Ohio, for example, "shirts were being made for 36 cents a dozen . . . the rules of one establishment paying such wages, employing a large number of females, required that the day's labor should commence and terminate with prayer and thanksgiving."[8]

According to a 1905 survey, women's wages averaged $5.25 a week, from which most paid at least $2.25 for board and lodging, if single, and with which many women tried to support families. Often they did not earn even this amount. If they had worked steadily over the year, their average wages would have totaled $273.00, but industries where women worked seldom provided a full year's employment. Although men averaged yearly earnings of $440.00, almost twice those of women workers, even this did not come close to the figure of $800.00 that was considered the minimum a family of four needed to maintain itself.[9]

Women in the Steam Laundries

How would you like to iron a shirt a minute? Think of standing at a mangle just above the washroom with the hot steam pouring up through the floor for 10, 12, 14 and sometimes 17 hours a day! Sometimes the floors are made of cement and then it seems as though one were standing on hot coals, and the workers are dripping with perspiration. Perhaps you have complained about the chemicals used in the washing of your clothes, which cause them to wear out quickly, but what do you suppose is the effect of these chemicals upon the workers? They are . . . breathing air laden with particles of soda, ammonia, and other chemicals! The Laundry Workers Union . . . in one city reduced this long day to 9 hours, and has increased the wages 50 percent. . . .[10]

Investigations turned up not only low wages and workweeks 78 hours long, but found that women were fired for refusing to perform overtime at no pay. Illinois factory inspector Florence Kelley reported women fainting at their work: "Girls have been removed from the laundry to the hospital suffering exhaustion after working sixteen, eighteen, and even twenty hours in heat and dampness in ill-ventilated laundries."[11]

In San Francisco in 1900, laundry workers "lived in," each laundry providing board and lodging for its employees.

The dormitories were stretched places, with four beds in each small room. The food was poor and scanty, and even though the girls worked until midnight or after, no food was allowed after the evening meal at 6 o'clock. Half an hour only was allowed for lunch. Early in the morning, the women were routed out in no gentle manner and by 6 o'clock the unwholesome breakfast was over, and every one hard at work. . . .[12]

These laundry workers earned no more than $8.10 in cash wages each month, in addition to their room and board. Those who lived at home could expect from $17.50 to $25.00 a month. So many letters of complaint were received by newspapers and by the California State Labor Commissioner about conditions in these laundries that the state decided to investigate. Inspectors found violations of the law forbidding work after 10:00 P.M., with women often on the job until 2:00 in the morning. As a result a new ordinance was passed forbidding work after 7:00 at night.

By this time laundry workers had realized that no law would be enforced unless they themselves got together to demand it. Three hundred women applied to the Laundry Workers International Union for a charter. Although the men in the laundries did not want women in their union, to its credit the parent International Union insisted that the women be admitted.

The organizing campaign was conducted secretly, as Hannah Mahony (later Nolan) realized that many of the women were too intimidated by the employers to join the new union openly. Within sixteen weeks a majority had signed up, along with the men. Not until the union was strong did it announce its demands: elimination of the boardinghouse system, shorter hours, wages of $6 to $10 a week, nine holidays a year, time-and-a-half for overtime, and a regular lunch hour with a fine imposed on those not taking it.

By the time these demands were presented to the employers, it was too late for them to fight the union. Among later gains that workers won was the 9-hour day. For years this laundry union thrived, even surviving the tragic San Francisco earthquake and fire of 1906, which destroyed its union headquarters and two-thirds of the city's laundries.

In 1907 the union presented new demands for the 8-hour day and higher wages. When the owners refused, 1,100 workers from fourteen laundries walked out. The union was able to hold out for eleven weeks, supporting its members, and reached a compromise settlement that brought workers the 51-hour week, to be reduced gradually until the 8-hour day was in place by April of 1910. There was to be no work before seven in the morning. All work after 5:00 at night was to receive overtime, except on Mondays, when laundries worked until 6:00. By 1912 the San Francisco laundry workers had brought up wages by 30 percent, installed safety measures in the plants, and organized all the city's steam laundries.

Few unions in such a low-wage, unskilled industry had ever lasted so long or accomplished so much.[13]

Elizabeth Butler, who studied the steam laundries of Pittsburgh in 1907, found that 2,185 of the 2,402 workers were women. Wages in the steam laundries had risen after the turn of the century, because employers in Pittsburgh competed for labor, even trying to steal workers from each other. But the work was physically hard and unhealthy. Steam from huge vats that boiled all day long rose from the washrooms in the basement to the floor above. There was no relief from the steam, for the windows had to remain closed against the soot from the city's iron and steel mills, which would soil the clothes even before they were out of the tubs.

Poor drainage in the basements meant flooding, so that workers stood in water all day long. While the men ran the washing machines, the women hand-washed items too delicate to put in the vats. Basement work paid $1 for a 10-hour day. Although this was higher than in some trades, the work was so unhealthy and respiratory disease so common that women preferred almost any other work and came to the laundries as a last resort.

Mangle operators also worked in unbearable heat for $3.00 to $3.50 a week. "Shakers" took the wet clothes as they were brought from the washroom and shook them out to be fed into the mangle.

> Every one of the hundred and twenty-five girls worked with frenzied energy as the avalanche of clothes kept falling in upon us and were sent with lightning speed through the different processes, from the tubs to the packers' counters. Nor was there any abatement of the snowy landslide—not a moment to stop and rest the aching arms.[14]

Wet sheets and towels made this heavy work. In fact, women did not last long in laundry work, perhaps two to four years. Mangles were dangerous machines even when the inadequate guards were installed, which they frequently were not. After an exhausing day of work, women easily caught fingers, hands, and even arms in the machinery.* Ironers' and pressers' work carried an additional hazard: the heavy irons were gas-heated. In England this gas had been found so dangerous that ventilation standards were prescribed by law, but in the United States in the early 1900s no such laws covered laundries.

Men and women competed for the elite laundry jobs, sorting and

---

* Elizabeth Butler found just one laundry with good working conditions, including seats for its workers, ventilated workrooms, and decent wages. She discovered that this company did the laundry for the Pullman cars and for towel companies and restaurants, and required perfect work. The women who worked in this laundry did turn out high-quality work and at a faster rate than in the other laundries. Butler credits the good working conditions and wages with bringing in steady, competent workers on whom the firm could rely.

checking. Men who held these jobs earned $12 to $20 dollars a week; women earned $5 to $12 for performing exactly the same work.[15]

Canning Moves to the Factory

One of the new and often dangerous industries which offered increasing employment for women in the early years of the new century was that of canning and food processing. Because the industry was seasonal, manufacturers were able to get exemptions from hours limitations for their workers. From the start, women made up over half the work force in canning. At first the factories were located at the edges of towns, and women who worked during the day in the fields picking the fruit or vegetables would come to the factories at night to do the canning. Farmers' wives and daughters, sometimes whole families, were employed. Some manufacturers preferred to hire newly arrived immigrant women. As one owner told an investigator, "They are the best workers I have; they keep at it just like horses."[16]

Most cannery workers were young women sixteen to twenty years old. While men in the factories did the cooking, the women prepared the raw vegetables and fruits, washed, filled, and labeled bottles, and cut and labeled the tin cans. Labelers, as Elizabeth Butler found in her 1907 study, earned 60 cents a day; skilled bottlers might make as much as $1.25. Women averaged no more than $3.50 to $4.00 a week for six 11-hour days that stretched to 14 hours or more during the rush season.[17] Butler points out that the workweek of 72 hours was at the time 12 hours above the legal limit for women's work in Pennsylvania.

In one Pittsburgh factory Butler came upon women tinning molasses.

> Girls are employed for everything in connection with the canning of molasses. . . . The women who fill the cans work, four at a machine, in a dark room, where floor and walls, machines and girls, are sticky with the exudations of syrup, and a visitor can scarcely walk without being fastened like a fly to what ever spot he touches. . . . Molasses comes in a continuous stream from the spout of the machine and spatters the girls as well as every exposed spot of floor or wall nearby. One girl pushes the cans under the spout, another takes them out and puts the tops on, a third clamps the top at another machine, and a fourth puts the can on a chain which takes it to the labeling table. The machine which puts the tops on the cans is difficult to adjust, yet if it is a sixteenth of an inch out of gear, the molasses splashes all over the girls and the floors. . . .[18]

One of the most vivid descriptions of conditions in the canning and bottling industry was given by Mother Jones (Mary Harris Jones), United Mine Workers organizer and a legend in herself. During the 1905–1911 period, when she was not on the organizing payroll of the Mine Workers, she often worked in different industries to help support herself, and in 1910 spent two months alongside women who washed bottles in a Milwaukee brewery. In the *Miner's Magazine* she reported the conditions she found:

> Condemned to slave daily in the wash-room in wet shoes and wet clothes, surrounded with foul-mouthed, brutal foremen . . . the poor girls work in the vile smell of sour beer, lifting cases of empty and full bottles weighing from 100 to 150 pounds, in their wet shoes and rags, for they cannot buy clothes on the pittance doled out to them. . . . Rheumatism is one of the chronic ailments and is closely followed by consumption. . . . The foreman even regulates the time [the girls] may stay in the toilet room, and in the event of overstaying it gives the foreman an opportunity for indecent and foul language. Should the patient slave forget herself and take offense, it will cost her the job. And after all, bad as it is, it is all that she knows how to do. To deprive her of the job means less crusts and worse rags. . . . Many of the girls have no home nor parents and are forced to feed and clothe and shelter themselves . . . on $3.00 per week.
>
> No matter how cold, how stormy, how inclement the weather, many walk from their shacks to their work, for their stipend precludes any possibility of squeezing a street car ride out of it.
>
> An illustration of what these poor girls must submit to, one about to become a mother told me with tears in her eyes that every other day a depraved specimen of mankind took delight in measuring her girth and passing . . . comments.
>
> While the wage paid is 75 to 85 cents a day, [they] are not permitted to work more than three or four days a week, and the continual threat of idle days makes the slave more tractable and submissive. . . . Often when their day's work is done they are put to washing off the tables and lunch room doors and the other odd jobs, for which there is not even the suggestion of compensation. . . .[19]

Still another view of women in the canning industry was that provided by Bessie (Mrs. John) Van Vorst, who came to Pittsburgh in 1902 to work in a canning factory. During the early years of the twentieth century several women of comfortable means exchanged their fine clothing for inexpensive working-class dress, disguised themselves as women seeking jobs, and shared the lives of factory women. What they learned as they wrestled with sewing machines or stuffed pickles into jars ten or more hours a day, they shared with the public through books and magazine articles they wrote afterward. Bessie Van Vorst set out to

> discover and adopt their [working women's] point of view, put ourselves in their surroundings, assume their burdens, unite with them in their daily effort . . . to give a faithful picture of things as they exist, both in and out of the factory, and to suggest remedies that occurred

to me as practical. My desire is to act as a mouthpiece for the women labourer. . . .

. . . Before leaving New York I assumed my disguise. . . . With the aid of coarse woolen garments, a shabby felt sailor hat, a cheap piece of fur, a knitted shawl and gloves I am transformed into a working girl of the ordinary type.[20]

She also adopted an alias, and became Esther Kelley as she boarded the train for Pittsburgh. When she arrived she had not "a friend or an acquaintance within hundreds of miles."[21] Her one concession to the possibility that she might not find a job was to pin inside her skirt a small silk purse which contained an emergency reserve fund to see her home again to New York. But she resolved not to touch this money except in absolute need, and to get along entirely on her own earnings.

They were hiring in the pickle factory and she applied for a job. After her first day at work she wrote:

I have become with desperate reality a factory girl, alone, inexperienced, friendless. I am making $4.20 a week and spending $3 of this for board alone, and I dread not being strong enough to keep my job. . . .

. . . My hands are stiff, my thumbs almost blistered. . . . Cases are emptied and refilled; bottles are labeled, stamped and rolled away . . . and still there are more cases, more jars, more bottles. Oh! the monotony of it . . . ! Now and then someone cuts a finger or runs a splinter under the flesh . . . and still the work goes on. Once I pause an instant, my head dazed and weary, my ears strained to bursting with the deafening noise. Quickly a voice whispers in my ear: "You'd better not stand there doin' nothin'. If *she* catches you she'll give it to you."

After what seemed like an interminable day, Van Vorst could report: "I have stood ten hours; I have fitted 1,300 corks; I have hauled and loaded 4,000 jars of pickles. My pay is seventy cents." She discovered that each Saturday afternoon the women spent four hours on their hands and knees scrubbing the tables and stands and "every inch of the factory floor." She also learned that the men hosed down their workrooms, but refused to get down on their hands and knees to scrub. Not long afterwards she found that men were furnished a hot lunch for ten cents, while women had to bring their own sandwiches. She learned that the lowest-paid man earned more than the highest-paid woman. While she wondered why the women did not stand up and complain as the men did, she never reached the conclusion that a union might be the answer. Instead, she reasoned that the men fought for their rights because *all* of them were breadwinners, whereas only some of the women depended on their earnings for a livelihood; also, that the availability of women willing to work for so little dragged down the wage level for all of them. Her solution was industrial schools to train women for more skilled jobs.[22]

Bindery Women

Women in bookbinding in the early 1900s provided a sharp contrast to the average factory worker. They were for the most part American-born and were better educated. Of the 14,000 bookbinders reported by the United States Census in 1900, just over half were women. They did not compete for jobs in the industry with the men, who completed a four-year apprenticeship while the women performed only the less skilled work. Although no rule prevented women from serving such apprenticeships, they were never offered them.

The International Brotherhood of Bookbinders formed in 1892, and by 1910 had 130 affiliated locals, of which 24 included both men and women members. Twenty-five percent of all women bookbinders were unionized. By and large, the women organized separately. The most famous of their locals, Women Bookbinders Local 43 of New York City, is still in existence. This unusual local began with 50 members in 1895 and grew to have 1,400 by 1910. Women from its ranks who served as elected officers developed effective collective bargaining machinery, established the six-day, forty-eight-hour week, preferential hiring for union members, and time-and-a-half pay after fifty-four hours if overtime was required. This contrasted sharply with conditions in unorganized binderies. In one such establishment, four girls who worked on the "night force" one day each week reported their longest day's labor as 16¾ hours, 20½, 22½, and 24½ hours. Such "long days" occurred once and sometimes twice a week for a period of 16 to 26 weeks.[23]

Mary Van Kleeck, who studied and wrote about a number of women's occupations for the Russell Sage Foundation, tried to determine the source of the strength of the bindery women. She decided their success was due to the way the local kept track of each member to ensure that union women were the first hired in union shops, ahead of any non-union workers; in effect, the local served as a hiring hall. In addition, all permanent workers had to join Local 43 after two weeks on the job; the women had achieved a "union shop." Van Kleeck found that all the women seemed to share a pride in the union's victories, and those she spoke with wanted to be sure she understood that they had done it for themselves, without much help or cooperation from the men. Even employers she interviewed confirmed that the women deserved full credit for the wages and working conditions they had achieved.[24]

Cracker Packers

Few women workers were as strongly organized as the bookbinders. Conditions in the cracker-packing industry* showed the effect of lack of unionization on women workers. In 1907, Elizabeth Butler investigated Pittsburgh cracker packers who worked in the five cracker factories of that city. Of the 1,810 workers in these plants, 928 were women. The men who mixed the dough (from a "secret formula" told to no one else) were the only skilled workers in the trade. Women tended the machines that stamped out the crackers, iced the cookies, and packed and labeled the cans and boxes. The hottest work in the factory was tending the ovens, most often a woman's job. This involved standing no more than six feet from the intense heat of the oven all day long, and was highly paid, for the woman who held it usually lasted no more than a couple of weeks.

Butler reported her observations of the cracker packers, who worked a 10-hour day and averaged $5 to $6 a week on piece rates:

> The pace of each worker is pitched to the highest point. I noticed especially one small girl with flushed cheeks and white lips who was folding the ends of soda cracker boxes and putting on each end a red stamp. She earned $.01 a dozen, and if she could make a hundred dozen a day, she would get a $.10 bonus, altogether $1.10. Her teeth were set, and her breath came hard, like that of an overspent runner at the end of a race; yet it was only ten o'clock in the morning. Her arms moved irregularly, jerkily, as if she were spurring her nervous energy to its limit. The office boy who was standing near watching her, said casually, "She's lucky if she makes her bonus. I was in this department a while ago and I seen these girls get so tired their arms was ready to drop off at night but they wouldn't make no hundred boxes."[25]

"Women Who Wait"

Long hours and poor pay are the general lot of unorganized waitresses. They often work 14 hours a day and 7 days a week. In many of these unorganized restaurants they have to provide uniforms and aprons of special fashion, and must pay for the laundering. They have to purchase the material from their employer at a higher cost than it can be had in the open market. In some places they are still compelled to pay for all breakages, however little they may be responsible. When not actually waiting on table, they have to clean silver, pick berries, iron napkins, and so forth. It is estimated that a waitress walks 10 miles

* This included both cracker and cookie packing.

in a "10-hour watch," and that she carries 1,500 pounds during that time.

The organized waitresses have their uniforms and aprons, and the laundering of these furnished them. They have established the 10-hour day and the 6-day week, and every other afternoon they are off duty from 2 to 5 o'clock. They have increased wages . . . and give their members $3 a week sick benefit for 13 weeks, and a $50 death benefit.[26]

Fewer than 5 percent of the 41,178 waitresses in 1900 belonged to a labor union, compared to 58 percent of all waiters. The first local union of waitresses to join the Hotel and Restaurant International Alliance was organized in Seattle, Washington, in 1900, when fifty women led by Alice Lord established Local 240. The following year the international union welcomed its first woman convention delegate, Bertye Breene, from Waitresses Local Union 249 in St. Louis. By 1910, the international union counted 962 waitresses as members.[27*]

The Chicago waitresses' local was one of the strongest in the international union. Organizing secretly in 1902, the women all showed up at work one day with union badges, demanded shorter hours and a pay raise—and won both. During the next seven years the Chicago union's membership fell from 1,500 to 300, owing in part to high turnover, inexperienced leadership, and employer opposition, but the waitresses seem to have maintained their favorable working conditions notwithstanding. This local was a prime mover in lobbying for the 8-hour day in the state legislature, enlisting the support of the Women's Trade Union League and other Illinois labor unions, particularly women's locals. The bill it supported, known as "The Girls' Bill," passed, but only after a compromise on 10 hours rather than 8 as the legal working day for women.[28]

Maud Younger, the founder and first president of the Waitresses Union of San Francisco, was another of the turn-of-the-century, well-to-do women who learned about wage-earning women by joining them. As a society debutante traveling through New York in the summer of 1901 on her way to Europe, she asked to spend a few days in the famous College Settlement House in the heart of the slums of the Lower East side. She stayed for five years. Moved by what she saw, she decided to get a job as a waitress. Much later, she recounted in *McClure's Magazine*:

> It was a great surprise to me to find how hard it is to "get a job." I always supposed that anyone who was willing and able to work could get one. . . . But for three days I walked along street after street and

---

* The difference in the figures given by Andrews and Bliss (2,000 unionized waitresses) and those issued by the international union at about the same time may be accounted for by independent locals of waitresses unaffiliated with the international.

went without success into every restaurant and lunchroom I saw. . . .
Sometimes [the manager] looked me over as though I were a horse,
while I stood by, boiling with rage.[29]

Every restaurant manager asked her whether she was experienced as a
waitress, and since she was not, she said so. After the tenth manager had
turned her down, she asked him how she was ever to get experience if no
one hired her. "Well, perhaps I'll give you some," he answered, "but you
must work for nothing for a while."[30] She did, then went on to paying
jobs and joined the New York Waitresses Union. When she returned to
her home city of San Francisco in 1908, she again worked as a waitress
and organized that city's waitresses' union, becoming its first president
and representing it as a delegate to the city's Central Trades and Labor
Council.

Younger, a strong advocate of the 8-hour day for women, mobilized
California unions to lobby for its passage by the state legislature. She is
credited with organizing the Wage Earners' Equal Suffrage League in
California, getting labor backing for the state's woman suffrage amendment, which passed in California in 1911 though it failed in a number
of other states at about the same period. Coming East again, she worked
as a member of the Women's Trade Union League to help the ILGWU
in the 1912 strike of white-goods (underwear and negligee) workers.
Through the league she gained her first experience in congressional lobbying in the fight for protective legislation for women workers, and later
used this expertise to campaign for woman suffrage and in the 1920s for
passage of the Equal Rights Amendment. She remained active in support
of these causes until her death in 1934 at the age of sixty-seven.[31]

Flower Makers

One group with little opportunity to organize were the artificial-flower
makers. Their trade, a subsidiary of hat trimming, was a tenement sweatshop industry located primarily in New York, where three-fourths of the
country's artificial flowers were produced as of 1913. Most flower makers
were women and children. The trade, a seasonal one, operated on a piece-
rate system where rates were cut during slow periods. Mary Van Kleeck,
in a Russell Sage Foundation study of this industry published in 1913,
described one of the many families that she found making these flowers:

In a tenement on MacDougal Street lives a family of seven—grandmother, father, mother and four children ages four years, three years,
two years and one month respectively. All excepting the father and
the two babies make violets. The three year old girl picks apart the
petals; her sister, aged four years, separates the stems, dipping an end

of each into paste spread on a piece of board on the kitchen table; and the mother and grandmother slip the petals up the stems.

"We all must work if we want to earn anything," said the mother. They are paid ten cents for a gross, 144 flowers, and if they work steadily from eight or nine o'clock in the morning until 7 or 8 at night, they may make twelve gross, $1.20. In the busy season their combined earning are usually $7.00 a week. During five months, from April to October, they have no work.[32]

The youngest worker she found in the industry was a child eighteen months old, who had been taught to separate the petals and was working right beside the other members of the family.

Even the few pennies that young children could earn working alongside other family members in the tenement sweatshops were necessary for family survival.

Women in Packingtown

Upton Sinclair, in his novel *The Jungle*, brought conditions in the Chicago stockyards and packing plants to the attention of the public. He writes of Marija, a young woman who had been fired from her job painting cans in a meat-packing plant because of union activity. She spent four weeks and half the fifth combing the packing plants without finding any job.

> She had about made up her mind that she was a lost soul, when somebody told her of an opening, and she went and got a place as a "beef trimmer." She got this because the boss saw that she had the muscles of a man, and so he discharged a man and put Marija to do his work, paying her a little more than half what he had been paying before.

When she first came to Packingtown, Marija would have scorned such work as this. She was in another canning factory, and her work was to cut up the diseased cattle. . . . She was shut up in one of the rooms where the people seldom saw the daylight; beneath her were the chilling rooms, where the meat was frozen, and above her were the cooking rooms; and so she stood on an ice-cold floor, while her head was often so hot she could scarcely breathe. Trimming beef off the bones by the hundredweight, while standing up from early morning to late at night, with heavy boots on and the floor always damp and full of puddles, liable to be thrown out of work indefinitely because of a slackening in the trade, liable again to be kept overtime in rush seasons, and be worked till she trembled in every nerve and lost her grip on her slimy knife, and gave herself a poisoned wound—that was the new life that unfolded itself before Marija. But because Marija was a human horse she merely laughed and went at it; it would enable her to pay her board again, and keep the family going.[33]

The Jungle produced such an outcry from the public that a major investigation into the food-packing industry resulted—but the outrage was over the unsanitary and diseased food that was being sold to the public, not the dangerous, inhuman conditions under which it was produced. The investigation was followed by the passage of federal legislation calling for meat inspection, a host of safeguards, and the labeling of food and drugs. These were all inadequately enforced, and life continued in Packingtown as before.

It was left to the workers themselves to organize. Women had worked as meat packers as early as 1876, but about 1902 they appeared in the meat-packing plants as "petticoat butchers."[34] In an early study (1905) of labor organization among women published by the University of Illinois, Belva Mary Herron described the work of the 5,000 women in the packing plants. Some of them painted and labeled cases, sewed hams into canvas bags, and boxed chipped beef. These were the "clean" jobs, and invariably it was American women who held them. Such jobs were not open to immigrant women, who might find work in the hot and noisy canning department, where men also worked. The most dangerous jobs were in the sausage department, working with knives and machinery at constant risk of infection from unclean meat; Lithuanian and Polish women began to be employed there about 1902 or 1903. For the first time women competed directly with the men for these jobs and were hired because they worked for less money, averaging perhaps $1.25 a day compared with the $1.75 paid to men.[35] It is small wonder that their entrance into the sausage department was viewed with alarm, yet the men never considered organizing the women when they formed the Amalgamated Meatcutters and Butcher Workmen's Union.

Women first struck over repeated cuts in the piece rate. Maggie Condon, one of the fastest packinghouse workers, noticed that whenever her take-home pay went above a certain amount, her rate was cut, and that the rate cut went all down the line. This meant that the slowest workers suffered for the speed of the fastest. The fast workers began to organize, holding back on their production to protect their fellow workers. Hannah O'Day, who had been packing meat since she was eleven years old but was not one of the fast workers, joined the group. They did not take long to decide that they needed a union. However, they got no encouragement from the men, not even when Hannah O'Day raised her red handkerchief on a stick, motioned the women to follow her, and led hundreds of women out on a spontaneous strike. The women won nothing, but managed to stay together by forming a club, called the Maud Gonne Club after an Irish patriot. But the club might never have evolved into a union if Maggie Condon had not read a newspaper account of a talk given by Mary Mc-Dowell, head of the University of Chicago Settlement House, which was located right near the stockyard. McDowell had described the terrible conditions of the women working in the packing plants. Condon and O'Day, feeling that here at last was someone who understood, began a series of discussions with her that came to include other women from the plant. Out of these grew Local 183, which in 1903 was finally granted a charter by the Amalgamated Meatcutters and Butcher Workmen. Although the local included few if any of the immigrant women from the packing plant as members, when the Meatcutters' convention took up a motion that these women be prohibited from working in the sausage department as meat trimmers, Local 183 delegates firmly opposed the motion and saw to it that it was defeated.

This local was one of the first in the union to admit blacks on an equal basis. One evening, so the story goes, a black woman came shyly to the local's meeting. The doorkeeper was Hannah O'Day, who shouted to the local's young president, Mollie Daley: "A colored sister is at the door; what'll I do with her?" "I say, admit her at once and let yez give her a hearty welcome," was the reply, and the new member of Local 183 was greeted with applause as she entered the hall.[36]

In 1904 a general strike of packinghouse workers occurred, with the women supporting the men who had walked out. This strike was a major defeat, and Local 183 went down with the men. Hannah O'Day had believed firmly that "we ought to organize for them that comes after us,"[37] but it would be a long time before packinghouse workers could regroup and rebuild their union.

However, women workers had made some progress. Although few were union members, more than a dozen unions now admitted women and most no longer segregated them by sex. Shoeworkers and waitresses, bookbinders, garment, tobacco, and laundry workers, women in textile mills, and glove sewers were beginning to organize. Gradually unions were coming to see the importance of including women workers.

Where Black Women Worked

Almost no black women were union members. While the AFL's stated policy in 1886 was to organize all workers, black and white, it followed this policy only until 1895. That year the federation ran into a major conflict with the International Association of Machinists—one of a number of unions that did not admit black workers—and after Gompers's defeat on the issue of opening national union membership to blacks, he retreated in favor of a policy of organizing first, reforming unions later.*

Few black women workers were eligible for union membership in any case, since they were seldom permitted to work in skilled occupations that organized. They were concentrated in Southern agricultural and domestic service jobs, in laundries, and in tobacco factories, particularly in tobacco stripping.

> The stripping . . . is done by women, some of them very old, others crippled. They carry their tobacco in amounts varying from 30 to 60 pounds in aprons or sacks tied around their waists, from a central point to their benches, and after it has been stripped, to the scales to have it weighed. The strippers' benches are very low, without backs or rests of any kind; the floors are very dirty, the light is poor, and the women have to lean over their work. Twice a day they get new supplies of tobacco.[38]

There were tobacco strippers in the North, too, but it was often a home industry. Elizabeth Butler, in her study of women in the Pittsburgh trades, describes the tenements in which women worked:

> The only source of air was a narrow door leading by a flight of steps up to the street. A tiny slit of a window at the far end was close barred, and two thirds of the cubic space in the room was occupied by bales of tobacco and cases of stripped stock. Pools of muddy water stood on the earth floor, and the air was foul beyond endurance.[39]

Of the 523 tenement tobacco strippers in Pittsburgh whom Butler found, all but 18 were women earning from 60 cents to $1.00 a day working piece rate. There was no union to help them, for the Tobacco Workers International Union, founded in 1895, did not—or could not—organize home workers, isolated from each other, poor, and often frightened. It

---

* By the time of World War I, total black membership in the AFL was perhaps 55,000, or 3.6 percent of the federation's million and a half membership. Philip Foner, *Organized Labor and the Black Worker, 1619–1974* (New York: Praeger Publishers, 1974), p. 127.

is worth noting, however, that the two largest locals of this international union were the one in Detroit, where women outnumbered men by more than two to one, and the one in Richmond, Virginia, where 236 men and 131 women, all black, maintained a successful union.[40]

Where black women did work in mills, it was at the heavy labor jobs or as janitresses, not at the machines. In the South, the only jobs they could get were those white workers refused to do, while white workers went into the cotton mills. Poor as the wages and working conditions in these mills were, white workers struck thirty-one times between 1882 and 1900, not to organize unions, but to keep black workers from being hired to work on machines.[41]

After the Civil War many black women worked in the fields alongside the men, just as they had done as slaves. Laboring from dawn to dark, men might earn $3 a week, women $2. Often men could not find any jobs at all, especially in the cities, and the burden of family support fell on black women, who worked as laundresses, seamstresses, scrubwomen, or cooks. Census figures from 1890 indicate in general where black women were employed:[42]

Agriculture	38.74%
Domestic service	30.83%
Laundry work	15.59%
Manufacturing	2.76%

One household worker described her life as a Southern domestic servant:

> I frequently work from fourteen to sixteen hours a day. I am compelled ... to sleep in the house. I am allowed to go home to my children, the oldest of whom is a girl of 18 years, only once in two weeks, every other Sunday afternoon—even then I'm not permitted to stay all night.[43]

In addition to 24-hour-a-day care of four children, one only eleven months old, her duties including helping the cook, mending the family's clothes, watering the lawn, mopping, dusting, and sweeping. For her work she received $10 a month. "I live a treadmill life," she said, and added that if it were not for the "service pan"—the leftover food that Southern servants were permitted to take home—many black families would have starved.

Black women prisoners were used as convict labor. Dressed in men's clothes, they were farmed out along with men prisoners to work in the fields. Black men and women in tenant farming and sharecropping were not much better off. Those who could manage it headed North—by 1910 some 400,000 of them had moved to Northern cities.[45] There they found domestic service open to them and little else. Though the 1890 census reported 11,846 black women working as seamstresses and 7,586 more as dressmakers, many black seamstresses were hired to fill a servant's role.

The first entry of black women into factory sewing was usually as scabs in labor disputes. A study done in 1900 showed that in New York City's leading industry for women, dressmaking, only 813 black women were employed out of a total of 37,514 women in this trade. The same study revealed the degree to which unemployment attended black men when they moved North, for 25 percent of all married black women were found in New York's work force, as compared with only 5 percent of married white women.[46]

In an 1899 study of black workers in another major city, Philadelphia, W. E. B. Du Bois described how an *employed* man, woman, and grown child lived. Three rooms of their seven room-house were rented out to boarders. The family's budget is revealing:[47]

Income

Husband, a hod carrier and day laborer. Earned $1.25 to $2.00 a day, when he found work. Average: $3.00 a week	$150 per year
Wife: laundress, October–March, $5.00–$6.00 a week; April–September, $1.50–$2.00 a week	$180 a year
Son, office building porter, $2.50 a week and meals	$125 a year
	$455

Expenses

Rent (net), $8.00 a month	$ 96
Food, $3.50–$4.00 a week	190
Fuel	35
All else, clothes, medical, church, savings: $134.00	$134
	$455 a year

In contrast to that family Du Bois described another, also a family of three, from a dismal slum area of the city. They lived in one room twelve by fourteen feet, poorly furnished and badly ventilated. The wife earned $3 a week as a domestic servant. Their $3-a-week rent was for three rooms, but boarders lived in two and they lived in just one. They had $1 a week for food, and 56 cents a week for fuel in winter. Of the $125 to $150 it cost this family to exist for a year, the wife earned $100 or more.

Men's wages in Philadelphia, Du Bois found, averaged from $2.61 a week for a bellboy to $8.58 a week for a coachman, while women's earnings ranged from $2.00 weekly for an errand girl to $4.06 for a janitress.

Cook and laundress were the only other occupations that averaged $4.00 a week or a few cents more. He found black women employed as dressmakers and seamstresses, errand girls, children's nurses, chambermaids, waitresses, ladies' maids, laundresses, cooks, janitresses, undertakers, and general workers. The highest wages Du Bois recorded for a black woman were those of a child's nurse and a cook, who earned $10.00 a week. Black people lost their jobs more rapidly than white, paid more for housing of poor quality, had to take insults and accept poor service, and watched their children grow up in the face of constant discrimination.

Although light-skinned black women had an easier time finding skilled employment, they were fired as soon as it was learned that they were not white. Du Bois found that one out of every ten domestic workers had some high school education and was qualified to hold a more skilled job— but could find none. A few black women managed to enter professions such as nursing, teaching, social work, medicine, journalism, or the law. Since almost all professions were barred to them, it took tremendous energy, talent, and courage to achieve a professional education and then to break into the field itself.

It is hard to appreciate properly the accomplishments of these women. More often than not, if a black woman wanted to work as a settlement house worker, she would have to establish the settlement house first, as did Janie Porter Barret, the daughter of ex-slaves. Born in 1865, she attended Hampton Institute, became a teacher, and decided to work with sharecroppers in the rural South. Later she conducted night classes at Hampton. In 1889 she married, and made Hampton her home for many years, in 1890 founding the South's first settlement house for blacks, the Locust Street Social Settlement. Girls who were in trouble with the law became her major interest, and in 1914 she established the Virginia Industrial School for Colored Girls to provide these young women with a home, guidance, and training in job skills. By 1920 this industrial school was rated as one of the five top schools of its kind in the country.

Lucy Craft Laney founded the Haines Institute in Augusta, Georgia. Born in 1854 of parents who had once been slaves, she graduated from high school at the age of fifteen and from Atlanta University at nineteen. After teaching school for some twelve years, she opened a private school for black children to test the ideas that she had developed about education. She taught her students Latin and algebra at a time when black people were supposed to learn only the service trades and farming. One of her goals was to train as many good teachers as she could to go out and prepare black children for college. Within two years after she opened the school in 1886, she had 300 students, but unfortunately few could pay their own way, while she would not turn down anyone who wanted to learn. She put all her savings into the school and then was forced to beg and borrow money to keep it operating, often going without food so that her students could eat.

Among her educational innovations, virtually unknown in black schools of her day, were a kindergarten, a school orchestra, and a training school for black nurses that she established in an old building the city of Augusta gave her for a hospital. A strict disciplinarian, she made it her teaching goal to instill in her students a pride in their race and faith in themselves.[48]

The leading black spokeswoman of her time was Ida Wells-Barnett, editor, journalist, lecturer, clubwoman, and community organizer, who fearlessly carried on a nation-wide antilynching campaign in a period marked by almost daily hangings and burnings of black men and women. Ida Wells, born in 1862 in Holly Springs, Mississippi, was orphaned at the age of fourteen when both her parents and three siblings died of yellow fever. Left to support four younger brothers and sisters, she gave up school and, as historian Eleanor Flexner describes it, "let down her skirts, put up her hair, and claiming to be eighteen, got a position teaching in a rural school at $25 a month."[49]

Soon she began writing newspaper articles under the pen name of "Iola." In 1891 she lost her teaching job when she criticized the poor education provided black children in the South, and joined the staff of the Memphis, Tennessee, *Free Speech* as part-owner. Her career as journalist and editor had begun. The following year three young friends of hers were lynched. Using the pages of her newspaper to print detailed accounts of other lynchings, she began what became her lifelong crusade against this horror. Soon she was forced to flee Memphis: her newspaper was broken into and the presses smashed in retaliation for her exposure of several white businessmen in connection with the lynching of her three friends.

A brilliant lecturer, she took her campaign for antilynching laws to a number of Northern cities, and later published her *Red Book*, the first in-depth study of lynching in America. While working in Chicago on the *Conservator*, she met and married Ferdinand Lee Barnett, a Chicago lawyer who shared her deep concern and joined in her crusade. Together they inaugurated a number of important clubs, some of them to assist blacks coming to Chicago from the South. She served as an officer in the National Afro-American Council, promoted women's suffrage, founded the first black women's suffrage association, and worked with Jane Addams to prevent Chicago from setting up separate schools for black children. Active all her life in community and social organizations, she died in 1931 at the age of sixty-nine.[50]

Until World War I, black women moved but slowly into factory jobs. Some entered the garment industry, some the packing plants in the Chicago stockyards; some worked in crab picking, others in canning factories; and there was almost always employment for them in the growing number of steam laundries. In the South, tobacco and cigarette factories employed black women in the least desirable jobs. Few black women could get office or sales jobs or work for the telephone company. Only during World War I did opportunities to work in industry open for black women, although rarely at the same jobs and almost never side-by-side with white women.

13

WOMEN IN TEACHING AND WHITE-COLLAR JOBS

> I tell you that 'tis very wrong.
> It is cruel and not right,
> To keep the girls upon their feet
> From morning until night.
> Then let the girls sit down, I pray;
> Oh, let the girls sit down;
> Don't keep them on their feet all day—
> Oh, let the girls sit down.
>
> My neighbors and myself have met,
> And talked the matter o'er;
> And we've resolved, and firmly too,
> To patronize no more
> Those barbarous establishments
> Not one of them in town—
> That keep the girls upon their feet,
> And let them ne'er sit down.
>
> —"Oh, Let the Girls Sit Down," *Labor Standard*
>   August 19, 1876

Women rushed to fill the openings created by expanding business and the use of the typewriter. Where there had been just 19,000 women office workers of all kinds in 1870, there were 75,000 in 1890, and 503,000 in 1900—an increase of 2,700 percent in thirty years.[1] From holding 4.5 percent of the stenographers' and typists' jobs in 1870, women came to hold 40 percent of such jobs ten years later and by 1900 were found in 76.7 percent of all jobs in these categories.[2] Like their sisters in factory and domestic work, they were young and single, but there was one major difference: women in office jobs were invariably native-born, and so were their parents. It was rare for an immigrant, the child of an immigrant, a black woman, or a Jew to get a white-collar position.

Young Florence Cohen was typical of those who tried but failed. Eighteen years old and eager to succeed, she took a six-month course at Strayer's Business College in Baltimore, Maryland, and was one of the few who stayed long enough to finish the entire curriculum of Pitman

A sign of the times: typists taking a civil service examination in 1909, as the field for office workers burgeoned.

stenography, typing, spelling, and letter writing. The college sent her, certificate in hand, to the Remington Typewriter Agency, which placed typists and stenographers in jobs where their machines were used. From there she was sent for an interview to the Levinson and Zenith Furniture Company, even though the company did not hire Jews. The agency gambled on Florence's skills and intelligence to win her the chance to take the company's test. When she arrived for the interview and gave her name, she was told at once that the firm never employed Jews. "No," said the interviewer, "Jews are not ever permitted to work here. They are all troublemakers."[3]

Therefore women often went to great lengths to hide their parentage or place of birth from prospective employers, changing their names and lying about their addresses so that the area of the city in which they lived would not give them away.

The appeal of office work was real: it was cleaner and less strenuous than factory work, and socially much more acceptable. Workers were paid a weekly salary rather than hourly wages, and work tended to be regular, layoffs less frequent. Most important for young women at that time, it meant working for men on an individual basis, which provided at least the possibility of finding a husband.

That was the credit side of the ledger. On the debit side were the long hours, the often low salaries, the need to dress well (an added cost), and working conditions that ranged from poorly lit desks to rooms filled with cigar smoke from the men who shared office space with the women. Then there were the advances of men who felt the young women were fair game and would not dare to protest.

Women office workers tried as early as 1882 to take united action to protect themselves. The first white-collar union on record was the Brotherhood of Telegraphers, which organized that year into an assembly of the Knights of Labor.

Elsie Diehl of Local 11,655 of the Stenographers and Typewriters Union, AFL, pointed out one of the key reasons why women typists (still called "typewriters") and stenographers were organizing: "We ought to have a union in order to get matters equalized. . . . We want quiet girls who are not charmers to get as good pay for the same work." Later she added discreetly: "Professional services instead of 'companionship' in business offices is one of the main matters that should receive our attention."[4] Soon the AFL began to charter federal locals for stenographers, typewriters, bookkeepers, and office assistants. But even though women were entering each of these job categories in increasing numbers, and the Chicago office workers' local formally requested that the AFL send in a woman organizer to help it recruit women, the AFL executive council was not yet interested in pushing unionization of this field and let the suggestion die.

At the Switchboard

Women worked in telegraphy from the start. The reader will recall that in 1846 Sarah Bagley of Lowell became the country's first telegraph operator. By 1870 women had established themselves nation-wide in this field, and the first class of Western Union operators had been graduated from the Cooper Union training school in New York City, launched the year before. As in other occupations, women's earnings were about one-half of men's: $30 to $50 a month, while men, still in a majority in telegraphy, received $75 to $100 for the same work.[5]

At the Philadelphia Centennial Exposition in 1876, Alexander Graham Bell exhibited his new invention, the telephone. Soon the first telephone line began operation between Somerville, Massachusetts, and Boston, three miles away. By January 1878, New Haven, Connecticut, boasted the country's first commercial telephone exchange, employing boys as operators, a carryover from the pattern established in telegraph offices.

Employers soon discovered that young women could do the work just as well for less money. Within ten years almost all daytime exchanges

The first telephone switchboard operators were men. In 1879 they connected telephone calls manually on the horizontal bar line.

By 1888 the scene had changed, and switchboards were operated almost entirely by women, except for the night shift.

were operated by women, though men and boys continued on the night shift until the early years of the twentieth century. Census reports for the years 1870 to 1900, recording telegraph and telephone operators as one group, show the tremendous jump in the employment of women during that thirty-year period. In 1870 only 350 women were counted—all in telegraphy, of course. By 1900, 21,980 women worked as telegraph and telephone operators, an increase from 4.3 percent of all the industry's workers in 1870 to 29.3 percent by the turn of the century.

That this increase was largely among telephone operators is confirmed after 1900, when each group was recorded separately. In 1902 the industry reported 37,333 female telephone operators and 2,525 male; in 1907, 76,638 female operators, and 3,576 male. More than 90 percent of these women were young and single, most of them under twenty. Another 5.7 percent were married; 3.2 percent more were widowed and supporting themselves. Only six-tenths of 1 percent were reported as divorced, reflecting in part the industry's attempt to preserve this up-and-coming white-collar occupation for "genteel" young women before they married.

While the work may have been "genteel"—that is, sedentary and clean—it was far from easy. The women spent long workdays seated with their noses against large switchboard jacks into which they reached and stretched to fit the proper plugs. They took from 250 to 350 calls an hour. Supervision was rigid. Mistakes spelled disaster. A spy system helped the company maintain discipline, and women were not permitted to talk among themselves. Sanitary facilities often were poor, and the time allowed for using them was rigorously controlled.

The young women, inexperienced though most of them were, chafed under these strict controls. As soon as the International Brotherhood of Electrical Workers (IBEW) in New England, the union organizing men who worked at the phone company, could be persuaded to open its doors to women operators (which it did in 1909), the women joined. Just four years later they made labor history during a much-publicized New England telephone workers' strike. The women in particular won the support of the public and of the labor movement in the Boston area when the phone company began to import strikebreakers, wining and dining them extravagantly and paying them large bonuses for scabbing. The Waiters Union refused to serve meals to the scabs, while other Boston unions closed ranks behind the strikers and threatened a sympathy strike. In the settlement that followed, workers gained a grievance board to handle future disputes and complaints.[6]

Before long, women in the Boston IBEW began to resent their second-class status in the local. Their leader, Julia O'Connor, a trained Women's

Trade Union League activist, voiced their dissatisfaction and succeeded in working out with the IBEW a separate department for the women operators, and separate locals. Because they earned less money than the men, their union dues were less and so were their benefits. The women found also that their voting rights were just half those of the men.[7] However, they did not let this affect their militancy, and before long Julia O'Connor headed the union's national division of women telephone operators.

Behind the Counter

When the reader last met the woman retail-store worker, she was just gaining entrance into the industry. By the turn of the century she was firmly entrenched, the number of women salesclerks having grown from just 10,000 in 1870 to 100,000 in 1890. Twenty percent of all store

Millinery store workers display an array of the latest hats, about 1890.

workers now were women.[8] Store wages (1909 figurse) ranged from $6 or $7 a week for saleswomen to $3 for cashiers. Stock girls might earn up to $3.50, while cash girls, who ran between the saleswomen and the cashiers with the customer's change, were paid only $1.50 to $2.00 a week. Long hours matched the low wages: 60 to 80 hours a week depending on the store, with even longer hours during holiday and inventory seasons. The large demand for such jobs enabled employers to keep wages low and to fire employees at will. Store work was no bargain, yet because it was considered "genteel," young women who could not afford business-school training spent their last pennies on outfitting themselves for a store-job interview. Their failure to obtain the post meant that they would be headed for the factory or domestic service.

Frances Donovan, who took a job as saleswoman to learn about the life of wage-earning women, wrote about her experiences:

> Never in my life had I been so conscious of my feet. . . . During that first week I would have been willing to increase their size fourfold if it could have lessened the dull, feverish throb with its agonizing persistence.
> Next to the feet, was the pain in the small of my back. . . . There is no doubt that there is both a physical and a mental strain in department store work.

Such agonies of store work as inventory season, when work lasted from 8:45 in the morning until far into the night, led Donovan to comment on the changing attitudes she saw in the saleswomen: "It is in such ways and under such conditions that the 'salesladies' become class-conscious and tend to cast in their lot with the rest of the world that labors."[9]

Saleswomen stood for twelve or more hours a day and sometimes fainted from exhaustion. Legislation to help them was passed by some states before 1900. Maryland, for example, enacted a law in 1896 that seats in stores must be provided for saleswomen. Companies complied, but did not allow the clerks to use them. In 1904 the law was amended to state specifically that women might sit down if they were not busy doing other work. These state laws did little good—as evidenced by one store in Baltimore which installed 2 seats for 85 saleswomen. During her investigation into department stores in Baltimore, Elizabeth Butler witnessed this scene:

> The sight of a frail little white-faced girl leaning against the counter occasioned from a customer the remonstrance, "Why don't you sit down?" "If we sat down, we'd get the grand bounce," was the reply,— a threat sufficient to keep any tired child "at attention."[10]

Lack of adequate toilet facilities was another major problem. One Baltimore store had only one toilet room on the third floor of its annex for all its customers and the 282 women it employed in both its six-story annex and its four-story main building. A saleswoman could not get back to her counter before her five minutes (the usual time allowance) ran out. Not only that, but she usually found a line at the toilet room, which made it impossible for her to return even in twice the time allotted. Moreover, she had to get a pass from a supervisor—almost always a man—and faced embarrassing comments, especially if she were late in returning. This effectively prevented many women from using the toilets at all, so that they frequently developed kidney ailments and related problems during their years in store work.

Butler's store investigations also took her to Pittsburgh, where she found similar conditions. Here she probed more deeply, and learned that many saleswomen left the stores in desperation and became prostitutes. Department-store dress requirements left them little money for food, and they went hungry much of the time. Male supervisors and floorwalkers took advantage of their plight and urged individual women to give them "concessions." If a woman refused, her job was in jeopardy. Butler writes:

> Rosa ——— was employed at the ribbon counter. She had a mother and two sisters dependent upon her, and her mother was always urging her for more money. She began while still in the store to "make money on the side." The management discovered this and dismissed her. She left for a city in Ohio; went into a house of prostitution there from which she sends her mother money. Her wages at the ribbon counter were $6.00 a week. . . .

> Vera ——— is 20 years old. Four years ago she was employed as a salesgirl at $3.50 a week. After a year she left for another store where she was employed as a cashier at a salary of $10.00 a week, making concessions to her employer. After two years she left the store for a house of prostitution.[11]

Help for the store worker was on its way with the formation of the Working Women's Society, founded in New York in 1886 by garment worker Leonora O'Reilly and several public leaders like Josephine Shaw Lowell. Organized to support working women on strike, it promoted legislation for adequate factory inspection and lobbied for the appointment of women factory inspectors. Most of all, it educated the public about the conditions under which the city's wage-earning women lived and worked.

Attention focused on women store workers following a mass protest meeting they held over their low wages and long hours. When the findings of an investigating committee confirmed the poor working conditions in New York's retail stores, Lowell decided to devote her full time to helping the saleswomen. She recruited eminent New York philanthropists, settlement house leaders, and reformers and in 1890 they launched the Consumers League of New York. The League evolved a plan to mobilize consumers and educate the public in the techniques of selective buying to support stores that agreed to maintain at least minimum working conditions and wages. It proposed that consumers purchase only from stores that agreed to:

six dollar a week minimums for workers with experience
a ten-hour day
a ¾-hour lunch break
a six-day week
a half-day off every week during the summer
a week of paid vacation
no children hired for store work
seats for saleswomen
a locker room
a lunch room[12]

When the Consumers' League issued its first "White List" to guide purchasers, it found just eight stores that complied with these standards.

By 1899 a National Consumers' League was established, with Florence Kelley as its general secretary. A former settlement-house worker from Chicago's Hull House, Kelley had worked with Elizabeth Morgan on the Illinois sweatshop investigations and held the post of chief factory inspector for Illinois under Governor Peter Altgeld. She was what one admirer called a "guerrilla warrior" in the "wilderness of industrial wrongs."[13] Florence Kelley campaigned vigorously for wage-and-hour laws to protect women and for an end to child labor. With Louis Brandeis and Josephine Goldmark, she helped to prepare the historic brief that led to the Supreme Court decision affirming the constitutionality of Oregon's 10-hour law limiting the workday for women (*Muller* v. *Oregon*, 1908). She organized the National Child Labor Committee in 1904, rejoicing when, in 1912, the United States set up the Children's Bureau for which she had worked so hard.

A founding member of the National Association for the Advancement of Colored People, Kelley also fought for maternal and child-care legislation and industrial safety laws. She vigorously opposed tenement labor, both because it destroyed the health of sweatshop workers and because it forced down the wages of factory workers competing with sweated labor for work. "Our industrial epoch," she wrote, "has corroded our morals and hardened our hearts as surely as slavery injured its contemporaries, and far more subtly. There is grave reason to fear that it may have unfitted us for the oncoming state of civilization."[14]

The New York Consumers' League did not rely solely on consumer boycotts, but supported efforts of saleswomen to organize, working with the Retail Clerks' union during its 1913 drive to unionize New York stores. In its campaign to publicize wages and working conditions in these stores, the league employed an unusual technique. Its most socially prominent members distributed leaflets, got themselves arrested, and then granted interviews to reporters to explain why they were leafleting and picketing. To call maximum attention to their cause, they chose the busiest streetcorners and made sure to block traffic. Even with their enthusiasm and publicity, however, this New York campaign did not muster sufficient consumer support to help the saleswomen win.

Two major strikes of saleswomen outside New York City were more successful. One in Lafayette, Indiana, in 1912 lasted for seventeen months, but the clerks won a $5 weekly minimum and shorter hours. The second of these strikes, in Buffalo in 1913, involved 4,000 retail workers, 80 percent of them women. There was violence on the picket line when the company brought in scabs, but ultimately the women won a $6 a week minimum (the men won a $12 minimum) and an 8½-hour day. However, they could not win union recognition.[15]

At their height, sixty Consumers' Leagues worked in twenty states, but they gradually died out when federal and state legislation for which they had fought was passed. An example was the 1898 Mercantile Inspection Act of New York, which limited the hours for women under twenty-one and boys under sixteen to 10 a day, 60 a week, with 7 A.M. and 10 P.M. the earliest and latest hours that stores might be open. However, for women who needed every penny they could earn, this was not an unmixed blessing; wages paid by the hour were reduced accordingly as hours were shortened.

The Retail Clerks' International Protective Association, one of the early unions to organize in an industry employing so large a number of women, at first reached out just for the men in the stores. They were paid more than the women, could afford to pay union dues, and were more likely to stay in store work. Union leaders felt that they could represent women's interests quite adequately without women in the union, a sentiment expressed by the editor of the union's newspaper, The Advocate, when he wrote: "What is really needed is some sort of labor organization that will give women the same salary as the man receives and place her in the position she is adapted to by nature."[16] The implication here is that men would then receive the jobs while women would stay at home.

When the union did open its doors to saleswomen, it established them in separate locals—at least until it realized that separate women's locals did not work well and accepted increasing numbers of women into men's locals. Women leaders such as Mary Burke played important roles in building the organization. The Chicago Tribune reported one meeting where Local 222's secretary, Catherine Schultz, following her fiery speech the night of March 6, 1902, led a parade through downtown Chicago to demand shorter workdays. "Miss Schultz, Joan of Arc of Retail Clerks, Appealing for Early Closing in Blue Island Avenue," ran the headline, and under it the Tribune carried a picture of Schultz silhouetted dramatically against a blazing bonfire, surrounded by a crowd of men and women waving their hats in the air.[17]

By 1904, twenty-six locals of Retail Clerks had organized in Chicago alone, with 6,000 members, and had been able to win reasonable closings. However, as so often happened following a downswing in the economy, the membership dropped from a national high of 50,000 members in 1903 to just 14,000 by 1909.[18]

Women in Nursing and Teaching

The overwhelming majority of those who worked in the professions of nursing and teaching were women. While they acquired status in these occupations, they shared low standards of pay with other working women and, in addition, found themselves hemmed in by rigid rules and restrictions that governed their behavior and frequently forced an end to their employment when they married or, at the very latest, when they had children.

Few of the 40,000 nurses and midwives who were counted in the census for 1890 had formal professional training. A nursing education was still largely on-the-job training in hospitals, with second-year students teaching the incoming first-year crop.

Working conditions for hospital nurses were as poor as their pay. They lived in, with room and board counted as part of their wages, although the dormitories in which they were crowded were often cold, bare, and inadequate and the food served them inedible. Nurses averaged $1 a week to start and gradually moved up to $4 a week after two years of training. Even supervisors of nurses could expect to earn no more than $500 a year. Long workdays accompanied the low pay, with minimum shifts of twelve or more hours the rule. Only private-duty graduate nurses earned higher wages, perhaps $15 a week. While that was good money at the time, it involved a seven-day week of 24-hour-a-day responsibility.[19]

At the turn of the century nursing had not yet become a respected profession. As late as 1898, during the Spanish-American War, it was not to the Nurses' Associated Alumni (shortly to become the American Nurses Association) that the government turned for recruiting and training nurses, but to the Daughters of the American Revolution.

In the teaching profession, women outnumbered men almost three to one. Half a million women taught school, many of them still in one-room schoolhouses, but thousands in established city school systems. Women began to enter teaching in substantial numbers as early as the 1830s. As opportunities increased during the nineteenth century for women to attend school, this became *the* profession for middle-class women. The supply of teachers was plentiful, and school boards were happy to hire them for one-half to one-third of what they would have had to pay men. Most women teachers were young and single. In fact, this could almost be assumed, for in most cases marriage was an automatic bar to teaching for a woman. A New York City law, for example, still held that "Should a female teacher marry, her place shall thereupon become vacant."

While some teachers had normal-school training and a few had completed college, many had as little as six or eight years of formal schooling. It was not until 1907 that Indiana became the first state to insist that its licensed teachers have completed high school.[20]

Associations of teachers formed as early as 1845, when the Massachusetts State Association of Teachers was organized, and twenty-two others formed over the next dozen years. This movement culminated in 1857 in the formation of the National Teachers Association. Thirteen years later the National Education Association was founded. That same year (1870) the National Labor Union numbered a Cincinnati Colored Teachers Cooperative Association among its affiliates.[21]

Teachers protested sporadically against arbitrary supervisors, or petitioned for pensions and for salary adjustments, but they achieved few concrete gains. In 1893 a Teachers' Club to "professionalize" the job of teaching was organized in Chicago. This formalized the search of teachers for acceptance as "professionals," and for higher standards for entry into teaching as a life career. The club's major focus, however, was on the interests of high school administrators, principals, and teachers, few of whom were women. It considered bargaining for money undignified, an activity mainly for working-class labor organizations with which the club was not eager to be identified. Nor did the club do much more than tolerate the elementary school teachers, who were viewed as part-time and temporary, transients in a genteel occupation for middle-class young women before they married and for spinsters. The public shared this view of the grade school teacher. So did the legislature, which paid them accordingly and set almost no standards for entry into the field.

It was therefore no surprise to elementary school teachers to find the Teachers Club promoting a pension fund and pushing the Illinois legislature to set up a teacher retirement plan—two programs that did not meet their needs. Their chances of being in the school system long enough to collect a pension were slim and their needs immediate: higher salaries, relief from the arbitrary rule of supervisors and from favoritism, and more equitable work loads. In 1897 Catherine Goggin, leader among the elementary school teachers of Chicago, took 300 teachers with her out of the club to organize the Chicago Teachers Federation, and within a year,

2,500 teachers had joined. With her friend and co-worker, Margaret Haley, Goggin began the long, uphill fight for teacher gains.

The first step was to break away from the 1877 salary scale under which teachers had been paid for twenty years; 3,567 teachers signed a petition for higher wages. But the Board of Education, which granted the increases in 1898, reported at the same time that it could not afford to pay them, as the city's tax structure could not support it.[22] Skeptical of this report, the teachers investigated on their own and discovered that for years a number of corporations had paid no taxes at all to the city, either on their stock, capital, or franchises. If these taxes were collected, the money to pay teacher increases would be available to the Board of Education.

The teachers sued for the wages due them. The city fathers of Chicago were livid with anger, and so was the state. In retaliation, legislators tried— unsuccessfully—to destroy the teachers' pension system. However, the teachers won their wage suit, including the award of $249,000 in back taxes to the Board of Education from the city. The story did not have quite as prompt a happy ending as it should have, however. The board took the tax money but failed to allocate it to teacher salaries, so that the federation had to go to court again. Finally, in 1904, six years after they won their increase, the teachers received the money due them.[23]

In 1902, Chicago teachers affiliated with the city Federation of Labor (AFL). This move, designed to join the teachers to the strength of the Chicago labor movement, frightened some teachers still fearful of close associations with working-class activities* and it infuriated the city's offi- cials. The *New York World* described the move as the officials saw it: "the servants of the city . . . organized against the interests of the city."[24] But one paper, the *Chicago Herald*, saw the reason for the teachers' move to affiliate with the labor federation as quite different:

> The urgencies which drove the teachers to affiliate with the Chicago Federation of Labor date back two decades.
>   The Teachers' Federation was born in the rooms of the school board, and the city of Chicago is its parent.
>   Picture the conditions of that time. Witness a meeting of the school board. Into their presence comes a committee of timorous women. The leader of the group speaks for them. She makes an appeal for higher salaries. She pleads that it is impossible for teachers to support them- selves at a reasonable standard of living on the wages paid.

* It is interesting, however, that even while some teachers still scorned union affiliation and felt it would affect their ability to be impartial in the classroom—as well as lower their status—it was the labor movement that always supported funds for free public edu- cation and better salaries for teachers. Since teacher salaries were set by state legislatures, this support has been essential.

The board members listen to the committee. The gentlemen are silent and their granite countenances do not betray their thoughts.

The teachers are ushered out. When the door closes laughter breaks the silence.

A few years later, after other experiences as discomforting, the teachers affiliated with the Chicago Federation of Labor.[25]

The city fathers, determined to thwart teacher affiliation with the AFL, adopted what became known as the "Loeb Plan," named after the Board of Education member who designed it. The old "yellow-dog contract" in a new guise, it declared that no Chicago Teachers' Federation member would be hired as long as the federation remained affiliated with the AFL. Although the teachers obtained a court injunction against this edict, the Illinois Supreme Court reversed the lower court, giving to the Board of Education the "absolute right to decline to employ or re-employ an applicant for any reason whatever or for no reason at all."[26] To save its members' jobs, the Chicago Teachers Federation was forced to withdraw from the AFL, but the damage had been done. Other state courts followed the Illinois example and affirmed the absolute right of boards of education to fire teachers. It became such an effective tool against teacher unionization that in the first decade of the twentieth century only nine teachers' locals affiliated with the AFL.

In New York, teachers fought on another front: equal pay for equal work. When Brooklyn became part of New York City in 1898, the New York legislature set $600 a year as the scale for women teachers in the newly unified school system, and $900 for men, with annual increases of no less than $40 a year for women and $105 for men.[27] The Interborough Association of Women Teachers was organized in 1906 around the issue of equal pay. This association succeeded in getting an equal-pay bill through the legislature, but New York City's mayor disapproved and the law could not take effect. The legislature repassed the bill, and this time Governor Charles Evans Hughes vetoed it, pointing out that women were paid less throughout state institutions and that he saw no reason for women who taught in New York City to be treated any differently.[28]

A survey of New York City schools in 1910 found that of the 15,333 teachers, 14,751 were women. While only three men were paid less than $1,000 a year, 7,619 women were. By 1912 equal pay had been instituted for high school teachers, but separate scales were still in effect for teachers through the eighth grade. Most male teachers were found on the high school level, while almost the entire classroom teaching staff of elementary schools was female. School superintendents and principals were men. When they married, women teachers were still forced to work as permanent substitutes, at lower pay, rather than as regularly licensed teachers.

One of the biggest battles loomed over the right of women to keep their regular jobs when they married. Mary Murphy's case was one of the first to test whether married women would be allowed to teach. A Brooklyn teacher since 1891, she married in 1901, was charged with misconduct and promptly fired. She took the case to court, where the lower court upheld the Board of Education but on appeal was overruled, the judge holding that marriage was not misconduct. In 1904, Murphy was reinstated with back pay.[29]

It had always been the rule that teachers were fired when they became pregnant. About 1913, teachers began to take issue with this edict. One teacher who needed her job desperately managed to conceal her pregnancy from school authorities and to give birth to her child over a weekend. Not as fortunate as she thought, she was discovered and suspended for "conduct unbecoming a teacher." Mrs. Bridget Pexitto handled her pregnancy differently, telling authorities she had an eye infection and could not come in to work. When she was found out and fired, it was for being absent for childbirth "without the permission of the Board of Education."[30]

To reinforce its position that good mothers should stay home with their children, the Board of Education ordered city board employee Dr. William Maxwell to search through the schools for pregnant teachers. He must have been embarrassed, and did so reluctantly. Nonetheless, he found fourteen pregnant teachers, all of whom were promptly suspended.

Infuriated, Henrietta Rodman, a high school English teacher and unionist, charged the Board of Education with "mother-baiting" in a letter to the *New York Tribune*, for which she was suspended. The board miscalculated in the case of Rodman. She took it on over the issue of free speech, and finally won reinstatement as a teacher—though only after losing a term of employment and accepting a transfer to another high school.

Nor did Bridget Pexitto accept her dismissal without a fight. She challenged the board's decision and won her case in the lower court. When it was reversed on appeal and her dismissal upheld, Pexitto went to the court of appeals, which recommended that she go directly to the state commissioner of education. By this time her case had attracted wide attention, and the commissioner ordered her reinstated.

Not until 1915 did the Teachers' League win a partial victory on the free-speech issue or get maternal-leave policies altered. Its battles, however, forged it into a militant organization, and in 1916 it voted to become a labor union, the fifth and largest local of the American Federation of Teachers, and to affiliate with the AFL.

While New York and Chicago teachers were organizing, life for rural and small-town teachers continued in the same restricted pattern of the preceding century. For example, when Iva McDaniels, a Massachusetts schoolteacher for fifteen years, came back after spending a Thanksgiving holiday with friends in a nearby town, she found she had been fired for ignoring two of the ten rules governing the behavior of female school-teachers. She had left town without the permission of the school board, and she had violated rule number 7 below.

Rules for Female Teachers

1. Do not get married.
2. Do not leave town at any time without permission of the school board.
3. Do not keep company with men.
4. Be home between the hours of 8 P.M. and 6 A.M.
5. Do not loiter downtown in ice cream stores.
6. Do not smoke.
7. Do not get into a carriage with any man except your father or brother.
8. Do not dress in bright colors.
9. Do not dye your hair.
10. Do not wear any dress more than two inches above the ankle.[31]

Such stringent guidelines to behavior, however, had not plagued the women who packed up family belongings and prepared for the grueling, tedious, and dangerous journey West.

14

WORKING WOMEN
OF THE WEST
1800–1900

She is known by every cowboy on the Pecos River wide,
They know full well that she can shoot, that she can rope and ride.
She goes to every round-up, every cow work without fail,
Looking out for her cattle, branded "walking hog on rail."

She made her start in cattle, yes, made it with her rope;
Can tie down every maverick before it can strike a lope.
She can rope and tie and brand it as quick as any man;
She's voted by all cowboys an A-1 top cow hand.

—"The Pecos Queen," cowboy ballad

While women in the seaboard cities of the East were moving into factory and office jobs, into retail stores and telephone exchanges to find work, women on the frontier moved back in time. Through the nineteenth century, men continued the westward trek, seeking a new life on the land or perhaps their fortune in the goldfields of California. Women went too, sometimes on their own, more often as wives. For a hundred years the vastness of a continent opened before them until finally there was no more new land to explore and the frontier came to an end.

It was not the ordinary American who could pack up and head West. It took capital, about $1,500, to outfit a wagon, buy supplies, and tide the family over until the land began to produce. This was an impossible sum for most working-class families to come by.[1] Thus it was the skilled worker, the small businessman, and the farmer who headed West. The women who accompanied them were young—most were under thirty—and usually strong. They had to be.

For most women the journey West was one long test of endurance; nor was it over when they reached their destination and a cabin, sod hut, or tent became "home." Whether out of a need to communicate their private hopes and fears, or out of a sense of history, or both, these women kept journals and diaries. Often their accounts detailed the day-to-day minutiae that make the history of the settling of the West so vivid and real:

Early in the morning of May 15, 1855, we began yoking the oxen. There were twenty head and two cows, and only one pair had ever been yoked before. It was a great undertaking and it was four o'clock in the afternoon before it was done.[2]

When it is realized that the average team pulled a wagon only fifteen or twenty miles in a day, there is agony in those two simple sentences!

Charting the Vast Beyond

The story of the frontiers of the nineteenth century can be said to have begun with the purchase of Louisiana from France in 1803 by President Thomas Jefferson, which doubled the size of the United States, incorporating lands from the Mississippi River all the way to the Rocky Mountains. On May 14, 1804, Jefferson launched Meriwether Lewis and William Clark on a remarkable journey across the Great Plains, over the high Rockies, and on to the Pacific, with instructions to explore, to establish friendly relations with the Indians they met, and to keep a precise record of everything they encountered.

The good relationships with the Indians that Lewis and Clark enjoyed during their travels were due in large part to the only woman on the expedition, Sacajawea, a Shoshone Indian woman and wife of one of their guides, Toussaint Charbonneau. Born about 1787, Sacajawea had been captured as a young girl by a war party of the Hidatsa tribe and taken to its village in what is now North Dakota. There she was sold to Charbonneau and lived with him and his wife, also a Shoshone. When she was seventeen or eighteen, Charbonneau married her as well.

Sacajawea is mentioned frequently in the Lewis and Clark journals. In 1805, during the expedition, her son was born, and the explorers halted for a few days while she regained her strength. She strapped her infant to her back, and continued with them. In addition to her role as interpreter and guide, she did all the expedition's laundry and cooking, gathering and preparing wild vegetables to accompany the fish and game that composed most of their diet.[3] The men counted on her as nurse and doctor as well, because of her knowledge of the use of herbs. Farther west, in Idaho, Lewis and Clark named a river after her, the "Sah-ca-ger we-ah or bird woman's River, after our interpreter the Snake woman."[4] *

At the close of the journey Charbonneau was paid for his services. Sacajawea received nothing. However, William Clark promised that whenever she and Charbonneau wished, he would adopt the child and

---

* The Snake River, a tributary of the Columbia River, flows through much of Idaho to form part of the boundary between Idaho and Oregon. Today two cities on its route through Washington to join the Columbia are Lewiston, Idaho, and Clarkston, Washington.

see that he received an education. On December 20, 1812, Sacajawea died, leaving an infant daughter as well as her son, and Clark became guardian for both children.[5]

With the charting by the Lewis and Clark expedition of lands previously known only to trappers, hunters, and Indians, the opening of the West began. Not many years later another Indian guide, Marie Dorion, of the Iowa tribe, helped to lead a 3,500-mile overland expedition into Oregon to the fur-trading area on the Columbia River founded by John Jacob Astor and known then as Astoria.[6]

Women on the Western Trail

While not all pioneers chose the overland route to the West, across the Great Plains, the desert, and the high Rockies, most did.* The wheels of all the wagons wore deep ruts in muddy weather that hardened in the baking sun. The woman on the board seat behind the oxen breathed in the clouds of dust their hoofs stirred up when the weather was dry. Sometimes it must have seemed that the household necessities for the trip would engulf her—

> a basket of potatoes to rest her feet upon, in her arms a child not quite two years old, in one hand an umbrella to screen her throbbing head from the oppressive heat of the sun, and in the other a bundle of sundries that could find no place secure from falling overboard, from the rocking to and fro of the ponderous vehicle.[7]

When the wagons came to rivers, they could be floated across, passengers and all, but not always. Narcissa Whitman, traveling to Oregon as a missionary in 1836, described one alternate method:

> I can cross the most difficult streams without the least fear. There is one manner of crossing husband has tried, but I have not. Take an elk skin and stretch it over you, spreading yourself out as much as possible, then let the Indian women carefully put you in the water and with a cord in the mouth they will swim and drag you over.[8]

The discovery of gold in California in 1849 and silver in Colorado and Nevada ten years later launched mad scrambles to stake out claims. With the 42,500 men who rushed to California in the one year of 1849 came 5,000 women, some of them prepared to stake out claims too, and 2,500 children.[9] Mrs. Lodisa Frizzell, one of those who made the trip,

---

* Two other routes were used by those bound for California, one the long boat trip around Cape Horn and up the west coast of South America, the other the three-stage journey by boat to Panama, on muleback across the Isthmus, and by boat again up the coast to California. Each route had its dangers and drawbacks. There was no easy way west.

confided to her journal as the group prepared to tackle the mountain passes:

> We are about fifteen ms. [miles] from South Pass, *we are hardly half way*. I felt tired and weary. O the luxury of a house, a house! I felt what some one expressed, who traveled this long and tedious journey, that, "it tires the soul." . . . That this journey is tiresome, no one will doubt, that it is perilous, the deaths of many will testify, and the heart has a thousand misgivings, & the mind is tortured with anxiety, & often as I passed the freshly made graves, I have glanced at the side boards of the waggon, not knowing how soon it might serve as the coffin for some one of us. . . .[10]

So many wagons headed west that by 1855, the trail along the Platte River was 100 feet wide, and the trailside was littered with cast-off articles that had become too heavy to haul. Carcasses of dead oxen littered the way. As wagon trains tackled the Rockies, all extra weight was jettisoned. Often women and children walked, while all those who could helped to push and pull the wagons. At times footings had to be cut for each step the oxen took, an agonizing task to the men who were in a hurry to cross the mountains before fall and the dreaded ice and snow storms of the Rockies began.

When the wagon train camped, the women would unite to plead for an extra day's halt to do the laundry.

> If she had no soap, and quite often she did not, she started the day by soaking a batch of hardwood ashes, preferably oak, in a kettle of water. When the water boiled and became lye, she dipped it into another kettle, stirring until a white, flaky scum appeared. This indicated that the water was "broken" and after clearing away the scum she poured it into washtubs, leaving it to stand until a sediment formed. The water was not clean and soft, but all this work used up the first half of her washing day.[11]

Even after the clothes were washed, a strong residue of lye remained, making life miserable for the infants still in diapers. Chafing and rashes rubbed their skin raw, and glycerine was a priority medication without which no mother started West.

Women found ways to bake, too, even under the most trying conditions. One determined woman in a party on the Oregon trail is described by traveler James Clyman (the spelling is his):

> . . . and here let me say there was one young Lady which showed herself worthy of the bravest undaunted poieneer of [the] West for after having kneaded her dough she watched and nursed the fire and held an umblella over the fire and her skillit with the greatest composure for near 2 hours and baked bread enough to give us a very plentifull supper. . . .[12]

In addition to the housekeeping chores they performed along the trail, women became expert at hitching and driving oxen, and at emergency tasks like shoeing them. Lydia Waters described how she and her husband did this on their way across Wyoming. They began by digging a trench as long as the ox.

> The animal was then thrown and rolled over so that its backbone lay in the trench and all four of its legs were up in the air. In this position it was helpless and the shoes were nailed on readily.[13]

A sisterhood developed on the trail, out of a need for companionship and an interdependence in time of sickness or trouble, reminiscent of the colonial period two centuries earlier. As women walked beside the wagons, cooked over shared campfires, or waited while wagon axles were repaired, they talked and comforted each other. Many had started out reluctantly, given little choice about whether or not the family moved West by husbands who rarely asked their opinion. They knew what to expect, from newspaper stories, magazine articles, and letters from those who had gone ahead.

The women knew of the loneliness and isolation they faced, the small chance they had of ever seeing family or friends again, the physical hardships, the possibility of Indian attack, the fact that they would have to produce almost everything their families used, and the probability that they would bear their children alone and unattended. No matter how well prepared they thought themselves for the experience, for the majority the reality proved worse. Thoughts of the home she left behind were with the pioneer woman constantly. In Indiana, her cabin might be a "barbarous rectangle of unhewed and unbarked logs, bound together by a gigantic dovetailing called notchings."[14] On the Nebraska plains, where wood was scarce, it was likely to be a hut of sod cut in great chunks and piled up in layers, covered over with a coating of mud. Whichever kind of home, it was small and crowded.

> You can imagine a crowded twelve or fourteen feet square, furnishing a bed-chamber for as many people. . . . A huge sack laid upon the planks served as the family bed. The mother and the oldest daughter would lie down on it at the opposite ends, so that each other's feet and head would be in contact, were it not for the little children, whom, to the number of three or four, we have seen stowed in . . . like mortar between the stones, to keep all tight.[15]

When the New York–Chicago railroad run began in 1852, women who could do so traveled to the Midwest and later as far as Nebraska by rail, meeting the wagon trains there. But railroad travel was sooty, hot, and uncomfortable. One Montana woman recalled later the backless benches, the cars without springs that lurched from side to side. "I got tired and wished to sleep," she wrote, "so I stretched out on the floor under the seats. I remember the conductor kicking my feet, which were sprawled out into the aisle."[16]

Women in the West dressed to suit the life they led. One traveler described the first woman he saw working on a frontier farm:

> A strange figure emerged from the tall rank weeds into the road before us. . . . at bottom it seemed to be a man, for there were a man's tow-linen breeches; at top, a woman; for there was the semblance of a short gown, and indeed a female kerchief on the neck and a sun-bonnet on the head. . . . It originated in the necessities of a new country, where women must hunt cows hid in tall weeds and coarse grass on dewy or frosty mornings.[17]

On the trail, too, women soon found it wise to dress for the rough life. If they could, they outfitted themselves with "specially made men's boots of smaller sizes" and knickerbockers that went to the boot tops. They "concealed this outlandish garb with knee-length skirts. Any woman starting west in a silk dress," wrote Dee Brown in *The Gentle Tamers*, "was immediately suspected of being a prostitute."[18] This is not the image of the madonna of the Trail that is often portrayed, but considering the hazards of the journey, it is likely that most women decided to be practical, at least until they reached civilization again.

That many did not reach "civilization," but only a new form of pioneer existence, is clear from accounts such as that of Anna Howard Shaw, minister, doctor, and suffrage leader, who moved to the northern Michigan woods in 1859 when she was a child of twelve:

> We were one hundred miles from a railroad, forty miles from the nearest post-office, and half a dozen miles from any neighbors save Indians, wolves, and wildcats. . . . [We were] unlearned in the ways of the woods as well as in the most primitive methods of farming . . . we lacked not only every comfort, but even the bare necessities of life . . . we must begin, single-handed and untaught, a struggle for existence in which some of the severest forces of nature would be arrayed against us. . . .[19]

The family at that point included her younger brother of eight, two older sisters and an invalid mother; her father had returned East to his job, from which he sent them money when he could. The cabin he had begun for them in the woods had four walls, but only holes for windows and another for a door. The nearest sawmill was nine miles away, the nearest store, forty. Once the shock of their situation had worn off, the family huddled in the cabin and assigned chores to each member. To Anna and her brother, she recalled years later, fell all the outside work, including finishing the cabin and building its furniture, as well as turning the virgin soil and planting and harvesting their first crops.

Working Women in the West

"I reckon women are some like horses and oxen," said an Illinois farmer about mid-century; "the biggest can do the most work, and that's what I want one for."[20] However, he was likely to be grateful for almost any woman, since there was such a shortage of them, and if he had a choice would pick one who was a widow experienced at farming, with several children who could help out with the work.

The 1870 census reported 384,898 men over the age of twenty-one in the Western states and territories,* and 172,145 women, but California had 99,688 of the women, more than half the total. The ratio of men to women in the population differed sharply from place to place, so that while New Mexico and Utah had almost equal numbers of men and women, in Idaho and Montana the ratio was 8 men for every woman. The gap closed rapidly, however: in California in 1850 there were 23 men for every woman in the state; in 1870, 2.28 men for every woman.[21]

Of the women over the age of twenty-one living in the West in 1870, 20,625 were listed as gainfully employed. This count did not include prostitutes, who composed the second largest group of wage-earning women. Domestic servants constituted the largest, with 10,758, or more than half the total. Other leading occupations for women included teaching (with 2,305 reported in that field), laundering, needlework, dressmaking, and nursing and midwifery. Women ran boardinghouses and hotels, farmed, and worked in the cotton and woolen mills that had begun to appear. The census listed two women as miners and another as a wheelwright. Since many women younger than twenty-one also were wage-earners, the census understated the numbers of women in the work force.[22]

By 1890, when national figures showed 17 percent of all adult women in the United States working outside the home, the percentage for the West was only 13. Not only was there little industry in the West to pull large numbers of women into the work force, but the Western woman still played a vital economic role as home producer for her family. However, women in the professions were represented in the West out of all proportion to their numbers nationally. With 5 percent of the nation's population and 4 percent of its adult women, the West in 1890 had 17

* In 1870 the Western states included California, Oregon, Nevada, and Texas. The territories were Washington, Utah, Idaho, Wyoming, the two Dakotas, New Mexico, Colorado, Montana, and Arizona.

percent of all the country's actresses; 15 percent of its women authors; 14 percent of all female lawyers; and 10 percent of all women doctors and journalists. Eight out of every 100 women workers in the country as a whole were in the professions, but 14 out of every 100 women in the West.[23]

While wages for women in some occupations where a shortage continued, as in teaching, remained higher than in the East, it cost more to live in the West, and it is likely that the two balanced out.* In the territory of Wyoming in 1869 and in the state of California in 1873, laws were passed guaranteeing equal pay for teachers regardless of sex. Though not enforced, these laws indicated a status accorded women that was not found in the East at the time.

Western women found themselves unhampered by many of the restrictions placed on their Eastern sisters. So it was that numbers of women who came West turned their traditional homemaking talents into successful businesses. One California woman wrote to a Boston newspaper in 1852 that she had "baked and sold $18,000 worth of pies, about one third of which was clear profit."

> I dragged my own wood off the mountains and chopped it, and I never had so much as a child to take a step for me in this country. $11,000 I baked in one little iron skillet, a considerable portion by a campfire, without the shelter of a tree from the broiling sun. But now I have a good many "Robinson Crusoe" comforts about me. I bake about 1,200 pies per month and clear $200. . . .[24]

A Mrs. Washington sold home-cooked meals to army men from Fort Phil Kearney in Wyoming who flocked to her house every payday. In 1878, women in Fresno County packed the first California raisins to be produced and shipped East, while Minna E. Sherman, perhaps on a dare to prove it could be done, packed and shipped table grapes to the East, and turned a tidy profit on the venture.[25]

An article, dated 1872, reported that, in the West,

> women are gradually filling all departments of labor. The latest occupation is that of Mrs. Sarah I. Aiken, who is making postal currency and independence (i.e., her living) by rowing over the Mississippi and transferring passengers from Clinton, Iowa to Garden Plain, Ill. . . .[26]

The article urged readers to watch the column "Notes Concerning Women" in future issues of *The Women's Journal* for new ideas about the kinds of work women "can do and undertake" in the West.

---

* The average pay for teachers nationally, according to an 1898–1899 report of the U.S. Bureau of Education, was $45.25 a month for men, $38.14 for women. In the West it was $61.04 for men and $50.58 for women. T. A. Larson, "Women's Role in the American West," *Montana, The Magazine of Western History* 24, no. 3 (summer 1974): 6.

Women rode the range and broke and trained horses. Mary Meagher won fame as a rancher in Washington Territory, a "tall, majestic woman about thirty years old who liked to play poker." Arizona Mary drove a sixteen-yoke ox team carrying freight in the Southwest. Charlie Pankhurst drove a stagecoach for twenty years. Only on the day she died in 1879 was it discovered that she was "Miss" Pankhurst and not Charlie.[27]

Calamity Jane, whose real name was Martha Jane Canary (Burke), is said to have warned men not to risk "calamity" by insulting her. She rode the rails, and served as an army scout and a pony express rider. Legends grew up around her, stories of her skill in handling horse teams and cattle and of the cheap cigars she smoked. Those who knew her best appreciated her ability as a gentle and accomplished nurse.[28]

The famed Annie Oakley (Phoeby Ann Oakley Mozee) became a crack shot at the age of nine through shooting game to help feed the family. In 1875 she pitted her skill against that of marksman Frank Butler in a shooting match, and married him a year later. The two spent their lives touring Europe and America in breathtaking shows that demonstrated their ability.[29]

People found it hard to believe that tiny Martha Maxwell, under five feet tall and an expert taxidermist, shot and trapped all the animals that she stuffed in the course of her work. Ambulance driver Laura Winthrop Johnson wrote a book about her exploits. Luella Day, a Chicago doctor, decided in 1898 to seek gold in the Alaskan Klondike, America's last frontier. She ended up fighting so hard for honest government there that four attempts were made to murder her. The last came close to succeeding. Escaping just in time, she returned to the United States in 1904 to write a book about the region's corruption.[30]

Kate Barnard, the first woman to hold state elective office in Oklahoma, was the chief of its Department of Charities and Corrections. An agitator for legislative reform, she supported child labor laws, fought for compulsory education, and sought prison reform. Early in her career she earned a reputation as a labor organizer, setting up a union of unemployed men and serving as its delegate to the Oklahoma City Trades Council and the State Federation of Labor.[31]

The democracy of the West, evidenced by the acceptance of women in a wide range of jobs and careers, did not extend to blacks. As early as 1850 the constitution of Indiana barred them as well as mulattos from coming into the state or settling there. Nor could those already there vote. A similar regulation barred blacks from the territory of Oregon. This caused a special problem when George William Bust and his wife and family, blacks who had guided the first group of American settlers to explore north of the Columbia River, wanted to settle there. It took strong

pressure from the white leaders of the expedition and a special act of
Congress to grant Bust the customary 640 acres of land that Oregon offered families who agreed to come to the territory to settle.*[32]

Some of the most interesting working women of the West were
black women. As a slave, Grandma Biddy Mason trudged behind her
master's three-hundred-wagon train on the route to California, tending
livestock all the way. When they arrived in 1854, she and her three
daughters were freed, and they settled in the new community of Los
Angeles, which had only eight white families and two black, including
hers. Through her good business sense, she accumulated valuable real
estate and became quite wealthy. The reputation that grew up around
her, however, centered on her generosity to the poor, the churches she
built, the schools she established for nurses, and her own work as a maternity nurse.[33]

Mary Fields, born a slave in Tennessee, found her way West and in
1884 took a job as freight hauler in Cascade, Montana. Six feet tall, fast
on the draw, and as strong as a man, she was as likely as any cowpuncher
to settle her quarrels with a shoot-out. A stint at running a restaurant
failed, but she found an occupation that suited her when, in her sixties,
she became a stagecoach driver carrying the United States mails. No
matter what route she was assigned or what the weather, she saw that her
mailcoach came through. In her seventies she opened her own laundry
business, spending her leisure hours at the local Cascade saloon, smoking
cigars and drinking alongside the men. When she died in 1914 and was
buried in Cascade's Hillside Cemetery, she had become one of the town's
beloved citizens.[34]

One of the most unusual careers in the West was that of Nettie Elizabeth Mills (West), a black woman born in 1880 on a Nebraska farm.
She became a boardinghouse operator, a saleswoman for *Collier's*, a member of the Omaha Stock Exchange, and the first woman to own and operate an oil drilling rig.[35]

Although a number of women of the West held colorful and adventurous jobs, the majority worked to make a home for their families, to
produce the food and clothing they needed, to raise the chickens and the
children, and to nurse and comfort those less fortunate than they. Gradually their first homes—a tent, a zinc shack in the goldfields, a tepee purchased from the Indians, a sod hut, or even a cave cut out of a hillside—
were replaced by frame or adobe houses. The settling-in process had
begun.

---

* Single women were offered 320 acres.

Wyoming's Women

While the movement for woman suffrage had been born in Seneca Falls, New York, back in 1848, it was the women of Wyoming who made their territory the leader in granting women the vote. In a series of "firsts" that astounded the country, they turned the territory into the Mecca of the suffrage movement.

> In Wyoming, our sisters fair
> Can use the ballot well,
> Why can't we do so everywhere,
> Can anybody tell?

To Esther McQuigg Morris, a rangy woman six feet tall, goes the credit for initiating and guiding through the Wyoming legislature the bill granting women of the territory the right to vote. From the start the territory was aware of its unique place in American history, so that the name of the first woman to vote, early that morning of September 6, 1870, is known. She was Louisa Ann Swain, a seventy-year-old resident of Laramie. Humorist Bill Nye reported: "No rum was sold, women rode to the polls in carriages furnished by the parties, and every man was straining himself to be a gentleman because there were votes at stake."[37]

In 1870, Wyoming became the first territory *or* state to impanel women jurors. During a period of lawlessness in the state, when men jurors were afraid, or at least reluctant, to hand down indictments, someone suggested putting women, now eligible to serve under Wyoming's new suffrage law, on the grand jury. Not only were the eyes of the country upon the first six women who agreed to serve, but the nation's press, particularly back East, was prepared to amuse its readers with the story. Justice John H. Howe, for the first time addressing twelve jurors as "Ladies and Gentlemen of the Grand Jury," promised them:

> You shall not be driven by the sneers, jeers and insults of a laughing crowd from the temple of justice, as your sisters have from some of the medical colleges of the land. The strong hand of the law shall protect you . . . it will be a sorry day for any man who shall so far forget the courtesies due and paid by every American gentleman to every American lady as to even by act or word endeavor to deter you from the exercise of those rights with which the law has invested you.[38]

The judge could not protect the women jurors from the inquiring press, with its cartoons and jingles such as "Baby, baby, don't get in a fury, / Your mamma's gone to sit on the jury."[39] When the women refused to let newspaper photographers take their picture, artists were sent into the courtroom to draw them. The women, in turn, put on heavy veils.

For three weeks the jury sat, bringing in indictments and setting a tone that guaranteed women jurors a place in Wyoming's system of justice from that time on.

In a similar vein, Esther Morris, elected to a term as justice of the peace, carried on in spite of Eastern newspaper cartoons showing her with her feet on her desk, a cigar in her mouth, and a jackknife for whittling in her hand. She earned such a reputation for fairness that not one of the forty cases she handled during her term was appealed.[40]

When Wyoming applied for statehood in 1889, there was some question whether Congress would admit it because it had granted suffrage to women. The Wyoming state legislature wired Washington: "We may stay out of the Union a hundred years, but we will come in with our women."[41] Wyoming was admitted to statehood, but the margin was narrow. In the House the vote was 139 to 127; in the Senate, 29 to 18.

In 1910, Wyoming's Mary G. Bellamy became the first woman elected to a state legislature, and the nation's first woman governor, another Wyoming woman, was Nellie Tayloe Ross (1925), who filled the unexpired term of her husband. President Franklin Delano Roosevelt named her director of the United States Mint in 1933, the first woman to serve in this post.

Wyoming was proud of its women and its record as a suffrage state. But other tireless leaders, women who worked, supported families, and still found time to campaign for the vote, came out of the West.* One of these was Abigail Scott Duniway, teacher, farmer, newspaper editor and publisher, writer, and suffragist. She knew the rigors of the trail West, for in the spring of 1852, as she later wrote,

> my father decided to emigrate to Oregon. My invalid mother expostulated in vain; she and nine of us children were stowed away in ox-wagons, where for six months we made our home, cooking food and washing dishes around campfires, sleeping at night in the wagons, and crossing many streams upon wagon-beds rigged as ferry-boats. When our weary line of march had reached the Black Hills of Wyoming my mother became a victim to the dreadful epidemic, cholera, that devastated the emigrant trains in that never-to-be-forgotten year, and after a few hours' illness her weary spirit was called to the skies. . . . But ten weeks after, our Willie, the baby, was buried in the sands of the Burnt River Mountains. Reaching Oregon in the fall with our broken household, I engaged in school-teaching till . . . I allowed the name of "Scott" to become "Duniway."[42]

After her marriage, Duniway gave up schoolteaching to devote herself to making a home and raising children. But when her husband met with

---

* Utah granted women the vote in 1870, and Colorado and Idaho in 1893 and 1896 respectively. In fact, the first dozen states to grant woman suffrage were all in the West.

an accident, it was she who, during most of the rest of her life, supported the family by taking in boarders, teaching, and opening a millinery business. When her sons were old enough to take on the family's support, she turned to writing. In the prosuffrage paper the *New Northwest*, which she published from 1871 to 1893, and later in her autobiographical account of the suffrage movement in the Pacific coast states, she wrote of the loneliness and isolation of the early years of her married life:

> We have ourself lived, during four consecutive winters, upon a farm where, for four months of each year, we did not see the face of a woman. Nobody need tell us that such a state of life is natural or right. . . .[43]

> I, if not washing, scrubbing, churning or nursing the baby, was preparing their meals in our lean-to kitchen. To bear two children in two and a half years from my marriage day, to make thousands of pounds of butter every year for market, not including what was used in our free hotel at home; to sew and cook, and wash and iron; to bake and clean and stew and fry; to be in short, a general pioneer drudge, with never a penny of my own, was not pleasant business for an erstwhile school teacher.[44]

Although Duniway had an extraordinary career, the issues on which she spoke were those of the ordinary women of the West, strong women who had endured the hardships of pioneer life and proved ingenious and inventive in the battle for survival. By the close of the nineteenth century, the challenge of the mountains and the plains was at an end. The sharp contrast between life on the frontier and life in the "civilized" world of the East began to diminish. As the lands were tamed, so were the people on them. A new migration was about to begin, that of the young Western woman who, joining her country cousins from the North, South, and East, would move into the cities of America in the search for work.

Part 5

EMERGENCE OF THE TRADE UNION WOMAN *1900–1914*

In the years between 1900 and the First World War, the Progressive movement took firm hold. Journalists wrote spine-chilling accounts of the conditions and wages of workers, and exposés of big business and corporate might. They detailed the lives of workers in stockyards and steel mills, in tenements and factories. The Settlement House movement brought together some of the most dedicated and literate women of that day or any day, who opened the doors of settlement houses to working people, particularly immigrant workers.

The leaders of these movements battled for legal reforms and finally found a listening ear among a number of liberal federal and state legislators. Studies and investigations following tragedies such as the Triangle Shirtwaist Company fire, and industrial strife such as the strike of the Lawrence textile workers, provided the basis for laws on factory safety and inspection and on limiting hours of work.

One of the leading organizations to emerge during this period of ferment was the National Women's Trade Union League of America (NWTUL), the only national organization of its time to concern itself primarily with the organization of working women into trade unions. For years this organization would be *the* voice that spoke out for women workers seeking entrance into AFL unions. Through league doors in the major cities across the country passed many of the working women who became organizers and leaders in their unions during the first half of the twentieth century.

Organizing the women clustered in low-wage, unskilled jobs was slow, hard work. Therefore the WTUL also lobbied for protective laws that would limit women's hours of work and monitor their working conditions. They pointed out that 10 hours in the factory, plus 2 or more hours a day spent in travel, left women too little time and energy to perform their many household tasks and bear and rear healthy children. It was no wonder women's life expectancy averaged less than forty-eight years.

The league walked a constant tightrope, on the one hand dependent on the AFL for funds and support, and on the other faced with the demands of members and leaders who were often critical of conservative AFL attitudes toward women and toward much of the legislation the league supported. In a time when union organization was not widely accepted even for men, the league reached out to the most downtrodden of all workers and supported their efforts to organize. Its leaders risked arrest, walked endless picket lines, traveled day and night on uncomfortable trains, bullied legislators, wrote reams of articles, and begged money from the rich and from labor unions alike to further the cause of working women. Upper-class society frowned on many of their efforts, and would have scowled even more deeply had not some of the leading league members come from their own ranks.

The WTUL's most lasting achievements were in educating women for leadership. At the end of the 1930s, League secretary-treasurer Elizabeth Christman, a former glove worker, could point to 2 women secretaries of national unions, 18 general executive board members, 27 secretaries of central labor unions, one secretary of a state federation of labor, and 273 local union officers, all elected officials who had been trained by the league. This was in addition to the numbers of women union organizers, education and other appointed staff, and community and government officials who had been league-trained.

15

WORKING WOMEN IN THE NATIONAL WOMEN'S TRADE UNION LEAGUE *1903–1914*

The working girls in the morning are going to work—long
   lines of them afoot amid the downtown stores and factories, thousands with little brick shaped lunches wrapped
   in newspapers under their arms.
Each morning as I move through this river of young-woman life
   I feel a wonder about where it is all going, so many with
a peach bloom of young years on them and laughter of red
   lips and memories in their eyes of dances the night before. . . .

—Carl Sandburg, "Working Girls"

Beginnings

Since 1894, Mary O'Sullivan had lived in Boston and successfully combined the raising of a family with her work in the labor movement there. The reader will recall her as Mary Kenney, the Chicago bindery worker who helped establish Ladies Federal Labor Union No. 2703 of the AFL, and as the AFL's first woman organizer for a brief six-month period in 1892. She and her labor-editor husband, Jack O'Sullivan, had a marriage unusual for its time. Not only did Jack O'Sullivan insist that his wife keep on working after their marriage, even after the couple had several children, but he helped with the work at home to make it possible for her to do so.

So it was that, night after night, she met with other labor leaders and settlement-house workers at Boston's Denison House to talk over the difficulties women workers had in organizing effectively without the support of established unions behind them. Out of these discussions came the idea for a national organization that would bring together working women from different industries and occupations so that they might reinforce each other's efforts for better wages and working conditions. Specifically, the new organization would help them form unions. As their model they took the British Women's Trade Union League, which had already been

Mary Kenney O'Sullivan, first woman organizer of the AFL
and founding member of the Women's Trade Union League,
shown with her three children.

active for almost thirty years before its American counterpart was organized.

When the AFL convention opened in Boston in mid-November 1903,
Mary O'Sullivan sought out her old friend, President Samuel Gompers.
Combining her knowledge of how the labor movement operated and her
own persuasiveness, she asked a favor: the opportunity to announce from
the convention speakers' platform the founding meeting for this new
organization of women workers, to be held that night, November 14, in
Boston's historic Faneuil Hall. Gompers agreed. The presidents of several
unions with large numbers of women members came to the meeting
along with women from the International Ladies' Garment Workers'
Union, the Retail Clerks, the Amalgamated Meatcutters, the Shoe Workers, the United Garment Workers, and the Textile Workers. They were
joined by settlement-house and reform leaders. Out of that evening's
meeting emerged the National Women's Trade Union League.

In the three days following its historic founding meeting, the Women's
Trade Union League adopted a constitution and elected Mary Kehew,
Boston philanthropist and organizer of women workers, as its president

Emblem of the National Women's Trade Union League.

and Jane Addams of Chicago's Hull House as vice-president. Bindery worker Mary O'Sullivan and shoeworker Mary Donovan became secretary and treasurer respectively. On its first board were Leonora O'Reilly (ILGWU), whose experience in the Working Women's Society of New York proved invaluable; Ellen Lindstrom (United Garment Workers); and Mary Freitas (Textile Workers). Although the league's constitution called for the formation of a board with a majority of worker members, this did not happen until 1907.

The nascent organization opened its headquarters in Chicago: one small desk in the office it was invited to share with the labor paper, the *Union Labor Advocate*. From here it coordinated the activities of branch leagues that gradually organized in cities across the country. The *Advocate* also provided the National League with access to a regular column, the "Women's Department." Soon all League publications and notices carried its seal and motto: "The eight-hour day; a living wage; to guard the home," and the statement "Endorsed by the A.F. of L." For Gompers had endorsed the league from the start, although this carried little financial support with it.

League leaders knew they would have to work as closely as possible through existing labor unions and the AFL to avoid any appearance of establishing a dual union structure. But league membership was open to all individuals, whether members of unions or not, and unions could affiliate as organizations, paying a per capita dues on the basis of their membership. Union women joined and so did wage-earning women not yet organized. "Allies," women not in the work force but committed to the goal of trade unions for working women, also were welcomed as members. The "allies" brought a tremendous resource to the league. Well educated, they usually had experience in setting up and running organizations and in dealing with politicians, legislators, and the press. They knew how to speak before groups. They were informed about the law and the rights of workers, limited as these were. They had access to money, both to support the new organization and to provide bail funds for women arrested during the many strikes in which the WTUL found itself involved. Still, it was the union women who sparked the establishing of WTUL branches, kept the league program focused on the concerns of working women, and were its organizers.

By 1905 the league was ready to hold its first national conference, set for New York in a strategy move to build ties to the city's unions. Samuel Gompers was invited to keynote its meeting. In a vigorous speech he told the women that the AFL would support their work,

> not as a mere compliment, not from a mere desire to please, but . . . as a matter of right and fraternity. [The League] broadened the work of the unions because it has had the cooperation of the other women and other men who sympathize with them. It is not a work of charity. It is not a work of endowing someone with a gratuity. It is instituted so that the girls and the women may be placed in a position where they may be helped to help themselves. What the workingmen want is less charity and more rights.[1]

However rousing his words on this occasion, Gompers's support for the WTUL vacillated. He was impressed with the high social position of many of the "allies," and his respect for status and wealth would override even his later hostility to the league, as long as socially prominent "ally" Margaret Dreier Robins was its president. When she resigned in 1922 and typographer Maud Swartz became WTUL president, Gompers became less receptive to the league.

The League at Work

By 1907 the WTUL had adopted a sweeping set of guiding principles:

> To provide a common meeting ground for women of all groups who endorse the principles of democracy and wish to see them applied to industry.

To encourage self-government in the workshop.

To develop leadership among the women workers, inspiring them with a sense of personal responsibility for the conditions under which they work.

To insure the protection of the younger girls in their efforts for better working conditions and a living wage.

To secure for girls and women equal opportunity with boys and men in trades and technical training and pay on the basis of occupation and not on the basis of sex.

To secure the representation of women on industrial tribunals and public boards and commissions.

To interpret to the public generally the aims and purposes of the trade union movement.[2]

As it went about its business of organizing women workers, the WTUL developed special techniques and approaches to reach them. As shoe-worker and league organizer Mary Anderson wrote in her autobiography:

> The men met in halls that were often back of a saloon, or in questionable districts, dirty and not well kept. I remember the so-called labor temples that were anything but temples. The girls would not go to meetings in these places and we could not ask them to go under the circumstances. Then, when it came to paying dues at the headquarters of the union, the girls found it very distasteful to go where there were large groups of men playing cards and hanging about. . . .[3]

The league found meeting rooms where women could talk about factory problems and organizing in a social atmosphere of coffee, cake, and companionship. It opened "rest" rooms downtown where waitresses could come between their split shifts to nap, read, talk, or sew.[4] A good time to distribute their leaflets announcing meetings, or urging women to report violations of state labor laws where they worked, turned out to be after church services. League workers would attend Mass respectfully, then afterwards stand outside the door to hand out their fliers.

One league committee focused on health problems, providing women doctors to examine women workers, a program which city health clinics later took over. Another committee helped the immigrant workers coming to the Chicago area.

Still another committee concentrated on organizing picket-line assistance and bail money for strikers.[5] Picket-line duty was not something that any woman assumed lightly, for it was tiring, dangerous, and humiliating. The women faced "unspeakable abuse," wrote Mary Brown Sumner. " 'Streetwalker' is one of the terms that the police and the thugs apply daily to the strikers."[6]

Part of the WTUL's job was interpreting the needs of women workers

to union men. It was not easy. League officers were less than popular
with the AFL when they urged the federation to admit women to policy-
making councils, boards, and committees in affiliated unions. It seemed
to the league—and probably to the AFL as well—that the WTUL waged
a constant battle to open union doors to women workers. Whenever
the league was unsuccessful in finding an AFL union that would
accept women it had organized, it tried to obtain charters from the
AFL directly. Sometimes this worked, but more often, the league was
faced with telling the women that the union of their trade would neither
admit them nor permit the AFL to charter them as a directly affiliated
local. While the women did the best they could alone, without adequate
support from a parent organization they had little staying power or influence.

To inform the public about conditions under which women in industry
worked, the league published a handbook both as a guide to its chapters
in their organizing work and as a source of information to the public. For
example, the handbook described women in the textile mills:

> Standing in thick cotton dust in the card room the speeder-tender may
> have 1,000 bobbins in the upper part of her machine and 500 in the
> lower part, and William Hard tells us that "each bobbin, in each
> machine, in each alley, is whirling like a dervish at almost unimagin-
> able speed, and screaming like the whistle on a peanut stand." And
> the weavers, the ringspinners, the speeder-tenders, work in heat which
> is like the intense heat of the tropics, and at the end of the day's work
> face the bitter cold nights of our northern winters. What a price we
> are paying for our cotton sheets and our calico![7]

But the heart of the league's program was organizing the unorganized.
As an editorial in its new journal, *Life and Labor*, put it:

> Women workers do not organize as fast as they should. If the women
> who labor could only realize that the union movement means more to
> them than any other force! . . . Better wages mean a home—a real home
> —and shorter hours mean family life, a life where father, mother and
> the children have time to be with one another and learn together and
> play together.
> But the best part of the union is that it makes you think! And we
> working women have got to do some thinking. Long hours, working
> for barely enough to live on, make it hard to do any thinking! And
> the boss knows it. That is why he wants us to work long hours. If six
> million working women should really think, something would hap-
> pen. . . .[8]

The New York league developed street meetings as one of its most
successful techniques for reaching working women. Helen Marot, New
York league secretary, describes them:

We had the best sort of a time at them. You don't have to send out notices. You just take a platform along, put up a banner and begin to talk. While someone is speaking others go round and distribute circulars among the girls and ask questions. These circulars are in Yiddish, Italian and English and we vary them. The last one we got was on getting married. . . . It is helpful in time of strike to hold street meetings . . . we . . . talk to the scabs when they come out [of the factories]. . . . It gives tremendous courage to the union girls to have us talk there. . . . I think these street meetings are something we can all get courage out of. We make great friends with the policemen in New York. Miss O'Reilly has already converted one policeman.[9]

Following its involvement in the shirtwaist workers' strike of 1909–1910,* the WTUL published a guide for all its future participation in strikes of women workers. WTUL branches were instructed to enter a strike situation only when invited by the union involved, and to verify that it was a duly authorized AFL strike. The WTUL required that two of its representatives sit on the strike committee and attend all policy meetings. The league, in turn, agreed to handle strike publicity, assist on the picket line, raise bail money for those arrested, help raise strike relief funds, and set up the necessary kitchens and relief stations.

To augment its organizing efforts, the WTUL brought together union women for mutual support and labor education. It taught them how to administer their locals and keep their books, how to conduct meetings, how to speak in public, how to take up shop grievances. A school for leadership training was the dream of Margaret Dreier Robins, who became president of the National League in 1907. She believed that union women made the best organizers and needed only education and practice to develop their skills. At the 1913 WTUL convention she urged that a school to train leaders be established.

The best organizers without question are the trade-union girls. Many a girl capable of leadership and service is held within the ranks because neither she as an individual nor her organization has money enough to set her free for service. Will it be possible for the National Women's Trade Union League to establish a training-school for women organizers, even though in the beginning it may be only a training class, offering every trade-union girl a scholarship for a year?[10]

Through the doors of the league school that began in 1914 went forty-four women, a few each year. During the twelve years that the school operated, they spent a year combining classroom work with practical league organizing experience. Almost all went on to leadership or staff roles in their trade unions.

The National WTUL made several significant, far-reaching contribu-

* See chapter 16, pp. 293–309.

tions when it lobbied to get the government, specifically the Bureau of Labor, to undertake an in-depth investigation into the conditions of women and children in industry. Begun in 1907, this study lasted four years and resulted in a historic nineteen-volume series of reports detailing for the first time both the conditions of women workers and the industries in which they were employed. It included a history of women in trade unions from the early nineteenth century to 1911, the year the study was published.[11] The data this study yielded on child labor led to the achievement of another WTUL goal, the establishment of the Children's Bureau, with social worker Grace Abbott as its first director (1912). It also helped to get passed—some years later, to be sure—laws regulating the age and hours of work for children under sixteen. It was not until 1920 that yet another of the WTUL's efforts came to fruition, the Women's Bureau in the Department of Labor, with league stalwart Mary Anderson at its head.

Women of the WTUL

Who were the women of the WTUL? This organization, the first to combine over a period of time the resources and organizational experience of middle-class women and the energy and talents of working women, was one in which women leaders thrived. To an outside observer it might have seemed that there were as many leaders as members. In fact, the impact of the league was far greater than its numbers might otherwise have warranted. Dedicated in word and deed to organizing wage-earning women, the league needed workers trained to do the job.

Undoubtedly this led to conflicts within the league. The working women whom it trained were young, active socialists for the most part. Most of the middle-class women, the "allies," were somewhat older, liberal to be sure, but not given to the soapbox oratory in which the young working women excelled. The more self-confidence these young women gained, the more articulate and outspoken they became and the more they pushed to keep the league responsive to their needs. Action was their keystone. Sometimes legislative routes to reform, while necessary to win limits on hours and decent sanitary conditions in the factories, seemed long and tortuous, as did the painstaking negotiations needed to maintain cordial relations with the AFL.

They were a daring lot, these women, defying tradition and society's edicts. They often gave up marriage and a home because they did not have time for it, or because they could not find men who were bright enough for them or who saw the importance of their continuing their work. Among them a sisterhood of friendship and conviviality developed. When they had any time off they would go hiking together, or attend forums on

Rose Schneiderman, garment worker who devoted her life to the Women's Trade Union League and the labor movement, shown here in 1912.

key issues of the day, or meet at a neighborhood settlement house for an evening of good food, good conversation, and song.

It was during the 1904 strike of the Cap Makers' Union in New York City that one of these young women, only four feet six inches tall, with flaming red hair, joined the WTUL. Rose Schneiderman had come to America from Russian Poland in 1891 as a child of nine. On her first job as cash girl in a department store she netted $2.16 for a 64-hour week, until she was fired for an error she had not made. When she changed trades and worked at sewing cap linings, she earned $6.00 her first week—but had to buy her own sewing machine.

In 1903 she and fellow capmaker Bessie Braut organized their shop. As president of this new local, Schneiderman attended the 1904 convention of the Cap Makers' Union where, at the age of twenty-two, she was elected to the union's executive board. Before long she was involved in a thirteen-week strike of capmakers. It was during that strike that she was invited to attend her first New York Women's Trade Union League meeting and met its president, Mary Dreier. Dreier in turn visited strike headquarters to offer the league's help, and out of this came the strike's first press coverage, a major boost indeed. Rose Schneiderman would work with and for the league during most of the rest of her life, becoming president first of the New York chapter, then of the National WTUL.

In 1907 two young Chicago glove workers emerged in WTUL leadership roles. Agnes Nestor was the first woman to become president of an international union, the International Glove Workers Union, and Elizabeth Christman succeeded her in the post of secretary-treasurer, making these two women among the very few who have ever held such high elected posts.

Nestor gave the appearance of frailty, which was misleading. A tireless worker and expert administrator, she proved a good lobbyist as well, working in Illinois for the 10-hour law and similar legislation. In 1913 she became head of the Chicago Women's Trade Union League, a post she held until her death in 1948. Christman, as energetic as she was beautiful, was described by her friend and long-time league and trade union associate, Pauline Newman, as "the most loyal person to the labor movement I ever saw in all my life."[12] In 1921 Christman became secretary-treasurer of the National Women's Trade Union League, and held that post until 1951, when the league was dissolved.

One of the most unforgettable WTUL activists was Leonora O'Reilly, a third-generation shirtworker and the league's most famous orator. Her union career started earlier than most, since her mother, Winifred, always an active unionist, often carried her infant daughter to union meetings with her. Leonora grew up in stark poverty. Her father died in 1871, when she was only a year old, and her mother worked in a garment factory by day and brought bundles home to sew at night to support herself and her daughter. When she was thirteen, Leonora became a collar sewer, and when she was sixteen she joined the Knights of Labor.

Leonora O'Reilly attracted people like a magnet. In 1886, the same year that she joined the Knights, she organized the New York Working Women's Society, and before long had gathered around her middle-class reformers like Josephine Shaw Lowell, men and women who provided financial support and helped to organize working women. One of the results of their efforts was the country's first factory inspection law.

Agnes Nestor, one-time president of the International Gloveworkers Union and active WTUL worker and suffragist.

Two generations of shirtworker unionists: Leonora O'Reilly and her mother, Winifred, shown on the lawn of their Brooklyn, New York, home about 1910.

A shirtwaist worker, O'Reilly organized a local trade union of the United Garment Workers, and it was as a UGW member that she attended the founding meeting of the National WTUL in Boston and was elected to its first executive board. Already a popular speaker on public issues, she returned to New York and turned her talents to launching the New York branch of the league. Before long she had brought into the league two women who turned out to be so important to the organization over the next two decades that it is possible the league might not have survived without them: Mary Dreier and her sister Margaret, best known as Margaret Dreier Robins.* Capable, dedicated, and generous with their own funds, these two "allies" devoted their lives to the cause of the league and working women.

Nonetheless, though O'Reilly counted "allies" as among her closest friends, she was often suspicious of them, fearing they would turn the WTUL into a "lady bountiful" organization. She disliked "do-gooders" and was sensitive about the language many of the middle-class women used when speaking of workers and their problems. Twice she resigned from the league, accusing some of its leaders of viewing it as a charity organization.

There is no doubt that O'Reilly's first love was the labor movement. Her friend and fellow WTUL member Pauline Newman recalls her as an enthusiastic, if dogmatic, person, determined to see justice done on behalf of workers. "Never say die; the work is the thing," she wrote Newman. "There is nothing like leather, says the cobbler. The Labor Movement for mine. . . ." And another time, in her colorful, lively, very Irish style: "To be sure, Paul dear, 'tis a topsy turvy world. But steady yourself in your seat, tuck your hat tight down on your head with one hand, hold

---

* Mary Dreier became president of the New York league, while Margaret Dreier Robins moved to Chicago and in 1905 was elected president of the Chicago league and, in 1907, of the National WTUL.

tight to the pilot wheel of labor, now use your long-range field glass—
It has been a long uphill trudge from 1776. . . ."[13]

In 1909 Mary Dreier made it possible for O'Reilly to devote full time
to league work through a lifetime annuity that she set up for her. For
a while O'Reilly traveled almost constantly, giving one or more speeches
a day, working to keep the league focused on the problems of wage-
earning women. At the WTUL convention that year she lashed out
against the program of the Chicago league, which provided women doctors
to examine women workers as part of its sick-benefit plan. O'Reilly felt
this smacked of charity:

> I feel often that all this sick benefit is welfare work. The workers toil
> for just a chance to be able to pay their way in the world! . . . I couldn't
> sit in my seat and hear that we too were trying to get cheap doctors
> rather than go out in the open and fight. The position we ought to
> take is that of the girl whose boss remarked to her: "Now that she has
> got cake, she wants ice cream." The girl's response was: "I never
> thought of ice cream before. But now that you remind me, I shall
> not stop until I get it."[14]

While her sensitivity stemmed from an early childhood spent in poverty
on the Lower East Side of New York, and the "charity" she saw working-
class families forced to accept, it is likely that some personality conflicts
with one or more of the Chicago league leaders in part caused her strong
reaction to this Chicago program. League stalwart Emma Steghagen,
Chicago shoeworker, answered her:

> Almost all progressive trade unions have benefits attached to them.
> . . . I do not consider it is welfare work when done by the union.

However, O'Reilly's attitude also reflected prevailing views of the
times, which had not been introduced to or accepted the idea of social
insurance. A St. Louis shoeworker, speaking on the same issue, indicated
that the $5 a week sick benefit her members received through the union
was mistakenly regarded as charity. Women would work until they
dropped rather than accept it, she reported, not realizing that they had
paid for it themselves through their union dues.[15]

The years 1909 and 1910 proved unusually busy ones for O'Reilly.
She was deeply involved in the shirtwaist workers' strike in New York,
the "Uprising of the 20,000." Just a year later she joined the Socialist
Party and became an active worker in its cause. She also threw her weight
behind the suffrage movement, in which she had long believed, by accepting the chairmanship of the Industrial Section of the New York State
Suffrage Party. The connection between the ballot for working women
and legislation on their behalf was clear to her. She answered critics of
votes for women:

You may tell us that our place is in the home. There are 8,000,000 of us in these United States who must go out of it to earn our daily bread and we come to tell you that while we are working in the mills, the mines, the factories and the mercantile houses we have not the protection that we should have. You have been making laws for us and the laws you have made have not been good for us. Year after year working women have gone to the Legislature in every state and have tried to tell their story of need. . . . They have gone believing in the strength of the big brother. . . . They have seen time after time the power of the big interests come behind the big brother and say to him, "If you grant the request of these working women you die politically."[16]

Mary Dreier, beloved president of the New York Women's Trade Union League.

She accused legislators of neglecting women's concerns because those who *had* the votes also had the power to remove the legislators from office. Women wanted that power too.

This concern over the ballot and its close connection with legislation was sharpened for her after the Triangle Shirtwaist Company fire of 1911* in which 146 workers, mostly women, lost their lives. O'Reilly headed a league committee to investigate factory conditions and to propose safety and inspection legislation to ensure that such a tragedy could never happen again, only to find that, in spite of the huge public outcry, state legislators took years rather than months to pass even watered-down versions of the laws workers needed to protect them.

After 1914, O'Reilly's health began to fail, and gradually she had to give up many of her activities for the league. She died in 1927.

One of the most celebrated league members, Mary Anderson, came to America from Sweden in 1889 at the age of sixteen. By the time she was twenty-two years old she was an experienced shoeworker, president of Stitchers Local 94, and a member of the International Boot and Shoe Workers executive board. Its only woman member, she was also the only board member who did not hold a paid union staff post, and she was forced to beg the foreman of her shop for time off to attend board meetings.

* For the 1909 shirtwaist workers' strike and the Triangle fire, see chapter 16.

Her experiences with night work made an indelible impression on her. In 1903 she worked in a shoe factory, where suddenly one afternoon at five the foreman announced to the workers that they would have to work overtime until nine o'clock. With their families not knowing where they were and no food to eat for supper, the women devised their own way of handling the problem. The next day many stayed out "sick." When the foreman ordered a late night again, one-third of the entire work force became "sick" the next day. The third time it happened, fully one-half stayed out. The fore-

Mary Anderson, shoeworker and WTUL organizer, in 1920 became the first director of the Women's Bureau of the United States Department of Labor.

man got the message and abandoned further emergency night work. When, as director of the Department of Labor's Women's Bureau, she called for limiting night work for women workers during World Wars I and II,[17] she recalled this experience.

Perhaps more than anyone else it was WTUL President Margaret Dreier Robins who held the organization together. In a real way she was a bridge. Beautiful and articulate, she was able to communicate her fierce anger over the exploitation of wage-earning women to the social workers and middle-class "allies" of the league and keep them both active and contributing funds. At the same time she smoothed over the conflicts between worker members and "allies," radiating confidence that the working women could assume leadership responsibility while providing them the training to help them do so. Many a worker who started out shyly agreeing to be secretary of a committee ended up as a labor union organizer, a state factory commission member, or, as in Mary Anderson's case, the first director of the Women's Bureau. "She gave us our chance," said Mary Anderson years later in her autobiography.

A dynamic public speaker, Robins joined the worker members in speaking at streetcorner meetings and rallies, a role many "allies" did not find comfortable. She won her soapbox spurs in 1911, when she spent countless lunch hours and evenings outside restaurants and hotels informing waitresses about the new 10-hour law the state of Illinois had passed. And as early as 1906 she had led a parade of 20,000 workers to protest the arrest of "Big Bill" Haywood, Industrial Workers of the World leader, who had been taken by force, along with two other labor leaders, across the state line from Colorado to Idaho.

The Women's Trade Union League
and the Suffrage Movement

Through the urging of WTUL President Robins and "allies" like Jane Addams and Florence Kelley, the suffrage movement began to reach out to working women. These women not only saw in votes for working women the potential for gaining legislation that would protect women, but they believed that unless suffragists supported both the organization of working women into unions and the legislation these women needed,

Margaret Dreier Robins, president of the National Women's Trade Union League and of the Chicago league, in a 1907 photograph.

union women would never believe the suffrage movement relevant to their cause. Therefore they set about convincing leaders in the suffrage movement that it needed the support of working women to succeed.

Working women became involved in the suffrage campaign as early as 1910. Agnes Nestor, then secretary-treasurer of the International Glove Workers, joined the "Suffrage Special," the train heading from Chicago to Springfield, to pressure legislators to pass the state suffrage bill. She spoke at whistle stops along the way, wherever industrial workers gathered.

Other union women in the league spent most of their time on the campaign. Leonora O'Reilly, Maggie Hinchey, a laundry worker with a keen sense of humor, and Rose Schneiderman were among the most popular speakers. Schneiderman wrote in her autobiography about how she answered a state senator who claimed giving women the vote meant they would lose their femininity.

> I pointed out to him, not too gently I hope, that women were working in the foundries, stripped to the waist because of the heat, but he said nothing about their losing their charm. Nor had he mentioned the

women in laundries who stood for thirteen and fourteen hours a day
in terrible heat and steam with their hands in hot starch. I asked him
if he thought they would lose more of their beauty and charm by
putting a ballot in the ballot box than standing around all day in
foundries or laundries.[18]

To reach unionists on the suffrage issue, the league organized a special
suffrage division, the Wage Earners' Suffrage League. The need for separate organizations to pursue the same suffrage goals was demonstrated in
the clash between San Francisco unionists and suffrage leaders. Mrs.
Louise La Rue of the San Francisco Waitresses Union reported at the
1909 WTUL biennial convention:

> The Working Girls' Suffrage League was organized just before our
> last legislature. We were at first with the National Woman's Suffrage
> League in San Francisco and got along fine with them; we endorsed
> everything they did; but the street car strike came along, and of course
> we had to walk. Some of those women objected to walking. So you
> can just imagine how we felt about it. We had to pull out from them
> but we thought it quite important that we should have a suffrage
> League, so we organized a Working Girls' Suffrage League.[19]

New York City's Wage Earners Suffrage League, organized in 1911, was
chaired by garment worker Leonora O'Reilly, with Clara Lemlich as
vice-chairman, two experienced organizers. That membership in this organization was open only to working women, "to preserve harmony of purpose and . . . freedom of discussion at meetings,"[20] is evidence of the
depth of feeling that existed toward the largely middle-class suffrage movement. This is not without its parallel today. Union women organized in
the Coalition of Labor Union Women (CLUW) did not officially join
forces with the women's movement organizations to support passage of
the Equal Rights Amendments until late in 1975, even though CLUW
had supported the amendment all along.

Pauline Newman was one of the WTUL activists who traveled widely
to speak on suffrage. She recalls that she was almost always heckled. " 'Go
home, feed the kids,' was what they'd shout, and I loved it," she told the
author. "I could always answer them back, and get the group with me."
She carried her soapbox with her, stepped up on it, and talked—and
talked. "Sometimes until rather late, too, I'm afraid," she laughed.

> One time a police officer at one of my streetcorner meetings in Niagara
> Falls came over and tugged at my sleeve. When I turned to see what
> he wanted he said to me, "Hey miss, don't you think it's time to go
> home? It's after midnight!"[21]

* In 1908 Newman campaigned for Eugene V. Debs, Socialist Party candidate for president of the United States, aboard his whistle-stop train, "The Red Special." Two years
before women gained the vote, she was Socialist candidate for Congress from New York's
eighteenth congressional district, and ran ahead of the Socialist Party ticket in the number
of votes cast for her.

WOMEN and HOME

VOTES AND POVERTY

Voters

Influence

Legislators

Protection

for Women

and Children

PAULINE M. NEWMAN,

OF NEW YORK,

HOMES OR FACTORIES

WHICH FOR WOMEN?

AT _____

ON _____

Miss Newman has been General Organizer for the International Garment Workers' Union for a number of years. She speaks from experience in mill and factory. Do not fail to hear her give reasons for supporting the

SUFFRAGE AMENDMENT

ELECTION DAY, NOVEMBER 2.

All Welcome.   Women Especially Invited.

SENTINEL PRINTING COMPANY,   429—440 WASHINGTON ST, READING, PA

State suffrage for women was on the ballot in Pennsylvania in 1915, and young Pauline Newman was a favorite pro-suffrage labor speaker.

League speakers would travel wherever a state suffrage bill was pending. In 1912 it was Ohio, where Rose Schneiderman took an active part.

> Here in Cincinnati everyone I think who is interested at all is working like a Trojan. But no one has ever touched the hearts of the masses like Miss Rose Schneiderman . . . she spoke to the largest crowds, I hear, of any speaker that has been here lately. . . . We have had splendid speakers here but not one who impressed the people as she did. Strong men sat with the tears rolling down their cheeks. Her pathos and earnestness held the audiences spellbound.[22]

The Women's Trade Union League and the AFL

The WTUL as a national organization faced its most difficult problem in its relationship with the American Federation of Labor, which offered for the most part only polite encouragement and often found the league's program an embarrassment. Because of its concern for the conditions of working women, most of them not in labor unions and without protection of any kind, the league supported wide-ranging legislation which the AFL opposed. WTUL reformers and union women, many from a socialist background, combined at the league convention as early as 1909 to vote down a resolution supporting the Alien Exclusion Act, running counter to the AFL position that Orientals should be barred from the United States. Only a few years later the WTUL adopted resolutions calling for a system of national unemployment insurance, national, state, and municipal labor exchanges with a women's department in each, guaranteed safe transportation for workers sent to areas where jobs were available, public works and government loans to states for such work, and municipal commissaries, "so that when a man works part time and receives three, four or five dollars a week he can spend the money at a municipal grocery store where he can get all the money he calls for without giving the middleman a profit."[23] It recommended that each local league study the unemployment situation, furnish speakers for conferences on the subject, and keep a file of related information for the use of league members.

None of this pleased the AFL. Gompers was suspicious of any government interference in what he felt was the individual liberty of workers. He opposed protective labor laws, believing they might endanger the hours and earnings of men. Furthermore, whatever the government provided in benefits, he argued, they could just as easily take away. The only security lay in trade unions setting the working conditions of their members through collective bargaining. He was not overly concerned about the large masses of working men and women who had no unions to bargain for them. More than once he warned the WTUL not to pursue its program of special legislation for working women.

> We should view with apprehension present sentiment in favor of setting up public and political agencies for securing industrial benefits for wage-earning women. These agencies would constitute a restriction upon freedom of action capable of serious abuses. . . . We cannot encourage too enthusiastically or too fully efforts of women to help themselves, to secure for themselves needed reform, and to associate themselves in trade unions which protect individual freedom and promote the general well-being.[24]

True, following the 1909–1910 shirtwaist worker's strike the league's contribution to the union's success was acknowledged. Gompers went on record afterwards in support of unionizing women workers, extolling "the capacity of those misused toilers to suffer, fight, and dare that justice might be done."[25] But the AFL and its union affiliates were wary about the National League. Nor did the AFL like being pushed to put women on its staff (which it did in 1908, but briefly) nor to add women to its executive board (a suggestion it flatly rejected).

Gompers was most unhappy when, in 1909, the WTUL went on record supporting a labor party, an idea that he discouraged within the AFL, advocating instead the policy that unions support their friends and punish labor's enemies. But the League not only passed a strongly worded resolution on the subject; it presumed to suggest to the AFL how it should go about forming such a party!

> Resolved. That the delegates of the National Women's Trade Union League, in convention assembled, do urge the American Federation of Labor to take action toward the formation of a Labor Party . . . pledged to forward the higher interests of the toiling millions as against the selfish interests of a privileged minority, and which shall welcome to its membership all persons of whatever other affiliations who shall subscribe to the above line of action. . . .[26]

It is not surprising, therefore, that relationships with the AFL continued to be a problem for the league. On the one hand, in 1910 the St. Louis convention of the AFL recommended that "in cities where there is a branch of the WTUL . . . the central body . . . give the League their cooperation and support to the end that the women workers of the country may be organized."[27] On the other hand, the AFL withheld its monthly organizing contribution to the league following the 1912 strike of Lawrence textile workers, supported by the Industrial Workers of the World.*

* See chapter 19 for the story of the Lawrence strike and the IWW. This revolutionary labor federation believed in one union for all workers and was at this time organizing unskilled, mainly immigrant workers in mills and factories of the East. It is more than likely that Mary Kenney O'Sullivan, one-time AFL organizer, provoked considerable AFL

In this strike the league reluctantly obeyed AFL orders to withdraw strike support, even though it lost one of its most trusted founding members, Mary Kenney O'Sullivan, over this issue. O'Sullivan resigned from the league in protest and remained in Lawrence to help the strikers. Following the Lawrence strike the AFL declared WTUL women "not qualified to organize,"[28] irreligious, and under the influence of the IWW.

In 1914, complaints from the United Garment Workers again brought a confrontation between the AFL and the WTUL. A league delegation, headed by UGW member Mary Haney, called on Gompers to ask why the league was so often blamed for actions that, when investigated, it was found innocent of committing. Here the UGW had accused it of agitating for worker rejection of a contract proposal in the big Chicago clothing strike of 1910, when in fact it had not done so, and of siding with the renegade Chicago garment workers against the UGW in its 1914 dispute.* Gompers conceded:

> . . . it is not fair . . . the Women's Trade Union League is doing a good work; it makes some mistakes, but neither is our American Federation of Labor perfect, but the Women's Trade Union League is the best thing we have got here, and when we realize that there are big institutions getting the girls together in clubs, singing societies and welfare organizations, and the women of the trade union leagues are the only people on the other side who are bringing the women together in the cause of labor, instead of criticizing the National Women's Trade Union League you ought to go in and help them.[29]

The AFL in 1914 had voted a one-cent-per-member special tax earmarked for the organizing of women workers, and in 1915 agreed to finance one league organizer. However, leaders of the WTUL believed that their repeated conflicts with the AFL would mean few close working relationships with federation leaders in the future. They were correct.

Women's Place

In 1908 the American Federation of Labor, after much urging from the WTUL, appointed a woman organizer, Annie Fitzgerald of the Upholsterers Union. When Fitzgerald sought the help of union men in her organizing efforts, she found that most of them still believed woman's place was in the home, not at work, and certainly not in the union hall.

---

ire by her article in *Survey* of April 6, 1912, "The Labor War at Lawrence." In introducing her to the readers, *Survey's* editorial note stated: "Mrs. O'Sullivan is the first of the old-line labor leaders in America to challenge the organizations which have built up the trade union movement of the United States, to adjust their policies and spirit to the industrial changes which have been going forward in the last twenty years . . ." (p. 72).

* See chapter 17 for a fuller discussion of both the strike and the dispute that led to the founding of The Amalgamated Clothing Workers of America.

She tried to persuade the men to accept the fact that women workers were already there and to

> apply the only remedy at hand, organization. Organize them. Apply the rule of equal pay for equal work for both sexes, and organize, keep on organizing. Do this and I hold that much of the evil complained of in the matter of women workers will be minimized. . . . The women can be organized. Will you men do your share in the necessary work? Speaking for the women, I can say, we will do our share, if given proper encouragement.[30]

She did not have too long a time to change any minds, however; she was not continued on the AFL staff for more than six months.

Nor was it only the men who felt that women's place was at home. Men who could not support their wives and families felt ashamed, and this shame spilled over to women who had to work. Since women who worked invariably held the lowest-paid, least skilled jobs available, which few men, unless forced by circumstances, would have accepted, attempts by women to organize were not viewed by the men as important, even in the same industry, as long as men performed the skilled work.

Where women were employed at similar work, men viewed them as a threat. They were paid half men's wages, and could be used to replace men during strikes or, indeed, at the whim of the employer. Increasingly unions responded to this threat in two ways. Some barred women from membership and attempted to get closed-shop agreements where only union members could work at particular jobs. This forced employers to lay off those women they had hired. The second approach, gradually adopted by unions as the numbers of women in the work force increased, was to include women as members, often in separate women's locals, so that when the men struck, so would the women. While women received some benefits and protection through these locals, they found that the system also locked them into "women's jobs," and their demands and concerns were often ignored when the time came to negotiate new contracts.

But at best it was difficult to organize women. The great ambition of most young girls was to get married and leave the factory. "The only security women could see was in marriage," wrote Mary Anderson in her autobiography, "and that made it difficult to get them into the trade union movement."[31] But often marriage was no escape. Women found themselves forced to contribute to the family's support, or to take it over altogether, and they worried about what would become of them when they were no longer able to earn a living. "We were never able to get ahead," Anderson said. Working women with family responsibilities had no time for union organization, and few could risk job loss and the blacklist by trying to organize a union.

Helen Marot summed it up in her book *American Labor Unions,* written in 1914:

> The real problem of the organization of women in labor unions is not discrimination, but the position of women in their domestic relations and industry. This is complicated by a special attitude assumed toward women, of which their attitude toward themselves is a part.[32]

But she also commented that attitudes differed depending on the area of the country: "The trade union men of California . . . take the organization of women for granted, and welcome them in administration affairs, while the trade union men of New York are, at best, politely skeptical."

But few of the women who devoted themselves to careers in the labor movement were as fortunate as Mary Kenney O'Sullivan or Margaret Dreier Robins, whose husbands shared their enthusiasm and encouraged them to continue their careers. Mary Anderson wrote somewhat wistfully:

> I thought, as a young girl, that I would get married, too, but somewhere I lost myself in my work and never felt that marriage would give me the security I wanted. I thought that through the trade union movement we workingwomen could get better conditions and security of mind.[33]

When Rose Schneiderman took her first job as a union organizer, her mother voiced disapproval and concern. She feared that her daughter never would get married, and indeed she did not.

The degree to which their jobs were totally demanding is revealed in a letter Rose Schneiderman received during the summer of 1910, when she had left New York on a badly needed vacation. Helen Marot, New York league secretary at the time, wrote her after she had been gone just two weeks:

> Dear Rose:
>
> I have been restraining myself for two weeks, but I can't keep to my resolution to leave you undisturbed. There is a critical turn of affairs down in the Shirt Waist Makers Union which none of us can manage but you. We have been needing you all through the month, and now I fear must have you. Could you possibly come back next Wednesday and see us at the League on Thursday and be ready for a meeting of the Shirt Waist Makers Thursday night. This leaves your month uncompleted . . . but I don't see what we are going to do without you.
>
> Love from us all,
>
> Helen
>
> I hope and pray dear that you are rested or have had a chance for rest. The work ahead of you is so appalling! You must—must have strength or what shall we do?[34]

Of course Schneiderman returned to New York. Personal lives were submerged; the great work needed to be done.

In her autobiography, Schneiderman described some of the frustrations of her work and how the endless demands on her time robbed her of any personal life.

> I found out that organizing is a hard job, too, and often very frustrating. You work and work and seem to be getting nowhere. Just when you feel that it is no use going on, something happens.
>
> You organize a group and set up a local. Then you have to nurse the members along so they won't get discouraged and quit before the union is strong enough to make demands on the employers. All this could be terribly discouraging if you didn't have faith in trade unionism and didn't believe with every cell in your body that what you were doing in urging them to organize was absolutely right for them. . . .
>
> Organizing also means hours and hours of standing on corners in all sorts of weather to distribute handbills to the women as they come from work. I must have given out millions in my lifetime. It means calling an endless number of meetings and never knowing if anyone will show up. And on top of all this, you never have a life of your own, for there is no limit to the time you can put into the job.[35]

Pauline Newman organized extensively for the International Ladies' Garment Workers' Union. In letters that she and her friend Rose Schneiderman wrote to each other while on assignment in different parts of the country, their sense of excitement and fulfillment in their work can be felt, but also the aching loneliness of the life of a woman labor organizer. Newman wrote:

> The road from St. Louis to Cleveland was simply wonderful! How I wished to have some one near me who should share my admiration! I felt very lonely all the way. And I could not help coming to the conclusion, that while my life, and way of living is *very interesting*—it is at the same time a very lonely life. Always alone. Except when you are out doing your work. I made a hit in St. Louis I am sure of that; no one to share it. I have so many plans to carry out, so much work to do—work that shall live after I am gone—yet no one to help me, no one to advise me. Always alone. It is dreadful. Yet it seems that there is no way out of it—at least for the present.
>
> I am just thrown about like a wave. From one city to another. When will it end?[36]

The Later Years

The WTUL's influence far exceeded its membership. In 1911 the three largest of its eleven branches, those in New York, Boston, and Chicago, counted 1,859 union women and "allies" as members, and sixty-one affiliated unions.[37] While these unions did represent many thousands of members and, through a small per capita payment, contributed in part to the league's support, most of its work was carried on by a relatively small number of intensely loyal individuals.

Organizing and lobbying went on simultaneously. Increasingly league leaders saw how hard it was to unionize women in low-wage industries, and they turned to legislation as the only way to improve working conditions and wages. For WTUL members, the classes conducted by the league branches were equally important, and included courses in English and social issues, and basic trade union education. The league produced a steady stream of writings, while its speakers took advantage of every opportunity to educate the public about working women and children, constituting a major influence in promoting protective legislation.

Rank-and-file women unionists, trained by the league, went on to help build the labor movement throughout the first half of the twentieth century. In 1920 the Women's Bureau of the United States Department of Labor was established, in part because of WTUL persistence, and WTUL leader Mary Anderson was named its first director.

During the 1920s the league faced attacks similar to those visited on other progressive organizations by Attorney General A. Mitchell Palmer's postwar anticommunist campaign. It was accused of socialist leanings and of having dictated the appointment of a foreign-born head of the newly created Women's Bureau. The twenties proved a difficult period for other reasons. In 1922 Margaret Dreier Robins stepped down as WTUL president and Maud O'Farrell Swartz of New York Typographical Union Number 6 became the first worker member to head the organization. Robins had never collected a salary as president, but Maud Swartz could not afford to leave her job as printer to take on full-time league work. It was Elizabeth Christman, as national secretary-treasurer, who had to handle the day-to-day administration of the organization's affairs. As noted earlier, Gompers's interest in the organization waned sharply at this point. Budget problems plagued the league and much of Christman's time had to

Maud Swartz, member of the International Typographical Union, became the first rank-and-file worker to be president of the National Women's Trade Union League, succeeding Margaret Dreier Robins in 1922.

Elizabeth Christman, gloveworker, was secretary, treasurer and lobbyist for the Women's Trade Union League. After the league folded in 1951, she became legislative representative for the Amalgamated Clothing Workers of America in Washington, D.C.

be devoted to raising money. League support of protective legislation ran into opposition from the women's movement, which saw protective laws for women as inconsistent with the campaign for the Equal Rights Amendment, introduced for the first time in 1924. The league, on the other side, felt that the Equal Rights Amendment would invalidate the laws that protected women who had no unions or other means of protecting themselves. The battle between the two groups was often bitter.

Nor did the WTUL succeed on the legislative front. The National Association of Manufacturers and the Chamber of Commerce joined forces to defeat the Child Labor Amendment and the Sterling-Reed Education Bill, both of which the league strongly supported. Little organizing was possible during the anti-union drives of the 1920s, and the league had to change its tactic, mounting "education campaigns" rather than its traditional organizing drives, especially in the South. It focused at the same time on opening men's unions to women. While it did not succeed in gaining entrance to the printing union for copyholders, nor to the baker's union for candymakers, it had better luck with the barbers' union, who admitted women barbers and beauticians to its ranks.

Gradually it became clear during the late 1920s and 1930s that the WTUL was failing to attract younger members. With the founding of the Congress of Industrial Organizations in 1938 following the split in AFL ranks, league leaders were divided in their loyalties, although they held themselves ready to assist either federation whenever called upon. But as new unions began to reach out for women members, there seemed less need for the league as an organizer of women workers.

The Roosevelt administration, however, found itself frequently consulting league leaders, both past and present, for league member Eleanor Roosevelt invited them to the White House, brought their talents as well as their concerns to the attention of the president, and paved the way for WTUL members to serve on numerous New Deal boards and committees. At last, in the 1930s, legislation the league had long supported passed, putting a floor under wages, limiting hours of work, providing social security and unemployment insurance, and most important, granting workers the right to organize into labor unions.

During this period WTUL branches began to fold, one by one, almost as if their mission were completed. Rose Schneiderman continued to maintain an active league office in New York City during the 1930s and 1940s, but it, too, closed its doors for the last time in 1951, forty-eight years after the WTUL had begun. Not for a generation would union women form another national organization: in 1974 the Coalition of Labor Union Women emerged to work within the labor movement for goals not unlike those the league had called its own.

The next chapter turns to a period when the WTUL had just come of age. During the winter of 1909–1910, 20,000 New York shirtwaist workers walked out in what is now famous as "The Uprising of the 20,000," and the league stepped in to organize strike relief on a mammoth scale. Seventy-five league "allies" joined the picket lines each day for the thirteen weeks of the strike as witnesses of police brutality and arrests so that they could testify in court on behalf of the strikers. The league raised bail money, provided legal counsel for strikers, handled publicity, and organized the registration of the thousands of new members who joined the International Ladies' Garment Workers' Union during the first few weeks of the strike. While the league went into the strike a relatively young and inexperienced organization, it emerged from those thirteen weeks with an expertise it would put to work almost immediately in the 1910 clothing workers' strike in Chicago.

The story of the shirtwaist workers of New York is more than an account of the WTUL's involvement, important as that was. It is the story of the birth of a strong, stable union of garment workers. Even though the victory of the shirtwaist workers was less than complete, the union's membership could view with pride the fact that their union had emerged from the strike as the third largest union in the American Federation of Labor. What was most unusual about this union, however, was the fact that a majority of its members were women.

16

THE RISE OF THE WOMAN GARMENT WORKER NEW YORK, 1909–1910

> In the black of the winter of nineteen-nine
> When we froze and bled on the picket line,
> We showed the world that women could fight
> And we rose and won with women's might.
>
> Hail the waistmakers of nineteen-nine
> Making their stand on the picket line,
> Breaking the power of those who reign,
> Pointing the way, smashing the chain.
>
> —"The Uprising of the 20,000"

Pauline Newman is nearing ninety and still walks every day from her apartment on West 12th Street to her office at the health center of the International Ladies' Garment Workers' Union on 25th Street, where she is education director. She has worked for this union since 1909.* One evening in 1975 she talked with a group of trade union women studying the role of women in American labor history, to tell them about the "Uprising of the 20,000," the historic strike of New York shirtwaist workers during the winter of 1909–1910.[1] That strike provided the

Pauline Newman, veteran shirtwaist striker and ILGWU organizer, describes the "Uprising of the 20,000" to union women in a class on women in American labor history at Cornell University's Trade Union Women's Studies.

* How Newman began her work with the ILGWU is recounted here. Following the 1909 strike she continued on the union's staff, becoming the first woman organizer in the ILGWU.

293

membership base for the modern ILGWU. In her measured, resonant voice she said:

I'd like to tell you about the kind of world we lived in 75 years ago because all of you probably weren't even born then. Seventy-five years is a long time, but I'd like to give you at least a glimpse of that world because it has no resemblance to the world we live in today, in any respect.

That world 75 years ago was a world of incredible exploitation of men, women, and children. I went to work for the Triangle Shirtwaist Company in 1901. The corner of a shop would resemble a kindergarten because we were young, eight, nine, ten years old. It was a world of greed; the human being didn't mean anything. The hours were from 7:30 in the morning to 6:30 at night when it wasn't busy. When the season was on we worked until 9 o'clock. No overtime pay, not even supper money. There was a bakery in the garment center that produced little apple pies the size of this ashtray [holding up ashtray for group to see] and that was what we got for our overtime instead of money.

My wages as a youngster were $1.50 for a seven-day week. I know it sounds exaggerated, but it isn't; it's true. If you worked there long enough and you were satisfactory you got 50 cents a week increase every year. So by the time I left the Triangle Waist Company in 1909, my wages went up to $5.50, and that was quite a wage in those days.

All shops were as bad as the Triangle Waist Company. When you were told Saturday afternoon, through a sign on the elevator, "If you don't come in on Sunday, you needn't come in on Monday," what choice did you have? You had no choice.

I worked on the 9th floor with a lot of youngsters like myself. Our work was not difficult. When the operators were through with sewing shirtwaists, there was a little thread left, and we youngsters would get a little scissors and trim the threads off.

And when the inspectors came around, do you know what happened? The supervisors made all the children climb into one of those crates that they ship material in, and they covered us over with finished shirtwaists until the inspectors had left, because of course we were too young to be working in the factory legally.

The Triangle Waist Company was a family affair, all relatives of the owner running the place, watching to see that you did your work, watching when you went into the toilet. And if you were two or three minutes longer than foremen or foreladies thought you should be, it was deducted from your pay. If you came five minutes late in the morning because the freight elevator didn't come down to take you up in time, you were sent home for a half a day without pay.

Rubber heels came into use around that time and our employers were the first to use them; you never knew when they would sneak up on you, spying, to be sure you did not talk to each other during working hours.

Most of the women rarely took more than $6.00 a week home, most less. The early sweatshops were usually so dark that gas jets (for light) burned day and night. There was no insulation in the winter, only a pot-bellied stove in the middle of the factory. If you were a finisher and could take your work with you (finishing is a hand operation) you could sit next to the stove in winter. But if you were an operator or a trimmer it was very cold indeed. Of course in the summer you suffocated with practically no ventilation.

There was no drinking water, maybe a tap in the hall, warm, dirty. What were you going to do? Drink this water or none at all. Well, in those days there were vendors who came in with bottles of pop for 2 cents, and much as you disliked to spend the two pennies you got the pop instead of the filthy water in the hall.

The condition was no better and no worse than the tenements where we lived. You got out of the workshop, dark and cold in winter, hot in summer, dirty unswept floors, no ventilation, and you would go home. What kind of home did you go to? You won't find the tenements *we* lived in. Some of the rooms didn't have any windows. I lived in a two-room tenement with my mother and two sisters and the bedroom had no windows, the facilities were down in the yard, but that's the way it was in the factories too. In the summer the sidewalk, fire escapes, and the roof of the tenements became bedrooms just to get a breath of air.*

We wore cheap clothes, lived in cheap tenements, ate cheap food. There was nothing to look forward to, nothing to expect the next day to be better.

Someone once asked me: "How did you survive?" And I told him, what alternative did we have? You stayed and you survived, that's all.

There had been emphemeral unions of garment workers for years before the founding of the ILGWU in 1900.[2] A strike of New York cloakmakers in 1885, for example, had involved over 1,500 men and women, but the union disappeared the following year. However, in 1890 the movement for organization among the New York garment workers gained momentum. Many of the immigrant workers in the industry had escaped from Czarist Russia and fled to America. They shared a socialist background and a strong sense that oppression must be fought. As conditions in the trade grew more unbearable, the workers felt that something had to be done about it.

For instance, before new spools of silk were given out, the old empty spools had to be returned; if they were lost, a fine of 50 cents had to be paid for each, the real value being nothing; for the loss of a "number" ticket the fine was 25 cents; if an employee lost a "trimmings" ticket before he had received the trimmings, he had to pay the full

---

* In 1907, as a teen-ager, Newman led her first strike, a rent strike. Her landlord tried to raise the rents in the tenement where she lived. Organizing the neighbors in the tenement and the three or four adjoining buildings, she urged that no one pay more rent unless the landlord agreed to put a toilet on each floor. He refused—but without emptying four or five buildings full of families, he could not charge more rent.

value of the trimmings, which were valued from $1 to $10. It was as though he had lost the trimmings and not the ticket. The ticket cost an extra fine of 25 cents; the loss of a special ticket was fined 50 to 75 cents. In some shops it was forbidden to bring cooked meals from home to the shop, a great hardship for the poor workers. . . .[3]

Three thousand workers walked out during January and February of 1890. Six months later the strike was still in progress, and the Manufacturers Association had instituted an industry-wide lockout. Strike support funds ran so low that the *New York Tribune* reported one occasion when the strike committee faced the problem of dividing $350 among 4,000 workers. But they did not give up.

On July 15 the cutters signed a separate agreement with the Manufacturers Association, specifying union recognition, but no one else was included. While the cutters were pleased, and prepared to return to work, the other strikers were infuriated and voted 1,536 to 20 to reject the contract and continue the walkout. One striker wrote:

> The enthusiasm was indescribable. Men and women jumped on the tables. Their voices could be heard ten blocks away. After the audience cooled off a little, the chairman declared that though everybody voted for the continuation of the strike, the thing most needed was money and that was lacking, and he advised the people to reconsider their decision. But he had hardly concluded his sentence, when one of the people walked up to the chairman's table and taking off a ring from his finger handed it over to the chairman with the request to sell it or pawn it and give the money to the strikers. In less time than it takes to tell it, the chairman's table became covered with rings, watches, ear-rings, brooches, and other pieces of jewelry. All were shouting that these offerings be sold and the strike go on.[4]

In spite of opposition from the public, lack of support by New York City unions, and the fact that the cutters had returned to work, the strike continued. At last, on July 25, seven months after the strike had begun, the manufacturers accepted the union's terms. The contract called for a closed shop, abolition of inside contracting, the firing of scabs (who could be rehired only if they joined the union), reinstatement of all workers, a board to settle grievances, and substantial wage increases. The ninth and final clause of the contract read: "No part of this agreement shall refer or apply to females employed by the Cloak Manufacturers' Association."[5]

Unions in the garment industry came and went. Only the small union of New York Cutters, men who constituted the elite in the trade, seemed stable. At the close of the nineteenth century the tenement sweatshop system that had flourished for so long began to give way to a hated "inside contractor" system that was more profitable for the employers. Under this system a contractor working in the shop would "contract" to do a particular order of work, and it would be up to him to arrange with a group of workers, usually women, how much they would get paid. It was to his advantage to pay as little as he could in order to keep as much of the agreed-upon price as he could for himself.

Shirtwaists came on the market about 1895, and after the turn of the century shirtwaist manufacturers enjoyed a big boom. White shirtwaists together with long dark skirts became the standard uniform of the white-collar worker, and her numbers in the work force were increasing rapidly. Women making shirtwaists worked in factories in small groups, each woman doing one part of the shirtwaist. It was important for the unionization of the industry that shirtwaists were *not* the product of tenement sweatshops, but that women worked on them in factories from the start. Only through their ability to have contact with each other and collectively to control production could a strong garment union have emerged.

How the Strike Began

The ILGWU was a young union in 1909. It had been founded only nine years earlier when a convention call issued by the United Brotherhood of Cloak Makers Union Number 1 was answered by eleven delegates, representing some 2,000 members nationally. They met in New York City on June 3, 1900, selected their name, the International Ladies' Garment Workers' Union, picked out a union label, and elected officers. The New York and Baltimore locals contributed the $30 with which the new union began its career. Initially, women were not as significant a part of the union as they would later become. In New York there were a number of small local unions, most of the members men in cutting, pressing, and skilled tailoring. It was through the strike of the shirtwaist workers, the "Uprising of the 20,000," that the union won a permanent foothold in the ladies' garment industry in New York and women their place in the union's membership.

Five hundred shirtwaist factories in New York employed upwards of 30,000 workers at the time of the strike in 1909. The conditions Pauline Newman experienced as a worker in the Triangle Shirtwaist Company are typical of those that prevailed in the industry generally. Work was seasonal, which meant weeks of unemployment each year. Employees paid for their needles and a fee for electricity, and often were charged for the boxes they sat on* and for coat lockers (when there were any). They paid for any damaged work and were fined if they were late. Clocks

---

* Pauline Newman points out that before the 1909 strike workers sat on boxes, and that not until the union succeeded in having a joint board of sanitary control established in 1910 could workers count on enforcement of the rule that they must be furnished chairs with backs.

The famous shirtwaist workers' march to City Hall during the 1909–1910 strike. Ten thousand strikers turned out on twenty-four hours' notice from the New York WTUL, organizer of the march.

were set back so workers would not be able to calculate how much over-time they worked. Frequently their paychecks were "short," but the process of correcting "mistakes" was so complex that it discouraged them from complaining. In 1909 the garment industry was back in business after an economic slump, and pushing workers hard for production. On July 2 of that year, 200 workers at Rosen Brothers walked out over a wage dispute—and won. Other workers soon followed their lead.

At the Triangle Shirtwaist Company, workers did not belong to the ILGWU but to a company union. Following a dispute with the em-ployer, several workers met in secret with ILGWU Local 25 officials to discuss joining the ILGWU. The story of how the Triangle Shirtwaist Company lockout and strike came about in September 1909 is reported by Alice Henry in her book *The Trade Union Woman*:

> One of the firm appeared before the girls and told them in kind phrases that the company was friendly to the union, and that they desired to encourage it, and that they might better give assistance, they would like to know what girls belonged to it. The girls, taken in by this speech, acknowledged their membership; only, instead of a few that the company had thought to discover and weed out, it developed that one hundred and fifty girls were members. That evening they were told,

in the same kind way, that, because of a lull in the trade, due to an uncertainty as to fashions in sleeves, there was for the time being no more work. The girls took their discharge without suspicion; but the next morning they saw in the newspaper advertisements of the company asking for shirt-waist operators at once. Their eyes opened by this, the girls picketed the shop, and told the girls who answered the advertisement that the shop was on strike. The company retaliated by hiring thugs to intimidate the girls, and for several weeks the picketing girls were being constantly attacked and beaten. These melees were followed by wholesale arrests of strikers, from a dozen to twenty girls being arrested daily.[6]

It was not a peaceful strike. The company hired prostitutes to stand at the factory door and fight off pickets so that the scabs could get in to work. At the Leiserson shop, also on strike, the company used the same tactics.

At the point when the spirits of the women were lowest, when all but 19 of the 98 who had been arrested had been fined and the union's treasury almost wiped out, the New York WTUL entered the picture, joining picket lines at the Triangle and Leiserson shops as witnesses to the unlawful arrests. When on November 4 police arrested Mary Dreier, New York league president and a prominent society woman, the incident made excellent copy for the newspapers. For the first time the wages and working conditions of the shirtwaist workers were revealed to the public.

Local 25, together with the United Hebrew Trades, a Jewish labor group assisting the strikers, began to consider the possibility of a general strike, partly to boost drooping morale, partly to organize the rest of the shirtwaist industry. However, the local's treasury contained approximately four dollars, while the local itself had only about one hundred regular dues-paying members.[7] Nonetheless, prostrike sentiment grew. The first meeting to discuss such a move, held October 21, voted a general strike and chose a committee of five, including two women, to develop a plan. As talk of the proposed general strike mounted, solidarity grew among the workers. Sewers at the Diamond Waist Company discovered they were working on garments for the struck Triangle firm and walked out. As October drew to a close, the Local 25 strike committee appeared before the general executive board of the ILGWU to ask its endorsement of the strike. Instead of all-out support, ILGWU Secretary John Dyche urged caution, while the international union appointed a committee to investigate conditions in the industry.

Discouraged but undaunted, the five strike-committee members called for an open meeting to discuss the general strike. Set for November 22 at Cooper Union Hall, it was announced by "sandwich men," who blanketed the Garment District with thousands of leaflets in English, Italian, and Yiddish calling all garment workers to the meeting. The program was to

include speeches by AFL President Samuel Gompers, New York league
President Mary Dreier, and more than seven prominent men from union
and socialist organizations.

The night of the meeting the "Great Hall" at Cooper Union was filled
early. Workers overflowed into Beethoven Hall, Manhattan Lyceum, and
several other meeting rooms. One speaker after another addressed the
crowd both in English and in Yiddish, the leaders from the ILGWU continuing to urge moderation. Their reluctance to support general strike
action stemmed in part from a realization of the intense suffering such
a strike would mean, since workers had little or no savings to draw on and
the union no treasury to support them. The new union was far from
strong. Thus the workers were urged "to use due deliberation, and to be
sober in their decision, but to be loyal to each other, and when they did
decide to strike to stand by their union until all demands were granted"[8]—
a confusing set of directives.

After about two hours, a young striker rose and interrupted the speaker,
Jacob Panken, to ask for the floor. Clara Lemlich was a young heroine
of the Leiserson strike, a gifted orator with a big following among the
workers. She was just recovering from a beating she had received on the
picket line two days earlier. Still in her teens, she was not new to strikes,
nor was this the first time she had been beaten during one. As a member

Samuel Gompers, president of the AFL, addresses the strike meeting at Cooper
Union Hall, November 22, 1909, that began the historic "Uprising of the
20,000."

Clara Lemlich in her teens was already an experienced striker and something of a folk heroine among the garment workers when, at the Cooper Union meeting, she called for a general strike of shirtwaist workers.

of the Local 25 executive board, she had been involved in the endless discussions pro and con the general strike. ILGWU historian Louis Levine describes what happened next:

Making her way to the platform, she delivered a "philippic in Yiddish." "I am a working girl, one of those who are on strike against intolerable conditions. I am tired of listening to speakers who talk in general terms. What we are here for is to decide whether we shall or shall not strike. I offer a resolution that a general strike be declared—now." Instantly, in the words of the reporter, "the big gathering was on its feet, everyone shouting an emphatic affirmative, waving hats, canes, handkerchiefs, anything that came handy. For five minutes, perhaps, the tumult continued; then the chairman, B. Feigenbaum, made himself heard and asked for a seconder of the resolution. Again the big audience leaped to its feet, everyone seconding. Carried off his feet by the emotional outburst, the chairman cried: "Do you mean faith? Will you take the old Jewish oath?" And up came two thousand hands, with the prayer: "If I turn traitor to the cause I now pledge, may this hand wither from the arm I now raise."[9]

The strike had begun. Pauline Newman from the Triangle Shirtwaist Company, already on strike, describes the feeling of the workers:

Thousands upon thousands left the factories from every side, all of them walking down toward Union Square. It was November, the cold winter was just around the corner, we had no fur coats to keep warm, and yet there was the spirit that led us on and on until we got to some hall to keep warm and out of the wind and out of the cold at least for the time being.

I can see the young people, mostly women, walking down and not caring what might happen. The spirit, I think, the spirit of a conqueror led them on. They didn't know what was in store for them, didn't really think of the hunger, cold, loneliness, and what could happen to them. They just didn't care on that particular day; that was *their* day.[10]

Then came the picket-line arrests. One judge, sentencing women carrying signs reading "We strike for justice," told them, "You are on strike against God and Nature, whose prime law it is that man shall earn his bread in the sweat of his brow."

A member of the WTUL sent this comment to British Socialist writer George Bernard Shaw by cablegram, and he wired back:

> Delightful. Medieval America always in the intimate personal confidence of the Almighty.[11]

Meanwhile, the women were taken off to Blackwell's Island to serve a two-week workhouse sentence scrubbing floors.

The union estimated that perhaps 3,000 workers would join the strike. Over 20,000 did. Workers in five hundred shops walked out. The job of signing up over 1,000 new members a day was enormous; the street outside the tiny union office overflowed with young women eager to join the union. Picket lines had to be set up in front of each of the five hundred shops that were affected, bail money arranged for the many who were arrested, meetings conducted in three languages (Yiddish, English, and Italian) in the twenty-four meeting halls needed to accommodate the huge numbers of workers, and still strikers spilled over into the streets. Strike relief was a necessity. The union had no prior experience in handling so many workers and no treasury to turn to. Into this confusion came the New York Women's Trade Union League, also new to such a large strike but ready to put its talent, time, and money at the service of the union. It took over registration of new members.

League "ally" Bertha Poole Weyl became assistant to S. Shindler, who headed Local 25. Others from the WTUL opened an information office in the middle of the Garment District to register strikers for relief and help with their personal and legal problems. During the thirteen weeks of the walkout seventy-five "allies" posted themselves throughout the strike as picket-line witnesses in the event of unlawful arrest. Strike publicity was handled by league members, who also sent workers to speak to church and club groups and ask for strike-relief funds. Rich society women learned firsthand from women on strike what the dispute was all about. One young girl told Colony Club members:

> When a girl comes five minutes late at my shop, she is compelled to go home. She may live outside of the city, it does not matter, she must go home and lose a day.
>
> We work eight days in the week. This may seem strange to you who know that there are only seven days in the week. But we work from seven in the morning till very late at night, when there's a rush, and sometimes we work a week and a half in one week.[12]

The league made sure that pictures were taken—for release to the press—of young immigrant girls on picket lines watched by burly, club-swinging policemen, and of women on their way to the workhouse after sentencing. During the course of the strike the league raised some $20,000 in relief funds and supplied $29,000 in bail money.

At first confusion reigned in the striking union, but order finally came. Each struck shop had a chairman or chairwoman to keep workers in close touch with each other and the union. Esther Lobetkin was typical. A Jewish sewer recently arrived from Russia, she found the job of shop chairman a twenty-four-hour-a-day task. The workers from her factory had to be kept abreast of strike developments and watched over to be sure that none went back to work. A sandwich in the middle of a night-time meeting, an hour's sleep during the day—that seemed to keep her going. Time and again she was arrested on the picket line, and would call from the patrol wagon, "Don't lose courage, we'll win yet."[13]

Bessie Switski, Local 25 executive board member, and her sister took on the hardest picketing job of all in front of a shop that was known as "the storm center" of the strike. Strikers called the private detectives and guards stationed there "gorillas," and they did manage to frighten some of the women away from the picket line. But the Switski sisters returned day after day to fight the "gorillas," and are credited with the fact that eventually this employer came to terms with the union.[14]

It was not long before women assumed the bulk of the picket-line duty, hoping that because they were women the police would be easier on them than on the men. But the company responded by hiring prostitutes to make trouble for the pickets.

> Fannie [Zinsher] was arrested for speaking to one of these [prostitutes]. The officer pinched her arm black and blue as he dragged [her] to court. . . .
> The hiring of women thugs ended dramatically. Six of them attacked two young pickets, threw them to the ground and beat them until their faces streamed with blood. . . . This last incident was too much to endure and the whole street [i.e., all the factories on the block] went on sympathetic strike. In less than two days the prostitutes were removed.[15]

Nonetheless, between November 23 and Christmas, 723 women and girls were arrested, 19 of them receiving sentences. As much as $2,500 a day was needed to post bail.

Toward the end of the strike, when funds were desperately short, Esther Lobetkin begrudged every penny spent to pay her fines and vowed she would go to the workhouse rather than let the union pay out any more money for her. But because of the treatment women received after arrest, they often had little choice, as Lobetkin's account of one such occasion illustrates:

The officer wouldn't let us girls sit down on the benches because we were strikers. . . . One of our girls got so tired she went to crouch down to rest herself, when one of the officers came over and poked her with his club and says, "Here, stand up. Where do you think you are? In Russia?" . . .

Well, when I got before the judge I was so worn out I didn't care what they did to me. I just let the union pay the fine and went home. But I won't let them pay the fine next time! They can send me to jail; they can do what they like with me; but I ain't going to let any more money be paid into the court for me, when benefits are needed by the girls.[16]

Young women were embarrassed with humiliating and sexually suggestive questions, and placed in cells with prostitutes and narcotics addicts. To call these outrages to public attention, the league organized a mass parade on December 3 during which 10,000 men and women, led by three women strikers and three WTUL "allies," marched to City Hall to carry their protest to Mayor McClellan.

Money began to run out. Workers received strike benefits of $2.50 to $3.00 a week for those with dependents, $1.50 a week for those without. Many of the single women, however, turned back their strike money so those who had families could have it, and did without. Some were discovered to be living on just one meal a day. To raise strike funds, the union sent Pauline Newman to cover New York State and Rose Schneiderman New England, to ask unions and women's clubs for their help. Pauline Newman described how her assignment came about:

I was called by Secretary John Dyche and he told me, "You are going to Buffalo tonight." I told him I had never been out of town in my entire life [she was about 16 at the time] and didn't even have a suitcase. "You can have mine," he said. He brought me the suitcase, took me to the train, gave me a one-way ticket to Buffalo, and said, "Remember, we have no money. You must raise money."

I got to Buffalo on the coldest day of the year. It was snowing, hailing, and windy. The train was cold, and I had been up all night on it. I was cold; I didn't know where the Labor Council was. The trolley-car conductor told me where to get off, and there was the red-brick building that matched the address I had. I walked up one flight —dark stairs and a locked door. Another flight, the same thing. The third floor door was unlocked. I opened it, hoping to find someone there. The room was empty and chilly, but I sat down and must have dozed off.

When I woke up a young machinist was standing over me. He brought me coffee and sandwiches, lighted the stove, and I began to come to life. That night at the meeting of the Central Trades and Labor Council I spoke, and began to collect the money we so badly needed.

During the day I spoke to wealthy women's groups, at night to union meetings. Then I moved on to Rochester, then Syracuse. I collected what was at that time a big sum: $6,000.[17]

Ida Mayerson was dispatched to Washington, D.C., and the Pennsylvania coalfields to raise money for the strike. As a bookkeeper for a Philadelphia shirtwaist manufacturer, her job had not been affected—at first—when the strike spread to Philadelphia and waistmakers there walked out. However, one day at a meeting of the Philadelphia Manufacturers Association, where she had been sent to take notes, she overheard the association members planning to pay off the police to provoke violence on the picket line. Outraged, she went to the union with the story, and that night repeated what she had heard at a meeting of the Philadelphia Central Labor Union. The morning paper carried a picture of her speaking at this meeting, together with the story of what she said, so it came as no surprise to her when she lost her job. That began her union career, her first assignment being to seek money from the Washington, D.C., unions.

While in Washington she decided to visit President William Taft to urge him to arrange for arbitration that would get the strike settled. "In those days," she stated in a recent interview, "you would just enter the White House. I didn't get to see the President but I got either his aide or secretary, who came out and said that President Taft felt he couldn't say anything as he would be showing partiality between capital and labor." Heading next to the coalfields of Pennsylvania, Mayerson found that the miners were very generous. "I was collecting as much from these poor locals of the miners as I had from the 'aristocratic' locals [craft unions] in Washington."

Following the strike, Mayerson returned to her bookkeeping, working for the union in its Philadelphia office and later moving to its headquarters in New York.[18]

Fund raising was imperative, and in New York the league involved three of the wealthiest women in the city, Anne Morgan, Mrs. O. H. P. Belmont, and Mrs. Henry Morgenthau, in its efforts. Mrs. Belmont rented the Hippodrome for a rally attended by their society friends, who sat in the orchestra and boxes, as well as by strikers, who filled the gallery. Leonora O'Reilly and others spoke, describing why the garment workers were striking and their need for funds. Although the publicity the rally generated was useful, the amount of money raised at it was disappointing. One of those present, Theresa Malkiel, wrote in her *Diary of a Shirtwaist Striker*:

The most of our girls had to walk both ways in order to save their car fare. Many came without dinner, but the collection baskets had more

Theresa Malkiel, strike supporter in 1909, at the Socialist Party convention of 1912 in Indianapolis. Malkiel, Pauline Newman, Rose Schneiderman, and Mother Jones were just a few of the women labor leaders who joined the Socialist Party and played an active role in organizing its support for the major strikes that took place between 1908 and 1914.

pennies than anything else in them—it was our girls themselves who helped to make it up, and yet there were so many rich women present. And I'm sure the speakers made it plain to them how badly the money was needed, then how comes it that out of the $300 collected there should be $70 in pennies?[19]

During the strike, employers sought strikebreakers wherever they could find them, and at one point attempted to hire black women to scab. Mary White Ovington of the National Association for the Advancement of Colored People, an organization that she had helped to found, brought this move by employers to the attention of the interracial Cosmopolitan Club, a group of white and black community leaders who met regularly to discuss ways to improve race relations. The club passed a resolution urging black women not to let themselves be used as strikebreakers, and asked the union to admit black workers to its ranks and encourage their employment in the industry when the strike was settled.

Meredith Tax, who reports on this concern of the Cosmopolitan Club in her 1971 unpublished manuscript, "The Uprising of the 30,000" (sic) also mentions that the executive board of the WTUL passed a motion acknowledging its appreciation of the work of the National Association for the Protection of Colored Women, both in New York and

Philadelphia, in keeping "several hundred colored girls from being used as strikebreakers."[20]

That there were some black workers in at least a few of the waist shops in the city, and that they joined the strike, is clear from a letter that appeared in *The Horizon*, a Washington, D.C., publication, in March 1910, over the signature of Elizabeth Dutcher for the league. It answered a charge that unions in general and the ILGWU in particular were hostile to Negro labor. While she could not speak for labor unions as a whole, Dutcher wrote from her own knowledge about the role of black workers during the shirtwaist workers' strike.

> In both Philadelphia and New York, some of the most devoted members of the Ladies Waist Makers Union are colored girls. In Philadelphia several of the girls going on strike were colored girls and two of these were the best pickets the union had in that city. They were not only able to persuade the girls of their own race and color from acting as strikebreakers, but they were able to keep wavering white girls from going back to work.
>
> In New York, colored girls are not only members of the union but they have been prominent in the union. One . . . has been secretary of her shop organization all through the strike and has been very frequently at the union headquarters doing responsible work. . . . meetings were held during the strike at the Fleet Street Methodist Memorial Church (colored) in Brooklyn and St. Marks Methodist Church in Manhattan . . . in both, members of the Ladies Waist Makers Union said definitely and publicly that colored girls were not only eligible but welcome to membership.[21]

During December there were several attempts at arbitration. On December 23 the union and the employers tentatively agreed on a set of terms: the 52-hour week, no discrimination against strikers, employers to supply power and needles, equal division of work in slack season, four paid holidays a year, individual shop negotiations for wage rates, reinstatement of strikers as soon as possible, and an initial, though weak, grievance procedure. However, there was no mention of union recognition, nor a union-shop provision, nor industry-wide agreements. On December 27, at mass meetings held in five halls to vote on the contract, workers overwhelmingly rejected it, mainly because it lacked a union-shop clause. Although leaders attempted to keep the strike going after that, chances for total victory diminished as the weeks dragged on. Small shops settled; workers returned. Early in January the union offered arbitration again, but employers refused. One by one the larger shops settled, many without union recognition.

On February 15, 1910, the strike was officially called off, although

1,100 workers were still on strike. Some 339 shops had settled with the union; 19 remained open shops. In over 300, however, workers had achieved most of the terms they had asked.

Even though the strike drifted to an anticlimactic conclusion, and the union was unable to maintain either its gains or its members for very long afterward, in retrospect it must be seen as a great achievement. A heterogeneous group of workers had united against factory sweatshop conditions. Their employers had had the support of the police and the law. But garment workers, out of struggle and sacrifice, had laid the foundation for a strong union. The women had proved themselves. A majority of the strikers, they had assumed the heaviest picket duty and voluntarily accepted the lowest strike benefits. They suffered most of the arrests and workhouse sentences. Yet their support never wavered.

The WTUL emerged as a mature and tested organization. Without league assistance the strike might well have been lost. Rank-and-file women emerged from this strike experienced as leaders that the union would call on for years to come. Rose Schneiderman and Pauline Newman are only two of a number who later served the union in staff positions.

After the strike, Pauline Newman recalls:

> We tried to educate ourselves. I would invite the girls to my rooms, and we took turns reading poetry in English to improve our understanding of the language. One of our favorites was Thomas Hood's "Song of the Shirt," and another that meant so much to us was Percy Bysshe Shelley's "Mask of Anarchy."* The last two stanzas I will never forget. To us they represented all the women during the shirtwaist workers' strike.
>
>> And these words shall then become
>> Like Oppression's thundered doom
>> Ringing through each heart and brain,
>> Heard again—again—again!
>>
>> Rise like lions after slumber
>> In unvanquishable number!
>> Shake your chains to earth, like dew
>> Which in sleep had fallen on you—
>> Ye are many, they are few![22]

Only a few months later, on July 10 of the same year, 60,000 ILGWU cloakmakers walked out of 350 small and all the larger cloakmaking firms in New York. Seventy-five percent of these workers were men. The settlement they won established what became known as the Protocol of Peace in the garment industry, setting a precedent for garment-union agree-

---

* Written to commemorate a mass meeting of British citizens who were seeking parliamentary reform, and were attacked by soldiers on August 16, 1819. Several were killed, hundreds injured.

ments for the next few years. Workers won a 50-hour workweek, the abolition of inside subcontracting, and the elimination of all charges for electricity or thread. The Protocol established holidays with pay, weekly payment in cash, a joint board of sanitary control to police working conditions, a grievance committee, and a board to arbitrate disputes.

The shirtwaist workers who had been out the year before, though they had not won so handsome or complete a victory, took pride in their pioneering role. These stanzas of "The Uprising of the 20,000" commemorate their spirit:

> And we gave new courage to the men
> Who carried on in nineteen-ten
> And shoulder to shoulder we'll win through,
> Led by the I L G W U.
>
> Hail the waistmakers of nineteen-nine
> Making their stand on the picket line,
> Breaking the power of those who reign,
> Pointing the way, smashing the chain.[23]

Workers at the Triangle Shirtwaist Company returned to work without a union agreement in February 1910 following the "Uprising of the 20,000." For them the strike had been lost, largely because of the company's use of scabs. Two of their key demands, therefore, were never discussed with the firm: open, unlocked doors from the Triangle factory on the seventh, eighth, and ninth floors of the Asch Building to the street; and fire escapes that worked.

Most shirtwaist workers had won the 54-hour week following their strike—but not those of the Triangle Shirtwaist Company, who still worked 59 hours. So it was that each Saturday groups of union workers going home at noon had made it a custom to walk by the Asch Building and call up to the Triangle Company workers, "So long, until victory is yours!"[24]

The Triangle Shirtwaist Company Fire

> Sisters mine, oh my sisters; brethren,
> Hear my sorrow;
> See where the dead are hidden in dark corners,
> Where life is choked from those who labor;
> Oh, woe is me, and woe is to the world. . . .[25]

A muffled explosion at about 4:30 in the afternoon was the first warning anyone had that March 25, 1911, would be different from any other Saturday in industrial history. Smoke billowed from the eighth floor of the Asch Building on Greene Street and Washington Place, the middle floor of the three which housed the Triangle Shirtwaist Company. One passerby saw what he took to be "a bale of dark dress goods" being thrown out of a window. Another who saw it thought the factory owner was trying to save his cloth from the fire. But then the screams began. It had not been a bundle of cloth, but a human being, leaping from the window. Then came another, and then another.

The fire engines drove up, the horses drawing them frightened by the shouts and the smell of blood. Fire ladders were raised—and the crowd gasped in horror as they saw that these extended only to the sixth floor. Women from the ninth floor of the Triangle Company, where the fire was burning full force, tried the fire escapes, which twisted and broke under their weight and were useless. The workers were urged to jump into blankets held by men below, only to have the impact of their bodies rip through the blankets, leaving the women smashed and lifeless on the street. Fire nets meant to catch one body tore under the weight of three and four young girls, who would jump together, their arms wound around each other. The force of their fall was so great that the bodies broke right through the industrial glass sidewalk to the cellar below.

Of the 500 workers crowded into the top three floors of the Asch building, 146, most of them women and girls, jumped to their death, were burned, or suffocated that afternoon in a building where no fire drills had been held, where doors opened inward rather than out,* where factory doors were locked each working day to keep the women in and the union organizers out, where there was no sprinkler system, and where the city's fire-fighting equipment proved totally unequal to the rescue task required.

The building was quite new and "fireproof," and when the fire itself was put out the walls seemed unharmed. But bodies lay everywhere, charred beyond recognition in the factory above, broken and bleeding on the street below. William Shepherd of the United Press, who witnessed the entire tragedy and called in the story as it was happening, wrote: "The floods of water from the firemen's hoses that ran into the gutter were actually red with blood."[26] Doctors and policemen went through the piles of bodies, sometimes finding a worker alive and moaning underneath. Ambulances raced between the scene of the fire and the hospitals. Relatives and friends of workers caught in the fire rushed to the scene. A crowd of a thousand broke through police lines in an effort to search among the bodies for their loved ones. All through the night they waited, as the dead were carried down the stairs one by one.

The 26th Street pier became a giant morgue. By seven o'clock of the

---

* After the fire, city ordinances required that doors of commercial and public buildings open outward, so that a crowd pushing against the doors would force it open. The reverse had occurred in the Triangle Company, where the hysterical crowd pushing against the doors made them impossible to open.

night of the fire, 2,000 people had gathered there to wait for the wagons bringing the dead bodies. Police barred the way, letting the wagons through so that coroners, and doctors still searching for any who might be alive, could do their work. Not till midnight did the gates open to admit small groups of twenty at a time to identify the bodies. The process was slow, painful, agonizing. One mother tried to jump off the pier into the river when she found her dead daughter, so police boarded up the pier windows. By dawn only forty-three of the bodies had been identified. At the end of a week seven still were nameless.

Local 25 of the ILGWU organized a city-wide relief campaign at once to help families whose key wage earners were now gone. While $120,000 was contributed from rich and poor, the famous and the unknown, many families were too shocked to ask for help, others too proud. Yet burial costs had to be paid and children provided for. Widows and women dependent entirely on their daughters' earnings now had to be helped to find work so they could support their families.

A sense of public outrage swept the city. A protest meeting at the headquarters of the New York Women's Trade Union League launched an immediate study into conditions in the city's factories, including a confidential questionnaire for workers to fill out: were doors in their shops locked, fire escapes inadequate, scraps of fabric and oily rags lying about?

A second protest meeting, called by ILGWU Local 25, was attended by thousands of friends, relatives, and fellow unionists of those who had died. This meeting became so hysterical with anger and sorrow that Leon Stein, labor journalist and historian, described the hall as resounding "with a single, mass shriek of despair." Women fainted, and doctors and ambulances were called in to set up emergency treatment for those overcome with grief.

The memorial meeting that drew the most attention was held in the Metropolitan Opera House under the sponsorship of the New York Women's Trade Union League. It was open to the public; the great and near-great, public officials, league "allies," and workers filled the hall. Each speaker spoke of the tragedy and of the need for better factory inspection laws. A resolution was offered calling for a state bureau of fire prevention, additional inspectors, and legislation setting up workmen's compensation. Few of the crowd were satisfied with a mere resolution after such a tragedy. There were hisses; speakers from the floor urged a "political organization of the workers," the appointment of union leaders as factory inspectors, and a committee of trade unionists to promote immediate legislation to protect workers.[27] Unionists in the galleries began to shout, and it looked for a moment as if the meeting would break up in a near-riot.

Then tiny Rose Schneiderman moved to the speaker's podium, her long red hair hidden by her hat, her powerful voice now barely raised above a whisper. But the workers in the gallery loved their Rose and quieted to hear her. With the acoustics of the Opera House, her words carried to the uppermost gallery.

> I would be a traitor to these poor burned bodies if I came here to talk good fellowship. We have tried you good people of the public and we have found you wanting. . . .
>
> This is the not the first time girls have been burned alive in the city. Every week I must learn of the untimely death of one of my sister workers. Every year thousands of us are maimed. The life of men and women is so cheap and property is so sacred. There are so many of us for one job it matters little if 143 [sic] of us are burned to death.
>
> We have tried you, citizens! We are trying you now, and you have a couple of dollars for the sorrowing mothers and daughters and sisters by way of a charity gift. But every time the workers come out in the only way they know to protest against conditions which are unbearable, the strong hand of the law is allowed to press down heavily upon us.
>
> Public officials have only words of warning to us—warning that we must be intensely orderly and must be intensely peaceable, and they have the workhouse just back of all their warnings. . . .
>
> I can't talk fellowship to you who are gathered here. Too much blood has been spilled. I know from my experience it is up to the working people to save themselves. The only way they can save themselves is by a strong working-class movement.[28]

These protest meetings brought results. Immediately a commission chaired by State Senator Robert Wagner, with State Legislator Al Smith as vice-chairman, began to investigate and make recommendations for improved factory safety. (New York WTUL President Mary Dreier was the only woman member on this commission.) One of its chief investigators was Frances Perkins,* then secretary of the New York Consumers' League, who had been visiting in the area the afternoon of the fire and had witnessed it almost from its beginning. Years later Frances Perkins would write:

> Alfred E. Smith and Robert Wagner, who later became great leaders . . . in social justice achieved by legislative techniques, got their education as members of the Factory Investigation Commission. . . .
>
> I was an investigator for the . . . Commission and we used to make it our business to take Al Smith . . . to see the women, thousands of them, coming off the ten-hour night-shift on the rope walks in Auburn

---

* Frances Perkins later served as industrial commissioner under Governor Franklin D. Roosevelt and became the first woman member of a president's cabinet when she served as secretary of labor during the presidency of Franklin Roosevelt.

(New York). We made sure that Robert Wagner personally crawled through the tiny hole in the wall that gave egress to a steep iron ladder covered with ice and ending twelve feet from the ground, which was euphemistically labeled "Fire Escape" in many factories. We saw to it that the austere legislative members of the Commission got up at dawn and drove with us for an unannounced visit to a Cattaraugus County cannery and that they saw with their own eyes the little children, not adolescents, but five-, six-, and seven-year-olds, snipping beans and shelling peas. We made sure that they saw the machinery that would scalp a girl or cut off a man's arm. Hours so long that both men and women were depleted and exhausted became realities to them through seeing for themselves the dirty little factories.[29]

The commission's work took four years, but resulted in what Perkins called the "greatest battery of bills to prevent disasters and hardships . . . of laws the like of which has never been seen in any four sessions of any state legislature."[30] One of the first recommendations of the State Factory Investigating Commission was the 54-hour workweek for factory and mercantile establishments, finally enacted into state law in 1913. It took constant pressure from Frances Perkins, the New York Women's Trade Union League, and labor unions, but the commission's recommendations for a sweeping new industrial code also were enacted into law.

Rose Schneiderman and others from the WTUL took to the streets, holding open-air meetings every noon and evening to inform factory and store workers about the new safety laws that should now be enforced. They urged workers to cooperate with State Factory Commission investigators who might be checking their shops, and to report factory law violations to WTUL headquarters.

The city took a long time to recover from the tragedy. Within a week after the fire the dead who had been identified were buried. Finally only the seven who were still unknown remained. ILGWU Local 25 and the New York Women's Trade Union League made plans for a public funeral. However, Charities Commissioner Drummond and Mayor Gaynor decided not to release the bodies but to bury them quietly on April 5 in the city's plot at the Evergreen Cemetery in Brooklyn. The funeral committee went ahead with its plans for a massive funeral parade, set for the same day. The call went out for all workers to join in this final tribute.

April 5 dawned wet and rainy, a downpour that lasted all day. Several processions which began at different points in the city merged at Washington Square in sight of the Asch building. By 3:00 the square was filled with marchers. How many there were no one knows for certain. But at 3:20 in the afternoon the marchers, following an empty hearse, filed eight abreast under the Washington Square Arch and started up Fifth Avenue, and the last marchers did not pass under the arch until 6:00 that evening.

Hundreds of thousands of New Yorkers watched the rain-soaked march in tribute to the 146 garment workers who died in the Triangle Shirtwaist Company fire March 25, 1911.

They marched in silence, an estimated 120,000 men, women, and children, among them members from sixty trade unions. There were no bands, and only one streamer carried by garment workers that read: "We demand Fire Protection."[31] No one left the line of march. Most were hatless and thoroughly rain-drenched. Perhaps 400,000 lined Fifth Avenue to watch.

In April the owners of the Triangle Shirtwaist Company, Isaac Harris and Max Blanck, were indicted on first- and second-degree manslaughter charges. The trial did not begin until December 4, and lasted just over three weeks.

General Sessions Judge Thomas Crain charged the jury to find the owners guilty only if it believed *all* the doors in the factory had been locked; if the owners knew they had been locked; if they were locked at *all* times during the working day and leaving time; and if Margaret Schwartz, a dead worker who represented all those who had so died, would have lived if the doors had *not* been locked. The jury returned a verdict of "not guilty." Some jurors felt unhappy about their verdict. But not juror H. Houston Hierst, an importer, who said:

> I cannot see that anyone was responsible for the disaster. It seems to me to have been an act of the Almighty. . . . I paid great attention to the witnesses while they were on the stand. I think the girls who

worked there were not as intelligent as those in other walks of life and were therefore the more susceptible to panic.[32]

Protests over the acquittal came at once. A new trial with a new manslaughter indictment was ordered. However, Criminal Court Judge Samuel Seabury charged the jury to acquit the defendants without a trial since the offense for which the new trial was ordered was the same as the old one, although the name of Jake Kline had been substituted for that of Margaret Schwartz. The jury so acted.

Meanwhile, five days after the fire, inspectors visited another building where Harris and Blanck had lost no time in starting up the production of shirtwaists again, and found machines blocking worker access to fire escapes. Two years later, in August 1913, Inspector Dugan of the new Bureau of Fire Prevention brought Max Blanck in on the charge that he had locked the door of his factory with a chain while 150 women were at work in the shop. Blanck paid a fine of $20.[33] Three months later, the Consumers' League found the Triangle Shirtwaist Company was using an imitation of the league's fair-practice label in order to sell more of its shirtwaists, and the organization obtained a court injunction against the company's use of this label in the future.

Leon Stein writes in *The Triangle Fire* a postscript to the earlier tragedy. In 1958, in a seventy-seven-year-old loft building at Houston Street and Broadway, a textile-finishing factory caught fire. On the floor above was an underwear-manufacturing company. This six-story building "had no sprinklers, its fire escape was worthless, there had been no fire drills."[34] Stein, who witnessed the tragedy, reports that after the fire started in the textile-finishing concern, seven minutes elapsed before any alarm was sent in. The underwear factory filled with smoke. Soon the glass blocks in the middle of the floor worked themselves loose in the heat, and the entire floor of women workers fell into the inferno of the textile shop below. Twenty-four workers died, including those who, like the Triangle workers before them, jumped from the windows to the street below.

Another witness at the 1958 fire was Josephine Nicolosi, a former Triangle worker who had survived the 1911 fire. When she and Stein found each other in the crowd on Houston Street, she was weeping. Together they watched the bodies being lowered to the street. Stein relates, "She gripped me by the wrists and shaking me demanded with anger and despair: 'What good have been all the years? The fire still burns.' "[35]

Union growth is never a steady upward curve on a graph, and the ILGWU found that gains in the hundreds of small shirtwaist shops were hard to police and consolidate. By 1911 the membership of Local

25 had fallen from its poststrike high of almost 20,000 to only 3,800. But during the first half of 1913 it grew again, back to 23,000, while the International Union that year could claim 90,000 members. The union's growth came through vigorous organizing campaigns and the work and sacrifices of what Pauline Newman has called "the unknown soldiers" of the organization. Hattie Bunin was one of these whom Newman met through the drive to unionize a key Philadelphia firm during this prewar period.

One Friday—I will never forget that day as long as I live—it was cold and the snow was fierce. We used to leaflet in front of the plant every evening as the workers went home, but that night I told everyone to go home, and I had decided to stay in the office all night because of the weather. I didn't expect a soul to come in, but there she was. I said, "Go home, for the Lord's sake go home. This is no night to stand in front of a shop and distribute leaflets." I really argued with her. Before I had a chance to say much more she snatched the bag of leaflets and out she went. She stood in front of Haber's shop and passed out leaflets and got pneumonia. Within five days she was gone. She was one of those unknown soldiers in our ranks whose dedication was so deep that no matter what would happen to them they have a job to do to build the union, they feel, and they're going to do it.[36]

Josephine Casey inscribed this photo for Pauline Newman: "Yours in the Co(unty) Jail, June 4, 1912," referring to their shared experience in Kalamazoo, Michigan.

Josephine Casey, one of the most colorful organizers in the ILGWU at this time, was a former elevated-railway ticket taker and member of the WTUL. In February 1912 she found herself in Kalamazoo, Michigan, leading a strike of ILGWU corset workers. The Kalamazoo Corset Company, deciding to rid itself of the union, had refused to renew Local 82's contract and had fired twelve of the most active unionists. Six hundred workers, most of them women, had walked out. Arrests and the jailing of strikers followed the court injunction that the company obtained against picketing. So Casey began to conduct "picket prayers" outside the company gates instead, a technique which brought the union considerable publicity when it resulted in her arrest. Asking the workers to get down on their knees, she would pray:

> Oh, God, Our Father, Who are generous. . . . Our employer who had plenty has denied our request. He has misued the law to help him crush us. . . . Thou Who didst save Noah and his family, may it please Thee to save the girls now on strike from the wicked city of Sodom. Oh, help us to get a living wage. . . . Grant that we may win the strike . . . so that we may not need to cry often, "Lord, deliver us from temptation."[37]*

Gradually the ILGWU forged a powerful union, until by 1916 it could withstand a lockout in New York affecting 25,000 workers, call out two thousand more shops with 60,000 members on a fourteen-week general strike—and win. With America's entrance into World War I, the union moved to use its new strength, based in part on a period of full employment in the industry, to protect union contract standards in the face of increased demands for high production. It also began a drive for a shorter workweek. Its health center, the first union-sponsored preventive medical service in the country, thrived. The union would need all its strength, however, to survive its intra-union battles and the anti-union employer campaigns that came with the decade of the twenties.

---

* ILGWU organizer Pauline Newman was assigned to Kalamazoo shortly afterward, and described to the author late in 1975 what happened next. The employer continued to operate with scab labor and to refuse to recognize the union, even though ministers in town and other community leaders urged him to come to terms. The union then tried the only other method it could use: the boycott. Newman traveled through the Middle West organizing support of a boycott of this company's brand of corsets. The economic pressure was successful, but rather than sign with the union, the employer chose to go out of business.

17

WOMEN IN THE MEN'S CLOTHING TRADES
A New Union: 1910–1914

Our Amalgamated union is fulfilling destiny,
We are glad of it, we're proud of it,
She's making history.
Her star of hope shines glorious
In the economic sky,
"Amalgamated, evermore" we cry!

Glory, glory Amalgamated,
Glory, glory Amalgamated,
Glory, Glory Amalgamated,
We'll stick until we win.

> —Anthem of the Amalgamated
> Clothing Workers of America

The clothing industry and the sweatshop conditions it generated were not confined to New York City. Elizabeth Butler investigated the Pittsburgh garment industry as part of a government survey and found in 1910 that women's work in the needle trades there had changed little in twenty years. Sweatshop workdays were still 10 to 14 hours long, and earnings no more than $4 or $5 a week. Pittsburgh had its own variation of homework, called "outwork," where factories sent sewing into the surrounding countryside in what resembled a stepped-up version of the early-nineteenth-century "putting out" system. Butler described the home of one such outworker: two rooms and an attic for a family of nine people, six ducks, and twenty-four chickens, the latter living in the kitchen.

> In the other room were 6 [sewing] machines and there the family slept—I could not see where, unless it were on the piles of clothing. . . . Mrs. J. has worked on jeans for 20 years, she told me. Her husband used to be in the [steel] mill, but one of his hands was crippled and he lost his job. . . . The result was that husband and wife began to make jeans at home, and as fast as the children could hold a needle they were pressed into service. Besides the two oldest children (17 and 19) the second boy (15) and a girl of 13 now work at the machines, and the others who are still younger sew on buttons, make

buttonholes and pull out threads. (The littlest one . . . could only just walk, but was very dexterous at pulling threads.) The hours of work seem incredible: from four in the morning until nine at night.[1]

Chicago: Women Sewers

Even the strong winds that blow across Chicago off Lake Michigan could not clear the air of smoke from the city's factories or of the stench from its stockyards. In 1900, men found work in Chicago's heavy industry, while women filled many of the jobs in the men's and women's clothing factories, in printing, meat packing, and millinery. By 1905 the single largest employer of women workers in Chicago was the men's clothing industry, where over 10,000 women worked, more than three times the number of women in any other factory occupation in the city. They constituted 55 percent of Chicago's clothing workers. Almost 8,000 men also worked in that trade, as cutters, as pressers, and in the higher-paid hand-sewing and finishing jobs.[2]

The Chicago clothing industry had a turbulent history. Workers had tried to organize under the Knights of Labor, but, like so many others, their union lacked permanence. Even after the disintegration of the Knights,

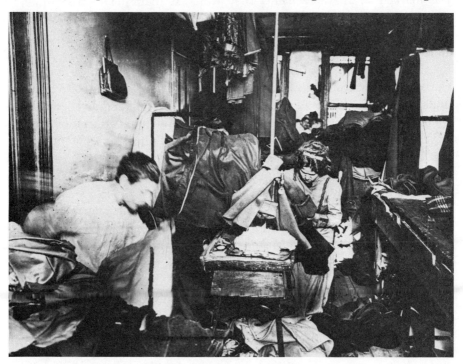

It was against the tenement sweatshop system and the hated contractors that the two major garment unions waged their most bitter campaigns.

15,000 Chicago clothing workers mobilized and struck in 1896, but after eight weeks were forced to admit defeat.

Two major changes in the industry began that year. First, skilled Scandinavian workers entered the trade. Second, manufacturers began taking orders from country stores for individual customers, and the special-order trade came into its own. Prompt delivery of finished suits became crucial, and garment sewer Ellen Lindstrom recognized the power—if they united to use it—that this gave the workers. She went to the recognized union in the trade, the United Garment Workers, an affiliate of the AFL, for help in organizing, but her request was ignored. So the women organized themselves, and a remarkable new—albeit brief—chapter in labor history opened.

Within two years, the Special Order Workers Union, whose membership was largely Swedish, had two, then three, then as many as nine locals and had formed a national organization. On its executive board of nine were five women and four men. The women, who were in a large majority, soon came to have the control and main guidance of the movement—apparently the only instance in American trade unionism up to 1910 of women directing more than a local organization.[3] Their progress was marked by the agreements they won. At their height, the union's 3,000 members, now calling themselves the Custom Clothing Makers, enjoyed a 9-hour day, a half-day off on Saturday, and wages that had almost doubled for many workers and increased as much as 80 percent for the lowest-paid. For the first time in the Chicago clothing industry, workers won a contract clause forbidding the employment of children under sixteen in the industry. The union also sought improved working conditions: better lighting, cleaner factories, and improved plumbing.

What happened next is important in understanding the reputation that the United Garment Workers had among Chicago clothing workers. In 1902 the Custom Clothing Makers Union was persuaded to apply for a charter from the American Federation of Labor. No sooner had it done so than the United Garment Workers stepped in, demanding that the union affiliate with them as the recognized union in the industry. Since the Custom Clothing Makers were reluctant, the UGW proposed— and the AFL convention of 1902 adopted—a resolution ordering the merger.

This may seem simple on the surface. However, at the same time a movement was under way by employers to subdivide the trade so that workers, instead of making most of an entire garment, would sew only a small part, thus permitting the employment of unskilled young girls at much less money. The Swedish union refused to allow this subdivision, while the United Garment Workers not only agreed to it but sold the UGW label to the employers to use instead of the label of the Custom Clothing Makers. Next, the employers turned to defeating the Swedish unionists, locking them out until, after seven weeks, they were forced to affiliate with the UGW and return to work under an agreement permitting subdivision of their work.

The Swedish workers managed to retain the right to handle their own affairs and extracted a promise that after October 1904, no section work would be done. There was little chance that they could enforce this proviso, and late in 1904 the struggle over section work began all over again. With the UGW lined up against them, the long strike in which they engaged—lasting until June of 1905—tolled the death knell of this spunky little union.[4]

The Amalgamated Clothing Workers of America:
From a Strike, a Union

The Chicago clothing industry now enjoyed a tremendous growth spurt. During the first decade of the twentieth century, it almost doubled in size. Floods of newcomers from Eastern Europe and Italy boarded the immigrant trains in New York City and headed to Chicago to find work. Among the men, women, and children on one of those Chicago-bound trains pulling out of Grand Central Station in 1905 was sixteen-year-old Bessie Abramowitz. She had left Grodno in White Russia following the Czarist pogroms that year. It is possible that she was also fleeing the marriage broker who had arranged marriages for her four older sisters and was due to visit her house soon to take care of Bessie. "Not on your life!" she is said to have declared, and hastened away to America.[5]

In Chicago she found work sewing buttons at 2½ cents a coat. One day the foreman scratched out the computations on her work sheet and lowered her piece rate by a fraction of a cent. The spirit that had brought her almost halfway around the world to Chicago now led her to recruit a committee of women on her section to complain to management. She was fired on the spot and also blacklisted. She soon discovered that no clothing plant in the Chicago area would hire her, and she had to leave town to get a job. When she returned to Chicago, it was under an assumed name. She managed to get a job at Hart, Schaffner, and Marx, the largest clothing company in the city, at Shop Number 5, sewing buttons on pants.

On September 22, 1910, her piece rate was arbitrarily cut from 4 cents to 3¼ cents a pair. Together with twelve other young women, Bessie Abramowitz and Anne Shapiro petitioned for a return to the old rate. When this appeal was ignored, they walked out of Shop Number 5 and sought help from the United Garment Workers, which had a small, elite local of clothing cutters within the Hart, Schaffner, and Marx plant. The union, uninterested in organizing young immigrant women, turned them away, and Bessie led her little band back to the factory to picket on their own. Most of their fellow workers paid little attention, although some refused to handle work coming from the department of the picketing women. In later years, as an Amalgamated Clothing Workers vice-president, Bessie Abramowitz Hillman would recall that the very men who became the leaders of the Amalgamated had walked right through the women's picket line for three weeks before they began to take it seriously. Sidney Hillman, the young man who became the ACW's first president, remembered that "we made fun of it."[6]

By the end of three weeks, the fourteen determined women who came back to picket day after day had generated a lot of interest. There were few workers who did not share their desperation over the wages and working conditions in the shop. About three weeks after they began picketing, the fourteen women called an evening meeting at Hull House of hand-picked rank-and-file leaders from different sections of the factory. About one hundred men and women attended, at the risk of their jobs if the company found out. The agenda consisted of only one subject: possible strike action. By the middle of October, almost 8,000 workers from the Hart, Schaffner, and Marx Company had walked out.

Of all the strikers, only the cutters and some select skilled craftsmen

Chicago, 1910. The clothing workers' strike began with 16 women stitchers at the Hart, Schaffner and Marx Company.

were members of the United Garment Workers. The union definitely was not interested in organizing such a large group of rebellious immigrant clothing workers, many of whom had fled political persecution and brought with them socialist ideas. But other men's clothing workers throughout the city now joined the strike. Toward the end of October, when 18,000 were out, UGW President Thomas Rickert could no longer ignore the letters and telegrams he had been receiving in his New York headquarters, and finally came to Chicago to meet with Hart, Schaffner, and Marx officials. The company offered to take the strikers back and listen to grievances but not to recognize the union. At a mass meeting where Rickert proposed these terms, workers shouted him down. "We want the union! Closed shop!" was the cry.[7] Finally Rickert agreed to support a general strike call for the clothing industry, Chicago's second largest employer. On October 27, between 35,000 and 40,000 workers poured out of the men's clothing plants.

Striking workers met in sixteen halls by language groups, the Poles in one, the Bohemians in another, Lithuanians, Italians, and Jews, all holding daily meetings to talk over their grievances and formulate demands. On one demand they all agreed: the closed shop. They also knew they needed help, and chose a committee, including Sidney Hillman, a cutter, to find it. The committee's first move was to turn to Chicago Federation of Labor President John Fitzpatrick, one of the great labor leaders of the day. Fitzpatrick's blue eyes under his bushy eyebrows looked right at Hillman and the clothing-strike leaders as he quickly sized up the situation. Suspicious of Rickert and the United Garment Workers, the strikers were vociferous and disorganized. They needed food and strike relief. Most of all, they needed leadership they could trust. Fitzpatrick suggested a joint strike conference committee to include the UGW as well as other factions among the strikers. Then he began to mobilize the Chicago labor movement to support the strike.

Two women representing the Chicago Women's Trade Union League sat on the strike committee, for the strikers had also turned to the league for help. Its Chicago chapter was a strong one, with 765 individual members and 32 union affiliates.[8] National WTUL President Margaret Dreier Robins, Jane Addams of Hull House, and Mary McDowell of the University of Chicago Settlement House all had close ties with the Chicago labor movement. The Chicago league had trained a number of women labor leaders, while the National WTUL, experienced after the shirtwaist strike of the preceding February, knew how to tackle the organizational problems of a strike of this dimension. It realized better than the young strikers what they would face on the winter picket line and what their needs for strike relief, legal assistance, and bail money would be. The league was also prepared to handle public relations. It was because of the league's new guidelines for assisting strikes where women workers were involved that it asked for, and after a preliminary argument obtained, its two seats on the Joint Strike Conference Committee.

Just as the Joint Strike Conference Committee was getting organized, Rickert announced on Saturday, November 5, that he had signed a settlement with Hart, Schaffner, and Marx providing for arbitration of the strike but not for union recognition. The workers learned about the proposed agreement from the newspapers that Saturday morning! At a mass meeting on Monday, Rickert presented the proposal to the strikers. Not only did they vote it down, but their anger at Rickert's "back-door" approach was so intense that he had to leave by one to avoid being mobbed.[9]

Labor unions and their friends now rallied to help, collecting coal and food as well as money. Spearheaded by Fitzpatrick, Chicago unions furnished supplies for four commissary stores. Doctors contributed free care for the many strikers injured on the picket line. Four hundred or more unionists were arrested, but lawyer Clarence Darrow came forward to defend them. Then, on December 3, striker Charles Lazinskas died from a bullet wound received on the picket line.

> I see Charley out there, walkin' in the
> line. Up comes a foreman, gives him a punch
> and yells, "Go home, trouble maker."
> An' Charley, he says, "I got my rights" . . .
>
> There was this sort of little scuffle,
> And then I heard the shot . . .
>
> People runnin' . . . an' Charley lyin' there, his
> blood spreadin' out across the snow . . .
>
> Rights, they gave him. A bullet in the
> head, they gave him.[10]

A procession of 10,000 silent marchers accompanied Charley Lazinskas to his grave. The city was alarmed. Leaders of every religious faith protested, while the Chicago City Council passed a resolution calling for arbitration. Clothing manufacturers refused. The Illinois state legislature moved to investigate the strike, and opened hearings on January 10, 1911.[11] Meanwhile Jane Addams of Hull House, where many of the strike leaders like Bessie Abramowitz had been meeting long before the walkout, sought a way to reach Joseph Schaffner, the financial wizard of Hart, Schaffner, and Marx. Schaffner was a philanthropist who, during the very weeks of the strike, was involved in endowing a program of night classes at Northwestern University for workers who could not at-

Young Bessie Abramowitz (Hillman), garment worker and union activist trained by the Chicago WTUL, with her friend, settlement-house leader Jane Addams.

tend daytime colleges. Addams felt that if he could be brought face to face with the suffering of the strikers and with the factory conditions against which the workers had rebelled, he might influence other members of his board to offer a settlement the workers could accept. The strike had now dragged on for five long weeks. She went to him and asked, "Mr. Schaffner, I wonder how long it's been since you saw with your own eyes the conditions under which these people work for you?" Schaffner agreed to go through the factory with her. He later admitted: "I wasn't surprised they went on strike. I was only surprised they waited so long."[12]

Schaffner took over the responsibility for the company's labor relations at that point and offered Rickert a settlement: an arbitration committee to take up all worker grievances, and the rehiring of all strikers except those who were found guilty of violence. In spite of their hardships, workers rejected this offer, and held out for union recognition.

The strike continued. During that winter, 1,250 babies were born to strikers and the wives of strikers. Mary Anderson of the Women's Trade Union League recalled:

> I remember Mrs. [Margaret Drier] Robins telling the story of the wife of a striker whom she visited. The woman was sick in bed, with several children to take care of. Her husband had been asked three times by the firm to come back to work, but he had refused to desert the union. When Mrs. Robins asked how she could bear the hardships for her children, she replied, "We do not live only on bread. If I cannot give my children bread, I *can* give them liberty."[13]

Then striker Frank Nagrekis was killed on the picket line. Again there was a massive, silent funeral procession, but this time it was attacked by the police. All Chicago rose up at the outrage.

Schaffner himself was distraught. Over his board's objections he came forward with a new proposal: all workers to be rehired, and a three-man board made up of one company representative, one UGW representative, and an impartial person chosen by the two, to handle all grievance issues. The Hart, Schaffner, and Marx workers accepted these terms. For them the sixteen-week strike was over.

On February 3, 1911, Rickert called off the strike for the rest of the Chicago clothing workers. He never consulted any of the strikers. Hillman described what this meant:

> Workers were forced to return to their old miserable conditions, through the back door; and happy were those who were taken back. Many who had participated in the 1910 strike were victimized for months afterward. They were forced to look for other employment and to wait until their record in the strike was forgotten.[14]

In order to consolidate the union in the Hart, Schaffner, and Marx plants and ensure fair grievance hearings for the members before the new arbitration board, Hillman volunteered to work full-time as a union representative for $10 a week plus $1 for expenses. Several far-seeing strike leaders from the shop guaranteed this sum each week, even if it had to come from their own pockets. This was an essential move, for the first Hart, Schaffner, and Marx agreement was born amidst great antagonism. Nor did the firm trust its workers, even after they had ratified the settlement, and asked for a "guarantee of good behavior," which John Fitzpatrick and Margaret Dreier Robins had to sign along with the union's leaders. Mary Anderson was asked by Robins to leave her factory job and represent the WTUL in working with the United Garment Workers to carry out the agreement. It took two years of hard work. Both the company and the union had to learn how to use grievance procedures and arbitration. Anderson and Bessie Abramowitz met each day with workers at lunchtime, urging them to come to evening meetings to talk over their grievances instead of walking out on the mini-strikes that occurred regularly for eighteen months following the strike. Finally workers agreed to select chairmen for each shop to handle grievances, and workers began to stay on the job while complaints were being settled.[15] In spite of continuing friction with the parent United Garment Workers, the clothing workers began at last to build a union in Chicago.

The Nashville Convention of 1914:
A New Union Emerges

In the years following the strike, the conservative UGW became increasingly unhappy about its new Chicago organization and the young, restless members who constantly urged it to help organize the rest of the city's clothing industry. Most alarming to the UGW, however, was the fact that here were 8,000 members of the union ready to join with dissidents from New York, Baltimore, and Boston who together made up two-thirds of the voting strength of the UGW.

As the October date for the 1914 convention approached, the young clothing workers were angry but not surprised when the UGW announced that it would be held in Nashville, Tennessee, far from any centers of the industry, hard to reach, and an expensive journey for garment workers, who would have to pay their own way. The UGW incumbents meant to assure their control over the union for the next few years. However, Bessie Abramowitz, now business agent for the vestmakers' local, packed her suitcase and traveled south along with the other delegates from Chicago. In Nashville, it became clear that dissidents were neither expected nor welcome. In fact, the UGW had requested standby police and detective contingents to keep order. The "progressives," including the Chicago delegates, met on the eve of the convention to discuss the rumor they had heard: that the UGW planned not to seat delegates who opposed its program and slate of candidates for office. The "progressives" made their own plans.

One of the Chicago delegates tried to convey his sense of excitement in a letter to a fellow unionist, Jacob Potofsky, who had not been able to come down to Nashville:

> Nashville, Tenn.
> Oct. 11, 1914 (10:30)
>
> Dear Jake:
>
> . . . Whatever the result may be, it will be for the best of the industry in the long run. Our boys are all doing their duty and showing the rest of the delegates that Chicago is not second to anyone. . . . I forgot to say about Bessie [Abramowitz], for she is not a boy, but she is working very nicely, in fact she [has become] one of our very important delegates.[16]

By the second day of the convention it was evident that 107 delegates would not be seated, over a third of the 305 who were present. Three of the Chicagoans, however, had been cleared and seated: Bessie Abramowitz, A. D. Marimpietri, and Frank Rosenblum. They took the floor in turn to call for a convention vote on the seating of the remaining delegates and demanded that delegates sent by their locals but barred by the UGW from the convention floor be permitted to vote from the gallery. Out of the chaos, Frank Rosenblum rose to move that all delegates who had been suspended, and their sympathizers on the convention floor, hold a convention of their own in the Duncan Hotel close by. One hundred thirty delegates left the hall to reconvene in this rump session. When they added up the number of UGW members they represented, they discovered that it came close to being three-fourths of the union's entire membership.

All through the night the Chicago contingent caucused to decide on its candidate for president of the insurgent union. Sidney Hillman was the choice, although he was now in New York as the International Ladies' Garment Workers' Union chief clerk, representing almost 50,000 New York ladies' garment workers, a big step up in his career. His Chicago friends sent urgent telegrams asking him to accept their nomination. One telegram was from Bessie Abramowitz, to whom he had become secretly engaged and who realized that he had taken the ILGWU post so that the higher salary might enable them to marry sooner. In answer to the question he had telegraphed to his friends in Nashville, whether the new job offered "the prospects of 'martyrdom' rather than the pleasures of office," she wired:

Understand that personal pledges (to me) must cease when sister organization at stake. To become a martyr I urge you to accept office.[17]

Hillman agreed to run, and the following day the rump convention unanimously elected him president of the new union. Two key goals the organization set were to unionize the 250,000 workers then in the clothing industry, and to establish one industrial union for all clothing workers rather than hierarchical craft organizations.

A long legal battle with the UGW followed over how the union's assets should be divided. One of the conditions in the settlement was that the new group should not also call itself "United Garment Workers." At the first official convention of this new union, held at Webster Hall in New York City on December 26, 1914, delegates from 68 locals representing 40,000 workers decided on the name Amalgamated Clothing Workers of America. Bessie Abramowitz was the only woman elected a vice-president on the union's first general executive board, and she was re-elected in 1916.

AFL President Gompers did not recognize the new organization. In fact, it was barred from the federation. It faced industry lockouts and strikes almost at once. Sidney Hillman, speaking of the struggles of those early years, commented, "In every city our dead are buried, and I bow to them."[18] With the New Year of 1915 the union set about proving itself equal to the tasks that lay ahead.

Women in the Early ACWA

Dorothy Jacobs, president of the buttonhole makers' union of Baltimore, Maryland, prepared a resolution[19] for the union's founding convention. Submitted on December 22, 1914, Resolution Number 20 read:

Mr. President and Delegates:
    The following resolution has been passed at a regular meeting of the Button Hole Workers Union, Local 170:
    Whereas, there are 19,784 workers engaged in the garment industry in the City of Baltimore, 10,183 of whom are women, and of whom only 800 are organized, and
    Whereas, with this preponderous majority of unorganized women in the trade the struggle for the maintenance of unions by the small organized minority is wrought with tremendous difficulties, and
    Whereas, experience has shown that with such a majority of unorganized women in the trade, strikes have few chances of being won, unions are always in danger of their existence, and wages consequently low, hours long, and conditions of work generally very unsatisfactory, Be it therefore resolved:
    That we, the Button Hole Workers Union, Local 170, call upon you to provide the City of Baltimore with at least one woman organizer.

Yours in the struggle for organization of the working class,

Margaret Ruppert, Rec. Sec'y.
Dorothy Jacobs, Pres. [author's italics]
H. Plinkman, 117
H. Blumberg, D. C. #3
Isreal [sic] Levine, Local 36
Frank Dvorak, Local 52
I. Bayer, Local 241

The convention committee considering this resolution reported on it favorably; the convention itself passed it. However, not until 1917 did the board implement the resolution and put a full-time organizer on its national staff: Dorothy Jacobs.

Dorothy Jacobs, born in 1894 in Latvia, was six years old when she came to America. She got her first job sewing buttonholes in a Baltimore clothing shop when she was thirteen, spending the first four weeks as a learner at no wages at all. After that she earned $3 a week. Almost immediately she started talking union to the women around her. However, the company regarded her as still a child and did not take her seriously, firing her one minute for agitating and reinstating her the next. By 1909, not two years later, she had organized the buttonhole makers and they had been chartered as Local 170 of the United Garment Workers. Elected president of that local in 1914, she led it out of the UGW and into the insurgent Amalgamated. As one of her local's two delegates to the founding convention of the union in Webster Hall, an event she referred to as "the coming of the smiling dawn,"[20] she heard her resolution on a woman organizer favorably reported on and passed. There were perhaps 5 women among the approximately 175 delegates attending the convention.

In 1915 she was elected secretary of the Baltimore joint board, and the following year, when she was just twenty-two, she was elected a vice-president of the union, and re-elected in 1918. She and August Bellanca,

Dorothy Jacobs (Bellanca), a button sewer from Baltimore, often called the "Joan of Arc" of her union, became the first woman vice-president of the new Amalgamated Clothing Workers of America in 1914.

a fellow organizer and ACW pioneer, were married that year, and after her marriage she resigned her board post because her husband was also a union vice-president.*

She dropped none of her union work, however. She and her husband organized together throughout the 1920s, especially assigned to follow runaway shops.† Throughout the 1930s, too, she was the union's leading

* In 1934 she was elected to the general executive board again, and from that time until her death in 1946 was the union's only woman vice-president.
† Runaway shops were those manufacturers who left New York for lower-wage, non-union areas like Connecticut, New Jersey, Pennsylvania, and upstate New York. Later, shops left these areas and New England for the South to escape the unions.
    Runaway shops were not new to the 1920s and 1930s. Alice Henry, editor of the WTUL's *Life and Labor*, described the same kind of situation in a letter dated March 7, 1914, to League Secretary Rose Schneiderman, urging her to travel to Montreal to help organize French-Canadian women during a strike of pantsmakers: "The manufacturers are

organizer. Wherever there was a picket line, she was there, and more than likely leading it. Yet she found time to take an active part in the Consumers' League of New York and the Women's Trade Union League throughout these two decades.

Those who knew Dorothy Jacobs Bellanca describe her as a beautiful, articulate, vibrant, and warm human being with a deep, resonant voice that made her an electric speaker. Her audiences, large or small, loved her. Her words showed how much she cared about the special problems of women workers:

> One of the most vital problems which the Amalgamated Clothing Workers must consider in a straightforward manner at its third biennial convention is the woman problem. The American Federation of Labor and, through it, the United Garment Workers, has bequeathed this sad heritage; The idea that women were to be considered as inferior beings. This idea was carried so far that, in certain labor centers, as in Philadelphia and even New York, in dealings between organizations and bosses the women were purposely excluded as if the female workers were beasts of burden unworthy of consideration. In other centers the women have been organized but with all restrictions of sex prejudices, being considered as dues payers and competitors and never as organization units with all the rights of initiative, cooperation, leadership and struggle enjoyed by the men. . . .[21]

In eulogizing her after her death in 1946, ACWA President Jacob S. Potofsky called her one of labor's greatest organizers: "Dorothy addressed more meetings, installed more newly-organized locals and spoke to a greater number of workers than any other leader of either the Amalgamated or the general labor movement in this country."[22]

The Amalgamated, like the ILGWU, had its ups and downs in its struggle to organize and to build a stable organization. During a bitter strike of 25,000 unorganized Chicago clothing workers in 1915, Hart, Schaffner, and Marx members assessed themselves 10 percent of their wages to support the walkout. Daily arrests and police brutality marked the dispute from the beginning. One woman was hospitalized with a fractured breastbone. A deaf-mute worker was shot. Spies infiltrated every union meeting. Finally, after ten weeks, Hillman had to tell those strikers still holding out that the union had reached the end of its resources: they must call off the strike. All he could promise was that someday the union would be back. Bessie Abramowitz wept as she sat in the audience with

---

gradually removing their factories outside of Montreal, and establishing them in the small outlying villages, where they are engaging the native French-Canadian girls, teaching them, and paying them much less than the operatives in the city." Rose Schneiderman Letters, Collection 18, Box 1, Folder 4, Tamiment Library, New York University, New York, N.Y.

A new union is born. In December 1914, garment workers who had seceded from the old United Garment Workers formed a new union organized on an industrial basis: the Amalgamated Clothing Workers of America.

the 3,000 who listened to Hillman that day. She remembered that meeting as "the saddest day of my life."[23]

But there were good times too. Each May Day since 1886 Chicago workers had marched in honor of working men and women. But May Day 1916 had its special romance. Thousands of clothing workers from Hart, Schaffner, and Marx trooped down Harrison Street, led by Sidney Hillman and Bessie Abramowitz, arm in arm, who had just announced their engagement. A crowd gathered afterward at the Hotel La Salle to greet the couple and wish them well. The city's newspapers headlined the labor romance of these two famous leaders who had known each other for six years and been secretly engaged for two, but who had not had the time to get married. After the wedding took place on May 3, the Hillmans proceeded immediately to Rochester for the union's second biennial convention. Although Bessie Hillman resigned from her post as business agent for Chicago vestmakers' Local 152 to move to New York, where the union had its headquarters, she continued to play an active role in the Amalgamated in an unpaid capacity for the rest of her life.

A graduate of the Chicago Women's Trade Union League training school and a former league organizer, she continued her interest in the New York WTUL and the Consumers' League when she moved East. But her major time was devoted to the union, whether in the shirtworkers' campaigns in Pennsylvania, upstate New York, and Cleveland in the 1930s, as education director for the Laundry Workers Joint Board of the Amalgamated (1937–1944), or working with the union's War Activities Department during World War II. She became known (and loved) throughout the South during the 1940s and 1950s in one organizing drive after another. Following the death of her husband in 1946, Bessie Hillman was elected a vice-president of the union, a post she still held at the time of her death in 1970.[24]

Increasing the role of women workers in the union was one of her major concerns. In 1961, at a labor-sponsored conference, she told participants:

> I have a great bone to pick with the organized labor movement in this country. In my opinion they are the greatest offenders as far as discrimination against women is concerned. Today women in every walk of life have bigger positions than they have in organized labor. There isn't a woman on the AFL-CIO council—only 31 men. There has never been a woman sent from the AFL-CIO to any conference board. There has never been a woman recommended to higher positions after a political campaign is over. . . .
> . . . don't take it for granted that just because you're active [in your unions] you are going to be picked by men for higher jobs. You have to assert yourself by being worthy and by standing up to all the tests in the labor movement—and then you're going to be recognized.[25]

A number of women leaders in addition to Bessie Abramowitz Hillman and Dorothy Jacobs Bellanca emerged during the early days of the Amalgamated Clothing Workers. Florence Wallin became secretary-treasurer of the Twin Cities Joint Board in Minnesota; Emma Saurer served as business agent in Louisville, Kentucky; Sadie Goodman helped organize a woman's local of 6,000 in Rochester, where every clothing shop had a "girl's committee"; Clara Leon was the president of the board of directors of the Chicago Joint Board.[26]

When the union took stock in 1918 it found over 100,000 of its members had had strike experience. It had become a seasoned union that would be able to meet the test of the anti-union drives by employers that began in earnest following World War I. But as one worker wrote to a union officer: "Listen, whatever you get, you have to fight for it. If I am wrong, if my information is mistaken, please correct me, which I will appreciate. Thank you."[27]

Chapters 16 and 17 have covered the birth of the two great unions of garment workers, the International Ladies' Garment Workers' Union and the Amalgamated Clothing Workers of America. Both unions made giant strides in eliminating sweatshop conditions and in initiating programs of health, welfare, and other benefits that union members had never before enjoyed.

Although women were in a majority in both these unions and played leading roles in their organization, both international unions were led by men. Women found the door open to their membership, but rarely to key positions of influence. Both unions have had one or another of their women leaders as vice-presidents, the ILGWU never more than one at a time. The ACWA, recently merged with the Textile Workers to form the Amalgamated Clothing and Textile Workers Union (ACTWU), counts 5 women among its 50 board members. Women have always held posts as local officers and shop leaders, organizers and union representatives. Some have served as joint board and district managers, sometimes of sizable and important areas. In the 1920s these unions hired one woman for every three men on their organizing staffs, a major change from the decade before when there were few women on any union payroll.

While the number of women staff in these unions has increased steadily since the 1920s, women have never made substantial inroads on the tradition of male leadership in the international union hierarchy, particularly on the general executive board of either union. During the period when these unions emerged, women were still viewed as temporary in the work force. Men looked forward to the time when they could support their families without their wives having to work. Women looked forward to this also, although many were forced to put economic need above any plans to "retire." The home remained the responsibility of women, and even after a long day of work in the shop they performed the major portion of all household and child-care duties. Conversely, men were freer to attend meetings and devote their time outside working hours to the union. It was the exceptional women such as Mary Kenney O'Sullivan, Margaret Drier Robins, Bessie Abramowitz Hillman, and Dorothy Jacobs Bellanca who were able to continue careers after marriage. The majority of women leaders with careers, women like Rose Schneiderman, Pauline Newman, and Leonora O'Reilly, never married.

It was expected that men would participate in their unions, where they got the experience that enabled them to run for union office and move into leadership posts. Women rarely had this opportunity. When they did attend membership meetings, their lack of experience in public speaking and parliamentary procedure and their lack of knowledge of how the union worked made them feel inadequate to participate. Most were content to accept secondary leadership roles at best. It seemed natural to vote for men for the major union jobs that required negotiating with management, taking cases to arbitration, or administering the union on a full-time basis.

In addition, the patriarchal tradition that many of the early garment workers brought with them from Europe led both men and women to assume that men would be the leaders. However, during strikes the women served on an equal basis with the men. Many were picket captains and held strike leadership roles. They were tenacious, dedicated, and loyal. After every strike involving women workers, the men were sure to comment publicly on this and thank them for their help—in itself a commentary on how they were viewed.

The two great organizations of garment workers were especially important as the first unions of substance, power, and durability to include large numbers of women and to effect changes in a low-wage, traditionally female sweatshop industry, although differentials between men's and women's wages would remain for a long time.

18

WOMEN OF THE MILLS AND MINES
1900–1914

No more shall I work in the factory
To greasy up my clothes,
No more shall I work in the factory
With splinters in my toes.

No more shall I hear the whistle blow
To call me up too soon,
No more shall I hear the whistle blow
To call me from my home.

No more shall I see the super come
All dressed up so fine;
For I know I'll marry a country boy
Before the year is round.

It's pity me, my darling,
It's pity me, I say,
It's pity me, my darling,
And carry me far away.

—"Song of the Girl Factory-Worker"*

Women in the Southern Mills

As the Southern textile industry grew, the increased demand for labor was met by mountain and hill families who, unable to make a living out of farming worn-out land, turned to the mills. Packing their few belongings on their backs, they trudged to the new cotton-mill towns seeking work. In 1890, women made up 40.6 percent of all the South's 36,415 textile workers, and children another 23.7 percent.[1] Between a quarter and a third of all this country's cotton mills now were located in the South, where company towns flourished and workers were forced to spend what little they earned in the company stores. Pay was usually

---

* This version of a common textile workers' folk song was collected about 1913 by John Lomax, "Some Types of American Folk Songs," *Journal of American Folklore*, vol. 28, 1915. The tune is plaintive and repetitive; the chorus adds to this effect, since it is sung after each verse. As with most folk songs, there are many versions, although the chorus is almost exactly the same in each.

monthly or semimonthly, in store scrip rather than cash, but agents collected rents for company-owned tenements and shacks every week. The millowners knew that their workers could not put enough aside from their slim pay to make monthly rent collections profitable.

One day in 1903 young Marie Van Vorst, writer and reformer, donned what she called her "simple work garb," took on her pseudonym of Bell Ballard, and headed for Columbia, South Carolina, to look for work in a cotton mill. She and her sister-in-law, Bessie (Mrs. John) Van Vorst, had each taken jobs in several different kinds of occupations to learn firsthand about the lives of factory women. Marie Van Vorst had come South from a job as a shoeworker in Lynn, Massachusetts, and found work at Excelsior, the largest cotton mill in the world. She quickly learned that she could not afford the town's one rather seedy hotel, for room and board cost $2.25 a week, more than her week's wages. She then set about looking for a room to rent in the mill village huddled around the factory. In her book, *The Woman Who Toils*, she later described the homes that took in boarders: "unpainted huts, raised on stilts from the soil, fever-ridden and malarious; this blank, ugly line of sun-blistered shanties, along a road, yellow-sand deep, is a mill village. . . . There is not a garden within miles, not a flower, scarcely a tree."[2]

After searching all over town she accepted the best boarding situation she could find, sharing a bed with a sick woman whose daughter also slept in the tiny garret room. Since the woman vomited all night and the child was fretful, it was not long before Van Vorst began to look and feel as worn-out as all the women she saw around her. Her lunch as a boarder consisted of salt pork and a "pile of grease-swimming spinach," but there was little time in which to eat it anyway, since fifteen minutes of the forty-five-minute lunch period was used in getting to the house and another fifteen minutes in returning to the mill. Supper was not too different: "One plate (in the middle of the table) is piled high with fish—bones, skin and flesh all together in one odourous mass. Salt pork graces another platter and hominy another."

Her first job in the mill was as a spooler, which was "hard on the left arm and the side."* She learned that heart trouble was an occupational disease of the older spoolers. As a result, children and young girls were assigned this work. She was also introduced to the custom of taking snuff and chewing tobacco.

> They all take it, old and young, even the smallest children. Their mouths are brown with it; their teeth are black with it. They take it and smell it and carry it about under their tongues all day in a black

* Spoolers run machines that wind the yarn from one rapidly turning spool onto another to make a continuous thread for the looms.

wad, spitting it all over the floor. . . . the air of the room is white with
cotton. . . . These little particles are breathed into the nose, drawn
into the lungs. Lung disease and pneumonia—consumption—are the
constant, never-absent scourge of the mill village. The girls expectorate
to such an extent that the floor is nauseous with it; the little girls
practise spitting and are adept at it.

Sickness and death were the daily companions of the millworkers.
Mr. Jones, her boardinghouse keeper and a former millworker, told her:
"You-all must of had good food whar you come from: your skin shows it;
'tain't much like hyar-'bouts. Why, I'd know a mill-hand anywhere, if I
met her at the North Pole—salla, pale, sickly."

With the blowing of the mill whistle each morning at 4:50, the village
awoke and by 5:30 Van Vorst and the other workers in her boardinghouse
had left for work. On their way to the mill they were joined by additional
men, women, and children headed in the same direction. One day a

An end to child labor was an early trade union goal. Nonetheless, the practice of employing children continued well into the twentieth century.

young boy of fourteen walked beside her, so thin, she wrote, that "his
bones threaten to pierce his vestments." He had only one arm; "cotton
clings to his clothes; his shoes, nearly falling off his feet, are red with
clay stains." He worked from 5:45 A.M. to 6:45 P.M., and made 50 cents
a day. "It keeps me in existence," he told Van Vorst.

The mill women wore dark felt bonnets or caps at work, pulled as far over their eyes as possible to protect their hair from the cotton flying about everywhere. They were covered with this lint when they left at night and still had wisps of it on them the next morning when they returned to work. Any free time that workers had they spent in "distraction." She heard a manufacturer once say, "We gave our millhands everything that we could to elevate them—a natatorium, a reading library—and these halls fell into disuse." In her book, Van Vorst asked:

> What time would he suggest that they should spend in the reading room, even if they have learned to read? They rise at four; at a quarter before six they are at work. The day in winter is not born when they start their tasks; the night has fallen long before they cease. In summer they are worked long into their evenings. They tell me that they are too tired to eat; that all they want to do is to turn their aching bones on to their miserable mattresses and sleep until they are cried and shrieked awake by the mill summons. . . .

It was the children, many of them illegitimate, that Marie Van Vorst found the most heartbreaking. In the midst of the grinding and pounding of the gigantic machines, she saw the children who had not yet been assigned work for the day sleeping against bales of cotton. A child of eight with "bare, filthy feet" worked next to her, the snuff she chewed drooling from her mouth. "Her hands and arms are no longer flesh colour, but resemble weather-roughened hide, ingrained with dirt." Describing her landlord's child, who worked in the mill, Van Vorst wrote:

> She is seven; so small that they have a box for her to stand upon. She is a pretty, frail, little thing, a spooler—"a good spooler, tew!" Through the frames on the other side I can only see her fingers as they clutch at the flying spools; her head is not high enough, even with the box, to be visible. Her hands are fairy hands, fine-boned, well-made, only they are so thin and dirty, and her nails—claws; she would do well to have them cut. A nail can be torn from the finger, *is* torn from the finger frequently, by this flying spool.

Van Vorst reported her talk with mill-town doctors, one of whom told her that he had "amputated the fingers of more than a hundred babies." A merchant told her of the many children he had seen whose hands had been cut off by the machinery.

She asked one young girl how old she was, and the child answered, "Ten." Van Vorst didn't believe her—she looked no more than six. But she found that the children were taught early to lie about their ages, both by the employers and by their own parents, who counted on the 40 cents a day the children earned to help sustain the family.

During her brief lunch period she often watched the children. They crouched on the floor to eat; some would fall asleep "between the mouthfuls of food, and so lie asleep with food in their mouths until the overseer rouses them to their tasks again. Here and there totters a little child just learning to walk; it runs and crawls the length of the mill."

The children all seemed malnourished, their stomachs distended and swollen, their bones "nearly through" their skin. Most of the children returned home at about 8:00 P.M., or later if the mill was working overtime.

> They are usually beyond speech. They fall asleep at the tables, on the stairs; they are carried to bed and there laid down as they are, unwashed, undressed; and the inanimate bundles of rags so lie until the mill summons them with its imperious cry before sunrise, while they are still in stupid sleep.

Van Vorst found that in one Alabama mill, where seventy-five children worked 12-hour shifts with a half-hour for lunch, the company sponsored a night school for the children. Fifty of the seventy-five children attended, but were so tired that many fell asleep at their books. Employers blamed the greed of parents for the fact that children worked in the mill; but mothers told Van Vorst that if they refused to send their children in to work they were evicted from their company-owned homes. She met some women with very young children who held the babies to them and claimed, "I would not let *my* little boy work in 'em! . . . He would go over my dead body." But in the end most families had to yield to a combination of economic need and company pressure. One of the few cheerful children she met in the entire mill village was the child of a woman who had managed somehow to keep her daughter from the mill and who told Van Vorst, "My little girl work? No, ma'am; she goes to school."

Absent workers who were ill were docked accordingly. If any took off for a day, a man hired especially for the purpose rode from house to house seeking them out, urging them "to rise, and if they are not literally too sick to move . . . hounds [them] out of their beds and back to their looms."

After Marie Van Vorst returned to the North, she discussed her mill experiences with a society acquaintance in New England who owned a half-interest in a large Carolina mill. She described for her as vividly as she could the children she had seen. Her friend responded: "Dear friend, I am going to surprise you very much. Those little children—*love the mill!* They *like* to work. It's a great deal better for them to be employed than for them to run the streets! Do you know that I believe they are really very happy." (The italics are Van Vorst's.) Van Vorst then asked her what she would think of a mill where workers had a 9-hour day, holidays, free evenings, schools, and recreational facilities. If all the cotton-mill owners agreed, her friend replied, it might be possible. For her mill alone to try it would mean "ruin." Van Vorst suggested, "Not ruin, a reduction of income." "Ruin," the friend fired back. "We couldn't compete. To compete, I must have my sixty-six hours a week!"

Van Vorst spoke to editors of Southern papers, to legislators, to mill-owners. No one wanted any outsider interfering with South Carolina's way of life. The state legislature voted down a bill restricting child labor. Absentee owners were concerned only with profits. The mill superintendents were quick to proclaim, "Labor unions cut no figure here!"

In her book, Van Vorst suggests not only protective legislation and an end to child labor, but unionization as one of the few hopes that mill-workers have.

> Go at night through the mills with the head of the Labour Federation and with the instigator of the first strikes in this district—with men who are the brain and fiber of the labour organization, and see the friendly looks flash forth, see the understanding with which they are greeted all through certain mills. Consider that not 200 miles away at the moment are 22,000 labourers on strike. Then greet these statements [of mill superintendents] with a smile!

Her Southern experiences led Marie Van Vorst to go on to write a novel, *Amanda of the Mill* (1905), which portrayed even more graphically the life of the Southern factory worker. Lecturer, writer, painter, and suffragist, she as well as her sister-in-law did much to publicize working conditions of women and children, although they did not come to substantive conclusions about solutions. But their courageous and unusual approach to the problems of factory women, their books and popular magazine articles, contributed to arousing the social conscience of America. This was one more step toward establishing a climate for legislation to correct the abuses they uncovered.

"Junior Unions"

> If a girl is caught looking out of a window her loom is stopped, and she is sent to the boss to explain, and very often she is docked for it. If a girl is discharged from any one department she cannot get employment in any other without first begging of her former boss permission to go to work, and they are not allowed to talk to one another during working hours, *or at noon time*, under penalty of being discharged. . . . They are not allowed to eat dinner together; even two sisters working in two different departments are not allowed to eat their meals together in the factory. . . .[3]

Southern employers were not the only exploiters of children, of course. Mine owners throughout West Virginia and Pennsylvania had always employed young boys in the coal mines. Toward the end of the nineteenth century, garment factories and textile mills began to open in the mining communities to take advantage of the low-wage labor supply: the wives and children of the miners. By 1900, in Pennsylvania alone some 120,000 children worked in mines and factories. Girls under sixteen, 17,000 of them, worked in Pennsylvania silk and lace plants, many on the 6:30 P.M. to 6:30 A.M. shift.

Miners were union men, and had been since the 1840s and 1850s. It was only natural for the children to emulate their fathers and organize "junior unions," as an article that appeared in *McClure's Magazine* in 1903 reported:

> Just as the boys in the mines had junior locals, so did their sisters in the mills have a union. The weekly meeting, it was reported, was the great event in the life of every child in the coal fields. When attending meetings members of the girls' unions wore "the same clothes that they would wear to church." The debates were about wages and hours and working conditions. Often the discussions led to serious action, strikes.
>
> The girls asserted themselves almost as often and with almost as much strength as the dirty, grimy miners. Sometimes an injustice done to one girl would arouse the feelings of her sisters.
>
> One strike was called when a very little girl began to grow crippled from operating a treadle. She became so lame and ill that she had to stay home for a week and go to bed. During that time a large boy was hired to do her work. He was, of course, paid more money. When the girl returned, the boy was fired and the girl put back on the treadle. The boss refused to find other work for her.
>
> In the words of a young leader of the union, "Shall we stand for it, girls, for seeing her grow up a cripple and the union not doing nothing, not reaching out no hand for to help? We that believes in the rights of man?"
>
> Some had fathers who were striking [at the time] but the vote was unanimous.
>
> "We had the resolution written out nice on a typewriter," the leader said. After two days the boss gave in. The boy worked at the treadle and the girl was placed at work at a bench.[4]

Mary Harris Jones, A Legend for All Time

A "widow lady" in a long, full skirt, a black silk blouse with a touch of lace at the neck, her hair escaping from her black flower-trimmed bonnet, applied for a job in one of the cotton mills of Cottondale.* In order to get hired she promised the millowner that her six children soon would be joining her and she would bring them to the mill to work.

---

* Perhaps Cottondale stands for all the mill towns in which Mother Jones worked during this period. She gives no state or clue to its location.

After a few weeks, when it became clear that no children were arriving, she was fired, only to move on to another mill town with the same story and another cotton-mill job. Thus Mary Harris Jones, or "Mother Jones," as she came to be known, carried on her own survey of Southern cotton-mill conditions. In her *Autobiography* she wrote of her experiences in the early 1890s:

> Sometimes it seemed to me I could not look at those silent little figures; that I must go north. . . . Little girls and boys, barefooted, walked up and down between endless rows of spindles, reaching thin little hands into the machinery to repair snapped threads. They crawled under the machinery to oil it. . . . Tiny babies of six years old with faces of sixty did an eight hour shift for ten cents a day. If they fell asleep, cold water was dashed in their faces, and the voice of the manager yelled above the ceaseless racket and whir of the machines.[5]

Conditions for women in the mills were no better. She recorded verbatim her conversation with one young mother coming home from her night work at the mill carrying her tiny baby cradled in one arm.

> "How old is the baby?"
> "Three days. I just went back this morning. The boss was good and saved my place."
> "When did you leave [work]?"
> "The boss was good; he let me off early the night the baby was born."
> "What do you do with the baby while you work?"
> "Oh, the boss is good and lets me have a little box with a pillow in it beside the loom. The baby sleeps there and when it cries, I nurse it."

In one mill Mother Jones found two little girls working beside their father for twelve hours a day and earning 10 cents; their father earned 40 cents. Another millworker had exactly $1 left at the end of a full year of work after the owner's deductions for rent and food from the company store. At yet another mill the owner opened a bank for the workers. When he found that they were saving 10 percent of their wages, he instituted a wage cut of just that amount. In Selma, Alabama, the daughter of a woman with whom Mother Jones boarded had been killed when her hair caught in an unguarded machine. The owner in one mill town charged prices for food and clothing in the company store and rent in the company tenements that always added up to more than a whole family could earn working seven days a week, fourteen hours a day. Thus they were continually in his debt and could never leave.

Angry beyond words, Mother Jones was moved to act. She abducted one family where the father had died of consumption and the family owed $36 to the company.[7] Years later she looked back on her cotton-mill days and said:

I wonder that armies did not stand forth to free those slaves. Poor
men and women and little children worked from morning to night
for bread, nothing but bread, no hope of anything better, only the
opportunity to prolong their miserable lives. No wonder that very
early in life I determined to wage war for the factory people.[8]

But Mother Jones never organized the women in the cotton mills.
Most of them were mothers, and she believed that women with children
should not work outside the home. She turned instead to organizing coal
miners, and quickly earned a reputation for mobilizing vigorous armies
of miners' wives, her only weapons her black umbrella and her long
hatpin.* "God! It's the old mother with her wild women!" the coal
operators would groan when Mother Jones appeared.[9]

More people probably have heard about Mother Jones than about
almost any other American labor hero or heroine. Who was she? So much
legend has grown up around this colorful, quotable woman that often it
is hard to separate fact from fiction. Her exact birthdate is not known, although she claimed to have been born on May 1, 1830, and to have come
to Toronto, Canada, from her native Cork, Ireland, when she was about
seven years old. Educated in Toronto, where her railroad-worker father
had a job, she taught school for a time in Michigan, then moved to
Chicago and became a dressmaker. Back in teaching, this time in Memphis, Tennessee, she met and married George Jones, an ironmolder who
was a strong trade unionist,† had one or more children (probably four) but
lost them all, and was widowed in a yellow fever epidemic that struck
Memphis in 1867. During that time she helped nurse fever victims, and
then moved back to Chicago to earn her living again in dressmaking.
When the Chicago fire of 1871 wiped out her shop, she seems to have
found solace at the Knights of Labor hall where she attended Knights'
meetings and sought companionship. Her union career probably began
in 1877 when she went to Pittsburgh to help strikers during the nation-
wide railroad dispute. The violence and brutality that she witnessed led her
to devote the rest of her life to workers and to the labor movement.[10]

Because she developed effective battalions of miners' wives to help the

* There seem to have been some exceptions. Folklorist Archie Green quotes John Far-
rance's story of Mother Jones in her Pennsylvania organizing days: "I saw her one time
in Monongahela. She was trying to organize the mines. She came down Pike Street in a
buggy and horse. Two company thugs grabbed the horse by the bridle and told her to
turn around and get back down the road. She wore a gingham apron and she reached
under it and pulled out a 38 special pistol and told them to turn her horse loose, and they
sure did. She continued on to the park and spoke to a large crowd of miners. She wasn't
afraid of the devil." ("The Death of Mother Jones," *Labor History*, vol. 1, no. 1 [winter
1960], p. 77).

† Historian Priscilla Long submits some evidence that he may have been a miner or an
organizer for the mine workers' union ("Mother Jones, Woman Organizer," unpublished
manuscript, p. 3, footnote).

men keep scab workers out of the mines during strikes, the United Mine Workers put her on their payroll as an organizer or "walking delegate." Mother Jones went from one mining town to another, living in the homes of the miners, partly to save money, partly because she was often denied hotel room in company towns. On occasion, families who gave her a room were evicted from their company-owned homes by the employers, yet no one turned her away. Sometimes she would stop at a home only long enough for a hot bath and a chance to do her laundry; then she was off again.

If we can believe that her birthdate was May 1, 1830, this remarkable woman lived to be one hundred years old, traveling up and down and across America almost until the end of her days. She probably logged more miles than all the labor organizers up to that time put together— and paid less train fare to do so, for the railroad workers, who loved her, stopped trains outside the towns to swing her aboard and rarely charged her a penny.

While Mother Jones is the most legendary and best known of the women who organized among the miners, each mining town had its "mother" who mobilized the women in support of the men in the mines. Some of them, like Mother Blizzard of Cabin Creek, West Virginia, never left the communities in which they lived, but they exerted a powerful influence. The mine women knew how to fight; Mother Jones did not teach them. The bucket-and-broom brigades that painted scabs with excreta did not arrive with Mother Jones, nor did the tin-pan noisemakers that frightened the mine mules. Women jailed in support of striking

Mary Harris Jones, known as Mother Jones, marches in Calumet, Michigan, in 1913 at the age of eighty-three to support striking iron miners and their families.

miners knew what to do; the more babies they took to jail with them and kept awake and crying all night by their singing, the shorter the length of time the women would spend behind bars.

However, Mother Jones was the most flamboyant and colorful of the women leaders. She was probably also the best public speaker. Her use of words was sharp, to the point, and earthy. The owners who opposed unionizing she called "high-class burglars."[11] Through one of the few verbatim accounts of any of her speeches, that given on the steps of the state capitol in Charleston, West Virginia, in 1912, we get the flavor of her language:

> But I warn this little governor that unless he rids Paint Creek and Cabin Creek of these goddamned Baldwin Felts mineguard thugs, there is going to be one hell of a lot of bloodletting in these hills.[12]

Her oratorical style must have been something to watch as well as hear. It was "revivalistic."

> Haranguing with an Irish lilt that could rise to a screech or fall to a whisper, she could move a crowd to fury even if she was the only English-speaking person present. She would shout, stamp, gesticulate, and throw in a few words of whatever languages seemed appropriate.[13]

"Incorrigible" was another word that described her. Once she was arrested in Pittsburgh during a steel strike and charged with streetcorner speaking without a permit. The judge asked her whether she had obtained the necessary permit, and she answered, "Yes, your honor, I have." "Who issued it to you?" asked the judge. "Patrick Henry; Thomas Jefferson; John Adams!" was her reply.[14]

Mother Jones saw the constant sorrow in workers' lives:

> Immigrants poured into the country and they worked cheap. Hours of work down under ground were cruelly long. Fourteen hours a day was not uncommon, thirteen, twelve. The life or limb of the miner was unprotected by any laws. Families lived in company-owned shacks that were not fit for their pigs. Children died by the hundreds due to the ignorance and poverty of their parents.
>
> Often I have helped lay out for burial the babies of the miners, and the mothers could scarcely conceal their relief at the little ones' deaths. Another was already on its way, destined, if a boy, for the breakers; if a girl, for the silk mills where the other brothers and sisters already worked.[15]

The biggest terror in mining communities was of mine accidents or fires, which so often left women and children helpless and forced little boys to take mine jobs to help support the family. When the accident bell rang out, anxious women gathered to watch and wait to learn whether the men in their families were among those killed or perhaps maimed for life. It

A typical scene: women and children wait outside the mine for word
of husbands and fathers, victims of a mine disaster. This one took place
in Cherry, Illinois, at the St. Paul Coal Company, November 27, 1909.

is small wonder that the women took part in the frequent and often war-
like strikes that swept the mining towns. Mother Jones was right with
them, wherever there was trouble.

> She spoke in open fields when halls were closed. She waded through
> Kelly Creek, West Virginia, to organize miners on the other side. Tried
> for violating an injunction, she called the judge a "scab" and proved
> it to him. She organized "women's armies" to chase scabs . . . [when]
> she was asked at a Congressional hearing: "Where is your home?" . . .
> she answered: . . . "My address is like my shoes. It travels with me.
> I abide where there is a fight against wrong."[16]

In 1903, Mother Jones resigned from the United Mine Workers over
an argument with UMW President John Mitchell. During the next
eight years, she supported herself on contributions from labor friends
and by taking jobs in a variety of industries in different parts of the
country. The spring of 1903 found her in Kensington, Pennsylvania,
outside of Philadelphia, where more than 75,000 textile workers were on
strike, 10,000 of them children. The children would come down to strike
headquarters, and once again she became aware of how many of them
were maimed. Many had fingers and even hands cut off by the machinery
and were bent over and old at less than ten years of age. She writes about
her fury:

I asked the newspaper men why they didn't publish the facts about child labor in Pennsylvania. They said they couldn't because the mill owners had stock in the papers.

"Well, I've got stock in these little children," said I, "and I'll arrange a little publicity."[17]

At a mass rally that she organized in Independence Park in Philadelphia, she showed the crowd the children, so many of them permanently injured, so many small enough for her to lift high over her head for the crowd to see. New York and Philadelphia papers gave her the publicity she sought, and stimulated discussions of child labor. But then interest lagged.

Looking for a way to create greater public pressure for legislation to end child labor, she got the idea during the summer of 1903 of a children's march to see President Theodore Roosevelt at his home in Oyster Bay, Long Island. She borrowed about seventy-five children from Kensington mothers, promising to return them safely in a week or ten days. Each child packed a little knapsack with a knife and fork, a tin cup and plate. With a few men to help her and a wash boiler to cook food for the little "army," they set out. The signs they carried read: "We want more schools and less hospitals"; "We want time to play"; "Prosperity is here. Where is ours?"[18]

After launching the march at a mass meeting in Philadelphia, the group started for New York, planning to stop off to visit J. P. Morgan, "out of politeness," said Mother Jones, because he owned the mines where the fathers of the children worked or had been killed. Some children were not strong enough for the march and had to be sent back home. But those who went on got all the publicity Mother Jones had planned.

In Princeton, New Jersey, the leading hotel fed the children. There Mother Jones spoke on "Higher Education" to a crowd outside the university.

I told them that the rich robbed these little children of any education of the lowest order that they might send their sons and daughters to places of higher education. . . . "Here's a textbook on economics," I said, pointing to a little chap, James Ashworth, who was ten years old and who was stooped over like an old man from carrying bundles of yarn that weighed seventy-five pounds. "He gets three dollars a week and his sister who is fourteen gets six dollars. They work in a carpet factory ten hours a day while the children of the rich are getting their higher education."[19]

In New York she marched the few children who were left in her "army" up Fourth Avenue to Madison Square and talked to a huge crowd on 20th Street. The children, placed in friendly homes, spent the next day at Coney Island, where another crowd heard Mother Jones compare child labor and slavery. Fifty years ago, she explained, there was a cry against slavery, but today white children were still sold into virtual slavery for two dollars a week. The only difference, said Mother Jones, was that "black babies were sold C.O.D. Today the white baby is sold on the installment plan."[20]

In some respects her march failed. Almost all the children had to return home before they got to Oyster Bay. President Roosevelt refused to see them, and did not even answer Mother Jones's letter. Nor did she raise much money for the Kensington textile strikers, who lost their fight. The children had to go back to the mills under the same terms as before. However, soon afterward Pennsylvania passed laws that forbade child labor under the age of fourteen. In terms of publicizing the conditions under which young children worked in the mills, her march had made history.

Mother Jones had an honored place with Lucy Parsons, widow of anarchist Albert Parsons,* at the founding convention of the Industrial Workers of the World in 1905, and for a time she was an IWW member. She thrilled women shirtwaist strikers in 1909 in New York when she addressed a mass rally and told them that every strike she "had ever been in was won by the women."[21] By 1911 she was back in the United Mine Workers' fold, again organizing miners' wives.

The massacre in Ludlow in 1914 moved her more deeply than almost any other event during her lifetime. Striking miners and their families were evicted from their homes, then their tent colony was brutally attacked by troops and set afire. Fifteen women and children and thirty miners were killed,[22] while scores were injured. Mother Jones began a nation-wide speaking campaign to report to the country what had occurred.†

In her nineties Mother Jones still moved through the hills of West Virginia, encouraging miners to organize. Interestingly, she never supported suffrage, prohibition, or the Women's Trade Union League. "The plutocrats have organized their women," she stated. "They keep them busy with suffrage and prohibition and charity," the last referring to the WTUL.[23] Her relationships with the miners honored the traditional roles of men and women that they knew and accepted. She promoted women's supportive positions as wives and mothers, their mops and brooms as their best weapons. Her commitment to them was based on her conviction that

---

* Labor organizer and martyr of the Haymarket Square bombing in Chicago in 1886, Albert Parsons was hanged for a crime he could not have committed. His wife, equally active in labor and political organizing, spent the rest of her life trying to clear his name.
† Mother Jones was not in Ludlow on April 20, 1914, the day of the massacre, but in Washington, D.C., testifying before the House Committee on Mines and Mining.

the hard, tragic lives they knew in the mining towns would be better if the men earned more and could win a union.

It has been said of Mother Jones that she much preferred the company of men, drinking with them in their smoke-filled saloons, even though her organizing work was largely around militant women. Even Elizabeth Gurley Flynn, labor leader, organizer, and orator, claimed that she was afraid of Mother Jones's biting tongue and caustic comments. But whatever her faults, Mother Jones was known and loved by thousands, and her name was a household word in workers' homes across America. Labor author and former miner Tom Tippett wrote of her after her death:

> For years she appeared in most of the major strikes, often by invitation of the leaders but many times by her ability to insinuate herself. . . .
> In the union office she was out of place, quarreling with officials, offering no constructive policy of her own and constantly violating union policy. It was in the field that she made her real contribution. With one speech she often threw a whole community on strike and she could keep the strikers loyal month after month on empty stomachs and behind prison bars. By virtue of her outstanding personality, intrepid daring and complete devotion to their cause, Mother Jones captured the imagination of the American workers as no other woman has yet done.[24]

Mother Jones would talk of "my army of women": her bravado was what the miners loved best. For example, when 2,000 to 3,000 miners' wives marched with her across the mountain from McAdoo, Pennsylvania, to Coaldale, they were stopped by the militia and held all night. Released at daybreak, they marched straight "to the kitchen of the hotel where the militia were quartered and ate the breakfast that was on the table for the soldiers."[25] It is not hard to imagine how this story was told and retold in mining town after mining town when the women returned.

In a time when travel was difficult, uncertain, and uncomfortable, Mother Jones was the most widely traveled organizer in America. Her partial itinerary for the year 1913–1914 included:

August 1913	Michigan Copper Strike
Labor Day, 1913	Texas
September 1913	Southern Colorado
October 1913	Washington, D.C.
December 1913	Colorado
January to April 1914	El Paso, Texas. Colorado: jailed in Trinidad for nine weeks; shipped to Denver; tried to return to Trinidad, jailed 26 days.
April 1914	Washington, D.C.
May 1914	New York City

If she was born in 1830, as she claimed, her age during this not atypical year could have been eighty-three or eighty-four. In 1916 she was active in the New York City transit strike, organizing the wives to "persuade" scabs who were running the streetcars to come out too. In 1919 she was involved in the big steel strike, and in 1921 she traveled to Mexico City to speak. That same year, at the age of ninety-one, she spoke to the miners of Charleston, West Virginia, and even addressed her friends and was recorded on newsreel film on her hundredth birthday, though she was weak and could not walk.

She died on November 30, 1930, mourned by thousands, and was buried in the Mount Olive cemetery in central Illinois. When a monument was dedicated to her in 1936, the ceremony was attended by 50,000 miners.[26] Not long after her death, this song began to circulate, first in the hills of West Virginia, then in mining communities wherever Mother Jones was known:

The Death of Mother Jones

The world today is mourning the death of Mother Jones;
Grief and sorrow hover around the miners' homes.
This grand old champion of labor has gone to a better land,
But the hard-working miners, they miss her guiding hand.

Through the hills and o'er the valleys in every mining town,
Mother Jones was ready to help them; she never let them down.
In front with the striking miners she always could be found;
She fought for right and justice; she took a noble stand.

With a spirit strong and fearless, she hated that which was wrong;
She never gave up fighting until her breath was gone.
May the workers all get together to carry out her plan,
And bring back better conditions for every laboring man.[27]

Mother Jones combined the drama in her soul and her eccentric personality to publicize the conditions of men, women, and children in the mines and factories of the early 1900s. She helped them to mobilize and act on their own behalf. A believer in industrial unionism, in 1905 Mother Jones attended the founding convention of the Industrial Workers of the World, an idealistic labor federation with the goal of organizing all workers into one big union. It was this federation that, in 1912, successfully led the textile workers in Lawrence, Massachusetts, through a difficult nine-and-a-half-week strike against tremendous odds. It developed and utilized original methods to meld a diverse group of thousands of immigrant workers.

The struggle in Lawrence made labor history. This was the first major strike to employ mass picketing effectively. The high level of organization and worker participation in this strike has rarely been matched. It became a model of discipline, solidarity, and devotion. The story of the Lawrence textile workers' strike underscores the fact that the conditions of millworkers in the South and throughout the coal-mining regions of Pennsylvania and West Virginia were not isolated examples of factory life of the 1900–1914 period. The New England textile industry offered its workers wages and working conditions that were little better and against which, finally, they were forced to rebel.

19

WOMEN IN THE INDUSTRIAL WORKERS OF THE WORLD
The Lawrence Strike, 1912

As we come marching, marching, unnumbered women dead
Go crying through our singing their ancient song of bread.
Small art and love and beauty their drudging spirits knew.
Yes, it is bread we fight for,
But we fight for roses, too.

—James Oppenheim, "Bread and Roses"

Women textile workers, carrying high their banners that proclaimed, "We Want Bread and Roses, Too!" made labor history in Lawrence, Massachusetts, in 1912. In a bitter struggle of nine-and-a-half weeks, they played such a key role that strike leader William "Big Bill" Haywood said of them, "The women won the strike."[1] The labor organization leading this strike of 20,000 mostly immigrant textile workers in Lawrence was the Industrial Workers of the World (IWW). Although no woman held a top office in the organization, the IWW had more women organizers and more women as public speakers and fund raisers than any other labor union up to that time.

The founding convention of the IWW on June 27, 1905, brought together workers from the Western Federation of Miners, anti-AFL unionists, socialists, and anarchists, who met in Chicago to form a new confederation of labor.* Haywood, the secretary of the Western Federation of Miners, chaired the meeting, calling for "a working class movement in possession of the economic powers, the means of life, in control of the machinery of

---

* At least three women were present at this founding convention: Mother Jones, Luella Twining, who later managed Haywood's 1908 trip around the country, and Lucy Parsons, who spoke as an anarchist on her conception of "the strike of the future. . . . [It] is not to strike and go out and starve, but to strike and remain in and take possession of the necessary property of production." In several instances the IWW employed the sit-down technique that would be used with such success by workers in the 1930s, most notably in the organizing drives of the CIO in the rubber and automobile industries. William D. Haywood, *Bill Haywood's Book* (New York: International Publishers Co., 1929), pp. 180, 183, 227; Patrick Renshaw, *The Wobblies* (New York: Doubleday & Co., Anchor Books, 1968), p. 56.

production and distribution without regard to capitalist masters."[2] The IWW believed in one big union for all, men and women, black and white, and promoted membership among black men and women as freely in the South as in the North or West. In a leaflet addressed "To Colored Workingmen and Women," it stated:

> If you are a wage worker you are welcome in the IWW halls, no matter what your color. By this you may see that the IWW is not a white man's union, not a black man's union, not a red man's union, but a workingman's union. All of the working class in one big union.[3]

The IWW kept few records, so the number of its women members is not known. Most of them came from the mills of the East. In the West, lumberjacks, miners, and migratory workers made up the bulk of its membership at different periods.[*] Wherever it could organize women workers, it was into industrial unions along with the men, not into separate women's locals. Although it disapproved of the National Women's Trade Union League approach and encouraged women to participate in all its organizational activities, it did hold separate strike meetings for women when that seemed necessary.

Its leading organizers included Katie Phar, a cripple with a lovely voice who sang Wobbly songs wherever she went; Matilda Rabinowitz, who looked so small and disarming, but whose arrival in town the local police invariably dreaded; and Vera Moller, one of several women who were Wobbly songwriters.[†] But none could compare with Elizabeth Gurley

---

[*] In the West, however, IWW women's auxiliaries and brigades gave active support to men on strike. Dues-paying membership in the IWW was never large. After the successful Lawrence strike, its membership among the textile workers there was 14,310 dues-paying men and women. By November 1913, this figure had fallen to 700, as will be discussed in this chapter. The influence of the IWW and the publicity it received far exceeded its size in importance. Robert Franklin Hoxie, *Trade Unionism in the United States* (New York: D. Appleton & Co., 1928 (1917), p. 140, n. 1.

[†] Vera Moller wrote her most famous song in prison, "We Made Good Wobs Out There," a parody on "Auld Lang Syne": "When we were out we did our bit/ To hasten Freedom's dawn./ They can't take back the seeds we spread,/ The truths we passed along./" Ethel Comer was the earliest Wobbly songwriter. Fred Thompson recalls that her first published song, "Stand Up Ye Workers," was written to a hymn tune. Rose Elizabeth Smith wrote one called "The Ninety and Nine"; Laura Payne Emerson, one titled "I Stood by a City Prison." Katie Phar of the beautiful voice was another to whom Joe Hill dedicated a copy of "The Rebel Girl," Thompson reports. Organizer Matilda Rabinowitz, active in the Little Falls, New York, textile strike following the Lawrence victory, moved on to Detroit, during the summer of 1913, where she carried her soapbox to the Ford plant gates to talk to auto workers and was involved in the Studebaker strike at the Delray plant. John Greenway, *American Folksongs of Protest* (New York: Perpetua Edition, A. S. Barnes & Co., 1960), p. 83, for Vera Moller's song. I am indebted to Fred W. Thompson for information about the other women songwriters of the IWW. Songbook editions of the *Little Red Book* in which their songs appeared are: 5th (p. 19); 9th (p. 19); 18th (p. 31). Haywood, *Bill Haywood's Book,* carries information about Matilda Rabinowitz (p. 257).

Flynn, the beautiful young organizer with the long dark hair and deep blue eyes to whom Wobbly Joe Hill dedicated his song "The Rebel Girl" in 1915.

The "Rebel Girl"

That's the Rebel Girl. That's the Rebel Girl.
To the working class she's a precious pearl.
She brings courage, pride and joy
To the Fighting Rebel Boy.
We've had girls before
But we need some more
In the Industrial Workers of the World,
For it's great to fight for freedom
With a Rebel Girl.[4]

Born in 1890 in New Hampshire, Gurley Flynn (as she came to be called) knew a number of towns and cities as home before her family finally settled in New York's South Bronx in 1900. The move to New York introduced her to city poverty: a cold-water tenement with no heat except the kitchen stove, with mice and roaches and bedbugs, with railroad yards across the street that were the scene of daily industrial accidents. In her autobiography she recalls her Irish mother, when things were at their worst, reciting a poem that Flynn attributes to Whittier:

When Earth produces free and fair the golden waving corn,
And golden fruits perfume the air and fleecy flocks are shorn,
Yet thousands cry with aching head the never-ending song,
"We starve! We die! Oh give us bread!"
There must be something wrong![5]

Brought up in a family that voted for Eugene Debs, Socialist Party candidate for president in 1900, Flynn accompanied her father regularly to political meetings. At the age of fifteen she gave her first public speech—on the rights of women—which launched her career as a speaker. From listening to streetcorner speakers like Rose Schneiderman, she learned how to cope with hecklers and how to answer such typical comments as "Go home and wash your dishes!" "How could women serve on juries and be locked up with men jurors?" "Who's taking care of your children?" "Imagine a pregnant woman running for office!"[6]

She was arrested for the first time in 1906, at the age of sixteen, when she and her father were accused of speaking without a permit. Free speech was to be an issue for which she fought all her life. By the time she was seventeen, she had been involved in the five-week strike at the American Tube and Stamping Company in Bridgeport, Connecticut, speaking all day and fund raising at street meetings during the evenings.

During the severe economic recession of 1907–1908, she organized the New York Propaganda League, which attempted to get help for unemployed workers. Already in demand as a speaker, she traveled widely for the IWW, and on one of her trips met Jack Jones, an IWW organizer then in his 30s, whom she married.

Gurley Flynn arrived in Spokane, Washington, during the IWW free-speech fight of 1909, and she was news. The city's papers described her as "frail, slender . . . pretty and graceful, with a resonant voice and a fiery eloquence that attracted huge crowds." Hundreds of IWW members poured into Spokane during this campaign and invited arrest to test their right to speak freely on issues of concern to them. But it was Gurley Flynn whom the authorities considered "the most dangerous and effective of Wobbly soapboxers."

> When a young attorney suggested to the city fathers that she not be tried along with the men on charges of criminal conspiracy, the local officials responded: "Hell, no! You just don't understand. She's the one we are after. She makes all the trouble. She puts fight into the men, gets them the publicity they enjoy. As it is, they're having the time of their lives."[7]

She was pregnant at the time of her Spokane arrest, and attracted attention by chaining herself to a lamppost to delay her removal while at the same time charging the city sheriff with using jailed women as prostitutes for his own profit.[8]

Gurley Flynn was brought to trial on charges of criminal conspiracy, along with Charley Filigno, a young Italian IWW member. When the jury found Filigno guilty and Gurley Flynn innocent, an angry prosecutor shouted at the jury foreman, "What in hell do you fellows mean by acquitting the most guilty, and convicting the man, far less guilty?" The jury foreman answered:

> She ain't a criminal, Fred, an' you know it! If you think this jury, or any jury, is goin' to send that pretty Irish girl to jail merely for bein' bighearted and idealistic, to mix with all those whores and crooks down at the pen, you've got another guess comin'.[9]

Later in the Spokane free-speech campaign Gurley Flynn was arrested again and this time jailed. Gleefully the press followed her to prison, and the experience she had there as a young pregnant woman was publicized from coast to coast. Too late the authorities realized the mistake they had made in tackling Gurley Flynn.[10]

Her son, Fred, was born after she and her husband had already decided to separate over the issue of his insistence that she stay home to raise their children. She continued her work with the IWW, and Fred was brought up for the most part by Gurley Flynn's mother.

When she came to Lawrence, Massachusetts, to help with the strike, Gurley Flynn was already an experienced organizer and an accomplished public speaker. But she always said that she learned how to talk to workers from listening to "Big Bill" Haywood during the mass meetings in Lawrence, "to use short words and short sentences, to repeat the same thought in different words if I saw that the audience did not understand. I learned never to reach for a three-syllable word if a one or two could do. . . . Words are tools and everybody doesn't have access to a whole tool chest."[11]

The "Bread and Roses" Strike: Lawrence, 1912

As we come marching, marching in the beauty of the day,
A million darkened kitchens, a thousand mill lofts gray
Are touched with all the radiance that a sudden sun discloses,
For the people hear us singing: "Bread and Roses! Bread and Roses!"[12]

The town of Lawrence, Massachusetts, was incorporated in 1847. By 1910 it had become a city of 86,000, some 35,000 of its inhabitants mill-workers who depended on the mills for their families' livelihood. Lawrence was not a pretty city. Workers lived in crowded tenement sections, and almost every family took in lodgers to help meet the rent in the company-owned buildings.

The American Woolen Company built the world's largest cloth-producing plant in Lawrence in 1905. It stretched for more than a third of a mile along the river and, during peak seasons, employed 10,000 workers. There were three additional mills belonging to the company in the city, and twenty-three other plants elsewhere.

One-half of all Lawrence children worked in the mills. Eleven out of every one hundred mill employees were boys and girls between the ages of fourteen and eighteen.[13] Massachusetts law made fourteen the legal minimum age for working in a factory, but there were men in every mill town whose business it was to forge "proofs" that children were over the legal age. Hungry families had to buy these false papers and send their children to work because wages of $8.76 a week* in the busy season, and as little as $2.50 a week in slack periods, could not cover rent and food.[14]

Mill hours were long, the spinning and weaving rooms hot and humid, the pace of work fast. The accident rate was high, especially for tired children at the end of a long day. Fingers and hands were easily crushed

---

* The figure includes the wages of skilled as well as unskilled workers, supervisors, and foremen. The figure also includes bonuses, which were not always added to the workers' pay since illness or producing "inferior" work could wipe out the bonus the worker had earned. An industrial survey of 1909 found that $900 was the lowest annual income on which the average family could live "and maintain efficiency," but that workers in the mills averaged $437.54 a year, the women and children considerably less. Bill Cahn, *Mill Town* (New York: Cameron & Kahn, 1954), pp. 74, 75.

Women and girls were sometimes scalped when their hair caught in the unguarded machinery. At government hearings following the Lawrence strike, one young woman who had been partially scalped testified that she had spent seven months in the hospital recovering, during which time she had been without any income at all.

The extent of poverty and near-starvation was appalling. Families depended on their wages to such an extent that pregnant women worked until just before their babies arrived, and some gave birth right in the mill between the looms.[15] Almost all the children had rickets: there was no money for milk. In 1909, the death rate for Lawrence children under one year old was 17.2 percent, exclusive of those who died at birth. Only six cities in a survey of forty had higher death rates, and three of these— Lowell, Fall River, and New Bedford, Massachusetts—were also textile-mill centers.[16]

Dr. Elizabeth Shapleigh, a Lawrence doctor familiar with the health problems of the millworkers, discussed their high death rate in an article on occupational diseases in the textile industry:

> 36 out of every 100 of the men and women who work in the mill die before, or by the time, they are 25 years of age. That means that out of the long line which enters the mill you may strike out every third person as dying before reaching maturity. Every fourth person in the line is dying from tuberculosis. And further, every second person, that is one alternating with a healthy person, will die of some form of respiratory trouble.[17]

The Strike

On January 1, 1912, a new Massachusetts law went into effect reducing the hours of work per week for women and children under eighteen from 56 to 54. Since this affected over half its employees, the American Woolen Company decided to reduce the hours for its entire work force. For weeks before the law took effect, workers wondered whether their first pay envelopes of the New Year would show a reduction in earnings as well as hours. A 3½ percent cut in earnings meant a critical loss for families so close to the edge of hunger.

Workers of twenty-five nationalities made up the bulk of the mill population. The largest ethnic group was Italian, but Poles, Lithuanians, Syrians, Russians, Germans, and Belgians were well represented. At this time, 208 millworkers paid dues to the United Textile Workers (AFL) and belonged to ten weak craft unions. The IWW had only about 300 paid-up members in its Lawrence local. Although the English-speaking IWW branch was small, early in January it sent several representatives to try to meet with company officials, and failing in that, wrote to President Wood of the American Woolen Company in Boston to learn what the company proposed to do about wages when the new 54-hour work-week went into effect. They never received a reply.

Their answer came, however, on January 11, when the Polish women opened their pay envelopes to find that they were 32 cents short. "Short pay, short pay!" rang out from all parts of the room, as workers stopped the looms and walked out of the mill. All through that day and the next, workers joined the walkout. "Flying squadrons" went through other mills shutting off power, urging workers out, in some cases cutting cables and smashing looms. The riot alarm sounded from the bell tower of the Lawrence city hall. By Saturday night, January 13, 20,000 mill-workers were on strike.

The pay cut triggered the strike, but it was, in fact, the last straw rather than the primary cause. Injustices on the part of section bosses, a hatred of the mill system, and hardships caused by a crippling rise in the cost of living were more basic. According to historian Melvyn Dubofsky, Lawrence strikers in 1912 had more of an understanding of the IWW philosophy and a greater hatred of the system than they are often credited with:

> IWW literature had affected them . . . they detested the conditions under which they labored and lived; and they despised the foremen and supervisors who treated them like cattle. . . . [They] wanted better wages, improved working conditions and decent homes; yet they also sought a social system better than the one they had—which was what the IWW and socialism promised them.[18]

Most burdensome of all was the vicious bonus system that made up, on the average, 8 percent of a worker's earnings. Under this system the weavers were constantly pressured for production by the loom fixers, who set their looms and who in turn were pressured by the foreman, as all their bonuses interlocked. Yet a worker who had produced over the standard and earned the bonus could lose it if he or she was ill more than one day in any four-week bonus period, or if the work produced was classified as "inferior" rather than of the finer grade.

As soon as the strike began, the IWW sent for Joseph Ettor, a member of its national board and a dynamic young organizer who spoke English, Italian, and Polish and understood Hungarian and Yiddish. The committee he formed had two representatives from each of the nationality groups and met daily to coordinate the strike. Workers decided on four demands: a 15 percent wage raise, the 54-hour week, double pay for overtime, and all strikers to be rehired without discrimination. During the first days of the strike six of the Italian workers were arrested, a militia was sent in by Lawrence's Mayor Scanlon, and the city got its first taste

IWW organizer Elizabeth Gurley Flynn with Joseph Ettor following
his release from prison after the 1912 strike of textile millworkers in
Lawrence, Massachussetts.

of mass picketing. Crowds of demonstrating workers, soaked with water
from fire hoses turned on them by firemen and police, retaliated by throwing chunks of ice. The result: thirty-six were arrested and most given one-
year prison terms. The IWW instituted strike discipline and a policy of
nonresistance to police violence.[19]

IWW poet Arturo Giovannitti came to Lawrence to organize strike
relief. As funds poured in from across the country, a system of strike
kitchens for each nationality group was set up. No one starved; strike relief of from $2 to $5 a week was paid throughout the ten weeks of the
strike.

John Golden of the United Textile Workers opposed the strike from
the start, calling it revolutionary and anarchistic. Nor did it receive the
sanction of the American Federation of Labor. Two weeks after the
strike started, the Women's Trade Union League opened a relief station
in cooperation with the Central Labor Union of Lawrence, and Mary
Kenney O'Sullivan from Boston came out to run it. Eight thousand strikers
received food and clothing.[20] But the WTUL found itself caught between the strikers and the UTW. Golden at first ignored the strike, then
for a brief time called his members out too. Sarah Conboy,* a carpet

* In 1912 following the Lawrence strike, Sarah Conboy became a national organizer for
the UTW and in 1915 the union's secretary-treasurer. She represented the AFL at numerous conferences, where she spoke on behalf of labor about the concerns of women
workers. Until she died in 1928 she remained as secretary-treasurer of the UTW, the

weaver and active UTW member, directed relief operations for the UTW. But Golden made a separate deal for the few skilled workers that the UTW represented and sent them back to work. Those who accepted UTW relief had to sign a pledge to return to the mills.

At that point, Golden ordered the WTUL to close its strike-relief operation and get out of Lawrence. Because of the WTUL's agreement with the AFL to work only with strikes the federation approved. Sue Ainslie Clark, president of the Boston league, complied, but wrote angrily to Margaret Dreier Robins:

> Many of those in power in the AFL today seem to be selfish, reactionary, and remote from the struggle for bread and liberty of the unskilled workers. . . . [In the future] we must be free to aid in the struggle of the workers wherever and however we find the "fight on."[21]

Mary Kenney O'Sullivan did not comply. She resigned from the Boston league and stayed on in Lawrence, helping throughout the remaining weeks of the strike.*

Lawrence city officials and a citizens' committee organized to oppose the strike, bringing in fresh units of militia as well as an immigration inspector to check all foreign-born workers for illegal papers. Arrests were made on any provocation.

The strike held firm. There was always singing. Journalist Mary Heaton Vorse commented, "They are always marching and singing,"[22] and Ray Stannard Baker recorded:

> It is the first strike I ever saw which sang. I shall not soon forget the curious lift, the strange sudden fire of the mingled nationalities at the strike meetings when they broke into the universal language of song. And not only at the meetings did they sing, but in the soup houses and

---

most influential elective post held by a woman in the labor movement up to that time. *Encyclopedia Americana*, 1968 rev. ed., vol. 7, p. 497, article on Sarah Conboy by Harvey Friedman.

* This struggle marked a turning point for the WTUL. Not long after the strike, on May 2, WTUL executive board members sat down with AFL President Gompers and Golden of the UTW to discuss future league relations with the AFL. Board members heard Golden explain that the UTW had not organized the unskilled workers in Lawrence because most of them were women and children who earned too little to afford union dues and it did not pay to organize them. Gompers, however, seems to have seen the advantage of locking the league into AFL policy, and agreed to forward $150 a month to the league for the specific purpose of putting a woman organizer into the field to organize textile workers. Out of a need for funds and to avoid the charge of dual unionism, the WTUL agreed to adhere faithfully to AFL policy and only enter strike situations sanctioned by the federation. This policy was tested almost immediately in the 1913 IWW textile strike in Paterson, New Jersey, where the league stayed on the sidelines while the silk workers struggled against overwhelming odds, only to go down in defeat. William O'Neill, *Everyone Was Brave* (Chicago: Quadrangle Books, 1969), p. 160.

in the streets. I saw one group of women strikers who were peeling potatoes at a relief station suddenly break into the swing of the "Internationale." They have a whole book of songs fitted to familiar tunes— "The Eight Hour Day," "The Banner of Labor," "Workers, Shall the Master Rule Us?" But the favorite of all was the "Internationale."[23]

Visitors to Lawrence were impressed with the almost religious spirit of the strikers, their zeal and the concern for each other that surmounted every language barrier. Some of those who visited never left. One such was Gertrude Marvin, a newspaper reporter, who wrote a sympathetic strike story for her Boston paper. Her editor crumpled it into a ball and shouted at her, "That big two-fisted thug [Haywood] has put it all over you!"[24] She resigned from her job and came to Lawrence to work for the strike publicity committee. Pearl McGill, an organizer of button workers from Muscatine, Iowa, was another who stayed, even though the AFL deprived her of her union credentials for doing so.

A week after the strike began, police reported finding dynamite in three locations in town and pointed to the IWW as the guilty party. As an attempt to discredit the strike, it failed.* Then on January 29, following one of the biggest demonstrations in the strike so far, a young woman striker, Anna LoPizzo, was killed. Years later, in his autobiography, IWW leader Bill Haywood described the incident:

> The police killed Anna LaPiza [sic]. The picket line was out that morning, 23,000 strong, an endless chain of pickets. And the police began to crowd them . . . until they were massed in so thick that they could not move back any further. Then the police began to club them. Some of the sympathizers threw coal from the windows. The strikers themselves threw snowballs and chunks of ice at the policemen. And one of the policemen was hit with a chunk of coal or a chunk of ice on the leg. It was the sergeant. He ordered the policemen to pull out the guns. And as they did, they fired. And officer Benoit is said to have fired the shot that killed Anna LaPiza. Nineteen witnesses saw him fire the shot. . . .[25]

Strike leaders Ettor and Giovannitti, who were three miles away at the time, were arrested and held in jail for eight months as accessories. So was Joseph Caruso, a striker from the picket line, who was accused of "inciting and provoking the violence."[26] The city declared martial law and moved in twenty-two more companies of militia. Strikers sent for Bill Haywood, who was met by 15,000 workers at the train station and taken to a mass rally where 10,000 more were waiting. Shortly after his arrival,

* Two years earlier, the country had been rocked by bombs exploding in the *Los Angeles Times* building, and late in 1911, labor leader John McNamara and his brother James had confessed to the bombing. Nothing could have been better designed to create hysteria in the city of Lawrence than the discovery of dynamite in the Syrian quarter in connection with an IWW strike. Ultimately it was proved to be a company-initiated plot.

several other veteran IWW organizers came to Lawrence, among them twenty-one-year-old Elizabeth Gurley Flynn. She began at once to organize special meetings focusing on the problems of the women workers.

> The women worked in the mills for lower pay and in addition had all the housework and care of the children. The old-world attitude of man as the "lord and master" was strong. At the end of the day's work—or, now, of strike duty—the man went home and sat at ease while his wife did all the work preparing the meal, cleaning the house, etc. There was considerable male opposition to women going to meetings and marching on the picket line. We resolutely set out to combat these notions. The women wanted to picket. They were strikers as well as wives and were valiant fighters. We knew that to leave them alone, isolated from the strike activity, a prey to worry, affected by the complaints of tradespeople . . . was dangerous to the strike.[27]*

IWW leaders found that schools and churches in Lawrence consciously tried to make the children ashamed of their foreign-born parents, of their way of talking and dressing, of their foreign newspapers, and, especially, of the strike. Through meetings for the school-age children of striking workers, the IWW tried to help the children understand the strike issues so they could take pride in what their parents were doing.

For nine-and-a-half weeks, strikers never wavered: not when the funeral procession for Anna LoPizzo was broken up by a cavalry attack; not when John Rami, an eighteen-year-old Syrian striker, was killed; not when Mrs. Annie Welzenbach and her fifteen- and eighteen-year-old sisters were arrested and dragged from their beds in the middle of the night to the police court; not when, on February 19, 200 police drew their clubs and went after 100 women pickets, knocking many to the ground and then beating them. Annie Welzenbach, the highest-paid worker in the mill, was the only woman on the ten-person strike committee and proved a particularly influential member.

As the clubbings by the police became more frequent and vicious, Haywood urged the women not to come out to the picket line. Instead of agreeing, an Italian woman at the meeting answered him:

> "To-morrow morning man no go on picket line. All man, boy stay home, sleep. Only woman, girl on picket line to-morrow morning. Soldier and policeman no beat woman, girl. You see," turning to her companion, she said, "I got big belly, she too got big belly. Policeman no beat us. I want to speak to all woman here."[28]

* In spite of the involvement of women in the strike, Helen Marot, former secretary of the New York WTUL, wrote afterward: "While the leaders of the Industrial Workers of the World show confidence in the part women have taken and will take in the industrial struggle, the women of Lawrence, Mass., observed that the officers of the local organization in that city have given them no better opportunity for taking part in the administration of union affairs than have the men of the American Federation." *American Labor Unions* (New York: Henry Holt & Co., 1914), p. 68.

A striking millworker is led off to jail during the Lawrence textile strike, 1912.

Haywood introduced her to the strikers, and she presented her idea. The next morning the women were out in full force, only to be so badly beaten by the police that the Italian woman who had spoken at the meeting and Bertha Crouse, another pregnant striker, lost their babies and almost died themselves.

Nor was this the only instance that caused Haywood to write, "The women strikers were as active and efficient as the men and fought as well." He recounted this story:

> One cold morning, after the strikers had been drenched on the bridge with the firehose of the mills, the women caught a policeman in the middle of the bridge and stripped off his uniform, pants and all. They were about to throw him in the icy river, when other policemen rushed in and saved him from the chilly ducking.[29]

This strike saw the use of a number of ingenious techniques for mobilizing the workers, keeping spirits high, and holding strikebreakers down to a minimum. Perhaps the best known was the mass picketing. To avoid arrest for loitering, strikers formed a human chain, a moving sidewalk, that wove around all the mills of Lawrence in an unbroken line. It was a twenty-four-hour-a-day operation involving anywhere from 5,000 to 20,000 workers, each picket wearing an armband saying "Don't Be a

Scab."[30] No strikebreaker could pass into the mill unless he or she broke through this human wall.

Worker morale was boosted by frequent parades. Every few days several thousand strikers marched around the city, singing to the accompaniment of brass bands. But toward the end of January, the town banned all mass meetings, the use of the village green, and parades. A new technique had to be devised. Strikers walked down the streets of Lawrence, arms locked, perhaps twenty, thirty, or even fifty abreast. Everyone and everything in the path of this building-to-building cyclone, known as a "sidewalk parade," would be swept aside. As police mobilized to halt this action, another was designed. Workers wandered in and out of stores in groups, never buying anything, but taking up all available floor space and terrifying storeowners, most of whom had aligned themselves with the city establishment against the strike.

When the going was most difficult, the suggestion was made that strikers' children be sent to other cities to be cared for by friendly families for the duration of the strike. This would remove a financial burden from the strike committee, provide wholesome food and warm homes for the children, and serve to publicize the strike story. The idea, a new one for United States workers but not for those who had come from Europe, caught on. Committees in New York and Philadelphia interviewed prospective families and made careful arrangements. Mrs. Margaret Sanger, a trained nurse (later to gain fame for her work in the field of birth control), headed the New York committee and came to Lawrence to take the first group of 119 children. On February 10, a crowd of 5,000 greeted the children in New York's Grand Central Station. The *New York Sun* reported:

> The committee had no trouble looking after suitcases and extra parcels for the reason that the travellers wore all the personal belongings they had brought along. There were few overcoats in the crowd. For the most part the girls wore cotton dresses partly covered with jackets or shawls, and worsted caps.[31]

Later Margaret Sanger would testify before the congressional committee: "Out of the 119 children, only four had underwear on . . . their coats were simply torn to shreds . . . and it was the bitterest weather we have had this winter."[32]

A small group of 40 children were sent to Barre, Vermont, another group of 92 to New York. So much publicity resulted that Lawrence authorities were alarmed and resolved to put an end to the exodus. Thus when 150 children were brought by their parents to the railroad station on February 24 to go to Philadelphia, they were met by 200 militia and police. One member of the Philadelphia committee who had come to Lawrence to escort the children described what happened next:

> When the time came to depart, the children arranged in a long line, two by two in an orderly procession with the parents near at hand, were about to make their way to the train when the police . . . closed in on us with their clubs, beating right and left with no thought of the children who then were in desperate danger of being trampled to death. The mothers and the children were thus hurled in a mass and bodily dragged to a military truck and even then clubbed. . . . We can scarcely find words with which to describe this display of brutality.[33]

Thirty-five women were forced with their children into patrol wagons, to be charged at the police station with "neglect." Ten of the children were sent to the Lawrence poor farm. The women from the Philadelphia committee were arrested and fined. Frightened, angry, desperate strikers converged on the police station. All America rose up in outrage.

When the uproar reached Congress, an investigation into the Lawrence strike began. Early in March over fifty strikers testified, showing through their pay envelopes how little they earned, testifying about the pregnant women who had been beaten by the police. All sixteen children who came as witnesses were strikers, and described the poverty that had led them to leave school and take jobs in the mill.

The American Woolen Company had no choice but to respond to the unfavorable publicity and yield to striker demands. On March 12 the Strike Committee of Nine* met with the company and got agreement to the workers' terms. Two days later 25,000 strikers gathered on the town green to hear Haywood discuss these terms and to vote approval. They had won wage increases (the largest increases to go to the lowest-paid employees), the 54-hour week with no cut in pay, premiums to be paid every two weeks instead of every four, and no discrimination against any striker. By the end of the month the rest of the Lawrence textile firms had agreed to substantially the same terms while the American Woolen Company had raised its wages in thirty-three other cities. Workers in Lowell and New Bedford then struck, and Elizabeth Gurley Flynn was assigned to each city in turn. The strikes were short and the workers successful. Between 175,000 and 200,000 workers in mills throughout New England won wage increases as a result of the Lawrence strike.

> As we come marching, marching, we bring the greater days.
> The rising of the women means the rising of the race.
> No more the drudge and idler—ten that toil where one reposes,
> But a sharing of life's glories: Bread and roses! Bread and roses!

* Actually the Committee of Ten, but Joseph Ettor, the tenth member, was in jail.

Despite their victory, the workers did not forget that Ettor, Giovannitti, and Caruso were still in prison in connection with the death of Anna LoPizzo. It took months of protest meetings across the country to raise the necessary money for their defense and to pressure for a trial. That the dynamite planted early in the strike was a company plot to discredit the union became clear with the confession of Ernest Pitman. A building contractor for the largest of the American Woolen Company mills in Lawrence, he admitted publicly that it had been a scheme of the textile corporations of Lawrence. Shortly after this confession, Pitman committed suicide.

The trial of Ettor, Giovannitti, and Caruso opened on September 30, 1912, in Salem, Massachusetts, and attracted world-wide attention. Each day for over two months the defendants sat in metal cages while testimony accumulated proving that none of the three had anything to do with the shooting of Anna LoPizzo. The jury voted acquittal and all three were freed. Victory seemed complete.

Yet less than a year later *Solidarity*, the IWW newspaper, would carry an editorial that stated:

> At present we are to the labor movement what the high diver is to the circus—a sensation marvelous and nerve-thrilling. We attract crowds . . . [but] as far as making industrial unionism fit the everyday life of the worker, we have failed miserably.[34]

The time had not yet come for industrial unionism to take hold. Nor could it succeed in the United States as long as it was attached to a political philosophy that attacked capitalism and demanded a revolutionary change in the economic and social order.

Lawrence: the Aftermath

The immediate effect of the Lawrence strike was felt throughout the mill towns of New England. Since millowners did not want a repetition of Lawrence in their factories, the IWW won wage increases in Lowell and New Bedford, Massachusetts, in Willimantic, Connecticut, and elsewhere. The IWW proved it knew how to organize and that unskilled workers were organizable. These workers found new courage and dignity; they surmounted language and nationality barriers to unite against the common enemy. The IWW taught picket-line discipline and preached passive resistance and nonviolence, even though in response to attacks by militia and hired thugs its strikes often involved considerable violence. IWW strikes sometimes led workers to victory, but equally important, they served to publicize the living and working conditions of the nation's most oppressed workers: unskilled factory hands, migratory farm laborers, miners, lumberjacks.

In Lawrence itself, victory was short-lived. In the aftermath of the strike, more than 14,000 textile workers belonged to the IWW, organized into fourteen different language locals or branches with individual shop committees, and for a time they remained active. The IWW focused most of its effort on freeing Ettor, Giovannitti, and Caruso, and at the time of the trial in September, IWW membership peaked at 16,000, with 10,000 dues-paying members. But following the trial the Lawrence organization declined rapidly.

Wage gains soon were offset by a 50 percent speedup of mill machinery that the union was unable to fight. The Catholic Church launched a campaign to discredit the IWW, harassing church members who belonged to the labor organization, while the Lawrence Citizens Association attacked the Wobblies as atheistic anarchists. Millowners, taking advantage of anti-IWW hysteria that followed a riot in Lawrence late in 1912, instituted a spy network in the mills and hounded IWW members unmercifully. By the fall of 1913, IWW membership in Lawrence had fallen to 700. The economic recession of 1913–1914 brought with it wage cuts and unemployment. IWW influence in Lawrence came to an end.

20

"IN UNVANQUISHABLE NUMBER..."

Now if you want equal wages let me tell you what you do
You got to work with your sisters in the shop with you.
You got to build you a CLUW* group, got to make it strong
If we all stick together now it won't be long . . .
We'll open up new jobs . . . win equal pay . . . make that seniority list.

It's not quite that simple—I know you know—
And a look at history sure does show,
We've a lot of experience on the picket line
We've backed up the men deep down in the mine,
We know about tear gas from the National Guard
We've fought and died for a union card—
And there've been times . . . they didn't even let us in their unions.

But now we're in and the door's ajar,
We've contracts and pensions and we've come far.
Let's not sit tight and think everything's set,
'Cause down the road a long way yet
Are millions of women like you and me
Who've got no union to set them free.
Thirty million of them . . . good lord, what an organizing job!

But back in Lawrence here's what they found,
And out in Chicago here's what they found,
And up in Flint, here's what they found,
And down in El Paso, here's what they found,
That if we stick together and they don't break us up,
If we fight for our rights and don't break up,
If we run for union office and don't break up,
And organize the unorganized and don't break up,
We'll win. What I mean, take it easy, but take it.

—Barbara Wertheimer,
" 'Talking Union' for Labor Union Women"

The long-run influence of the Lawrence strike, not to be underestimated, was that it planted the seeds for industrial organization. In the short run, however, all attempts to get Samuel Gompers to organize unskilled mass-production workers in the fast-growing industrial centers of the country failed. Mary McDowell, a Women's Trade Union League leader, expressed her fears in a letter to an AFL official in 1912:

* CLUW stands for Coalition of Labor Union Women, to be discussed later in the chapter.

It will be a great waste of time & energy if the AFL misses the point that has been so terribly emphasized at Lawrence, Mass. . . . In such industries as those of the steel, meat, textile & harvesters, etc., Industrial Unionism of a constructive type is surely the need of this moment. The AFL will lose out unless it wakes up and adds to the IWW's clever method, that of permanent and constructive organization.[1]

The strike of the Lawrence workers and their victory constituted the high point of women's organization for many years to come. Out of their need and their misery, 20,000 workers had united across multinationality lines in a struggle that is also symbolic. The conditions against which they rebelled did not differ substantially from those endured by factory workers throughout the country. In their battle against the might of the American Woolen Company, the Lawrence strikers represented all workers who fought for identity against the power of giant industry. But this one time everything worked. When leaders were needed, they were there. Strike discipline held. New techniques were devised to unite the strikers and keep the mills from operating: mass picketing, the moving sidewalk of bodies that built strike morale and proved its success as a strike weapon. Although workers suffered in the cold, and food and money were scarce, no one starved. Financial support from outside Lawrence did not fail them. At the darkest, when families sending their children to friendly homes in other cities met with police brutality, nation-wide publicity forced the government to hold hearings in Washington that brought new support and fresh funds. Ultimately the American Woolen Company could not withstand public pressure and yielded.

But an important signal went unrecognized at the time. Only when government intervened on behalf of workers, this time in the form of congressional hearings, could workers win against the power of industry. In the major labor conflicts of the twentieth century, government would make the difference between victory or defeat. Increasingly, it would be a third party in industrial disputes—though not always on the side of the workers. But workers alone, no matter what their sacrificial effort, could rarely succeed against employer might. The Lawrence victory contrasted sharply with the failure of the IWW-led strike of Paterson silk-mill workers in 1913, a strike doomed almost from the start. Leadership was torn by conflict. Financial help was never enough to keep the workers from near-starvation. Local government and the millowners collaborated to defeat the strike effort. After twenty-two weeks, 25,000 men and women—mostly women, some of whom earned as little as $1.85 for 56 hours a week of work—were forced to beg for their jobs back at any wages. Many who refused to beg, or who were blacklisted, left Paterson forever. Not until the 1930s would a textile union, under the banner of the Congress of

Industrial Organizations and with the protection of the Wagner Act, lead Paterson silk-mill workers to victory.

After 1914, and particularly with the entry of the United States into World War I, the IWW declined, and never fulfilled its promise of becoming a permanent organization of industrial workers. In opposing the war the IWW fell victim to the federal government's campaign to get rid of what it termed radical foreign influences. IWW leaders were jailed under the wartime espionage act and the organization's headquarters across the country were raided. These attacks did not end after the war. With the 1920s came the anti-Bolshevik hysteria following the Russian Revolution of 1917. United States Attorney General A. Mitchell Palmer led concerted attacks against unions, even against the Women's Trade Union League, substantially aiding companies in their all-out drive against almost every labor organization. During the 1920s trade unions lost a large proportion of their members, and except for isolated instances when garment and telephone workers struck successfully prior to 1920, many years would pass before any organizing efforts would approximate those of Lawrence or women workers would participate as totally to win a union.

The year 1914 nonetheless marked a watershed for women workers. Their work-force experience would be different from that point on. With World War I women entered industry in large numbers, and stayed. Not only were they on the threshold of gaining the vote, but the push for equality had begun, to gain momentum throughout the rest of the century.

While 1920 brought woman suffrage, in part acknowledging women's tremendous contribution to the war effort, the long-run impact of their vote seems negligible. Women did not vote as a power bloc—they still do not—nor were they uniformly liberal or even united on issues of special concern to women. The decade of the 1920s was only superficially the carefree period of the flivver and flapper. In reality it was a time of political reaction, weakened labor power, booming speculation, and rising unemployment. Poverty, as in the textile-mill towns in the South where thousands of women worked, gave the lie to the prosperity the country thought it was enjoying.

The year 1914, too, marked the point after which working women increasingly entered the same trade unions as men. They gained the strength of membership in permanent organizations. But there was a price. Once women had led unions of their own, ephemeral though these were. Women leaders had defied tradition to speak out on behalf of women workers. Now they would be absorbed into unions led entirely by men. This process was accelerated when the National Labor Relations

Act, passed during the Great Depression of the 1930s, at last gave workers the legal right to organize and bargain collectively. Breaking from the AFL, a Committee for Industrial Organization (later the Congress of Industrial Organizations) reached out to industrial workers, to blacks and other minorities, and to women.

However, dropping the bars to union membership for women did not mean that they were any more a part of union structure and leadership than they had been in the IWW, where women organizers and orators flourished but no women held high decision-making posts. True, in the thirties and forties women were more accepted as union organizers, as business representatives, and as labor educators. But only a few attained posts on international union executive boards, and of these a bare handful held positions that gave them any voice in setting policy.

Today in the 1970s, there is a new consciousness, and a drive has begun for increased participation of women at all leadership levels of the labor movement. This drive has climaxed the changes brought by two world wars, by the worst depression in the nation's history, by the birth of industrial unionism, by the civil rights and women's movements of the 1960s and 1970s, and by the unprecedented and continuing entrance of millions of women of all ages into the world of paid employment.

There are 37 million women in the work force, fully 40 percent of all workers. The fight for equal pay, led in the nineteenth century by men who saw in it a way to prevent jobs going to women workers, is now led by women who recognize their equal economic need and the justice of their cause. Today, too, women make up more than one out of every four union members. This is a new voice that must be attended. In as many as twenty-five international unions women make up at least half the membership. Women's grievances must be heard, their demands placed on the bargaining table and not traded off.

March 1974 saw 3,500 union women from across the nation demonstrate this new awareness when they met to launch a new organization, the Coalition of Labor Union Women, known as CLUW. Designed to move women toward their rightful place in the labor unions to which they belong, this organization set about to work within the framework of the labor movement toward the achievement of four main goals:

1. To increase affirmative action on the job and women's participation in their unions at every level.
2. To work for passage of legislation important to women workers.
3. To encourage women's involvement in the political process, including election to office.

4. To organize the millions of unorganized women workers in this country, without which the labor movement cannot grow.

Yet another landmark in women's perception of themselves as workers, CLUW's more than fifty chapters link union women from over sixty national and international unions. Together it is hoped they can muster support for health security legislation, for full employment, for safer work sites, for child care, for equal opportunity and pay through their union contracts, and for the enforcement of equal rights and equal pay laws.

Unlike the Women's Trade Union League of the past, CLUW is open only to union members. Its chapter and national structures parallel those of international unions and their affiliated locals. While the young organization numbers only some 3,000 members (as of late 1976), it has had a far greater impact than would be expected in view of the small percentage of women unionists who have joined. In three short years it has raised the consciousness of the men who run American labor unions and served notice—as the late Myra Wolfgang, vice-president of the Hotel and Restaurant Workers' union put it—that women in CLUW have not joined together to swap recipes! As a result of its chapter activities and the publicity that CLUW has received as an organization, international unions have begun to include women as convention speakers and have passed resolutions strongly supporting equal rights for women on the job and the equal rights amendment. In fact, CLUW was instrumental in getting the AFL-CIO to reverse its anti-ERA stance and to work for this amendment in states where it has not passed.

Because of this new voice of women in the labor movement, the AFL-CIO added a woman as associate director of its Civil Rights Department to focus particularly on women's activities. Since no department in the federation is headed by a woman except the library, this is a small step in the right direction. Similarly, international unions have begun to seek and support women for posts on their national executive boards and are increasing the number of women in staff jobs. Union newspapers now cover news by and about women members, where formerly they were virtually oblivious of many of their contributions. The trend is up, and encouraging. At the same time, it must be recognized that achieving the four stated goals of the coalition will be far from easy.

CLUW can play a seminal role in alerting union women to job discrimination and in encouraging their insistence on equal pay and job training opportunities. Its Task Force on Model Contract Clauses will provide women with guides for local as well as national bargaining.

Indeed, one key to increased participation by women in their own unions is their involvement in an organization like CLUW. CLUW chapters offer women the opportunity to develop and practice leadership skills, to cope with inner organizational politics that parallel those in their local unions, and to transfer their new skills to these locals. This may turn out to be one of CLUW's major contributions.

In mobilizing support for legislation in which working women have a special concern, CLUW can help women to develop as leaders through increasing their participation in the political process. Here CLUW will have to aim for local as well as national impact. For example, the Arkansas chapter of CLUW involved union women as never before in the campaign for repeal of the state's "right-to-work" law, an amendment on the November 1976 ballot. The thrust of the CLUW drive was to show how women workers in particular are hurt by a law that forbids union shops and piles up obstacles to union organization. Underrepresented in trade unions, women are the ones who are locked into low-paying jobs with non-union wages and working conditions through this kind of legislation. Although the amendments for repeal lost in the state referendum, CLUW women developed a "pride in what we've done," as Jeannie Lambie, their leader, reported, and earned a new respect from the Arkansas labor movement. The next time around, a trained, disciplined core of women unionists will be ready to play an even more effective part.

CLUW's most difficult goal is that of organizing the close to 30 million women workers not yet in labor unions. This challenge proved insurmountable for the WTUL, although the league cut its teeth on the two major strikes of garment workers, where its aid proved invaluable, and organized numbers of locals of women workers. However, many of these were refused admittance into the national union having jurisdiction in the occupation, and none of the locals that did not affiliate with a parent union managed to survive.

Today's labor movement does not organize women into separate local unions, and, in any event, CLUW is committed to working within the labor movement. Its chapters cannot proceed on their own to seek out unorganized women, and if they did, the charge of dual unionism would soon be raised. CLUW has as yet no mechanism for organizing the unorganized short of working through the union with jurisdiction in the field. Most unions today, as ongoing institutions, have staff who do not always take kindly to suggestions for extending their organizing efforts. Sometimes, too, more than one union claims jurisdiction. CLUW's present organizing activities, therefore, have been limited, by and large, to strike and picket line support and to consumer boycotts.

CLUW also tries to persuade union officers of the importance of assigning women as organizers, especially where women constitute the majority of workers in a plant or office to be organized. It is felt that women are more effective in reaching out to other women and helping them understand the value of belonging to a union. One technique employed by the WTUL that the coalition may yet utilize is the training school for women workers. Of the 44 women trained by the WTUL, over 30 went on to devote most of their lives to the labor movement. A training school for labor union women, this time union endorsed, could provide a pool of skilled organizers, education staff, and union representatives and would be one way to help unions reach out to the mass of women workers in occupations traditionally difficult to organize.

Whatever its problems, however, the Coalition of Labor Union Women could not have emerged at any other point in history. Three factors have combined to make this newest thrust possible: the impact of the women's movement; the effect of the equal-pay and antidiscrimination laws of the 1960s, which for the first time barred discrimination in employment and pay on the basis of sex; and the influx of new millions of women into the work force.

This renascence, however, owes its very existence to the women of the past: to the millwomen of Lowell who protested wage cuts in the 1840s and cried "Try Again!" in the midst of defeat; to the Lynn shoemakers whose banners read "American Ladies Will Not Be Slaves!"; to the garment workers on strike in 1890, who pawned their wedding rings so fellow strikers would not starve, only to find that no clause in the contract that was won applied to women; and to all the Sarah Bagleys and the Pauline Newmans who preceded and followed them.

The road to equality for women is still a long one. Although increasing numbers of women unionists hold local offices, few have achieved top leadership and policy-making positions, even in labor organizations where more than three-quarters of the membership is female. In the workplace, women earn on the average only 57 percent of what men earn for full-time, year-round work. Women who head families are far more likely to be poor than are men who head families: in 1975, 33 percent of all families headed by women were poor, compared with 6 percent of all families headed by men. Minority women still find themselves on the lowest rung of the job and pay ladders and bear the heaviest burden of unemployment. Although blue-collar and apprentice jobs are opening to more women, as yet we remain clustered in traditionally female jobs, primarily in those clerical and service occupations where women have always worked. Now, as in the past, women work out of economic need. But today more women are breaking out of the jobs that society traditionally had assigned them, using their new economic rights to break down old barriers. Again there is a price. A Washington, D.C., carpenter who recounted her two-and-a-half-year struggle to gain entrance into an apprentice program also told of the open resentment from the men on the job with which she has to contend every day. But she is staying—at far higher earning than her former work as a practical nurse could ever have provided.[2] Women working on Alaska pipeline construction crews or climbing telephone poles or digging coal relate similar stories, but they too stay. Nor do those women think of themselves as heroic, though many have been.

The working women of America are moving toward full participation for the first time. In the past, home responsibilities kept us from being active even when we had a union, and isolated us from each other. Our role at home, however, released men to take part in their labor union organizations and to run for political office. Now we seek a partnership role on the job, in the home, in those same labor unions, in politics. We make no predictions about how long this will take to achieve, nor do we know how women, as they win the opportunity to influence policy, will utilize their new power. But as we chart our way, point by point, we are committed to the belief that in our long journey to equality we will one day reach our goal. Our look to the past has shown where we came from and how far we have come. Surely we will continue to draw strength from those women who went before, knowing that for nearly four hundred years of America's history women have been part of the story. From the beginning, we were there.

NOTES

PART 1. Two Centuries into the New World

Prologue. The First American Women

1. Captain John Smith, *History of Virginia*, ed. David F. Hawke (Indianapolis: Bobbs-Merrill Co., 1975), p. 7.
2. Carolyn Thomas Foreman, *Indian Women Chiefs* (Norman: University of Oklahoma Press, 1954), pp. 6, 7.
3. Frederick Webb Hodge, *Handbook of the North American Indian*, 2 vols. *Annual Report*, Bureau of American Ethnology (Washington, D.C.: Smithsonian Institution, 1937), provides detailed tribal information for the student of Indian affairs.
4. Judith K. Brown, "Economic Organization and the Position of Women Among the Iroquois," *Ethnohistory*, vol. 17, nos. 3–4 (summer–fall 1970), p. 164. Also see Alanson Skinner's *Indians of Greater New York* (Cedar Rapids, Iowa: Torch Press, 1915), and Marcus Wilson Jernegan, *The American Colonies, 1492–1750* (New York: Frederick Ungar Publishing Co., 1959).
5. Anne Terry White, *Indians and the Old West* (New York: Simon and Schuster, 1958), p. 16.

Chapter 1. Working Women in Seventeenth- and Eighteenth-Century America

1. Eugenie Andruss Leonard, Sophie Hutchinson Drinker, and Miriam Young Holden, *The American Woman in Colonial and Revolutionary Times, 1565–1800* (Philadelphia: University of Pennsylvania Press, 1962), pp. 16, 17.
2. Julia Cherry Spruill, *Women's Life and Work in the Southern Colonies* (1938; paperback ed., New York: W. W. Norton & Co., 1972), p. 4.
3. Richard N. Current, T. Harry Williams, and Frank Freidel, *American History: A Survey*, 3rd ed. (New York: Alfred A. Knopf, 1971), vol. 1, p. 25.
4. Mary Beard, *America Through Women's Eyes* (1933; reprint ed., Westport, Conn.: Greenwood Press, 1969) vol. 1, p. 13.
5. Clarence Senior, *The Puerto Ricans, Strangers—Then Neighbors* (Chicago: Quadrangle Books, 1961), p. 17.
6. Chester Wright, *Economic History of the United States* (New York: McGraw-Hill Book Co., 1941), pp. 65, 66.
7. Andrew Sinclair, *The Emancipation of the American Woman* (New York: Harper & Row, 1965), p. 3. Governor William Bradford's own account of "Plimoth" tells us that the first house to be built was a Common House, where bedrolls were placed one next to the other for all the Pilgrims. The house, twenty feet square, had a lean-to shed attached and a thatched roof that promptly caught fire and was destroyed.
8. This and other related material is from William Franklin Atwood, *The Pilgrim Story* (Plymouth, Mass.: Memorial Press, 1940).
9. William Bradford, *History of Plimoth Plantation, 1606–1646* (New York: Charles Scribner's Sons, 1908), p. 146.
10. Current and others, *American History*, vol. 1, p. 27.

377

11. Abbott Emerson Smith, *Colonists in Bondage* (1947; paperback ed., New York: W. W. Norton & Co., 1971), p. 336.
12. A. E. Smith, *Colonists in Bondage*, pp. 20, 21.
13. *Ibid*, p. 12.
14. Foster Rhea Dulles, *Labor in America*, 3rd ed. (New York: Thomas Y. Crowell Co., 1966), p. 6.
15. See Beard, *America Through Women's Eyes*, p. 19, for the story of Hannah Dustin, and Linda Grant DePauw, "The Forgotten Spirit of 1776: Women of the Revolutionary Era," *Ms.* Magazine, July 1974, p. 52.
16. Edith Abbott, *Women in Industry* (New York: D. Appleton & Co., 1910), p. 13.
17. Edna Yost, *Famous American Pioneering Women from the Seventeenth Century to the Present* (New York: Dodd, Mead & Co., 1961), p. 29.
18. Abbott, *Women in Industry*, p. 17.
19. Leonard and others, *American Woman*, p. 81.
20. Abbott, *Women in Industry*, p. 20.
21. Selden Rodman, ed., *One Hundred American Poems* (New York: New American Library, 1948), p. 35.
22. Spruill, *Women's Life and Work*, pp. 13, 14.
23. Abbott, *Women in Industry*, pp. 21, 22.
24. Dulles, *Labor in America*, p. 14; Abbott, *Women in Industry*, p. 22.
25. Abbott, *Women in Industry*, p. 23; Dulles, *Labor in America*, p. 14.
26. As quoted by Philip Foner, *History of the Labor Movement in the United States* (New York: International Publishers Co., 1962), vol. 1, p. 26.
27. Quoted by Page Smith in *Daughters of the Promised Land* (Boston: Little, Brown & Co., 1970), p. 54.
28. Abbott, *Women in Industry*, p. 27.
29. Spruill, *Women's Life and Work*, pp. 288, 289.
30. Annie Nathan Meyer, *Woman's Work in America* (New York: Henry Holt & Co., 1891), p. 279.
31. Spruill, *Women's Life and Work*, p. 264.
32. Yost, *Pioneering Women*, p. 32. Much of the information about Katherine Goddard comes from this source.
33. Yost quotes Lawrence Wroth, an authority on printers of the colonial period in American history, *Pioneering Women*, p. 37.
34. This differed totally from established English law, according to which any printed attack against a government official could be held libelous. See Current and others, *American History*, vol. 1, p. 80.
35. "A Young Girl's Day's Work, 1775," from Sydney G. Fisher, *Men, Women and Manners in Colonial Days* (1897), as quoted in Eve Merriam, *Growing Up Female in America* (New York: Dell Publishing Co., 1971), p. 257.
36. Spruill, *Women's Life and Work*, p. 324. This book has excellent coverage of indentured women servants.
37. A. E. Smith, *Colonists in Bondage*, p. 253.
38. "The Trapan's Maiden, or The Distressed Damsel," from C. H. Firth, ed., *An American Garland: Being a Collection of Ballads Relating to America, 1563–1759* (Oxford: Oxford University Press, 1915), quoted in Nancy Cott, *Root of Bitterness* (New York: E. P. Dutton & Co., 1972), p. 31.
39. Abbott, *Women in Industry*, pp. 34, 32.
40. Leonard and others, *American Woman*, p. 48.
41. Wright, *Economic History of the U.S.*, p. 72.

Chapter 2. Black Women in Colonial America

1. Lerone Bennett, Jr., *Before the Mayflower* (Baltimore: Penguin Books, 1964), p. 30.
2. August Meier and Elliott Rudwick, *From Plantation to Ghetto* (New York: Hill & Wang, 1966), p. 37. As early as 1650, sales of Negro servants were for life and this status was passed on to their children.
3. Robert Goldston, *The Negro Revolution* (New York: Macmillan Co., 1968), p. 43; Meier and Rudwick, *From Plantation to Ghetto*, p. 40.

4. Benjamin Quarles, *The Negro in the Making of America* (New York: Macmillan Co., Collier Books, 1969), p. 36.
5. William Loren Katz, *Eyewitness: The Negro in American History* (New York: Pitman Publishing Corp., 1968), p. 10.
6. Bennett, *Before the Mayflower*, p. 40.
7. Reverend R. Walsh, *Notices of Brazil in 1828 and 1829* (London: Frederick Westley & A. H. Davis, 1830), vol. 2, 479–86.
8. As quoted by Bennett, *Before the Mayflower*, p. 32.
9. *Encyclopaedia Britannica*, 14th ed. vol. 20, p. 779.
10. Wright, *Economic History of the U.S.*, pp. 71–3.
11. Bennett, *Before the Mayflower*, p. 74.
12. *Ibid*, p. 74, quoting a South Carolina planter.
13. *Ibid*, p. 81.
14. Spruill, *Women's Life and Work*, p. 57. From *Maryland Gazette*, April 14, 1750; *South Carolina Gazette*, Dec. 31, 1764; and *Georgia Gazette*, Oct. 1, 1766.
15. Langston Hughes and Arna Bontemps, eds., *The Poetry of the Negro, 1746–1970*, rev. ed. (Garden City, N.Y.: Doubleday & Co., Anchor Books, 1973), p. 14.
16. See Herbert Aptheker's *American Negro Slave Revolts* (1943; reprint ed., New York: International Publishers Co., 1969).
17. Katz, *Eyewitness*, p. 35, quoting George H. Moore, *Notes on the History of Slavery in Massachusetts* (1866), pp. 75–9.
18. Quarles, *Negro in the Making of America*, p. 45.
19. Katz, *Eyewitness*, p. 24.
20. *Ibid.*, p. 39.

Chapter 3. Working Women in the American Revolution

1. Foner, *Labor Movement in the U.S.*, vol. 1, p. 207.
2. Andrew S. Berky and James P. Shenton, *The Historians' History of the United States* (New York: Capricorn Books, 1966), vol. 1, p. 207.
3. *Ibid.*, p. 306.
4. Thomas Paine, *Common Sense*, part 3, "Thoughts on the Present State of American Affairs," from Harry Hayden Clark, ed., *Thomas Paine: Representative Selections* (New York: American Book Co., 1944), p. 18.
5. Foner, *Labor Movement in the U.S.*, vol. 1, p. 36.
6. "A New Song—Address'd to the Sons of Liberty on the Continent of America, 1768," as quoted in *ibid.*, pp. 35–6.
7. Foner, *Labor Movement in the U.S.*, vol. 1, p. 36.
8. Spruill, *Women's Life and Work*, pp. 244–5. Quotation is from *Virginia Gazette*, Sept. 21, 1776.
9. Beard, *America Through Women's Eyes*, p. 54.
10. Frank Moore, *Songs and Ballads of the American Revolution* (1855; reprint ed., New York: Arno Press, 1969), p. 208.
11. Broadus Mitchell, "The Rise of Cotton Mills in the South," *Johns Hopkins University Studies in Historical and Political Science*, series 39, no. 2 (1921), pp. 13, 14. From *City Gazette Daily Advertiser*, Charleston, S.C., Jan. 24, 1779.
12. Beard, *Through Women's Eyes*, pp. 55–6.
13. Linda Grant DePauw, *Four Traditions: Women of New York During the American Revolution* (Albany: New York State Bicentennial Committee, 1974), pp. 25, 21.
14. Walter Hart Blumenthal, *Women Camp Followers of the American Revolutionary War* (Philadelphia: MacManus Co., 1952), pp. 15–51, for these and other accounts. Also Beard, *Through Women's Eyes*, p. 56.
15. Edward T. James and Janet W. James, eds., *Notable American Women: A Biographical Dictionary* (Cambridge, Mass.: Belknap Press, 1971), vol. 3, pp. 227–9.
16. Beard, *Through Women's Eyes*, p. 59.
17. The letters are excerpted from Mary M. Beard, *Through Women's Eyes* (1933; reprint ed., Westport, Conn.: Greenwood Press, 1969), pp. 60–72, and Anne Firor Scott, ed., *Women in American Life* (Boston: Houghton Mifflin Co., 1970), p. 22. For the complete letters of this correspondence, see Charles Francis Adams, ed.,

Familiar Letters of John Adams and His Wife, Abigail Adams, During the Revolution (Boston: Houghton Mifflin Co., 1876).

18. James and James, eds., *Notable American Women,* vol. 3, p. 7.
19. Roi Ottley and William Weatherby, *The Negro in New York* (New York: New York Public Library and Oceana Publications, 1967), p. 38. From a letter by Dr. Solomon Drowne to his sister, June 24, 1776.
20. Quoted by Chester Wright, *Economic History of the U.S.,* p. 216.
21. Arthur M. Schlesinger, *New Viewpoints in American History* (New York: Macmillan Co., 1922), p. 132.
22. Louis E. Lomax, *The Negro Revolt* (New York: New American Library, Signet Books, 1963), p. 24.
23. Quarles, *Negro in the Making of America,* p. 56.
24. Bennett, *Before the Mayflower,* p. 62.
25. Meier and Rudwick, *From Plantation to Ghetto,* p. 47.
26. Article 1, section 2., (3) "Representatives and direct taxes shall be apportioned among the several states which may be included within this Union, according to their respective numbers, (which shall be determined by adding to the whole number of free persons, including those bound to service for a term of years), and excluding Indians not taxed, (three fifths of all other persons)."

   Article IV, section 2., (3) "(no person held to service or labor in one State, under the laws thereof, escaping into another, shall in consequence of any law or regulation therein, be discharged for such service or labor, but shall be delivered up on claim of the party to whom such service or labor may be due.)"
27. Linda Grant DePauw, "Forgotten Spirit of '76," *Ms.* Magazine, July 1974, p. 56.
28. *Ibid.,* p. 53.
29. Spruill, *Women's Life and Work,* p. 245.

Chapter 4. The Transition: *1783–1815*

1. Beard, *America Through Women's Eyes,* p. 86.
2. De Pauw, *Four Traditions,* p. 37; Sinclair, *Emancipation of the American Woman,* p. 30.
3. Gerda Lerner, "The Lady and the Mill Girl: Changes in the Status of Women in the Age of Jackson," *American Studies* vol. 10, no. 1 (spring 1969), pp. 8, 9.
4. Arthur Summerfield, *U.S. Mail* (New York: Holt, Rinehart, & Winston, 1960), p. 49.
5. In 1812 Mary Clarke of the Indiana Territory won a court decision and her freedom when the court declared that indentured servants were held involuntarily, contrary to the Northwest Ordinance. This marked the beginning of the end of bonded servitude; by 1831 indentured service had disappeared. See Joseph G. Rayback, *A History of American Labor* (New York: Free Press, 1966), p. 40.
6. J. Leander Bishop, *A History of American Manufactures from 1608 to 1860* (Philadelphia: Edward Young & Co., 1864), vol. 1, p. 419.
7. *Ibid.,* p. 420.
8. Abbott, *Women in Industry,* p. 41.
9. *Ibid.,* p. 43.
10. Aleine Austin, *The Labor Story* (New York: Coward-McCann, 1949), p. 8.
11. Elizabeth Faulkner Baker, *Technology and Women's Work* (New York: Columbia University Press, 1964), p. 4, n. 4, quoting Matilda Joselyn Gage "Woman as an Inventor," *North American Review,* May 1883; also see Meyer, *Women's Work in America,* pp. 279–80, and Bishop, *History of American Manufactures,* vol. 1, p. 48.
12. Wright, *Economic History of the U.S.,* p. 272.
13. Quoted by Eleanor Flexner in *Century of Struggle* (New York: Atheneum Publishers, 1970), p. 21. From a compilation by Theodore and Angelina Grimké Weld, *American Slavery As It Is: Testimony of a Thousand Witnesses* (1839), p. 175.
14. Quarles, *Negro in the Making of America,* pp. 66, 67.
15. Meier and Rudwick, *From Plantation to Ghetto,* p. 52.
16. *Ibid.,* p. 54, for a more detailed summary of strictures regulating the slave population.
17. DePauw, *Four Traditions,* pp. 34, 35.
18. Leonard and others, *American Woman,* p. 53.

19. Wright, *Economic History of the U.S.*, p. 275.
20. Abbott, *Women In Industry*, p. 87.
21. Helen L. Sumner, *History of Women in Industry in the United States* (Washington, D.C.: Government Printing Office, 1910), pp. 47, 49, 50.
22. As quoted by Abbott, *Women in Industry*, pp. 51–9.
23. Sumner, *History of Women in Industry*, p. 55; Stanley Lebergott, *Manpower in Economic Growth* (New York: McGraw-Hill Book Co., 1964), pp. 510, 520.

PART 2. Working Women of the Nineteenth Century

1. Almond H. Davis, *The Female Preacher, or Memoir of Salome Lincoln, Afterwards the Wife of Elder Junia S. Mowry* (1843; reprint ed., New York: Arno Press, 1972), pp. 51–2, 161.
2. Current and others, *American History*, vol. 1, p. 225.
3. Wright, *Economic History of the U.S.*, p. 409; Sumner, *History of Women in Industry*, p. 27; Abbott, *Women in Industry*, p. 120.
4. Norman Ware, *The Industrial Worker, 1840–1860* (1924; reprint ed., Quadrangle Books, 1964), pp. 26, 7.
5. Lebergott, *Manpower in Economic Growth*, p. 520.
6. *Ibid.*, pp. 510, 520.

Chapter 5. The Factory Bell: 1815–1860

1. *Encyclopaedia Britannica*, 14th ed. (1929), vol. 14, p. 443; Abbott, *Women in Industry*, p. 90.
2. Abbott, *Women in Industry*, pp. 374–5.
3. *Ibid.*, pp. 94–95, 125–7.
4. "The Lowell Factory Girl," *Southern Exposure*, vol. 2, no. 1 (spring–summer 1974), p. 42.
5. Sumner, *History of Women in Industry*, p. 102, from *Voice of Industry*, May 7, 1847.
6. Caroline F. Ware, *The Early New England Cotton Manufacture* (Boston: Houghton Mifflin Co., 1931), pp. 214, 221. The Hamilton Company's agent is quoted by Ware as having written in 1845: "I should have mentioned to you yesterday that the proprietors of the *Lowell Offering* have recently made a request to the agents of the mills here for some aid to relieve them from the embarrassment they find themselves in. . . . It has been thought advisable to aid them by purchasing a lot of the back numbers to the amount of a thousand dollars. . . . It was thought best that assistance should be rendered to them in the way proposed . . . so that it might not be said that the concern is at present supported by the corporations or under their influence" (p. 222, from the *Hamilton Company Papers*).
7. Abbott, *Women in Industry*, pp. 377–8, from Appendix, Seth Luther's "Address to the Workingmen of New England" (1836).
8. John B. Andrews and W. D. P. Bliss, *History of Women in Trade Unions*, Bureau of Labor Report on Conditions of Women and Child Wage-Earners in the United States, vol. 10 (Washington, D.C.: Government Printing Office, 1911), p. 24. Quoting *Mechanics Free Press*, Jan. 17, 1829.
9. *Ibid.*, p. 23, quoting *National Gazette*, Jan. 7, 1829.
10. *Ibid.*, p. 27, quoting *Lowell Journal* and *Essex Tribune*, Feb. 22, 1834.
11. *Ibid.*, p. 28, quoting *The Man*, Feb. 22, 1834.
12. *Ibid.*, pp. 25–26.
13. *Ibid.*, p. 26, quoting *The Man*, March 11, 1834.
14. Harriet H. Robinson, *Loom and Spindle, or Life Among the Early Mill Girls* (New York: Thomas Y. Crowell & Co., 1898), pp. 84–5.
15. *Ibid.*, p. 84.
16. Andrews and Bliss, *Women in Trade Unions*, p. 30, from *National Laborer*, Oct. 29, 1836.
17. Robinson, *Loom and Spindle*, p. 85.

18. Foner, *Labor Movement in the U.S.*, vol. 1, p. 110. Taken from "An Address on the Origin and Progress of Avarice, and its Deleterious Effects on Human Happiness" (Boston, 1834).
19. Published anonymously in *Voice of Industry*, Feb. 20, 1846; quoted in Sumner, *History of Women in Industry*, p. 69.
20. Andrews and Bliss, *Women in Trade Unions*, p. 71, from *Voice of Industry*, June 5, 1845.
21. Hannah Josephson, *The Golden Threads* (New York: Duell, Sloan & Pearce, 1949), p. 259.
22. N. Ware, *Industrial Worker*, p. 137, quoting Massachusetts House Document no. 50 (1845).
23. Andrews and Bliss, *Women in Trade Unions*, p. 74, quoting *Voice of Industry*, Jan. 9, 1846.
24. *Ibid.*, p. 74, quoting *Voice of Indutsry*, Nov. 28, 1846.
25. C. F. Ware, *New England Cotton Manufacture*, p. 280.
26. Andrews and Bliss, *Women in Trade Unions*, p. 72, from *Voice of Industry*, Feb. 27, 1846.
27. *Ibid.*, p. 72.
28. *Ibid.*, p. 79.
29. Dulles, *Labor in America*, p. 78. Also N. Ware, *Industrial Worker*, p. 10.
30. *Alistair Cook's America* (New York: Alfred A. Knopf, 1974), p. 275.
31. William Cahn, *A Pictorial History of American Labor* (New York: Crown Publishers, 1972), p. 43.
32. C. F. Ware, *New England Cotton Manufacture*, p. 260.
33. *Ibid.*, p. 261.
34. John R. Commons, ed., *A Documentary History of American Industrial Society* (New York: Russell & Russell, 1909), vol. 7, pp. 50, 51.
35. Foner, *Labor Movement in the U.S.*, vol. 1, p. 108.
36. Dulles, *Labor in America*, pp. 54, 55; John R. Commons, *History of Labor in the United States* (New York: Macmillan Co., 1918), vol. 1, p. 381. The significance of the 140 figure is seen when compared with the nine strikes that took place in 1837, the first year of the major depression that lasted until 1842.
37. Commons, ed., *American Industrial Society*, vol. 1, p. 285, from the National Trades Union Report of the Committee on Female Labor, Nov. 12, 1836.
38. Andrews and Bliss, *Women in Trade Unions*, p. 46.
39. *Ibid.*, p. 49.

Chapter 6. Binding Shoes and Other Trades

1. Annie Marion MacClean, *Wage-Earning Women* (New York: Macmillan Co., 1910), pp. 152, 153.
2. *Ibid.*, p. 18. Poem by Lucy Larcom of Lowell, Massachusetts.
3. *Ibid.*, p. 158; Sumner, *History of Women in Industry*, p. 168.
4. Abbott, *Women in Industry*, p. 166.
5. *Ibid.*, p. 168.
6. Harry A. Millis and Royal E. Montgomery, *Organized Labor* (New York: McGraw-Hill Book Co., 1945), pp. 503–4. Philip Taft, *Organized Labor in American History* (New York: Harper & Row, 1964), pp. 41–3.
7. N. Ware, *Industrial Worker*, p. 41.
8. Andrews and Bliss, *Women in Trade Unions*, pp. 41–3. Quotation from *Lynn Record*, Jan. 1, 1834, on p. 42.
9. *Ibid.*, p. 43, 44, quoting *Lynn Record*, Jan. 8, 1834.
10. *Ibid.*, p. 44.
11. Taft, *Organized Labor*, p. 28; Andrews and Bliss, *Women in Trade Unions*, p. 44; from *The Man*, June 19, 1835; Sumner, *History of Women in Industry*, p. 169.
12. Andrews and Bliss, *Women in Trade Unions*, p. 45, from *The Pennsylvanian*, March 28, 1836.
13. *Ibid.*, p. 60, from *The Awl*, July 17, 1844.
14. *Ibid.*, p. 108.

15. Dulles, *Labor in America*, p. 90.
16. Andrews and Bliss, Women in Trade Unions, p. 108; N. Ware, *Industrial Worker*, p. 47; Dulles, *Labor in America*, p. 90.
17. Information on the straw bonnet workers from Abbott, *Women in Industry*, p. 71. As late as 1845 and perhaps into the 1850s, more Massachusetts workers still manufactured goods under the domestic system in their own homes than in factories, according to George Rogers Taylor, in *The Economic History of the United States* (New York: Holt, Rinehart & Winston, 1951), vol. 4, p. 267.
18. Sumner, *History of Women in Industry*, p. 22, quoting *New York Tribune*, Aug. 19, 1845.
19. Abbott, *Women in Industry*, p. 81.
20. Andrews and Bliss, *Women in Trade Unions*, p. 40, quoting *Philadelphia Public Ledger*, Dec. 1, 1836.
21. *Ibid.*, p. 100.
22. Abbott, *Women in Industry*, p. 249.
23. *Ibid.*, p. 253.
24. *Ibid.*, p. 252, from "Women Printers and the Typographical Union," a 1906 publication of the Women's Trade Union League of Massachusetts.
25. Sumner, *History of Women in Industry*, p. 77.
26. *Ibid.*, pp. 178–80.
27. *Ibid.*, 181, from *Workingman's Advocate*, Jan. 9, 1830.
28. Sumner, *History of Women in Industry*, p. 125.
29. Abbott, *Women in Industry*, p. 218.
30. Joel Seidman, *The Needle Trades* (New York: Farrar & Rinehart, 1942), p. 14.
31. Andrews and Bliss, *Women in Trade Unions*, p. 36, quoting *Boston Transcript*, Feb. 22, 1831.
32. *Ibid.*, p. 37, quoting *Working Man's Advocate*, June 11, 1831.
33. *Ibid.*, p. 39.
34. Sumner, *History of Women in Industry*, p. 127; N. Ware, *Industrial Worker*, p. 50.
35. Sumner, *History of Women in Industry*, pp. 127–28; quotations from Carey's Miscellaneous Pamphlets, No. 12, To the Editor of the New York Daily Sentinel, Philadelphia, 1831.
36. *Ibid.*, p. 135.
37. Andrews and Bliss, *Women in Trade Unions*, p. 58.
38. N. Ware, *Industrial Worker*, p. 52; Andrews and Bliss, *Women in Trade Unions*, p. 59, quoting *Voice of Industry*, Nov. 7, 1845.
39. Commons, ed., *American Industrial Society*, vol. 8, p. 227 from *Working Man's Advocate*, March 8, 1845.
40. Andrews and Bliss, *Women in Trade Unions*, p. 59, from *Voice of Industry*, Sept. 4, 1846.
41. N. Ware, *Industrial Worker*, p. 53, quoting *New York Daily Tribune*, Feb. 23, 1850.
42. Andrews and Bliss, *Women in Trade Unions*, p. 60, quoting *New York Daily Tribune*, July 31, 1853.
43. *Ibid.*, pp. 82–3.
44. As quoted in Foner, *Labor Movement in the U.S.*, vol. 1, p. 220.
45. Seidman, *Needle Trades*, p. 15.
46. N. Ware, *Industrial Worker*, pp. 49–50.
47. *Ibid.*, p. 52, quoting *Voice of Industry*, Jan. 14, 1848.
48. For much of the material on prostitutes I have drawn from Dr. William Sanger's report, *The History of Prostitution: Its Extent, Causes, and Effects Throughout the World* (New York: Harper & Brothers, 1859), especially pp. 452–73 and 527–9.
49. Otto L. Bettmann, *The Good Old Days — They Were Terrible!* (New York: Random House, 1974), p. 98.
50. Doris Faber, *Petticoat Politics: How American Women Won the Right to Vote* (New York: Lothrop, Lee & Shepard Co., 1967), p. 177.
51. Gerda Lerner, *The Woman in American History* (Menlo Park, Calif.: Addison-Wesley Publishing Co., 1971), p. 84.
52. Sue B. Green, "Lucretia Mott—'Hicksite,' Abolitionist, Feminist," *Friends Journal*, July 1/15, 1974, pages unnumbered.
53. N. Ware, *Industrial Worker*, p. 77.

Chapter 7. In Factory and Field:
Black Women and Slavery in America, 1808–1860

1. Ray Marshall, *The Negro Worker* (New York: Random House, 1967), p. 4, table 1.1.
2. Sung by slaves when separated from their families and friends after auction sales; from Jacob Stroyer, *Sketches of My Life in the South* (Salem, Mass., 1879), vol. 1, pp. 29–31, quoted by Katz, *Eyewitness*, p. 113.
3. Richard Wade, "Slavery in the Cities," in Raymond A. Mohl and Neil Betten, eds., *Urban America in Historical Perspective* (New York, Weybright & Talley, 1970), p. 144.
4. Robert S. Starobin, *Blacks in Bondage* (New York: New Viewpoints, 1974), p. 5; Joanne Grant, *Black Protest* (Greenwich, Conn.: Fawcett Publications, 1968), p. 63; John Hope Franklin, *From Slavery to Freedom* (New York: Vintage Books, 1969), p. 176.
5. E. Franklin Frazier, *The Negro Family in the United States* (Chicago: University of Chicago Press, 1969), p. 35.
6. Moses Grandy, *Narrative of the Life 'of Moses Grandy; late a Slave in the United States of America* (1844; reprint ed., New York: Arno Press, 1968), in *Five Slave Narratives: A Compendium*, pp. 5, 6.
7. Franklin, *From Slavery*, p. 178.
8. Frederick Douglass, *Narrative of the Life of Frederick Douglass, An American Slave* (1845; paperback ed., New York: New American Library, Signet Books, 1968, p. 22.
9. Franklin, *From Slavery*, p. 181.
10. Robert S. Starobin, *Industrial Slavery in the Old South* (New York: Oxford University Press, 1970), p. 11.
11. Lewis Clarke, *Narrative of the Sufferings of Lewis and Milton Clarke* (Boston, 1846), p. 127, quoted by Frazier, *Negro Family*, p. 38.
12. Grandy, *Narrative*, p. 18.
13. Franklin, *From Slavery to Freedom*, p. 188.
14. *Ibid.*, p. 203.
15. From Herbert Aptheker, *A Documentary History of the Negro People in the United States* (1951; paperback ed., New York: Citadel Press, 1967), vol. 1, pp. 277–8.
16. Ann Petry, *Harriet Tubman, Conductor on the Underground Railroad* (1955; paperback ed., New York: Pocket Books, 1971), p. 86. Lerone Bennett, Jr., *Pioneers in Protest* (Baltimore: Penguin Books, 1968), pp. 131–49.
17. Meier and Rudwick, *From Plantation to Ghetto*, p. 116.
18. Petry, *Harriet Tubman*, pp. 220–1. Petry's book is an excellent short work on the life of Harriet Tubman. Other sources upon which I have drawn are discussed in the Annotated Bibliography.
19. Starobin, *Industrial Slavery*, pp. 13, 17–24, 165, 168. This is the most complete treatment I have found on the use of slaves in Southern industry before the Civil War.
20. Wade, in Mohl and Betten, *Urban America*, p. 154.
21. Saunders Redding, *They Came in Chains* (Philadelphia: J. B. Lippincott Co., 1950), p. 135, Frances Anne Kemble, *Journal of Residence on a Georgian Plantation, 1838–1839* (1863). Fanny Kemble, a noted English actress, had married a Southern planter, but was so disturbed by the system of plantation slavery that she left him, choosing a life of poverty and hardship rather than remain in Georgia.
22. Redding, *They Came in Chains*, quoting John H. Van Evrie's *White Supremacy and Negro Subordination* (1868), p. 134.
23. Quarles, *Negro in the Making of America*, p. 87.
24. Frazier, *The Negro Family*, p. 148.
25. Quoted by Philip Foner, *Organized Labor and the Black Worker, 1619–1974* (New York: Praeger Publishers, 1974), p. 6.
26. Katz, *Eyewitness*, p. 153; Flexner, *Century of Struggle*, pp. 38–40; James and James, eds., *Notable American Women*, vol. 1, pp. 399–401.
27. Redding, *They Came in Chains*, p. 145.
28. James and James, eds., *Notable American Women*, vol. 1, pp. 300–301.

29. Susie King Taylor, *Reminiscences of My Life in Camp* (1902), quoted in Katz, *Eyewitness*, p. 133.
30. James and James, eds., *Notable American Women*, vol. 1, pp. 511–13.
31. *Ibid.*, vol. 2, pp. 137–9; Hughes and Bontemps, *Poetry of the Negro*, p. 606.
32. Aptheker, *History of the Negro People*, vol. 1, p. 388.

PART 3. Working Women in War and Peace: *1861–1886*

Chapter 8. Women in the Civil War and Reconstruction

1. Current and others, *American History*, vol. 1, p. 366.
2. *Ibid.*, pp. 142, 143.
3. Flexner, *Century of Struggle*, p. 107.
4. Clement Eaton, *The Growth of Southern Civilization, 1790–1860* (New York: Harper & Row, 1961), p. 284.
5. Agatha Young, *The Women and the Crisis* (New York: McDowell, Obolensky, 1959), p. 134.
6. Hearings before the Special Committee on Aging, U.S. Senate, Aug. 10, 1971, p. 105. Remarks of Senator Jennings Randolph of West Virginia.
7. James and James, eds., *Notable American Women*, vol. 1, p. 104.
8. *Ibid.*, p. 145.
9. Young, *Women and the Crisis*, p. 367.
10. *Ibid.*, p. 97.
11. Vern Bullough, *The Subordinate Sex* (Baltimore: Penguin Books, 1974), p. 319; James Horan, *Desperate Women* (New York: G. P. Putnam's Sons, 1952), pp. 105, 137.
12. Katz, *Eyewitness*, pp. 223–4.
13. Young, *Women and the Crisis*, pp. 144–6.
14. Louise Terri Washington, "Sojourner Truth, A Black Woman in White America," unpublished term paper for Trade Union Women's Studies, Cornell University, New York State School of Industrial and Labor Relations, March 1975, p. 1.
15. Redding, *They Came in Chains*, p. 102.
16. As told by Lerone Bennett, Jr., *Pioneers in Protest*, p. 122.
17. *Ibid.*, pp. 123, 124.
18. Katz, *Eyewitness*, pp. 186–7; Bennett, *Pioneers in Protest*, p. 126.
19. Helen Stone Peterson, *Sojourner Truth, Fearless Crusader* (Champaign, Ill.: Garrard Publishing Co., 1972), p. 67.
20. Beard, *Through Women's Eyes*, pp. 231, 232.
21. Bennett, *Pioneers in Protest*, p. 127.
22. As paraphrased by Victoria Ortiz, *Sojourner Truth, a Self-made Woman* (Philadelphia: J. B. Lippincott Co., 1974), p. 121.
23. Bennett, *Pioneers in Protest*, p. 128.
24. Abraham Lincoln on the work of women in the Civil War, quoted by Schlesinger, *New Viewpoints in American History*, p. 144.
25. Horan, *Desperate Women*, pp. 52–3.
26. Quoted by Bullough in *The Subordinate Sex*, p. 319.
27. Schlesinger, *New Viewpoints*, p. 144.
28. Bell Irvin Wiley, *Southern Negroes, 1861–1865* (New Haven, Conn.: Yale University Press, 1938) p. 56.
29. *Ibid.*, pp. 5–7, 18–9, 58, 59, 61, 74–5.
30. Samuel Eliot Morison, Henry Steele Commager, and William E. Leuchtenberg, *The Growth of the American Republic* (New York: Oxford University Press, 1969), vol. 1, p. 719; Mary Elizabeth Massey, *Bonnet Brigades* (New York: Alfred A. Knopf, 1966), p. 142; June Sochen, *Herstory: A Woman's View of American History* (New York: Alfred Publishing Co., 1974), p. 182.
31. Bennett, *Before the Mayflower*, p. 187.
32. *Ibid.*, p. 187; Morison and others, *American Republic*, vol. 1, p. 732; Redding, *They Came in Chains*, p. 171.

33. Katz, *Eyewitness*, p. 251.
34. *Ibid.*, p. 242.
35. Wiley, *Southern Negroes*, p. 271, quoting a report of the Executive Board of Friends Association for the Aid and Elevation of the Freedmen, May 11, 1864.
36. *Ibid.*, p. 271.
37. *Ibid.*, pp. 274–5.
38. W. E. B. DuBois, *The Souls of Black Folk* (New York: New American Library, Signet Classics, 1969), p. 65.
39. Franklin, *From Slavery to Freedom*, p. 311.
40. Morison and others, *American Republic*, vol. 1, pp. 730–1.
41. Grant, *Black Protest*, pp. 148–9. Acts of the General Assembly of Louisiana Regulating Labor, 1865.
42. Bennett, *Before the Mayflower*, p. 212.

Chapter 9. Women on the Home Front and in the Industrial Era

1. Rayback, *History of American Labor*, p. 111; Meyer, ed., *Woman's Work in America*, p. 284.
2. Foner, *Labor Movement in the U.S.*, vol. 1, p. 341.
3. Andrews and Bliss, *Women in Trade Unions*, pp. 96, 97.
4. *Ibid.*, p. 97.
5. *Ibid.*, p. 96.
6. *Fincher's Trades' Review* for March 18, 1865, quoted in Commons, *American Industrial Society*, vol. 9, pp. 72, 73.
7. Andrews and Bliss, *Women in Trade Unions*, p. 99. This is the best account I have found of the many activities of sewing women during the 1860s.
8. Young, *Women and the Crisis*, p. 69.
9. Foner, *Labor Movement in the U.S.*, vol. 1, p. 342.
10. Stanley Feldstein and Lawrence Costello, *The Ordeal of Assimilation* (Garden City, N.Y.: Doubleday & Co., Anchor Books, 1974), p. 269; Flexner, *Century of Struggle*, p. 133.
11. Sumner, *History of Women in Industry*, p. 17; Foner, *Labor Movement in the U.S.*, vol. 1, p. 342.
12. Sumner, *History of Women in Industry*, p. 17, quoting *Daily Evening Voice*, March 2, 1867.
13. Baker, *Technology and Women's Work*, p. 64.
14. Sumner, *History of Women in Industry*, p. 235, quoting William Burns, *Life in New York, Indoors and Out of Doors* (1851); p. 237.
15. Reginald Wright Kauffman, *A House of Bondage* (selection) in Upton Sinclair, *The Cry for Justice* (New York: Upton Sinclair, 1915), pp. 54, 55.
16. Sumner, *History of Women in Industry*, p. 238.
17. Baker, *Technology and Women's Work*, pp. 65, 66; Sumner, *History of Women in Industry*, p. 238.
18. Sumner, *History of Women in Industry*, p. 239.
19. *Ibid.*, p. 240.
20. Table derived from figures in *ibid.*, pp. 240–1.
21. Baker, *Technology and Women's Work*, p. 73.
22. Morison and others, *American Republic*, vol. 1, p. 803.
23. James and James, eds., *Notable American Women*, vol. 3, pp. 148, 149; Baker, *Technology and Women's Work*, p. 62.
24. Commons, ed., *American Industrial Society*, vol. 9, pp. 204, 205; New York Congress of the National Labor Union, Sept. 21, 1868.
25. Sumner, *History of Women in Industry*, p. 29, quoting *Fincher's Trades' Review*, Oct. 1, 1864; p. 27, quoting *The Revolution*, Dec. 31, 1868.
26. Foner, *Labor Movement in the U.S.*, vol. 1, p. 387.
27. Commons, ed., *American Industrial Society*, vol. 9, p. 267.
28. Andrews and Bliss, *Women in Trade Unions*, p. 92.
29. Abbott, *Women in Industry*, pp. 192, 193.

30. Andrews and Bliss, *Women in Trade Unions*, p. 94, quoting *Cigar Makers' Journal*, May 10, 1878; p. 92.
31. Meyer, *Woman's Work in America*, p. 308.
32. Andrews and Bliss, *Women in Trade Unions*, p. 93.
33. *Ibid.*, p. 93.
34. *Ibid.*, p. 94.
35. Abbott, *Women in Industry*, p. 195.
36. George A. Stevens, *New York Typographical Union Number 6, Study of a Modern Trade Union and its Predecessors* (Albany, N.Y.: J. B. Lyon Co., State Printers, 1913, p. 422.
37. *Ibid.*, p. 442.
38. Flexner, *Century of Struggle*, p. 135, quoting *The Revolution*, Oct. 15, 1868.
39. Alma Lutz, *Susan B. Anthony, Rebel, Crusader, Humanitarian* (Boston: Beacon Hill Press, 1959), pp. 154, 153. Some accounts indicate that Augusta Lewis may have been fired from a job as typesetter on the *Revolution* for union activity. However, Anthony always denied this.
40. James and James, eds., *Notable Amercian Women*, vol. 2, p. 478, article by Eleanor Flexner. Flexner and Stevens do not agree on the year Augusta Lewis married; Stevens gives it as 1872, Flexner as 1874. Both agree it was on June 12.
41. Stevens, *New York Typographical Union*, p. 437.
42. *Ibid.*, p. 432, n. 2.
43. Andrews and Bliss, *Women in Trade Unions*, pp. 108, 109.
44. *Ibid.*, p. 109, quoting *American Workman*, April 30, 1870.
45. Abbott, *Women in Industry*, p. 236.
46. Alice Henry, *Women and the Labor Movement* (New York: George H. Doran, Co., 1923), p. 73.
47. Andrews and Bliss, *Women in Trade Unions*, pp. 106, 107.
48. *Ibid.*, p. 107; Foner, Labor Movement in the U.S., vol. 1, p. 383, quoting *New York Tribune*, Dec. 8–10, 1869.
49. Andrews and Bliss, *Women in Trade Unions*, p. 107.
50. Flexner, *Century of Struggle*, pp. 138, 139.
51. C. F. Ware, *New England Cotton Manufacture*, p. 255.
52. James and James, eds., *Notable American Women*, vol. 1, p. 362, article by Elizabeth Hoxie.
53. Andrews and Bliss, *Women in Trade Unions*, p. 103.
54. James and James, eds., *Notable American Women*, vol. 1, p. 362.
55. Andrews and Bliss, *Women in Trade Unions*, p. 103; Foner, *Labor Movement in the U.S.*, vol. 1, p. 455.
56. Ken Lawrence, "Mississippi's First Labor Union," Tougaloo, Mississippi, Deep South People's History Project, Freedom Information Service, 1974.
57. Foner, *Organized Labor and the Black Worker*, p. 34.
58. Rayback, *History of American Labor*, p. 129.
59. M. B. Schnapper, *American Labor, A Pictorial Social History* (Washington, D.C.: Public Affairs Press, 1972), p. 93.
60. Rayback, *History of American Labor*, p. 130.
61. William Cahn, *A Pictorial History of American Labor* (New York: Crown Publishers, 1972), p. 103.
62. Samuel Gompers, *Seventy Years of Life and Labor* (New York: E. P. Dutton & Co., 1943), pp. 97, 98.
63. Cahn, *Pictorial History of American Labor*, p. 130.

Chapter 10. Women in the Knights of Labor: *1881–1886*

1. Foner, *Labor Movement in the U.S.*, vol. 2, p. 15.
2. Janet Hooks, *Women's Occupations through Seven Decades*, Women's Bureau Bulletin no. 218 (Washington, D.C.: U.S. Department of Labor, 1947), pp. 33, 52.
3. Foner, *Labor Movement in the U.S.*, vol. 2, p. 21.
4. *Ibid.*, pp. 25, 26.

5. Andrews and Bliss, *Women in Trade Unions*, p. 113.
6. *Ibid.*, pp. 129–31.
7. Hooks, *Women's Occupations*, p. 34.
8. Andrews and Bliss, *Women in Trade Unions*, p. 131.
9. *Ibid.*, p. 126.
10. *Ibid.*, p. 125.
11. *Ibid.*, p. 116.
12. James J. Kenneally, "Women and Trade Unions, 1870–1920: The Quandary of the Reformer," *Labor History*, vol. 14, no. 1 (winter 1973), p. 43.
13. Foner, *Labor Movement in the U.S.*, vol. 2, p. 64.
14. Flexner, *Century of Struggle*, p. 196, quoting Frances Willard, *Glimpses of Fifty Years* (1892).
15. Andrews and Bliss, *Women in Trade Unions*, pp. 125–8; Flexner, *Century of Struggle*, pp. 195–6.
16. The material on Leonora Barry is from Andrews and Bliss, *Women in Trade Unions*, pp. 116–23; Flexner, *Century of Struggle*, p. 197; James and James, eds., *Notable American Women*, vol. 1, pp. 101–2, article by Eleanor Flexner.
17. Quoted by Annie Nathan Meyer in *Woman's Work in America*, p. 299.
18. Andrews and Bliss, *Women in Trade Unions*, pp. 118, 119.
19. *Ibid.*, p. 121.
20. *Ibid.*
21. *Ibid.*, p. 117; Kenneally, "Women and Trade Unions," p. 44.
22. Foner, *Labor Movement in the U.S.*, vol. 2, p. 65.
23. James and James, eds., *Notable American Women*, vol. 1, p. 102.
24. Grace Hutchins, *Women Who Work* (New York: International Publishers Co., 1952), p. 230.
25. Foner, *Labor Movement in the U.S.*, vol. 2, pp. 62, 64.
26. *Ibid.*, p. 63, quoting *John Swinton's Paper*, June 7, 1885.
27. *Ibid.*, p. 66.

PART 4. The Wage-Earning Woman: *1886–1910*

Statistics for the Introduction to Part Four are from:

Historical Statistics, Statistical Abstracts of the United States; Baker, *Technology and Women's Work*, p. 72; *1969 Handbook on Women Workers*, Women's Bureau, U.S. Department of Labor; Eli Ginzberg and Hyman Berman, *The American Worker in the Twentieth Century* (Glencoe, Ill., Free Press, 1963), p. 29; Taft, *Organized Labor in American History*, p. 162; Andrews and Bliss, *Women in Trade Unions*, p. 136; Abbott, *Women in Industry*, p. 379; Ann Oakley, *Woman's Work* (New York: Pantheon Books, 1974), p. 50; Foner, *Labor Movement in the U.S.*, vol. 2, pp. 225, 367.

Chapter 11. Women Workers and the Early American Federation of Labor

1. Dorothy Richardson, "Trades-Unions in Petticoats," *Leslie's Monthly Magazine*, March 1904, pp. 489–500.
2. Foner, *Labor Movement in the U.S.*, vol. 2, p. 94.
3. Henry, *Women and the Labor Movement*, p. 52.
4. Foner, *Labor Movement in the U.S.*, vol. 3, p. 190, quoting a letter to Chris Evans, AFL officer.
5. *Ibid.*, pp. 221, 222.
6. *Ibid.*, p. 227; Sarah Simpson to Samuel Gompers, March 13, 1903.
7. *Ibid.*, p. 226, P. Dolan to S. Gompers, Oct. 29, 1904.
8. *Ibid.*, vol. 2, p. 190.
9. *Ibid.*, p. 190, from 1891 AFL correspondence.
10. *Ibid.*, p. 191, 192; Ralph Scharman, "Elizabeth Morgan, Crusader for Labor Reform," *Labor History*, vol. 14, no. 3 (summer 1973), pp. 340–51.

11. Scharman, "Elizabeth Morgan," pp. 347–9.
12. Henry, *Women and the Labor Movement*, p. 54.
13. Andrews and Bliss, *Women in Trade Unions*, pp. 204, 206.
14. Foner, *Labor Movement in the U.S.*, vol. 3, pp. 225, 226. See pages 219–28 for a summary of AFL attitudes toward women workers.
15. Cott, *Root of Bitterness*, p. 332.
16. Andrews and Bliss, *Women in Trade Unions*, p. 156.
17. Mary Kenney O'Sullivan, "Autobiography," rough draft, typed, Schlesinger Library, Radcliffe College, gift of Oscar Handlin in 1959. James and James, eds., *Notable American Women*, vol. 2, pp. 655, 656, article by Eleanor Flexner and Janet Wilson James.
18. Andrews and Bliss, *Women in Trade Unions*, p. 156.
19. Foner, *Labor Movement in the U.S.*, vol. 2, pp. 193–5; Andrews and Bliss, *Women in Trade Unions*, p. 156. Some of the other women organizers who worked for the AFL in this early period include Annie Fitzgerald, appointed an organizer in 1908, who came out of the Upholsterers Union and was president of the International Women's Label League, an organization that promoted consumer support of products carrying the union label. She served for six months. Mary Kelleher held the post for six years, Melinda Scott, leader of the Hat Trimmers union, for four years. Anna Neary held the job for over four years. According to Alice Henry, from 1908 to 1923, when she wrote *Women and the Labor Movement*, 38 women had been organizers, many for as short a time as a few weeks or months during a special emergency.
20. Foner, *Labor Movement in the U.S.*, vol. 3, p. 224.

Chapter 12. Women's Wages, Women's Work

1. Robert W. Smuts, *Work in America* (New York: Schocken Books, 1959, 1971), p. 14. Mrs. John Van Vorst and Marie Van Vorst, *The Woman Who Toils* (Garden City, N.Y.: Doubleday, Page & Co., 1903), pp. 67–8.
2. Smuts, *Work in America*, p. 16.
3. *Ibid.*, p. 17.
4. Janet Hooks, *Women's Occupations through Seven Decades*, Women's Bureau Bulletin no. 218 (Washington, D.C.: U.S. Department of Labor, 1947), p. 39.
5. Elizabeth Beardsley Butler, *Women and the Trades, Pittsburgh 1907–1908* (New York: Charities Publications Committee, 1911), p. 212–13, 227.
6. *Ibid.*, p. 227.
7. Helen Campbell, *Women Wage-Earners* (Boston: Roberts Bros., 1893), pp. 216–222.
8. Quoting Helen Campbell, *Prisoners of Poverty* (Boston: Roberts Bros., 1887), p. 200.
9. Foner, *Labor Movement in the U.S.*, vol. 3, pp. 18, 19.
10. *Toward Better Working Conditions for Women*, Women's Bureau Bulletin #252 (Washington, D.C.: U.S. Department of Labor, 1953), p. 14, from the 1909 *Handbook* of the National Women's Trade Union League.
11. Florence Kelley, "Industrial Democracy," *Outlook*, Dec. 15, 1906, p. 926.
12. Alice Henry, *The Trade Union Woman* (New York: D. Appleton & Co., 1915), pp. 45–6, quoting Lillian Ruth Matthews.
13. *Ibid.*, pp. 46–50.
14. Dorothy Richardson, *The Long Day: The Story of a New York Working Girl* (1905; reprint ed., Chicago: Quadrangle Books, 1972), p. 240.
15. Information on Pittsburgh laundries is from Butler, *Women and the Trades*, pp. 161–91.
16. *Ibid.*, p. 33.
17. *Ibid.*, pp. 33–43.
18. *Ibid.*, pp. 42, 43.
19. Priscilla Long, "Mother Jones, Woman Organizer," unpublished manuscript about the relations of Mother Jones to the "wives of workers, to working women, and to the suffrage movement." Undated, this manuscript was prepared under a grant from the Louis Rabinowitz Foundation, and was lent to me in August 1974 by Joe Glazer, to whom I am most grateful.
20. Van Vorst, *The Woman Who Toils*, pp. 4, 5, 11.
21. *Ibid.*, p. 12.

22. *Ibid.*, pp. 22–6, 27, 33–5, 46, 54, 55.
23. Andrews and Bliss, *Women in Trade Unions*, p. 182; Mary Van Kleeck, *Women in the Book Binding Trade* (New York: Survey Associates, 1913), pp. 1, 2.
24. *Ibid.*, pp. 93, 94, 178–88, 188–92.
25. Butler, *Women and the Trades*, p. 65. For other material on cracker packers, see *ibid.*, pp. 60–70.
26. *Toward Better Working Conditions for Women*, pp. 14, 15.
27. Andrews and Bliss, *Women in Trade Unions*, pp. 186, 187; Matthew Josephson, *Union House, Union Bar* (New York: Random House, 1956), p. 36.
28. Andrews and Bliss, *Women in Trade Unions*, p. 216.
29. Lynn Sherr and Jurate Kazickas, "Maud Younger, Millionaire Waitress," *Ms.* Magazine, January 1973, p. 12, quoting *McClure's Magazine*, May 6, 1907.
30. *Ibid.*, p. 12.
31. James and James, eds., *Notable American Women*, vol. 3, p. 700.
32. Mary Van Kleeck, *Artificial Flower Makers* (New York: Survey Associates, 1913), pp. 94, 95.
33. Upton Sinclair, *The Jungle* (1905; paperback ed., New York: New American Library, Signet Books, 1960), pp. 107, 108.
34. Andrews and Bliss, *Women in Trade Unions*, p. 195.
35. Belva Mary Herron, "The Progress of Labor Organization Among Women, Together with some Considerations Concerning Their Place in Industry," *University Studies*, vol. 1, no. 10 (May 1905), p. 54 (p. 496). Schlesinger Library, Radcliffe College.
36. Henry, *Trade Union Woman*, p. 56.
37. *Ibid.*, p. 58. Also pp. 52–8.
38. Baker, *Technology and Women's Work*, p. 161, quoting 1911 report by the U.S. Bureau of Labor, vol. 18, p. 79, which notes that some tobacco factories that were clean and well lit were also found in the survey.
39. Butler, *Women and the Trades*, p. 83.
40. Andrews and Bliss, *Women in Trade Unions*, p. 181.
41. Redding, *They Came in Chains*, p. 189.
42. Gerda Lerner, *Black Women in White America* (New York: Pantheon Books, 1972), p. 252.
43. *Ibid.*, pp. 227, 228, "More Slavery at the South," by a Negro Nurse, from *The Independent*, Jan. 25, 1912, pp. 196–200.
45. Frazier, *The Negro Family*, p. 210.
46. Mary White Ovington, *Half a Man* (1911; reprint ed., New York: Schocken Books, 1969), p. 146.
47. W. E. B. DuBois, *The Philadelphia Negro, A Social Study* (1899; reprint ed., New York: Schocken Books, 1967), p. 175.
48. Beard, *America Through Women's Eyes*, pp. 244–9, from Mary White Ovington's *Portraits in Color* (New York: Viking Press, 1927).
49. James and James, eds., *Notable Women*, vol. 3, p. 565, article by Eleanor Flexner.
50. Milton Meltzer, *In Their Own Words: A History of the American Negro* (New York, Thomas Y. Crowell Co., 1964), pp. 154, 155; Aptheker, *History of the Negro People*, vol. 2, p. 792; James and James, eds., *Notable Women*, vol. 2, pp. 565, 567, article by Eleanor Flexner.

Chapter 13. Women in White-Collar Jobs

1. Baker, *Technology and Women's Work*, p. 78.
2. Margery Davies, "Woman's Place Is at the Typewriter," *Radical America*, vol. 8, no. 4 (July–Aug. 1974), p. 10; figures from the 16th Census of the United States, 1945.
3. Interview of Florence Cohen Gross by Dana Gross Schechter, Nov. 14, 1975. This incident actually occurred in 1912, and was typical of the prejudice prevailing.
4. Benjamin Solomon, "Early Movements of Unionization Among Salaried Employees," from unpublished materials (1969), White-Collar Union Research Project, at the University of Chicago Industrial Relations Center, p. 11, quoting *New York Tribune*, April 23, 1904.
5. See Sumner, *History of Women in Industry*, pp. 241, 242, for wage and employment statistics used in this section.

6. Solomon, "Early Movements of Unionization," p. 29.

7. *Ibid.*, pp. 27, 28.

8. Smuts, *Women and Work in America*, p. 27.

9. Frances Donovan, *The Saleslady* (Chicago: University of Chicago Press, 1929), pp. 27, 28, 79.

10. Elizabeth Beardsley Butler, *Saleswomen in Mercantile Stories, Baltimore, 1909* (New York: Charities Publication Committee, 1912), pp. 78, 105–10, 30.

11. Butler, *Women and the Trades*, pp. 305, 306.

12. Adapted from Flexner, *Century of Struggle*, pp. 208–9.

13. James and James, eds., *Notable American Women*, vol. 2, p. 319.

14. William O'Neill, *Everyone Was Brave* (Chicago: Quadrangle Books, 1969), p. 136, quoting Florence Kelley, *Modern Industry in Relation to the Family, Health, Education, Morality* (1914), pp. 133–4.

15. Solomon, "Early Movements of Unionization," pp. 20, 21.

16. George Kirstein, *Stores and Unions* (New York: Fairchild Publications, 1950), p. 33, quoting *The Advocate*, Feb. 1899, p. 8.

17. Retail Clerks *Advocate*, March 1975, p. 9; Solomon, "Early Movements of Unionization," p. 8.

18. Solomon, "Early Movements of Unionization," p. 9.

19. Smuts, *Women and Work in America*, pp. 20, 90.

20. *Ibid.*, pp. 19, 20; quotation from "Women as Teachers," *Educational Review*, vol. 2, 1891.

21. Solomon, "Early Movements of Unionization," p. 1.

22. *Ibid.*, p. 17a.

23. *Ibid.*, p. 18.

24. *Ibid.*, p. 18, quoting *Literary Object*, Oct. 2, 1915.

25. *Ibid.*, p. 19, quoting *Literary Object*, Oct. 2, 1915.

26. Philip Taft, *United They Teach: The Story of the United Federation of Teachers* (Los Angeles: Nash Publications, 1974), p. 7.

27. Thomas Brooks, *Toward Dignity* (New York: United Federation of Teachers, 1967), pp. 1, 2.

28. Taft, *United They Teach*, p. 11.

29. *Ibid.*, p. 12.

30. Brooks, *Toward Dignity*, p. 12.

31. From a 1915 Massachusetts school-department manual, quoted in Nancy Zerfoss, "Schoolmarm to School Ms.," *Changing Education*, summer 1974, p. 23.

Chapter 14. Working Women of the West

1. Philip T. Silvia, Jr., "The Position of Workers in a Textile Community: Fall River in the early 1880's," *Labor History* vol. 16, no. 2 (spring 1975), p. 235.

2. Dee Brown, *The Gentle Tamers* (New York: Bantam Pathfinder, 1958), p. 5, quoting Lydia M. Waters, "Account of a Trip Across the Plains in 1855," *Society of California Pioneers Quarterly*, vol. 6 (1929), p. 5.

3. Clark Wissler, *Indians of the United States* (Garden City, N.Y.: Doubleday & Co. 1940), pp. 252 8.

4. Bernard De Voto, ed., *The Journals of Lewis and Clark* (Boston: Houghton Mifflin Co., 1953), p. 113; "Woman Movement Typified by Indian Mother," *Life and Labor*, March 1917, p. 33.

5. Wissler, *Indians of the U.S.*, p. 258.

6. Marion Gridley, *American Indian Women* (New York: Hawthorne Books, 1974), p. 51.

7. Brown, *Gentle Tamers*, pp. 1, 2, quoting Julie Lovejoy, "Letters," *Kansas Historical Quarterly*, vol. 16 (1948), p. 302.

8. Beard, *America Through Women's Eyes*, pp. 114–15, quoting the diary of Narcissa Whitman. Narcissa Whitman was slain by an angry Indian tribe decimated by an epidemic of measles, unknown by the Indians before the white settlers arrived.

9. Brown, *Gentle Tamers*, p. 6.

10. William Forrest Sprague, *Women and the West* (Boston: Christopher Publishing House, 1940), pp. 105–6, from Victor H. Paltsists, ed., "Across the Plains to Cali-

fornia in 1852: Journal of Mrs. Lodisa Frizzell," *New York Public Library Bulletin*, April 1915, pp. 28, 29.

11. Brown, *Gentle Tamers*, p. 180.

12. Sprague, *Women and the West*, pp. 100–1, from a manuscript owned by the Henry E. Huntington Library, San Marino, California.

13. Brown, *Gentle Tamers*, p. 92.

14. Marshall B. Davidson, *Life in America* (Boston: Houghton Mifflin Co., 1951), vol. 1, p. 170.

15. Sprague, *Women and the West*, p. 45, quoting C. J. Latrobe, *The Rambler in North America* (1836), vol. 2, pp. 252–3.

16. Brown, *Gentle Tamers*, p. 100.

17. Sprague, *Women and the West*, p. 137, quoting B. R. Hall, *The New Purchase* (1855), p. 201.

18. Brown, *Gentle Tamers*, p. 92.

19. Beard, *America Through Women's Eyes*, p. 106, from Anna Howard Shaw, *The Story of a Pioneer* (1915).

20. Eliza Farnham, *Life in Prairie Land* (New York: Harper & Bros., 1846), p. 38.

21. T. A. Larson, "Women's Role in the American West," *Montana, The Magazine of Western History*, vol. 24, no. 3 (summer 1974), p. 5.

22. Based on data from the U.S. Census of 1870, Larson, "Women's Role," pp. 5, 6.

23. Larson, "Women's Role," p. 6.

24. Brown, *Gentle Tamers*, p. 228, from Walker D. Wyman, "California Emigrant Letters," *California Historical Society, Quarterly*, vol. 24 (1945), p. 348.

25. *Ibid.*, p. 229.

26. Phebe A. Hanaford, *Daughters of America, or Women of the Century* (Augusta, Maine: True & Co., 1882), p. 596.

27. Brown, *Gentle Tamers*, p. 230.

28. Martha Canary, *Life and Adventures of Calamity Jane by Herself* (Livingstone, Mont.: Post Printing, n.d., circa 1896, 8 pages).

29. Annie Fern Swartwout, *Missie, an Historical Biography of Annie Oakley* (Blanchester, Ohio: Brown Co., 1947).

30. Mary Dart Thompson, *On the Plains and Among the Peaks* (Philadelphia: Claxton, Remson & Haffelfinger, 1879); Laura Winthrop Johnson, *800 Miles in an Ambulance* (Philadelphia: J. B. Lippincott Co., 1889); Luella Day, *The Tragedy of the Klondike* (New York, n.p., 1906).

31. Leon Stein and Annette K. Baxter, eds., *Lives to Remember* (New York: Arno Press, 1974), from A. J. McKelway, "Kate, The Good Angel of Oklahoma," *American Magazine*, Oct. 1908, p. 588.

32. Katz, *Eyewitness*, pp. 75, 77, 78.

33. *Ibid.*, pp. 76, 77.

34. William Loren Katz, *The Black West* (Garden City, N.Y.: Doubleday & Co., Anchor Books, 1973), pp. 155–6.

35. Nettie Elizabeth Mills (West), *The Lady Driller: Autobiography of Nettie Elizabeth Mills* (New York: Exposition Press, 1955).

36. In a 1974 untitled manuscript by Joe Glazer for Retail Clerks *Advocate*, p. 3, copy in library of Trade Union Women's Studies, Cornell University, 7 East 43rd Street, New York, N.Y.

37. Brown, *Gentle Tamers*, pp. 220, 221, quoting "Bill Nye's Experience; Tells What He Knows About Woman Suffrage," *Annals of Wyoming*, vol. 16 (1940), p. 66.

38. *Ibid.*, p. 219, and Grace Raymond Hebard, "The First Woman Jury," *Journal of American History*, Nov. 4, 1913, pp. 1302–4.

39. Hebard, "The First Woman Jury," p. 1313.

40. Brown, *Gentle Tamers*, pp. 214, 215.

41. *Ibid.*, p. 223.

42. Elizabeth Cady Stanton, Susan B. Anthony, Matilda Joslyn Gage, eds., *History of Woman Suffrage*, vol. 3, 1876–1855 (Rochester, N.Y.: Charles Mann Printing Co., 1866), p. 768.

43. Larson, "Women's Role," p. 7, quoting *The New Northwest* (which Duniway founded and edited) June 16, 1871, pp. 1, 7.

44. Abigail Scott Duniway, *Path Breaking: An Autobiographical History of the Equal Suffrage Movement in Pacific Coast States* (1914; reprinted, New York: Schocken Books, 1971), p. 10.

PART 5. Emergence of the
Trade Union Woman: *1900–1914*

Chapter 15. Working Women in the National
Women's Trade Union League: *1903–1914*

1. Allen Davis, "The Women's Trade Union League: Origins and Organization," *Labor History*, vol. 5, no. 1 (winter 1964), p. 14, quoting Samuel Gompers, March 24, 1905, speaking to the WTUL conference at the Berkley Lyceum in New York City.
2. Henry, *Women and the Labor Movement*, p. 113.
3. Mary Anderson (as told to Mary N. Winslow), *Woman at Work* (Minneapolis: University of Minnesota Press, 1951), p. 66.
4. *Ibid.*, pp. 66, 69, 75, 76.
5. *Ibid.*, pp. 81–3.
6. Mary Brown Sumner, "The Spirit of the Strikers," *Survey* Jan. 22, 1910, p. 551.
7. "Toward Better Working Conditions," from the 1909 Handbook of the Women's Trade Union League, p. 12.
8. Anderson, *Woman at Work*, pp. 46–7. Editorial for *Life and Labor*, July 1911.
9. *Proceedings*, Second Biennial Convention, National Women's Trade Union League of America, Chicago, Sept. 27–Oct. 1, 1909, inclusive, p. 20.
10. Henry, *Trade Union Woman*, p. 156.
11. *Report on Condition of Woman and Child Wage-Earners in the United States*, 19 vols. (Washington, D.C.: Government Printing Office, 1911).
12. Interview with the author, Jan. 3, 1976.
13. Letters from Leonora O'Reilly to Pauline Newman, Nov. 9, 1918; March 18, 1919; May 9, 1919; lent to the author by Pauline Newman and used with her permission.
14. *Proceedings*, Second Biennial Convention, National Women's Trade Union League, p. 21.
15. *Ibid.*, p. 21.
16. Ida Husted Harper, ed., *History of Woman Suffrage* (1922; reprint ed., New York: Arno Press, 1969), vol. 5, p. 352.
17. Anderson, *Woman at Work*, p. 26.
18. Rose Schneiderman (with Lucy Goldthwaite), *All For One* (New York: Paul S. Eriksson, 1967), pp. 120, 121.
19. *Proceedings*, Second Biennial Convention, National Women's Trade Union League, p. 28.
20. Robin Jacoby, "The Women's Trade Union League and American Feminism," paper presented at the Second Berkshire Conference on the History of Women, Radcliffe College, Oct. 27, 1974, p. 12, quoting *Life and Labor*, 1912.
21. Conversation with the author, Jan. 3, 1976.
22. Letter to Mrs. Upton from Mrs. M. A. Sherwood, July 15, 1912, Rose Schneiderman Letters, Collection 18, Box 1, Folder 2, Tamiment Library, New York University, New York, N.Y.
23. *Proceedings*, Fifth Biennial Convention, National Women's Trade Union League of America, New York City, June 7–12, 1915, inclusive, p. 38.
24. Helen Marot, *American Labor Unions* (New York: Henry Holt & Co., 1914), p. 77.
25. James Kenneally, "Women and Trade Unions, 1870–1920: The Quandary of the Reformer," *Labor History*, vol. 14, no. 1 (winter 1973), p. 48, quoting article by Samuel Gompers, "The Struggle in the Garment Trades—from Misery and Despondency to Betterment and Hope," *American Federalist*, Feb. 1913.
26. *Proceedings*, Second Biennial Convention, National Women's Trade Union League, p. 42.

27. *Proceedings*, Third Biennial Convention, National Women's Trade Union League of America, Boston, June 12–17, 1911, inclusive, p. 17.
28. Kenneally, "Women and Trade Unions," p. 52.
29. *Proceedings*, Fifth Biennial Convention, National Women's Trade Union League, pp. 71, 72.
30. Philip Foner, *Labor Movement in the U.S.*, vol. 3, p. 231, from *Union Labor Advocate*, May 1905.
31. Anderson, *Woman at Work*, pp. 65, 66.
32. Marot, *American Labor Unions*, p. 68.
33. Anderson, *Woman at Work*, p. 65.
34. Helen Marot to Rose Schneiderman, Aug. 25, 1910, Rose Schneiderman Letters, Collection 18, Box 1, Folder 1, Tamiment Library, New York University, New York, N.Y.
35. Schneiderman, *All For One*, pp. 110, 111.
36. Letter from Pauline Newman to Rose Schneiderman, quoted by Robin Jacoby, unpublished course notes, Women in Labor History, University of Michigan Summer School for Women Workers, 1974, p. 12. Used here with the permission of Pauline Newman.
37. *Proceedings*, Third Biennial Convention, National Women's Trade Union League, pp. 18, 30, 32.

Chapter 16. The Rise of the Woman Garment Worker:
New York, 1909–1910

1. Pauline Newman spoke to union women from Trade Union Women's Studies, a program of the New York State School of Industrial and Labor Relations, Cornell University, in March 1975, as part of a course on women in American labor history, taught by the author.
2. Louis Levine, *The Women's Garment Workers* (New York: B. W. Huebsch, 1924). I am indebted for much of the chronology on the early years of the ILGWU to this detailed account. See especially chaps. 15, 21, 22, and 23.
3. *Ibid.*, p. 45, quoting the New York Bureau of Labor Statistics report of 1890.
4. *Ibid.*, p. 52, quoting A. Rosenberg, *Memoirs of a Cloakmaker*, p. 25.
5. *Ibid.*, p. 54, quoting the contract.
6. Henry, *Trade Union Woman*, pp. 90, 91.
7. Levine, *Women's Garment Workers*, p. 151.
8. *Ibid.*, p. 154.
9. *Ibid.*
10. Pauline Newman, taped talk. See note 1.
11. Levine, *Women's Garment Workers*, p. 159.
12. Henry, *Trade Union Woman*, pp. 94, 95.
13. Levine, *Women's Garment Workers*, pp. 156, 157.
14. *Ibid.*, p. 157.
15. Mary Brown Sumner, "The Spirit of the Strikers," *Survey*, Jan. 22, 1910, p. 553.
16. As quoted in Meredith Tax's unpublished manuscript, "The Uprising of the Thirty Thousand: The Waistmakers General Strike of 1909–1910," 1973, p. 34; quoted from *Progressive Woman*, Feb. 1910, p. 6. Copy of this manuscript in the Materials Center, Trade Union Women's Studies, Cornell University, 7 East 43rd Street, New York, N.Y.
17. Pauline Newman, taped talk, see note 1.
18. Pamela Allen, "Living Labor Heroines," *Union Wage*, Jan.–Feb. 1975, p. 11. Ida Mayerson, now eighty-seven, lives in Mill Valley, California. She was interviewed by Pamela Allen in 1974.
19. Theresa Serber Malkiel, *The Diary of a Shirtwaist Striker* (New York: Cooperative Press, 1910), pp. 40, 41.
20. Tax, "The Uprising," p. 42.
21. Quoted by Herbert Aptheker in *History of the Negro People*, vol. 2, pp. 844, 845.
22. Pauline Newman, taped talk, see note 1.
23. "The Uprising of the 20,000," dedicated to the Waistmakers of 1909, *Everybody Sings* (New York: International Ladies' Garment Workers' Union, May 1942), p. 21.

24. Rose Greenstein, composition written at the Bryn Mawr Summer School for Women Workers, 1930.
25. "Dirge" by Morris Rosenfeld, written four days after the Triangle Waist Company fire, March 25, 1911. From Leon Stein, *The Triangle Fire* (Philadelphia: J. B. Lippincott Co., 1962), p. 145.
26. Stein, *Triangle Fire*, p. 20. It is impossible to describe the fire in a few short pages. By far the best account of it is that by Leon Stein, editor emeritus of ILGWU *Justice*, who painstakingly traced and interviewed survivors and witnesses of the fire. His book, in paperback, should be required reading for students of American history.
27. Stein, *Triangle Fire*, p. 143.
28. Schneiderman, *All for One*, pp. 100, 101. From the *New York* article on May 3, 1911 that carried her speech.
29. Frances Perkins, *The Roosevelt I Knew* (New York: Viking Press, 1946), pp. 17, 22.
30. Frances Perkins, speech at the Fiftieth Anniversary meeting commemorating the Triangle Fire.
31. Stein, *Triangle Fire*, p. 154.
32. *Ibid.*, p. 199.
33. *Ibid.*, pp. 205, 206.
34. *Ibid.*, p. 213.
35. *Ibid.*, p. 214.
36. Pauline Newman, taped talk, see note 1.
37. Levine, *Women's Garment Workers*, pp. 221, 222.

Chapter 17. Women in the Men's Clothing Trades: *A New Union, 1910–1914*

1. Butler, *Women and the Trades*, pp. 136, 137.
2. The 1905 figures used may be found in U.S. Senate Report on *Conditions of Women and Child Wage-Earners in the United States*, vol. 2 (1911), p. 14. These figures reflect 1900 census data, and it should be remembered that the industry grew between 1900 and 1910, so that by the time of the strike in 1910 between 35,000 and 40,000 workers walked out. For their interesting study on "The Role of Women in the Organization of the Men's Garment Trade in Chicago, 1910–1919: Jewish Working Women," I am indebted to Anne Bobroff and Miriam Cohen, whose History 772 paper dated May 5, 1972, came to my attention in time to be useful. A copy of this paper is in the Materials Center, Trade Union Women's Studies, Cornell University, 7 East 43rd Street, New York, N.Y.
3. Andrews and Bliss, *Women in Trade Unions*, p. 164.
4. *Ibid.*, p. 167.
5. Jane Julianelli, "Bessie Hillman: Up from the Sweatshop," *Ms.* Magazine, May 1973, p. 16.
6. Matthew Josephson, *Sidney Hillman, Statesman of American Labor* (Garden City, N.Y.: Doubleday & Co., 1952), p. 47.
7. *Ibid.*, p. 49.
8. *Proceedings,* Third Biennial Convention of the National Women's Trade Union League of America, Boston, June 12–17, 1911, p. 32.
9. Josephson, *Sidney Hillman*, p. 50.
10. *The Inheritance,* script by Millard Lampell, 50th Anniversary of the Amalgamated Clothing Workers of America, 1961, p. 38.
11. Josephson, *Sidney Hillman*, pp. 50–2.
12. *The Inheritance*, p. 40.
13. Anderson, *Woman at Work*, p. 41.
14. Josephson, *Sidney Hillman*, pp. 53–57; quotation on p. 57.
15. This was a slow process. For a detailed and fascinating account, see *ibid.*, pp. 59–85.
16. *Ibid.*, p. 96; letter from A. D. Marimpietri to Jacob S. Potofsky.
17. *Ibid.*, p. 100.

18. *Ibid.*, p. 110.
19. Archives of the Amalgamated Clothing Workers of America, "Resolution for a Woman Organizer," Dec. 22, 1914.
20. *The Advance*, Sept. 1, 1946, pp. 1–4, "In Memoriam, Dorothy J. Bellanca," General Executive Board Report to the ACWA Convention, 1948, pp. xx–xxii; James and James, eds., *Notable American Women*, vol. 1, pp. 124–6, article by Herbert Gutman.
21. Dorothy Jacobs, "The Convention—Woman Problem," address to the Third Biennial Convention of the ACWA, Baltimore, May 1918.
22. *The Advance*, Sept. 1, 1946, p. 3.
23. Josephson, *Sidney Hillman*, p. 132.
24. *The Advance*, Jan. 15, 1971, p. 3.
25. Summary Report, "Problems of Working Women," Industrial Union Department, AFL-CIO, conference held at the Mayflower Hotel, Washington, D.C., June 12–14, 1961, p. 50.
26. Henry, *Women and the Labor Movement*, pp. 83, 84.
27. *The Inheritance*, p. 47.

Chapter 18. Women of the Mills and Mines, *1900–1914*

1. Broadus Mitchell, "The Rise of Cotton Mills in the South," *Johns Hopkins University Studies in Historical and Political Science*, ser. 39, no. 2 (Baltimore: Johns Hopkins Press, 1921), p. 80.
2. Mrs. John Van Vorst and Marie Van Vorst, *The Woman Who Toils* (New York: Doubleday, Page & Co., 1903), pp. 278–9. The material in this section, unless otherwise specified, summarizes Marie Van Vorst's experiences as reported in chapters 7 and 9 of that book.
3. Michael A. Gordon, "The Labor Boycott in New York City," *Labor History* (New York, Tamiment Institute), vol. 16, no. 2 (spring 1975), p. 212, quoting *New York Times* Feb. 22, 1885, and *Irish World*, March 7, April 4, 1885.
4. Cahn, *Pictorial History of American Labor*, p. 194.
5. Mary Harris Jones, *Autobiography of Mother Jones*, ed. Mary Field Parton (Chicago: Charles H. Kerr, 1925), p. 119.
6. *Ibid.*, p. 123.
7. *Ibid.*, p. 126.
8. Elizabeth Janeway, ed., *Women: Their Changing Roles* (New York: Arno Press, 1973); obituary of Mother Jones, *New York Times*, Dec. 1, 1930 (p. 166).
9. Elizabeth Gurley Flynn, *I Speak My Own Piece* (New York: Massas & Mainstream, 1955), p. 80.
10. James and James, eds., *Notable American Women*, vol. 2, pp. 286–8, article by Irving Dilliard and Mary Sue Dilliard Schusky; Flynn, *I Speak My Own Piece*, pp. 80, 81.
11. Janeway, ed., *Women: Their Changing Roles*, Mother Jones obituary, pp. 166, 167.
12. Long, "Mother Jones," p. 6, quoting Howard B. Lee in *Bloodletting in West Virginia* (Morgantown: West Virginia University Press, 1969), p. 27.
13. Long, "Mother Jones," p. 5.
14. Merriam, *Growing Up Female*, p. 212.
15. Jones, *Autobiography*, p. 30.
16. Flynn, *I Speak My Own Piece*, pp. 80, 81.
17. Jones, *Autobiography*, p. 71.
18. *Ibid.*, pp. 73, 74.
19. *Ibid.*, pp. 76, 77.
20. *Ibid.*, p. 80.
21. Long, "Mother Jones," p. 33, quoting *New York Call*, Dec. 10, 1909.
22. Flynn, *I Speak My Own Piece*, pp. 175, 176.
23. Jones, *Autobiography*, p. 204.
24. Tom Tippett, in *Encyclopedia of the Social Sciences* (New York: Macmillan Co., 1932), vol. 8, p. 415.
25. Jones, *Autobiography*, p. 92.
26. *Ibid.*, introduction by Fred Thompson to paperback edition, Feb. 1972, p. xiv.

27. Edith Fowkes and Joe Glazer, eds., *Songs of Work and Freedom* (Chicago: Roosevelt University, 1960), pp. 58, 59.

Chapter 19. Women in the Industrial Workers of the World: *The Lawrence Strike, 1912*

1. Bill Cahn, *Mill Town* (New York: Cameron & Kahn, 1954), p. 210.
2. Joyce L. Kornbluh, ed., *Rebel Voices, an IWW Anthology* (Ann Arbor: University of Michigan Press, 1968), p. 1, Proceedings of the first IWW Convention, 1905. For an authoritative collection of key documents, writings, and songs of the Industrial Workers of the World, accompanied by informative, perceptive commentary, the reader is referred to this excellent work. Lovingly organized, the book is also liberally illustrated and fortunately is available in paperback as well as hardcover.
3. Foner, *Organized Labor and the Black Worker*, pp. 110, 111.
4. Chorus from "The Rebel Girl," Joe Hill, *Songs of the Workers*, 34th ed. (Chicago: Industrial Workers of the World, May 1, 1973), p. 39.
5. Flynn, *I Speak My Own Piece*, p. 34.
6. *Ibid.*, p. 46.
7. Melvyn Dubofsky, *We Shall Be All: A History of the IWW* (Chicago: Quadrangle Books, 1969), pp. 180, 181; quotation from B. H. Kizer, "Elizabeth Gurley Flynn," *Pacific Northwest Quarterly*, vol. 57 (July 1966), pp. 110–12.
8. Fred Thompson, *The I.W.W.—Its First Fifty Years, 1905–1955* (Chicago: Industrial Workers of the World, November 1955), p. 49.
9. Dubofsky, *We Shall Be All*, p. 181, quoting Kizer, p. 112.
10. *Ibid.*, p. 182.
11. Flynn, *I Speak My Own Piece*, pp. 120, 121.
12. James Oppenheim, "Bread and Roses," written to commemorate the women of the Lawrence textile workers' strike. In Fowkes and Glazer, eds., *Songs of Work and Protest*, p. 70.
13. Samuel Yellen, "The Great Lawrence Strike," in Samuel Colton, ed., *Sagas of Struggle* (New York: Claridge Publishing Corp., 1951), p. 81; Foner, *Labor Movement in the U.S.*, vol. 4, p. 309.
14. According to a report by U.S. Commissioner of Labor Charles O'Neil, almost one-third of the Lawrence millworkers earned less than $7 a week, but this figure and the one cited of $8.76 included supervisors' and foremen's salaries. The average wages of the pieceworkers was somewhat less, and Bill Haywood reports that the workers who conducted the strike averaged $6 a week in wages (*Bill Haywood's Book*, p. 247).
15. Flynn, *I Speak My Own Piece*, p. 117.
16. Kornbluh, *Rebel Voices*, p. 169, from an article by Justus Ebert, "The Industrial Democracy Arrives." Ebert had charge of publicity for the IWW Lawrence Defense Committee. His statistics come from the report on the Lawrence strike based on government hearings held in March 1912.
17. *Ibid.*, p. 169, quoting *New York Call*, Dec. 29, 1912.
18. Dubofsky, *We Shall Be All*, p. 235.
19. Kornbluh, *Rebel Voices*, p. 159.
20. O'Neill, *Everyone Was Brave*, p. 159.
21. *Ibid.*, pp. 159, 160.
22. Kornbluh, *Rebel Voices*, p. 160.
23. *Ibid.*, p. 158, quoting Ray Stannard Baker, "The Revolutionary Strike," *American Magazine*, May 1912, p. 24.
24. Haywood, *Bill Haywood's Book*, p. 251.
25. *Ibid.*, p. 254. Flynn, in *I Speak My Own Piece*, p. 118, refers to her as Anna La Pizza.
26. Kornbluh, *Rebel Voices*, p. 160.
27. Flynn, *I Speak My Own Piece*, p. 122.
28. Haywood, *Bill Haywood's Book*, p. 251.
29. *Ibid.*, p. 249.
30. Selig Perlman and Philip Taft, *History of Labor in the United States, 1896–1932* (1935; reprint ed., Clifton, N.J.: Augustus M. Kelley, 1966), p. 272.

31. Flynn, *I Speak My Own Piece*, p. 127.
32. Kornbluh, *Rebel Voices*, p. 161.
33. *Ibid.*, p. 162, from Hearings on the Strike at Lawrence, Massachusetts, 62nd Congress, 2nd Session, House Document no. 671, 1912.
34. Paul F. Brissenden, *The I.W.W.: A Study of American Syndicalism* (1919; reprint ed., New York: Russell & Russell, 1957), p. 319, quoting *Solidarity* Aug. 23, 1913.

Chapter 20. "In Unvanquishable Number . . ."

1. Foner, *Labor Movement in the U.S.*, vol. 4, p. 350.
2. *Wall Street Journal*, July 6, 1976, p. 31.

BIBLIOGRAPHY

One of the pleasures of preparing this bibliography has been the chance it affords to share with the reader those books that have been especially useful. It also offers the opportunity to suggest additional reading for those who wish to dig further. In this bibliographical section will be found:

A list of additional bibliographies to consult.

Books that I found particularly helpful in the areas of labor and economic history.

Books in the area of women in industry and in trade unions that were invaluable in writing this work.

A selected listing of works consulted in writing *We Were There*, arranged according to the five major parts of the book.

Suggestions for further reading. These follow the listings for each of the five parts mentioned above.

I have tried to report reprint editions wherever these exist. In most cases I have not listed books more than once. The earliest reference to a work in the chapter footnotes determines the section of the Bibliography where it will be found.

Suggested Bibliographies

The most extensive bibliography on women in labor history is that by Martha Jane Soltow, Carolyn Forche, and Murray Masare, *Women in American Labor History, 1825–1935: An Annotated Bibliography* (Lansing: Michigan State University, School of Labor and Industrial Relations, 1972). This comprehensive work includes sources of archival collections relating to women and labor. For a comprehensive general bibliography of works in labor history, organized by period, topic, and industry, see Maurice Neufeld, *A Representative Bibliography of American Labor History* (Ithaca: New York State School of Industrial and Labor Relations, Cornell University, 1964). For works on Native Americans, see the *Index to Literature on the American Indian* (San Francisco: Indian Historian Press, 1972). For an outstanding bibliography on black women, see *Black Women in the Cities, 1872–1975: A Bibliography of Published Works on the Life Achievements of Black Women in Cities in the United States*, 2nd ed., prepared by Lenwood Davis for the Council of Planning Librarians, Exchange Bibliography no. 751–752, February 1975. This includes additional bibliographies, government documents, books, periodicals, and an extensive list of articles from periodicals. A fine bibliography on black history can be found in August Meier and Elliott Rudwick, *From Plantation to Ghetto: History of the American Negro* (New York: Hill & Wang, 1966). For in-depth exploration of the subject of women in early America, see Eugenie Andruss Leonard, Sophie Hutchinson Drinker, and Miriam Young Holden, *The American Woman in Colonial and Revolutionary Times, 1565–1800* (Philadelphia: University of Pennsylvania Press, 1962), for an annotated syllabus of works covering this period.

Books on Labor and Economic History

Beard, Mary. *The American Labor Movement: A Short History*. New York: Macmillan Co., 1939. Reprint. New York: Arno Press, 1969.

Berky, Andrew S., and Shenton, James P. *The Historians' History of the United States*. 2 vols. New York Capricorn Books, 1972.

Commons, John R., and others, eds. *A Documentary History of American Industrial Society* (to 1896). 10 vols. Cleveland: A. H. Clark Co., 1910. Reprint. New York: Russell & Russell, 1958.

———. *History of Labor in the United States* [to 1896]. New York: Macmillan Co., 1918. Reprint. Clifton, N.J.: Augustus M. Kelley, 1966. Vols. 1 and 2.

Current, Richard N., Williams, T. Harry; and Friedel, Frank. *American History: A Survey*. 3rd ed. New York: Alfred A. Knopf, 1971. Vol. 1, to 1877.

Dulles, Foster Rhea. *Labor in America: A History*. 3rd ed. New York: Thomas Y. Crowell Co., 1966.

Foner, Philip. *The History of the Labor Movement in the United States*. 4 vols. New York: International Publishers Co., 1947–65.

———. *Organized Labor and the Black Worker, 1619–1973*. New York: Praeger Publishers, 1974.

Millis, Harry A., and Montgomery, Royal E. *Organized Labor*. New York, McGraw-Hill Book Co., 1945.

Pelling, Henry. *American Labor*. Chicago: University of Chicago Press, 1960.

Perlman, Selig, and Taft, Philip. *History of Labor in the United States, 1896–1932: Labor Movements*. New York: Macmillan Co., 1939. Reprint. Clifton, N.J.: Augustus M. Kelley, 1966.

Rayback, Joseph. *A History of American Labor*. New York: Free Press, 1966.

Taft, Philip. *Organized Labor in American History*. New York: Harper & Row, 1964.

Wright, Chester. *Economic History of the United States*. New York: McGraw-Hill Book Co., 1941.

Women in Industry and the Early Trade Unions

Abbott, Edith. *Women in Industry*. New York, D. Appleton & Co., 1910. Reprint. New York: Arno Press, 1969.

Andrews, John D., and Bliss, W. D. P. *History of Women in Trade Unions*. Bureau of Labor Report on Conditions of Woman and Child Wage Earners in the United States, vol. 10. Washington, D.C.: Government Printing Office, 1911. Reprint, New York: Arno Press, 1974.

Baker, Elizabeth Faulkner. *Technology and Woman's Work.* New York: Columbia University Press, 1964.

Henry, Alice. *The Trade Union Woman.* New York: D. Appleton & Co., 1915. Reprint. New York: Burt Franklin & Co., 1973.

———. *Women and the Labor Movement.* New York: George H. Doran Co., 1923. Reprint. New York: Arno Press, 1971.

Meyer, Annie Nathan. *Women's Work in America.* New York: Henry Holt & Co., 1891. Reprint. New York: Arno Press, 1972.

Sumner, Helen. *History of Women in Industry in the United States.* Bureau of Labor Report on Conditions of Woman and Child Wage-Earners in the United States, vol. 9. Washington, D.C.: Government Printing Office, 1910. Reprint. New York: Arno Press, 1974.

Wolfson, Theresa. *The Woman Worker and the Trade Unions.* New York: International Publishers Co., 1926.

The books by Andrews and Bliss and by Sumner are two of the nineteen-volume series that resulted from the United States Bureau of Labor study launched in 1907, due in part to the continual urging of the Women's Trade Union League. Fortunately, several of the volumes and a number of other books important in the field but formerly out of print have been reissued by the Arno Press.

Several more recent books on aspects of women's history have good chapters on the early attempts of women to organize and on the conditions of women workers.

Flexner, Eleanor. *Century of Struggle.* New York: Atheneum Publishers, 1970.

James, Edward T., and James, Janet W., eds., *Notable American Women, 1607–1950: A Biographical Dictionary.* 3 vols. Cambridge, Mass.: Belknap Press, 1971; paperback ed. 1974.

Lerner, Gerda, ed. *Black Women in White America: A Documentary History.* New York: Vintage Books, 1973.

———. *The Woman in American History.* Menlo Park, Calif.: Addison-Wesley Publishing Co., 1971.

O'Neill, William. *Everyone Was Brave.* Chicago: Quadrangle Books, 1971.

Sinclair, Andrew. *The Emancipation of the American Woman.* New York: Harper & Row, 1965.

Smuts, Robert. *Women and Work in America.* New York: Columbia University Press, 1959. Paperback ed. New York: Schocken Books, 1971.

Part 1. Two Centuries into the New World:
Chapters 1–4, 1600–1815

Mary Beard, *America Through Women's Eyes* (New York, Macmillan Co., 1933; reprint ed., Westport, Conn.: Greenwood Press, 1969), includes both selected letters and writings of American women and valuable commentary by

Beard. Daniel J. Boorstin, *The Americans: The Colonial Experience* (New York: Vintage Books, 1958), is a classic in the field, offering excellent in-depth material on the period, with some discussion of women's position in colonial America and extensive bibliographical suggestions. Abbot Emerson Smith, *Colonists in Bondage: White Servitude and Convict Labor in America, 1607–1776* (Chapel Hill: University of North Carolina Press, 1947; paperback ed., New York: W. W. Norton & Co., 1971), covers the field of indentured service, including that of women, and provides excellent bibliographical material. Julia Cherry Spruill, *Women's Life and Work in the Southern Colonies* (1938; paperback ed., New York: W. W. Norton & Co., 1972), is one of the best and most comprehensive books on Southern women of this period, and is unusually rich in references to original source materials.

Other Sources Consulted, Part 1

Adams, Charles Francis, ed. *Familiar Letters of John Adams and His Wife Abigail Adams During the Revolution.* Cambridge, Mass.: Houghton Mifflin & Co., 1875. Reprint. Plainview, N.Y.: Books for Libraries Press, 1971.

Allen, T. O., ed. *Arrows Four: Prose and Poetry by Young American Indians.* New York: Washington Square Press Pocket Books, 1974.

Astrov, Margot, ed. *The Winged Serpent: An Anthology of American Indian Prose and Poetry.* New York: John Day Co., 1946. Paperback ed. New York: Fawcett World Library, 1973.

Atwood, William Franklin. *The Pilgrim Story.* Plymouth, Mass.: Memorial Press, 1940, 1963.

Austin, Aleine. *The Labor Story.* New York: Coward-McCann, 1949.

Bayliss, John F. *Black Slave Narratives.* New York: Macmillan Co., Collier Books, 1970.

Bennett, Lerone, Jr. *Before the Mayflower: A History of the Negro in America 1619–1964.* Baltimore: Penguin Books, 1964.

Bishop, J. Leander. *A History of American Manufactures from 1608 to 1860.* Philadelphia: Edward Young & Co., 1864, 1868. Vols. 1 and 2, 1864 ed.; vol. 3, 1868 ed. Reprint. New York: Johnson Reprint Corp., 1968.

Blumenthal, Walter Hart. *Women Camp Followers of the American Revolution.* Philadelphia: MacManus Co., 1952. Reprint. New York: Arno Press, 1974.

Bradford, William. *History of Plimoth Plantation, 1606–1646.* New York: Charles Scribner's Sons, 1908. Reprint. New York: Barnes & Noble, 1959.

Brown, Judith K. "Economic Organization and the Position of Women Among the Iroquois." *Ethnohistory*, vol. 17, nos. 3–4 (Summer–Fall 1970), pp. 151–64.

Cahn, William. *A Pictorial History of American Labor.* New York: Crown Publishers, 1972.

Cott, Nancy, ed., *Root of Bitterness.* New York: E. P. Dutton & Co., 1972.

De Pauw, Linda Grant. *The Four Traditions.* Albany: New York State Bicentennial Committee, 1974.

Dexter, Elizabeth Anthony. *Colonial Women of Affairs: Women in Business and the Professions in America Before 1776.* 2nd rev. ed. Boston: Houghton Mifflin Co., 1931.

Dingwall, Eric John. *The American Woman, An Historical Study.* New York: Rinehart, 1957.

Earle, Alice Morse. *Colonial Dames and Good Wives.* New York: Frederick Ungar Publishing Co., 1962.

Foreman, Carolyn Thomas. *Indian Woman Chiefs.* Norman: University of Oklahoma Press, 1954.

Franklin, John Hope. *From Slavery to Freedom: A History of Negro Americans.* New York: Vintage Books, 1969.

Goldston, Robert. *The Negro Revolution from its African Genesis to the Death of Martin Luther King.* New York: Macmillan Co., 1968.

Grant, Joanne. *Black Protest.* Greenwich, Conn.: Fawcett Publications, 1968.

Green, Harry Clinton and Mary Wolcott. *The Pioneer Mothers of America: A Record of the More Notable Women of the Early Days of the Country & Particularly of the Colonial and Revolutionary Periods.* 3 vols. New York: G. P. Putnam, 1912.

Hechtlinger, Adelaide. "Women in Early America." *Early American Life,* vol. 4, no. 2 (April 1973), pp. 20–27, 37.

Holliday, Carl. *Woman's Life in Colonial Days.* Boston: Cornhill Publishing Co., 1922. Reprint. New York, Frederick Ungar Publishing Co., 1960.

Hughes, Langston, and Bontemps, Arna, eds. *The Poetry of the Negro, 1746–1970.* Rev. and updated ed. Garden City, N.Y.: Doubleday & Co., 1970.

Jernegan, Marcus Wilson. *The American Colonies, 1492–1750: A Study of their Political, Economic, and Social Development.* New York: Frederick Ungar Publishing Co., 1959.

Jordan, Winthrop. *White over Black: American Attitudes Toward the Negro, 1550–1812.* Baltimore: Pelican Books, 1969.

Katz, William Loren. *Eyewitness: The Negro in American History.* New York: Pitman Publishing Corp., 1968.

Lomax, Louis. *The Negro Revolt.* New York: New American Library, Signet Books, 1963.

Marshall, Ray. *The Negro Worker.* New York: Random House, 1967.

Meier, August, and Rudwick, Elliott, eds. *The Making of Black America.* vol. 1. New York: Atheneum Publishers, 1969.

Meltzer, Milton. *In Their Own Words: A History of the American Negro.* Vol. 1 (1619–1865). New York: Thomas Y. Crowell Co., 1964.

Merriam, Eve. *Growing Up Female in America: Ten Lives.* New York: Dell Publishing Co., 1971.

Mitchell, Broadus. "The Rise of Cotton Mills in the South." *Johns Hopkins University Studies in Historical and Political Science,* Series 39, no. 2, 1921.

Montgomery, David. "The Working Classes of the Pre-Industrial City." In *Urban America in Historical Perspective,* edited by Raymond Mohl and Neil Betten. New York: Weybright & Talley, 1970.

Moore, Frank. *Songs and Ballads of the American Revolution.* New York: D. Appleton & Co., 1855. Reprint. New York: Arno Press, 1969.

Quarles, Benjamin. *The Negro in the Making of America.* New York: Macmillan Co., Collier Books, 1969.

Readings in American History, '73–'74. Annual Editions. Guilford, Conn.: Dushkin Publishing Group, 1973.

Redding, J. Saunders. *They Came in Chains.* Rev. ed. Philadelphia: J. B. Lippincott Co., 1973.

Schlesinger, Arthur M. *New Viewpoints in American History.* New York: Macmillan Co., 1922.

Schnapper, M. B. *American Labor, A Pictorial Social History.* Washington, D.C.: Public Affairs Press, 1972.

Scott, Anne Firor, ed. *Women in American Life, Selected Readings.* Boston: Houghton Mifflin Co., 1970.

Skinner, Alanson B. *Indians of Greater New York.* Little Histories of North American Indians, No. 3. Cedar Rapids, Iowa: Torch Press, 1915.

Smith, Captain John. *History of Virginia.* Edited by David F. Hawke. Indianapolis: Bobbs-Merrill Co., 1975.

Smith, Page. *Daughters of the Promised Land: Women in American History.* Boston: Little, Brown & Co., 1970.

Summerfield, Arthur. *U.S. Mail.* New York: Holt, Rinehart & Winston, 1960.

Walsh, Reverend R. *Notices of Brazil in 1828 and 1829.* Vol. 2. London: Frederick Westley & A.H. Davis, 1830.

White, Anne Terry. *Indians and the Old West.* New York: Simon & Schuster, 1958.

Yost, Edna. *Famous American Pioneering Women from the Seventeenth Century to the Present.* New York: Dodd, Mead & Co., 1961.

Suggested Supplementary Reading, Part 1

Blumenthal, Walter Hart. *Brides from Bridewell: Female Felons Sent to Colonial America.* Rutland, Vt.: Charles B. Tuttle Co., 1962.

Brooks, Geraldine. *Dames and Daughters of Colonial Days.* New York: Thomas Y. Crowell Co., 1900. Reprint. New York: Arno Press, 1974.

Earle, Alice Morse. *Home Life in the Colonial Days.* New York: Macmillan Co., 1906. Paperback ed. Stockbridge, Mass.: Berkshire Traveller Press, 1974.

Ellet, Elizabeth F. *The Women of the American Revolution.* New York: Baker & Scribner, 1848. Reprint. New York: Haskell House Publishers, 1969. A domestic history of the American Revolution, which attempts to put back into history the story of the role women played during the war.

Greene, Lorenzo Johnston. *The Negro in Colonial New England, 1620–1776.* New York: Columbia University Press, 1942. Paperback ed. New York: Atheneum Publishers, 1968.

Marrott, Alice, and Rachlin, Carol. *American Epic, The Story of the American Indian.* New York: New American Library, Mentor Books, 1969.

Morgan, Edmund. *The Puritan Family*. New York: Harper & Row, 1966.

Noyes, Ethel J. *The Women of the Mayflower and Women of Plymouth Colony*. Plymouth, Mass.: Memorial Press, 1921. Reprint. Ann Arbor, Mich.: Gryphon Books, 1971.

Russell, John H. *The Free Negro in Virginia, 1619–1865*. Baltimore: Johns Hopkins Press, 1913. Paperback. New York: Dover Publications, 1969.

Terrell, John Upton and Donna M. *Indian Women of the Western Morning, Their Life in Early America*. New York: Dial Press, 1974. Includes a good bibliography on Native American women.

Wharton, Anne Hollingsworth. *Colonial Days and Dames*. Philadelphia: J. B. Lippincott Co., 1895.

Williams, Selma R. *Demeter's Daughters: The Women Who Founded America, 1587–1787*. New York: Atheneum Publishers, 1976.

Part 2. Working Women of the Nineteenth Century: Chapters 5–7, 1815–1861

For an illuminating view of women in the textile mills of Lowell, Massachusetts, before the Civil War, see Thomas Dublin, "Women, Work and Protest in the Early Lowell Mills: 'The Oppressing Hand of Avarice Would Enslave Us,'" *Labor History*, vol. 16, no. 1 (winter 1975), pp. 99–117. There is a wealth of good material on the nineteenth-century mill women, although more information is available on the women of Lowell, where the boarding-house plan was in effect, than on workers in mills that operated on the family system. The following four books I have found most useful, and each gives a different perspective. Hannah Josephson, *The Golden Threads: New England's Mill Girls and Magnates* (New York: Duell, Sloan & Pearce, 1949), is a classic study of the Lowell mills. Harriet H. Robinson, *Loom and Spindle or Life Among the Early Mill Girls* (New York: Thomas Y. Crowell Co., 1898; reprint ed., New York: Arno Press, 1974), presents a fascinating retrospective account of life in the mills. Caroline Ware, *The Early New England Cotton Manufacture* (Boston: Houghton Mifflin Co., 1931), discusses the industry throughout New England, including the impact of periodic recessions on the mill workers. Norman Ware, *The Industrial Worker, 1840–1860* (Boston: Houghton Mifflin Co., 1924; reprint ed., Chicago: Quadrangle Books, 1964), focuses on the family system in the mills in some detail, and relates the struggles of American workers, including mill workers, to organize during this period.

William Sanger, *The History of Prostitution: Its Extent, Causes and Effects Throughout the World* (New York: Harper & Bros., 1859), reports on one of the first systematic attempts to look at the causes and consequences of prostitution. For a discussion of working women in a variety of occupations, see Annie Marion MacClean, *Wage-Earning Women* (New York: Macmillan Co., 1910; reprint ed., New York: Arno Press, 1974).

A number of excellent works on black Americans during the antebellum period are available. Among those I found particularly helpful are:

Bennett, Lerone, Jr. *Pioneers in Protest.* Baltimore: Penguin Books, 1968. An excellent treatment of Harriet Tubman and Sojourner Truth.

Douglass, Frederick. *Narrative of the Life of Frederick Douglass, An American Slave.* 1845. Paperback ed. New York: New American Library, Signet Books, 1968.

Frazier, E. Franklin. *The Negro Family in the United States.* Chicago: University of Chicago Press, 1948, 1969.

Grandy, Moses. *Narrative of the Life of Moses Grandy; late a Slave in the United States of America.* In *Five Slave Narratives: A Compendium.* Boston: O. Johnson, 1844. Reprint. New York: Arno Press, 1968.

Meier, August, and Rudwick, Elliott. *From Plantation to Ghetto.* New York: Hill & Wang, 1966.

Quarles, Benjamin. *The Negro in the Making of America.* New York: Macmillan Co., Collier Books, 1964.

Starobin, Robert S. *Industrial Slavery in the Old South.* New York: Oxford University Press, 1970. Starobin details the role of slaves, including women slaves, as workers in industry, an aspect of slavery not covered at any length in other books on the subject.

Wade, Richard. "Slavery in the Cities." In *Urban America in Historical Perspective,* edited by Raymond Mohl and Neil Betten. New York: Weybright & Talley, 1970.

Other Sources Consulted, Part 2

Aptheker, Herbert. *American Negro Slave Revolts.* New York: Columbia University Press, 1943. Reprint. New York: International Publishers, 1969.

———. *A Documentary History of the Negro People in the United States.* Vol. 1. New York: Citadel Press, 1967.

Berlin, Ira. *Slaves Without Masters: The Free Negro in the Antebellum South.* New York: Pantheon Books, 1974.

Brooks, Thomas. *Toil and Trouble.* Rev. ed. New York: Delacorte Press, 1971.

Commager, Henry Steele, ed. *Documents of American History.* 8th ed. New York: Appleton-Century-Crofts, 1968.

Cooke, Alistair. *Alistair Cooke's America.* New York: Alfred A. Knopf, 1974.

Davis, Almond H. *The Female Preacher, or, Memoir of Salome Lincoln.* Providence: Elder J. S. Mowry, at bookstore of I. Wilcox, 1843. Reprint. New York: Arno Press, 1972.

Delzell, Ruth. *Articles on the Early History of Women Trade Unionists of America.* Chicago: National Women's Trade Union League, 1915. Reprinted from *Life and Labor,* 1912–1914.

Eaton, Clement. *The Growth of Southern Civilization 1790–1860.* New York: Harper & Row, 1961.

Faber, Doris. *Petticoat Politics: How American Women Won the Right to Vote.* New York: Lothrop, Lee & Shepard Co., 1967.

Genovese, Eugene D. *Roll, Jordan, Roll: The World the Slaves Made.* New York: Pantheon Books, 1974.

Greenway, John. *American Folksongs of Protest.* New York: Perpetua Books, 1960.

Larcom, Lucy. *A New England Girlhood, Outlined from Memory.* Boston: Houghton Mifflin Co., 1889. Reprint. New York: Arno Press, 1974.

Lerner, Gerda. "The Lady and the Mill Girl: Changes in the Status of Women in the Age of Jackson." *Midcontinent American Studies,* vol. X, no. 1 (spring 1969), pp. 5–15.

Martineau, Harriet. *Society in America.* Edited, abridged, and with an introduction by Martin Lipset. Gloucester, Mass.: Peter Smith, 1962.

O'Neil, Elizabeth. "Rebel Girls and Union Maids." *Lithopinion,* no. 21 (spring 1971), pp. 56–63.

Petry, Ann. *Harriet Tubman, Conductor on the Underground Railroad.* New York: Pocket Books, 1971.

Seidman, Joel. *The Needle Trades.* New York: Farrar & Rinehart, 1942. Reprint. New York: Johnson Reprint Corp., 1970.

Starobin, Robert S. *Blacks in Bondage: Letters of American Slaves.* New York: Franklin Watts, New Viewpoints, 1974.

Taylor, George Rogers. *The Economic History of the United States.* Vol. 4. *The Transportation Revolution: Industry 1815–1860.* New York: Holt, Rinehart & Winston, 1951.

Suggested Supplementary Reading, Part 2

Brent, Linda. *Incidents in the Life of a Slave Girl.* Boston: published by author, 1861. Paperback ed. New York: Harcourt Brace Jovanovich, 1973.

Browne, Martha. *Autobiography of a Female Slave.* New York: Redfield, 1857. Reprint. Negro Universities Press, 1969.

Ellet, Elizabeth. *The Pioneer Women of the West.* New York: Charles Scribner's Sons, 1852. Reprint. Plainview, N.Y.: Books for Libraries Press, 1973.

James, Bessie Rowland. *Anne Royall's USA.* New Brunswick, N.J.: Rutgers University Press, 1972. This crusading journalist figured prominently during the years 1831–1854.

Lerner, Gerda. *The Grimké Sisters from North Carolina.* Boston: Houghton Mifflin, 1967.

Lutz, Alma. *Crusade for Freedom: Women of the Anti-Slavery Movement.* Boston: Beacon Press, 1968.

Still, William. *Underground Railroad.* Philadelphia: Porter & Coates, 1872. Reprint. New York: Arno Press, 1968.

Tannenbaum, Frank. *Slave and Citizen: The Negro in the Americas.* New York, Alfred A. Knopf, 1947. Paperback ed. New York: Vintage Books, 1970.

Whitton, Mary Ormsbee. *These Were the Women: USA 1776–1860*. New York: Hastings House, 1954.

Part 3. Working Women in War and Peace:
Chapters 8–10, 1861–1886

In addition to the general works cited earlier, I found the following provided especially useful material on the Civil War period: Horan, James D. *Desperate Women*. New York: G. P. Putnam's Sons, 1952. McPherson, James M. *The Negro's Civil War*. New York: Vintage Books, 1967. Ortiz, Victoria, *Sojourner Truth, A Self Made Woman*. Philadelphia: J. B. Lippincott Co., 1974. Wiley, Bell Irvin. *Southern Negroes, 1861–1865*. New Haven, Conn: Yale Historical Publications, 1938. Reprint. Yale University Press, 1965. Young, Agatha. *The Women and the Crisis: Women of the North in the Civil War*. New York: McDowell, Obolensky, 1959.

On the Reconstruction period, John Hope Franklin, *Reconstruction After the Civil War* (Chicago: University of Chicago Press, 1961), was most helpful, as was the work edited by Stanley Feldstein and Lawrence Costello, *The Ordeal of Assimilation: A Documentary History of the White Working Class, 1830's to the 1970's* (Garden City, N.Y.: Doubleday & Co., Anchor Books, 1974), for its material on immigrant workers and life in the cities. For additional material on labor organization during this period, especially the Knights of Labor, see Norman Ware, *The Labor Movement in the United States, 1860–1895* (New York: D. Appleton-Century Co., 1929; reprint ed., Gloucester, Mass.: Peter Smith, 1959), and John Bracey, August Meier, and Elliott Rudwick, *Black Workers and Organized Labor* (Belmont, Calif.: Wadsworth Publishing Co., 1971).

Other Sources Consulted, Part 3

Bullough, Vern L., and Bullough, Bonnie. *The Subordinate Sex: A History of Attitudes Toward Women*. Baltimore: Penguin Books, 1974.

Foner, Philip. *American Labor Songs of the Nineteenth Century*. Urbana: University of Illinois Press, 1975.

Gompers, Samuel. *Seventy Years of Life and Labor*. 1 vol. Introduction by Matthew Woll. New York: E. P. Dutton & Co., 1943.

Kugler, Israel. "The Woman's Rights Movement and the National Labor Union (1866–1872)." Unpublished Ph.D. thesis, New York University School of Education, 1954.

Lawrence, Ken. "Mississippi's First Labor Union." Tougaloo, Miss · Deep South People's History Project, Freedom Information Service, 1974.

Lebergott, Stanley. *Manpower in Economic Growth: The American Record Since 1800*. New York: McGraw-Hill Book Co., 1964.

Litwack, Leon. *The American Labor Movement*. Englewood Cliffs, N.J.: Prentice-Hall, 1962.

Luder, Hope Elizabeth. *Women and Quakerism*. Pendle Hill Pamphlet no. 196, August 1974.

Lutz, Alma. *Susan B. Anthony: Rebel, Crusader, Humanitarian*. Boston: Beacon Press, 1959.

Massey, Mary Elizabeth. *Bonnet Brigades*. New York: Alfred A. Knopf, 1966.

McCabe, James D., Jr. *Lights and Shadows of New York Life*. Philadelphia: National Publishing Co., 1872. Reprint. New York: Farrar, Straus & Giroux, 1972.

Meltzer, Milton. *Bread—and Roses*. New York: Alfred A. Knopf, 1967.

Montgomery, David. *Beyond Equality: Labor and the Radical Republicans, 1862–1872*. New York: Alfred A. Knopf, 1967.

Morison, Samuel Eliot; Commager, Henry Steele; and Leuchtenburg, William E. *The Growth of the American Republic*. 6th ed. Vol. 1. New York: Oxford University Press, 1969.

Silvia, Philip T., Jr. "The Position of Workers in a Textile Community: Fall River in the Early 1880's." *Labor History*, vol. 16, no. 2 (spring 1975), pp. 230–49.

Sinclair, Upton, ed. *The Cry for Justice: An Anthology of the Literature of Social Protest*. New York: Upton Sinclair, 1915. Reprint. Clifton, N.J.: Augustus M. Kelley, 1971.

Sochen, June. *Herstory: A Woman's View of American History*. New York: Alfred Publishing Co., 1974.

Suggested Supplementary Reading, Part 3

Alcott, Louisa May. *Hospital Sketches*. Boston: Redpath, 1863. Reprint. New York: Sagamore Press, 1957.

Cumming, Kate. *The Journal of a Confederate Nurse*. Edited by Richard Barksdale Harwell. Louisville, Ky.: J. P. Morton, 1866. Reprint. Baton Rouge: Louisiana State University Press, 1959.

Edmundson, Sarah Emma. *Nurse and Spy in the Union Army: Comprising the Adventures and Experiences of a Woman in Hospitals, Camps and Battle-Fields*. Hartford, Conn.: W. S. Williams, 1865.

Handlin, Oscar, ed. *Immigration as a Factor in American History*. Englewood Cliffs, N.J.: Prentice-Hall, 1959.

Haviland, Laura S. *A Woman's Life-Work: Labors and Experiences of Laura S. Haviland*. Cincinnati: Walden & Stowe, 1884. Reprint. New York: Arno Press, 1969.

Livermore, Mary Ashton. *The Story of My Life; or, The Sunshine and Shadow of Seventy Years*. Hartford, Conn.: A. D. Worthington & Co., 1897. Reprint. New York: Arno Press, 1974.

Lockwood, Rev. Lewis. *Mary S. Peake, First Missionary to the Freedmen at Fortress Monroe, 1862*. Boston: American Tract Society, 1863. Forten, Charlotte, *Life on the Sea Islands*. *Atlantic Magazine*, May–June, 1864. Reprinted together in *Two Black Teachers During the Civil War*. New York: Arno Press, 1969.

Penny, Virginia. *Employment of Women: An Encyclopedia of Woman's Work.* Boston: Wacher, Wise & Co., 1863.

————. *Think and Act: A Series of Articles Pertaining to Men and Women, Work and Wages.* Philadelphia: Claxton, Remsen & Haffelfinger, 1869. Reprint. New York: Arno Press, 1971.

Swint, Henry Lee. *The Northern Teacher in the South, 1862–1870.* Nashville, Tenn.: Vanderbilt University Press, 1941. Reprint. New York: Octagon Books, 1967.

Taylor, Susie King. *Reminiscences of My Life in Camp with the 33rd United States Colored Troops.* Boston: published by author, 1902. Reprint. New York: Arno Press, 1968.

Titus, Frances W. *Sojourner Truth, A Bondswoman of Olden Time: Narrative and Book of Life.* 1875. Reprint. Chicago: Johnson Publishing Co., 1970.

Part 4. The Wage-Earning Woman:
Chapters 11–14, 1886–1905

There are a number of excellent books on wage-earning women that cover this period. The Progressive Era sparked studies such as those of the Russell Sage Foundation, several of which have been particularly helpful. This was the period, too, when women identifying with wage-earning women took working-class jobs and wrote about the conditions they encountered. The net result is a wealth of information about the lives of women in a broad range of occupations, all of them low-paid, at the turn of the century. Of special value I have found:

Butler, Elizabeth Beardsley. *Saleswomen in Mercantile Stores, Baltimore, 1909.* New York: Charities Publication Committee, 1912.

————. *Women and the Trades, Pittsburgh, 1907–1908.* New York: Charities Publication Committee, 1911. Reprint. New York: Arno Press, 1969.

Campbell, Helen. *Women Wage-Earners: Their Past, Their Present, and Their Future.* Boston: Roberts Brothers, 1893. Reprint. New York: Arno Press, 1972.

Richardson, Dorothy. *The Long Day: Story of a New York Working Girl.* 1905. Reprint. Chicago: Quadrangle Books, 1972.

————. "Trades-Unions in Petticoats: What the Women Who Work in Chicago Have Done and Are Doing for Themselves Through Their Own Unions." *Leslie's Monthly Magazine,* March 1904. Courtesy of the Chicago Historical Society.

Solomon, Benjamin. "Early Movements of Unionization Among Salaried Employees." White Collar Research Project, unpublished, University of Chicago Industrial Relations Center, 1969. Copy available at Trade Union Women's Studies, Cornell University, 7 East 43 Street, NYC, 10017.

Stein, Leon, and Taft, Philip, eds. *Workers Speak: Self-Portraits.* New York: Arno Press, 1971. A collection of pieces originally published in *The Independent* between 1902 and 1906.

Van Kleeck, Mary. *Artificial Flower Makers*. New York: Survey Associates, 1913.

———. *Wages in the Millinery Trade*. Albany, N.Y.: J. B. Lyon Co., 1914.

———. *Women in the Book Binding Trade*. New York: Survey Associates, 1913.

Van Vorst, Mrs. John, and Van Vorst, Marie. *The Woman Who Toils*. New York, Doubleday, Page & Co., 1903.

The material available on the westward migration during the nineteenth century is splendid. I have chosen only seven of the most useful titles to list here. Additional works will be found among the other sources consulted, and supplementary-reading suggestions are made for those interested in further information on frontier women.

Brown, Dee. *Gentle Tamers: Women of the Old Wild West*. New York: Bantam Books, 1974.

Duniway, Abigail Scott. *Path Breaking: An Autobiographical History of the Equal Suffrage Movement in Pacific Coast States*. 1914. Reprint. New York: Schocken Books, 1971.

Gridley, Marion F. *American Indian Women*. New York: Hawthorn Books, 1974.

Larson, T. A. "Women's Role in the American West." *Montana, The Magazine of Western History*, vol. 24, no. 3 (Summer 1974), pp. 3–11.

Shaw, Anna Howard. *The Story of a Pioneer*. New York: Harper & Bros., 1915. Reprint. Millwood, N.Y.: Kraus Reprint Co., 1970.

Sprague, William Forrest. *Women and the West, A Short Social History*. Boston: Christopher Publishing House, 1940. Reprint. New York: Arno Press, 1972.

Wissler, Clark. *Indians of the United States*. Garden City, N.Y.: Doubleday & Co., 1966.

Other Sources Consulted, Part 4

Bettmann, Otto L. *The Good Old Days—They were Terrible!* New York: Random House, 1974.

Brooks, Thomas. *Toward Dignity*. New York: United Federation of Teachers, 1967.

Campbell, Helen. *Prisoners of Poverty: Women Wage-Workers, Their Trades and Their Lives*. Cambridge, Mass.: John Wilson & Son, 1887. Reprint. Westport, Conn.: Greenwood Press, 1970.

Cooper, Gary. "Stagecoach Mary." *Ebony*, vol. 14 (Oct. 1959), pp. 97–100.

Davies, Margery. "Woman's Place Is at the Typewriter." *Radical America*, vol. 8, no. 4 (July–August 1974), pp. 1–25.

Day, Luella. *The Tragedy of the Klondike*. New York: n.p., 1906.

DeVoto, Bernard, ed. *The Journals of Lewis and Clark*. Boston, Houghton Mifflin Co., 1963.

Donovan, Frances R. *The Saleslady*. Chicago: University of Chicago Press, 1929. Reprint. New York: Arno Press, 1974.

DuBois, W. E. B. *The Souls of Black Folk*. Chicago: McClurg, 1903. Reprint. New York: New American Library, 1969.

Ducatte, Nancy. "The Shirt and Collar Industry and Kate Mullaney." Undated paper, Troy, N.Y., 7 pages.

Farnham, Eliza. *Life in Prairie Land*. New York: Harper & Bros., 1846. Reprint. New York: Arno Press, 1972.

Gilman, Charlotte Perkins. *Women and Economics*. Boston: Small, Maynard & Co., 1898–1899. Reprint. Cincinnati: Collectors Editions, 1970.

Gordon, Michael A. "The Labor Boycott in New York City." *Labor History*, vol. 16, no. 2 (spring 1975), pp. 184–230.

Greeley, Horace. "The Plains as I Crossed Them Ten Years Ago." *Harper's Magazine*, vol. 38, no. 228 (May 1869), pp. 789–95.

Green, Annie Marie. *Sixteen Years of the Great American Desert*. Titusville, Pa.: F. W. Truesdell, 1887.

Hebard, Grace. "The First Woman Jury." *Journal of American History*, vol. 17 (Nov. 4, 1913), pp. 1293–1341.

Herron, Belva Mary. "The Progress of Labor Organization among Women, Together with Some Considerations Concerning their Place in Industry." *University Studies* (University of Illinois), vol. 1, no. 10 (May 1905).

Hooks, Janet. *Women's Occupations Through Seven Decades*. Women's Bureau Bulletin no. 218. Washington, D.C.: U.S. Department of Labor, 1947.

Johnson, Laura Winthrop. *800 Miles in an Ambulance*. Philadelphia: J. B. Lippincott Co., 1889. Autobiography of a woman ambulance driver.

Josephson, Matthew. *Union House, Union Bar*. New York: Random House, 1956.

Katz, William Loren. *The Black West*. Garden City, N.Y., Doubleday & Co., Anchor Books, 1973.

Ketchum, Richard, and others. *The American Heritage Book of the Pioneer Spirit*. New York: American Heritage Publishing Co., 1959.

Kirstein, George G. *Stores and Unions, A Study of the Growth of Unionism in Dry Goods and Department Stores*. New York: Fairchild Publications, 1950.

Mills, Nettie Elizabeth. *The Lady Driller: Autobiography of Nettie Elizabeth Mills*. New York: Exposition Press, 1955.

Rhine, Alice Hyneman. "Women in Industry." In Annie Nathan Meyer, ed. *Women's Work in America*. New York: Henry Holt & Co., 1891. Reprint. New York: Arno Press, 1972. Pp. 276–322.

Riis, Jacob A. *How the Other Half Lives*. New York: Charles Scribner's, 1890. Reprint. New York: Sagamore Press, 1957.

Sandburg, Carl. *Complete Poems*. New York: Harcourt, Brace & World, 1950.

Scharman, Ralph. "Elizabeth Morgan, Crusader for Labor Reform." *Labor History*, vol. 14, no. 3 (summer 1973), pp. 340–51.

Sherr, Lynn, and Kazickas, Jurate. "Maud Younger, Millionaire Waitress." *MS* magazine, vol. 1, no. 7 (Jan. 1973), pp. 12, 14–15.

Sinclair, Upton. *The Jungle.* New York: Doubleday, Page & Co., 1906. Reprint. New York: New American Library, 1960.

Stanton, Elizabeth Cady; Anthony, Susan B.; and Gage, Matilda Joslyn, eds. *History of Woman Suffrage.* Vol. 3, 1876–1885. Rochester, N.Y.: Charles Mann Printing Co., 1886. Reprint. New York: Arno Press, 1969.

Stein, Leon, and Baxter, Annette K., eds. *Lives to Remember: An Original Anthology.* New York: Arno Press, 1974.

Swartwout, Annie Fern. *Missie: An Historical Biography of Annie Oakley.* Blanchester, Ohio: Brown Co., 1947.

Taft, Philip. *United They Teach: The Story of the United Federation of Teachers.* Los Angeles: Nash Publishers, 1974.

Thompson, Mary Dart. *On the Plains and Among the Peaks.* Philadelphia: Claxton, Remson & Haffelfinger, 1879.

Wright, Carroll D. *The Working Girls of Boston.* Boston: Wright & Potter, 1889. From the 15th Annual Report of the Massachusetts Bureau of Statistics of Labor for 1884. Reprint. New York: Arno Press, 1969.

Suggested Supplementary Reading, Part 4

Adelman, William. *Touring Pullman.* Chicago: Illinois Labor History Society, 1972. Good, brief account of the Pullman strike, including the role of Jennie Curtis, Pullman Company worker.

Ames, Azel. *Sex in Industry: A Plea for the Working Girl.* Boston: J. R. Osgood & Co., 1875.

Carwardine, Rev. William H. *The Pullman Strike.* 1894. Reprint. Chicago: Charles H. Kerr & Co., 1973.

Collins, Elizabeth. *The Cattle Queen of Montana.* Spokane, Wash.: Dyer Printing Co., 1914. Autobiography of a woman who mined in New Mexico, was captured by Indians, ranched in Montana, and visited Alaska.

Cuzneau, Jane. *Eagle Pass; or Life on the Border.* New York: George Putnam & Co., 1852. Critical treatise on treatment of Indians, blacks; describes the peonage system on the Texas-Mexico border.

Everett, Dick. *The Sod House Frontier.* Lincoln, Neb.: Johnsen Publishers, 1954.

Hopkins, Sarah Winnemucca. *Life Among the Piutes: Their Wrongs and Claims.* Edited by Mrs. Horace Mann. Boston: for sale by Cupples, Upham, 1883.

Lindsey, Almont. *The Pullman Strike.* Chicago: University of Chicago Press, 1942, 1971.

Marshall, Ann James. *The Autobiography of Mrs. A. J. Marshall, Age 84 Years.* Pine Bluff, Ark.: Adams-Wilson Printing Co., 1897. The story of a frontier teacher.

Nathan, Maud. *The Story of an Epoch Making Movement.* New York: Doubleday, Page & Co., 1926. A history of the Consumers' League.

Ross, Isabel. *Ladies of the Press: The Story of Women in Journalism by an*

Insider. New York: Harper & Bros., 1936. Reprint. New York: Arno Press, 1974.

Ross, Nancy Wilson. *Westward the Women.* New York: Random House, 1944. Reprint. Plainview, N.Y.: Books for Libraries Press, 1975.

Tarbell, Ida. *All in the Day's Work: Autobiography.* New York: Macmillan Co., 1939.

Towle, Virginia Rowe. *Vigilante Women.* New York: A. S. Barnes & Co., 1966. Seven pioneer women of Montana, 1863–1864.

Wells, Ida B. *Crusader for Justice: The Autobiography of Ida B. Wells.* Edited by Alfreda M. Duster. Chicago: University of Chicago Press, 1970.

Yellen, Samuel. *American Labor Struggles.* New York: Harcourt, Brace & Co., 1936. Reprint. New York: Arno Press, 1969. Accounts of the railroad strike of 1877; Haymarket, 1886; Homestead strike of 1892; Pullman strike of 1894.

Young, Ann Elizabeth. *Wife No. 19.* Hartford, Conn.: Dustin, Gilman & Co., 1896. Reprint. New York: Arno Press, 1974. Brigham Young's nineteenth wife changed her mind about Mormonism and lectured against polygamy.

Part 5. Emergence of the Trade Union Woman: Chapters 15–20, 1900–1914

The material available to the student of this period in women's labor history is rich, in part because of the records kept by the National Women's Trade Union League, in part because a number of women activists wrote autobiographies that supplement the standard histories of the time. The books below only begin to illustrate the available literature.

Anderson, Mary, as told to Mary N. Winslow. *Woman at Work.* Minneapolis: University of Minnesota Press, 1951. Reprint. Westport, Conn.: Greenwood Press, 1973.

Brissenden, Paul. *The I.W.W.: A Study of American Syndicalism.* New York: Columbia University Press, 1919. Reprint. New York: Russell & Russell, 1957.

Davis, Allen. "The Women's Trade Union League: Origins and Organization." *Labor History,* vol. 5, no. 1 (winter 1964), pp. 3–17.

Dubofsky, Melvyn. *We Shall Be All: A History of the IWW.* Chicago: Quadrangle Books, 1969.

Fetherling, Dale. *Mother Jones: The Miners' Angel.* Carbondale: Southern Illinois University Press, 1974.

Flynn, Elizabeth Gurley. *I Speak My Own Piece.* New York: Masses & Mainstream, 1955. Reprinted as *The Rebel Girl.* New York: International Publishers Co., 1973.

Haywood, William D. *Bill Haywood's Book.* New York: International Publishers Co., 1929.

Jones, Mary Harris. *Autobiography of Mother Jones.* Edited by Mary Field

Parton. Chicago: Charles Kerr, 1925. Reprint. Chicago: Illinois Labor Historical Society, 1972.

Kornbluh, Joyce L., ed. *Rebel Voices: An IWW Anthology.* Ann Arbor: University of Michigan Press, 1968.

Lorwin, Louis (Levine). *The Women's Garment Workers.* New York: B. W. Huebsch, 1924. Reprint. New York: Arno Press, 1969.

National Women's Trade Union League of America. *Proceedings, Biennial Conventions 1909, 1911.* Chicago: National Women's Trade Union League, 1909, 1911.

Schneiderman, Rose, with Lucy Goldthwaite. *All For One.* New York: Paul S. Eriksson, 1967.

Stein, Leon. *The Triangle Fire.* Philadelphia: J. B. Lippincott Co., 1962.

Women's Bureau, U.S. Department of Labor. *Toward Better Working Conditions for Women, Methods and Policies of the National Women's Trade Union League of America.* Bulletin no. 252. Washington, D.C.: Government Printing Office, 1953.

Other Sources Consulted, Part 5

Abramowitz, Mimi. "The Effects of Early Protective Labor Laws on Women Industrial Workers, 1890–1920." Unpublished paper, Dec. 18, 1973, Columbia School for Social Work. Copy in library of Trade Union Women's Studies, Cornell University, 7 East 43rd Street, New York, N.Y.

The Advance, newspaper of the Amalgamated Clothing Workers of America, Sept. 1, 1946, pp. 1–4.

Amalgamated Clothing Workers of America. *Documentary History of the ACWA, 1914–1916.* New York: Amalgamated Clothing Workers of America, May 1, 1920.

———. *The Inheritance.* Script by Millard Lampell. New York: Amalgamated Clothing Workers of America, 1964.

AFL-CIO Industrial Union Department. *Summary Report,* "Problems of Working Women." Conference, June 12–14, 1961. Washington, D.C.: Industrial Union Department, AFL-CIO, 1961.

Aptheker, Herbert. *A Documentary History of the Negro People in the United States.* Vol. 2. New York: Citadel Press, 1951, 1967.

Cahn, Bill. *Mill Town.* New York: Cameron & Kahn, 1954.

Colton, Sam. *Sagas of Struggle.* New York: Claridge Publishing Corp., 1951.

Conlin, Joseph Robert. *Bread and Roses Too: Studies of the Wobblies.* Westport, Conn.: Greenwood Press, 1969.

Fowkes, Edith, and Glazer, Joe. *Songs of Work and Freedom.* Chicago: Roosevelt University, 1960.

Ginzburg, Eli, and Berman, Hyman. *The American Worker in the Twentieth Century.* Glencoe, Ill.: Free Press, 1963.

Green, Archie. "The Death of Mother Jones." *Labor History,* vol. 1, no. 1 (winter 1960), pp. 68–80.

Hoxie, Robert Franklin. *Trade Unionism in the United States.* New York: D. Appleton & Co., 1917. Reprint. New York: Russell & Russell, 1966.

———. "The Truth about the IWW." *Journal of Political Economy,* vol. 21 (Nov. 1913), pp. 785–97.

Jacoby, Robin. "The Women's Trade Union League and American Feminism." Paper presented at the Second Berkshire Conference on the History of Women, Radcliffe College, Oct. 27, 1974. Copy in Library, Trade Union Women's Studies, Cornell University, 7 East 43rd Street, New York, N.Y.

Elizabeth Janeway, ed., *Women: Their Changing Roles.* New York: Arno Press, 1973.

Josephson, Matthew. *Sidney Hillman: Statesman of American Labor.* Garden City, N.Y., Doubleday & Co., 1952.

Kelley, Florence. "Industrial Democracy: Women in Trade Unions." *Outlook,* Dec. 15, 1906, pp. 926–31.

———. *Modern Industry in Relation to the Family, Health, Education, Morality.* New York: Longmans, Green & Co., 1914.

Kenneally, James. "Women and Trade Unions, 1870–1920: The Quandary of the Reformer." *Labor History,* vol. 14, no. 1 (winter 1973), pp. 42–55.

Kraditor, Aileen S., ed. *Up from the Pedestal: Selected Writings in the History of Feminism.* Chicago: Quadrangle Books, 1968.

Long, Priscilla. "Mother Jones, Woman Organizer, and her Relations with the Wives of Workers, Working Women, and the Suffrage Movement." Unpublished manuscript, undated, funded by Louis Rabinowitz Foundation. Copy in library of Trade Union Women's Studies, Cornell University, 7 East 43rd Street, New York, N.Y.

Malkiel, Theresa Serber. *The Diary of a Shirtwaist Striker.* New York: Co-operative Press, 1910.

Marot, Helen. *American Labor Unions.* New York: Henry Holt & Co., 1914. Reprint. New York: Arno Press, 1969.

O'Sullivan, Mary Kenney. "The Labor War at Lawrence," *Survey,* April 6, 1912, pp. 72–4.

Ovington, Mary White. *Half a Man: The Status of the Negro in New York.* New York, Longmans, Green & Co., 1911. Reprint. Westport, Conn.: Negro Universities Press, 1971.

Perkins, Frances. *The Roosevelt I Knew.* New York: Viking Press, 1946.

Renshaw, Patrick. *The Wobblies: The Story of Syndicalism in the United States.* Garden City, N.Y.: Doubleday & Co., Anchor Books, 1968.

Schneiderman, Rose. Letters, 1910–1912, collection in the Tamiment Library, New York University.

Strong, Earl D. *The Amalgamated Clothing Workers of America.* Grinnell, Iowa: Herald-Register Publishing Co., 1940.

Sumner, Mary Brown. "The Spirit of the Strikers." *Survey,* Jan. 22, 1910, pp. 550–5.

Tax, Meredith. "The Uprising of the Thirty Thousand: The Waistmakers General Strike of 1909–1910." Unpublished manuscript, 1973. Copy in library of Trade Union Women's Studies, Cornell University, 7 East 43rd St., New York, N.Y.

Thompson, Fred. *The IWW, Its First Fifty Years (1905–1955)*. Chicago: Industrial Workers of the World, 1955.

Tippett, Tom. "Jones, Mary (Mother)." *Encyclopedia of the Social Sciences.* New York: Macmillan Co., 1967. Vol. 8, p. 415.

Wald, Lillian. "Organization Amongst Working Women." *Annals*, American Academy of Political and Social Sciences, vol. 27 (May 1906), pp. 638–45.

Suggested Supplementary Reading, Part 5

Addams, Jane. *Twenty Years at Hull-House.* New York: Macmillan Co., 1924. Paperback ed. New York: New American Library, Signet Classics, 1961.

Baker, Elizabeth Faulkner. *Protective Labor Legislation.* New York: Columbia University Press, 1925.

Bloor, Ella R. *We Are Many: Autobiography.* New York: International Publishers Co., 1940.

Boone, Gladys. *The Women's Trade Union League in Great Britain and the United States of America.* New York: Columbia University Press, 1942. Reprint. New York: AMS Press, 1968.

Brandeis, Elizabeth. "Labor Legislation." In *History of Labor in the United States*, edited by John R. Commons. Vol. 3, *Working Conditions*. New York: Macmillan Co., 1935. Reprint. Clifton, N.J.: Augustus M. Kelley, 1966.

Brandeis, Louis, and Goldmark, Josephine. *Women in Industry*, 1908 *Muller v. Oregon* Brief for the State of Oregon, reprinted for the National Consumers' League. New York: Arno Press, 1969.

Davis, Allen F. *American Heroine: Life and Legend of Jane Addams.* New York: Oxford University Press, 1973.

Donovan, Frances R. *The Woman Who Waits.* Boston: Gorham Press, 1920. Reprint. New York: Arno Press, 1974.

Dreier, Mary E. *Margaret Dreier Robins—Her Life, Letters and Work.* New York: Island Press Cooperative, 1950.

Goldmark, Josephine. *Impatient Crusader: Florence Kelley's Life Story.* Urbana: University of Illinois Press, 1953.

Life and Labor, magazine of the National Women's Trade Union League of America, 1911–1932. Includes numerous articles by and about working women and their struggle to organize unions.

Nestor, Agnes. *Woman's Labor Leader: An Autobiography.* Rockford, Ill.: Bellevue Books, 1954.

Yellen, Samuel. *American Labor Struggles.* New York: Harcourt, Brace & Co., 1936. Reprint. New York: Arno Press, 1969. Listed here for its account of the Lawrence strike of 1912 and the Ludlow (Colorado) Massacre of 1913.

INDEX

(Numbers in boldface type refer to illustrations)

About the Author

Barbara Mayer Wertheimer is on the extension faculty of Cornell University's School of Industrial and Labor Relations and is the director of its Working Women's Program for Research and Education, of which the best-known division is Trade Union Women's Studies. A former organizer for the Amalgamated Clothing Workers of America and director of its national education department, she has received two national awards for creative programming in adult education. A prolific contributor to national journals on the topic of women and work, she is the author (with Anne H. Nelson) of *Trade Union Women: A Study of Their Participation in New York City Locals.*

Barbara Mayer Wertheimer is on the extension
faculty of Cornell University's School of Industrial and Labor Relations and is the director of
its Working Women's Program for Research
and Education, of which the best-known division
is Trade Union Women's Studies. A former
organizer for the Amalgamated Clothing Workers of America and director of its national education department, she has received two national
awards for creative programming in adult education. A prolific contributor to national journals
on the topic of women and work, she is the
author (with Anne H. Nelson) of *Trade Union
Women: A Study of Their Participation in New
York City Locals.*